The Life of the Buddha

The Life of the Buddha

According to the Pali Canon

Translation from the Pali,
selection of material
and arrangement by

Bhikkhu Ñāṇamoli

BPS Pariyatti Editions Seattle

BPE

BPS Pariyatti Editions
P.O. Box 15926
Seattle, WA 98115, USA
www.pariyatti.com

Published by Buddhist Publication Society, Kandy, Sri Lanka, 1972, 1978, 1992.
Published with the consent of the original publisher.
Copies of this book for sale in the Americas only.

First BPS Pariyatti Edition, 2001
09 08 07 06 05 04 03 02 5 4 3 2 1

Publisher's Cataloging-in-Publication
(Provided by Quality Books, Inc.)

The life of the Buddha: according to the Pāḷi canon / translation from the Pāḷi, selection of material and arrangement by Bhikkhu Ñāṇamoli. — 1st BPS Pariyatti ed.

p. cm.
Includes bibliographical references and index.
Originally published: 3rd ed. Kandy, Sri Lanka : Buddhist Publication Society, 1992.
LCCN: 2001089640
ISBN:1-928706-12-6 (pbk.)

1. Gautama Buddha. I. Ñāṇamoli, Bhikkhu, d.1960.

BQ882.L54 2001 294.3'63
QBI01-200487

Cover design by Amy Cao
Cover photograph by Jeffrey Davis

Printed in Canada on acid-free paper.

Namo tassa bhagavato arahato sammā sambuddhassa

Sabba-pāpassa akaraṇaṃ, kusalassa upasampadā,
Sacitta-pariyodāpanaṃ; etaṃ buddhāna sāsanaṃ.

To do no evil deeds, to give effect to good,
To purify the heart; this is the Buddha's teaching.
D. 14

CONTENTS

Editor's Preface ix
Introduction xi
Map of Central and Eastern India xvi-xvii
Voices xviii

1. The Birth and the Early Years 1
2. The Struggle for Enlightenment 10
3. After the Enlightenment 30
4. The Spreading of the Dhamma 48
5. The Two Chief Disciples 70
6. Anāthapiṇḍika, The Feeder of the Poor 87
7. The Formation of the Order of Nuns 102
8. The Quarrel at Kosambī 109
9. The End of the First Twenty Years 120
10. The Middle Period 151
11. The Person 182
12. The Doctrine 206
13. Devadatta 257
14. Old Age 273
15. The Last Year 286
16. The First Council 333

Notes 347
List of Sources 360
Index 369
Table of Principal Dates 375
About the Author 376
Bhikkhu Ñāṇamoli: A Bibliography 377

KEY TO ABBREVIATIONS

Vin.	VINAYA PIṬAKA
Sv.	Sutta-vibhanga
Pārā.	Pārājika
Sangh.	Sanghādisesa
Pāc.	Pācittiya
Mv.	Mahāvagga
Cv.	Cullavagga

SUTTA PIṬAKA

D.	Dīgha-nikāya
M.	Majjhima-nikāya
S.	Saṃyutta-nikāya
A.	Anguttara-nikāya

Khuddaka-nikāya

Khp.	Khuddaka-pāṭha
Ud.	Udāna
Iti.	Itivuttaka
Sn.	Sutta-nipāta
Dh.	Dhammapada
Thag.	Theragāthā

References are to the chapter (*khandhaka*) and section number of the Mahāvagga and Cullavagga; to the rule number for the other books of the Vinaya Piṭaka; to the discourse by number or by group and number for the main books of the Sutta Piṭaka; and to verse number for the Dhammapada and Theragāthā.

EDITOR'S PREFACE

This volume is published from the posthumous papers of the late Venerable Bhikkhu Ñāṇamoli, whose life sketch appears at the end of this book. The bulk of the book had received its final form by the author himself and the typescript had been carefully and neatly prepared by him. The introduction, however, was marked as a draft and appendices mentioned in the manuscript were not found among the author's papers. More than half of the texts in this book had been published before, in serial form, in a fortnightly Buddhist periodical, *Buddha Jayanthi* (Colombo, 1954-1956), though some renderings were different. For the present version, the late author had revised and considerably expanded his translation of canonical texts and had added the ingeniously devised framework of the book, incorporating ample material from non-canonical sources. This arrangement of the book is explained in the prefatory section, "Voices."

He had also experimented with new renderings of a number of doctrinal and other terms. But in the case of five of these, the editor thought it advisable to return to the author's earlier renderings as they appeared in *Buddha Jayanthi* and in his translation of the *Visuddhimagga*. References to some of these few alterations have been made in the editor's footnotes. As shown by handwritten changes in the manuscript, the author had found that some of his new renderings could not be consistently applied in all contexts—a fact that contributed to the editor's decision to prefer the author's earlier renderings in those few instances.

NYANAPONIKA THERA

Forest Hermitage
Kandy, Ceylon
September 1971

NOTE TO THE THIRD EDITION

In this Third Edition of the Venerable Ñāṇamoli's now classic *Life of the Buddha* a few minor inconsistencies of rendering in the earlier editions have been corrected, and again, a very few minor awkward syntactical formations have been straightened out. In addition, several standard Pali doctrinal terms that the author had translated have been retained in the Pali, as they have already become sufficiently familiar to readers of Buddhist literature and are now integral to English-language Dhamma terminology. These terms are "Buddha" (almost always rendered by the author as "the Enlightened One," which occasionally has been kept here for special effect); "Dhamma" (rendered by him as "Law"); "Sangha" (rendered by him as "Community"); and "Nibbāna" (often rendered in the original edition as "extinction").

All notes to the text appear in the form of backnotes. Those notes followed by "Nyp." in parenthesis are by Nyanaponika Thera, those followed by "BB" are by myself. All others are the author's.

New to this edition, too, is the List of Sources, which should enable students of the Pali suttas to easily locate texts familiar to them from other readings. The original nucleus of this directory was compiled years ago by Bhikkhu Ñāṇajivako, but it has been expanded to make it as inclusive as possible.

BHIKKHU BODHI

INTRODUCTION

How little the European public at the end of the 18th century knew of the Buddha and his teaching was underlined by Gibbon in a footnote to Chapter LXIV of the *Decline and Fall*; he says that "the idol Fo" is "The Indian Fo, whose worship prevails among the sects of Hindustan, Siam, Thibet, China and Japan. But this mysterious subject is still lost in a cloud which the researches of our Asiatic Society may gradually dispel." The fact was that plenty of reliable information had actually come to Europe from the East, but it was not published and remained in manuscript form locked away in libraries. For example, the Jesuit missionary, Filippo Desideri, brought back a long and accurate account both of the Buddha's life and of his doctrine from Tibet in the first quarter of the eighteenth century: it remained unpublished for two hundred years. Other accounts had fared likewise.

Meanwhile, though, the "cloud" of mystery was dispersed by the researches of the nineteenth century only to be replaced by one of controversial dust raised by scholars' battles, in which the newly discovered personality of the historical Buddha seemed to vanish again. Nevertheless, this too thinned out, and by the turn of that century the Buddha's historical existence was no more questioned, documents were assessed and texts established. Of those documents (whose number is enormous) the Pali Canon, or *Tipiṭaka* as it is called, was, and is still generally considered to be the oldest: somewhat older than its Sanskrit counterpart, though some Sanskritists resist this opinion. With that, the Pali scholar T.W. Rhys Davids was able to write, a little over a century after Gibbon: "When it is recollected that Gotama Buddha did not leave behind him a number of deeply simple sayings, from which his followers subsequently built up a system or systems of their own, but had himself thoroughly elaborated his doctrine, partly as to details, after, but in its fundamental points even before, his mission began; that during his long career as a teacher, he had ample time to repeat the principles and details of the system over and over again to his disciples, and to test their knowledge of it; and finally that his leading disciples were, like himself, accustomed to the subtlest metaphysical distinctions, and trained in that wonderful command of memory which Indian ascetics then possessed; when these facts are recalled to mind, it will be seen that much more reliance may reasonably be placed upon the doctrinal parts of the Buddhist Scriptures than upon corresponding late records of other religions."

European literature on the history of Buddhism is now very extensive, and likewise on its literature and on its doctrines. The great measure of agreement achieved in the fields of history and literature, though, is still not reflected in that of doctrine. There have been, and are, numerous and various attempts made to prove that Buddhism teaches annihilation or eternal existence, that it is negativist, positivist, atheist, theist, or inconsistent, that it is a reformed Vedānta, a humanism, pessimism, absolutism, pluralism, monism, that it is a philosophy, a religion, an ethical system, or indeed almost what you will. Nevertheless, the words of the Russian scholar Theodore Stcherbatsky, written in the late 1920s, apply today: "Although a hundred years have elapsed since the scientific study of Buddhism has been initiated in Europe, we are nevertheless still in the dark about the fundamental teachings of this religion and its philosophy. Certainly no other religion has proved so refractory to clear formulation."

All the books in the Pali Tipiṭaka that contain historical matter and discourses are composed in the form of anthologies. The Book of Discipline (Vinaya Piṭaka) consists of collections of monastic rules with accounts of incidents, sometimes very long, relating in some way to their pronouncement. The Discourses in the Sutta Piṭaka are grouped together under many and various headings, but never historically (history for history's sake has not interested India much at any time). Consequently a consecutive chronological account of the Buddha's life has to be pieced together from material scattered all over the Vinaya and Sutta Piṭakas. That those books do contain a picture complete in itself and strongly contrasting in its simplicity with the ornate and florid later versions (the Sanskrit *Lalita Vistara,* for example, which inspired Sir Edwin Arnold's *Light of Asia,* or the less known introduction to the Pali Birth Stories in Ācariya Buddhaghosa's

Jātaka Commentary). Compared with these, the account it provides of the period up to the Enlightenment seems as lean and polished as a rapier, a candle flame or an uncarved ivory tusk.

In compiling this account all the canonical material (except the Buddhavaṃsa) dealing with the period from the Last Birth down to the second year after the Enlightenment, and that for the last year, which is practically all the chronology the Canon itself provides, has been included. What chronological evidence the Canon itself offers has been given first place. The next most authoritative Pali source (how reliable, it is difficult to say) is the Commentaries of Ācariya Buddhaghosa (sixth century A.C.), which place a lot more of the canonical stories in order down as far as the twentieth year after the Enlightenment, adding details, and also the Devadatta story. They add as well, a number of non-canonical incidents, which have not been included here. Lastly, there is a late Burmese work, the *Mālālankāravatthu* (fifteenth century? translated into English by Bishop Bigandet under the title *The Story of the Burmese Buddha*), which dates some more canonical incidents; but it has probably no real historical authority at all and has only been followed for want of other guidance. These are the three sources for the arrangement of events, themselves contained in the Tipiṭaka. Other canonical events of special interest, although undatable, have also been included here and there and in the "middle period." One or two incidents, notably the deaths of King Bimbisāra and King Pasenadi, which are only given in the Commentaries, have also been added (their source being clearly indicated) because they round off certain scenes. The principal aim in compilation has been to include all important events with complete coverage up till the twentieth year after the Enlightenment and the last year. Chapters 9 and 10 are unavoidably episodic. Chapter 11 has been devoted to descriptions of the Buddha's personality. But "personality" is a subject of central importance in Buddhist doctrine, and so Chapter 12, "The Doctrine," is necessarily implied by that. In Chapter 12 the main elements of doctrine have been brought together roughly following an order suggested by the Discourses. No interpretation has been attempted (see below, however, paragraph on "translation"), but rather the material has been put together in such a way as to help the reader to make his own. A stereotyped interpretation risks slipping into one of the types of metaphysical wrong view, which the Buddha himself has described in great detail. If Chapter 12 is found rather forbidding, let the last words of Anāthapiṇḍika (Ch. 6) be pleaded in justification for its inclusion, and those who do not find it to their taste will not read it, or all of it.

Pali (whose literature is very large) is a language reserved entirely to one subject, namely, the Buddha's teaching. With that it is unlike Buddhist Sanskrit or Church Latin: a fact that lends it a peculiar clarity of its own without counterpart in Europe. It is one of the Indo-European group and is closely allied to Sanskrit, though of a different flavour. The style in the Suttas (Discourses) has an economic simplicity, coupled with a richness of idioms, that makes it a very polished vehicle hard to do justice to in translation. That is the main problem; but there is also another, the special feature of the repeated verbatim passages, sentences and phrases, which occur again and again. This peculiarity is probably due originally to the fact that these "books" were intended for recitation (we in Europe are used to formal repetitions in symphonic music in the concert hall, and even to refrains in poetry, but in prose we find it strange). To the reader unused to them these repetitions, in the extent to which they appear in the Pali, seem disagreeable on a printed page. They have therefore for the most part been elided in translation by means of various devices, though always with particular regard to preservation of the original architectural form of the discourses, which is one of the most notable characteristics of the Buddha's utterances. At the same time, however, some repetitions have been retained, exploiting as they do the valuable technique of "discovery of the familiar." Such repeats, if verbatim in the Pali, are verbatim in the English too. In translation two principal aims have been literalness of rendering and idiomaticness of the rendered version: two aims not easy to reconcile. Any translation distorts. Great care, however, has been taken to render technical terms consistently (avoiding "elegant variation"), and the Pali for these will be found against the English equivalents in the Index. The choice of English equivalents has also been made with great care and with a view to assisting a coherent examination in its English form of material suitable for a study of ontology and a theory of perception and cognition that is embedded in the Discourses (not by accident, it would seem).

There are instances where the Commentaries' explanation of word-meanings conflicts with those given in the Pali Text Society's Dictionary. Preference has then, after consideration, been given to the former. The most important are dealt with in the notes.

The pronunciation of Pali words and names is quite easy if these simple rules are followed: Pronounce 'a' as in countryman, 'ā' father, 'e' whey, 'i' chip, 'ī' machine, 'u' put, 'ū' rude, 'g' girl (always), 'c' church (always), 'j' judge (always), 'ñ' onion; ṭ, ḍ, ṇ, ḷ, with tongue on palate; t, d, n, l, with tongue on upper teeth; 'ṃ' as in sing; 'h' always separately, e.g. 'ch' as in which house, 'th' as in hot-house, 'ph' as in upholstery, etc.; double consonants always separately as in Italian, e.g. 'dd' as in mad dog (not madder), 'gg' as in big gun (not bigger), etc.; all others as in English. An 'o' and an 'e' always carry a stress, e.g. Pasenadi of Kosala, otherwise the stress always falls on a long vowel, ā, ī, or ū, or with a doubled consonant or 'ṃ,' even if consecutive.

Lastly, a word about the form of this compilation. The form of a "broadcast" (not intended for broadcasting) was suggested by the material itself, which as has been said was originally orally recited. The Vinaya Piṭaka itself suggests the "Voices" (see Ch. 16 and list of Voices preceding Ch. 1), which "rehearsed" the Canon at the Councils. The two "Narrators" are, as it were, two compeers. In contrast to what the "Voices" have to say, the "Narrators" parts have been deliberately flattened in style as well as kept to the minimum length.

BHIKKHU ÑĀṆAMOLI

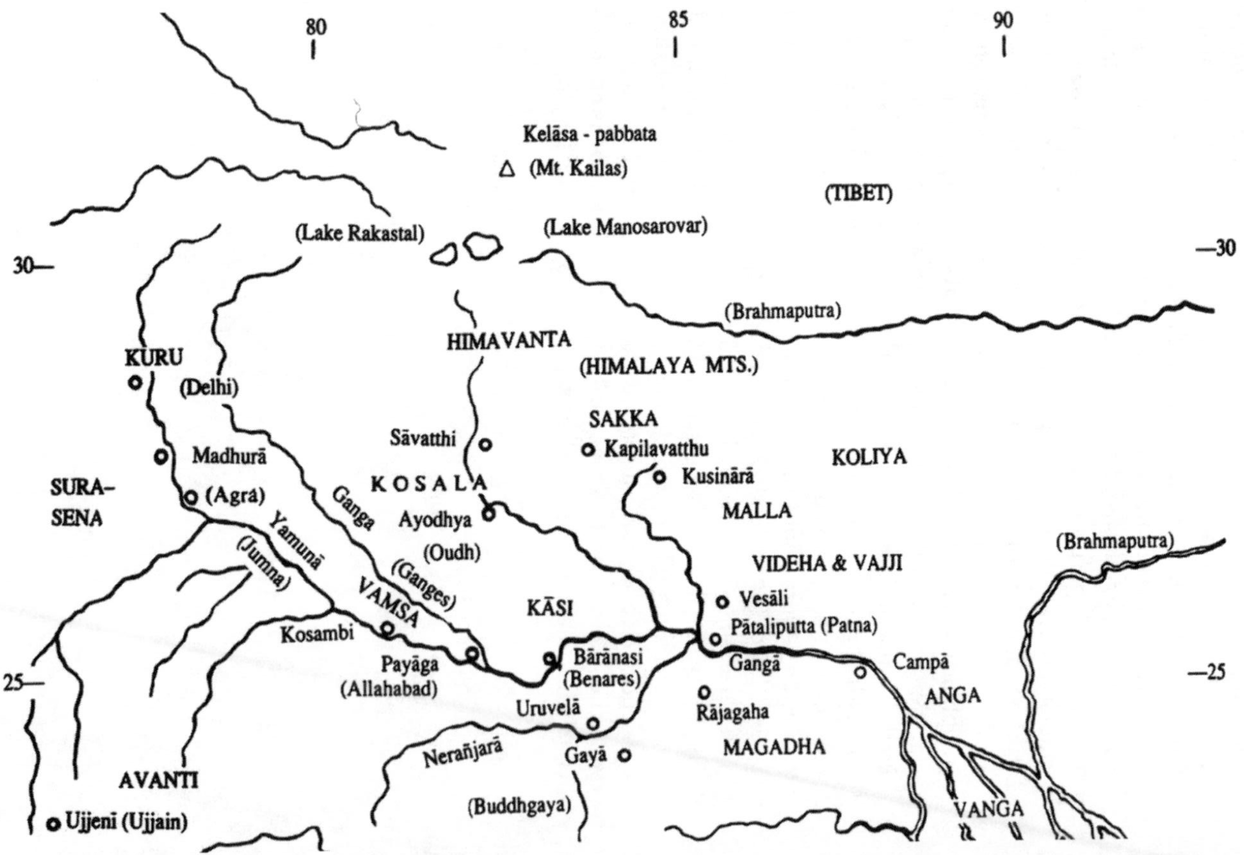
80
85
90
30—
—30
25—
—25
Kelāsa - pabbata
(Mt. Kailas)
(TIBET)
(Lake Rakastal)
(Lake Manosarovar)
(Brahmaputra)
HIMAVANTA
(HIMALAYA MTS.)
KURU
(Delhi)
SAKKA
Sāvatthi
Kapilavatthu
KOLIYA
Madhurā
Kusinārā
SURA-
SENA
(Agrā)
K O S A L A
Ganga
Ayodhya
MALLA
Yamunā
(Jumna)
(Oudh)
VIDEHA & VAJJI
(Brahmaputra)
(Ganges)
VAMSA
KĀSI
Vesāli
Kosambi
Pātaliputta (Patna)
Payāga
(Allahabad)
Bārānasi
(Benares)
Gangā
Campā
ANGA
Rājagaha
Uruvelā
MAGADHA
Nerañjarā
Gayā
AVANTI
(Buddhgaya)
VANGA
Ujjenī (Ujjain)

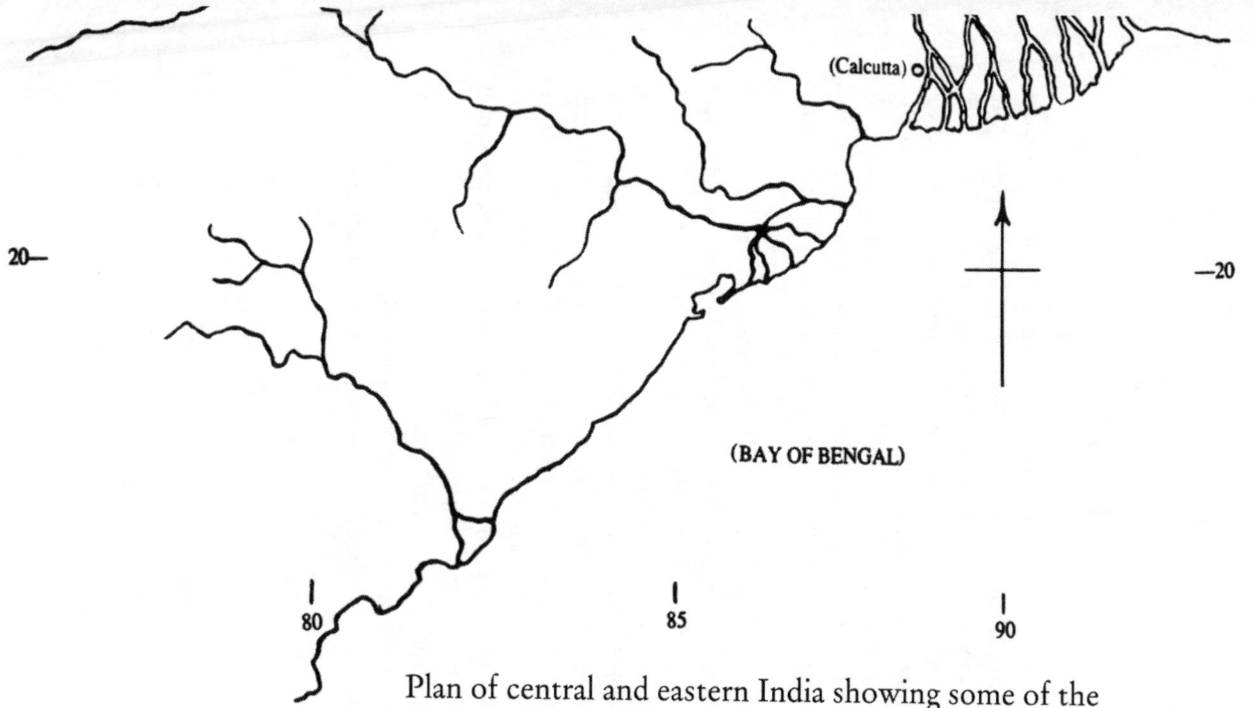

Plan of central and eastern India showing some of the principal place names mentioned in the Pali Tipiṭaka with modern names in brackets (Sources: *Cambridge History of India*. Vol 1 Map 5, T.W. Rhys Davids, *Buddhist India*)

VOICES

NARRATOR ONE. A commentator, or compeer, of the present time, who introduces the others, and who represents a dispassionate onlooker with some general knowledge of the events.

NARRATOR TWO. A commentator who supplies historical and traditional information contained only in the medieval Pali commentaries (mainly those of the fifth century by the Elder Buddhaghosa). His functions are to give the minimum of such material needed for historical clarity and, occasionally, to summarize portions of the Canon itself.

FIRST VOICE. The voice of the Elder Ānanda, the disciple and personal attendant of the Buddha, who recited the Discourses (or Suttas) at the First Council, held at Rājagaha three months after the Buddha's attainment of final Nibbāna.

SECOND VOICE. The voice of the Elder Upāli, disciple of the Buddha, who recited the Discipline (or Vinaya) at the First Council.

THIRD VOICE. The reciter of events that took place actually during, or after, the First Council. He appears only in Chapter 16, and represents a member of the Second Council held one hundred years after the Buddha's attainment of final Nibbāna.

CHANTER. A reciter of certain verses in the form of short epics or hymns in the Canon not introduced with the traditional words of the Elder Ānanda, "Thus I heard," or included within the Discipline.

1
THE BIRTH AND THE EARLY YEARS

NARRATOR ONE. Indian history actually begins with the story of the Buddha Gotama's life: or to put it perhaps more exactly, that is the point where history as record replaces archaeology and legend; for the documents of the Buddha's life and teaching—the earliest Indian documents to be accorded historical standing—reveal a civilization already stable and highly developed which can only have matured after a very long period indeed. Now the Buddha attained his complete enlightenment at Uruvelā in the Ganges plain, which is called the "Middle Country." As distances are reckoned in India, it was not very far from the immemorial holy city of Benares. His struggle to attain enlightenment had lasted six years, and he was then thirty-five years old. From that time onward he wandered from place to place in central India for the space of forty-five years, constantly explaining the Four Noble Truths that he had discovered. The final Parinibbāna took place as it is now calculated in Europe, in the year 483 B.C. (traditionally on the full-moon day of the month of May). The period through which he lived seems to have been outstandingly quiet with governments well organized and a stable society, in marked contrast with what must have gone before and came after.

NARRATOR TWO. Three months from the time of the Buddha's Parinibbāna his senior disciples who survived him summoned a council of five hundred senior monks in order to agree upon the form in which the Master's teaching should be handed down to posterity. Among these five hundred, all of whom had realized enlightenment, the Elder Upāli was the acknowledged authority on the rules of conduct for the Sangha or monastic order, which are called the "Vinaya" or "Discipline." In lay life a barber, he had gone forth into the life of homelessness along with the Buddha's cousin, Ānanda, and others. He was appointed to recite before the council the rules of conduct together with the circumstances that caused them to be laid down. The main part of the "Coffer of the Discipline" (the Vinaya Piṭaka) was composed there from his recitation.

When he had finished, the Elder Ānanda was invited to recite the Discourses. During the last twenty-four years of the Buddha's life he had been the Buddha's personal attendant, and he was gifted with an extraordinary memory. Almost the whole of the collections of discourses in the "Coffer of Discourses" (the Sutta Piṭaka) was composed from his recitation of them with their settings. The Elder Upāli began each account with the words *tena samayena* "the occasion was this," but the Elder Ānanda prefaced each discourse with an account of where and to whom it was spoken, beginning with the words *evaṃ me sutaṃ*, "thus I heard."

NARRATOR ONE. This narrative of the Buddha's life is taken from those two "Coffers." How they survived to this day is a story to be given later on; but here, to begin with, is the account of the Buddha's last birth, told by himself and related afterwards at the Council by the Elder Ānanda. The words were actually spoken in the Buddha's own language now known as Pali.

FIRST VOICE. Thus I heard. On one occasion the Blessed One[1] was living at Sāvatthi in Jeta's Grove, Anāthapiṇḍika's Park. Then a number of bhikkhus[2] were waiting in an assembly hall where they had met together on return from their alms-round after their meal was over. Meanwhile it was being said among them: "It is wonderful, friends, it is marvellous how the Perfect One's power and might enable him to know of past Buddhas who attained the complete extinction of defilement, cut the tangle, broke the circle, ended the round, and surmounted all suffering: such were those Blessed Ones' births, such their names, such their clans, such their virtue, such their concentration, such their understanding, such their abiding, such the manner of their deliverance."

When this was said, the venerable Ānanda told the bhikkhus: "Perfect Ones are wonderful, friends, and have wonderful qualities; Perfect Ones are marvellous and have marvellous qualities."

However, their talk meanwhile was left unfinished; for now it was already evening and the Blessed One, who had risen from retreat, came to the assembly hall and sat down on the seat made ready. Then he asked the bhikkhus: "Bhikkhus, for what talk are you gathered together here now? And what was your talk meanwhile that was left unfinished?"

What the bhikkhus and the venerable Ānanda had said was related, and they added: "Lord, this was our talk meanwhile that was left unfinished; for the Blessed One arrived." Then the Blessed One turned to the venerable Ānanda: "That being so, Ānanda, explain the Perfect One's wonderful and marvellous qualities more fully."

"I heard and learned this, Lord, from the Blessed One's own lips: Mindful and fully aware the Bodhisatta, the Being Dedicated to Enlightenment, appeared in the Heaven of the Contented.[3] And I remember that as a wonderful and marvellous quality of the Blessed One.

"I heard and learned this, Lord, from the Blessed One's own lips: Mindful and fully aware the Bodhisatta remained in the Heaven of the Contented.

"For the whole of that life-span the Bodhisatta remained in the Heaven of the Contented.

"Mindful and fully aware the Bodhisatta passed away from the Heaven of the Contented and descended into his mother's womb.

"When the Bodhisatta had passed away from the Heaven of the Contented and entered his mother's womb, a great measureless light surpassing the splendour of the gods appeared in the world with its deities, its Māras and its Brahmā divinities, in this generation with its monks and brahmans, with its princes and men.[4] And even in those abysmal world interspaces of vacancy, gloom and utter darkness, where the moon and sun, powerful and mighty as they are, cannot make their light prevail—there too a great measureless light surpassing the splendour of the gods appeared; and the creatures born there perceived each other by that light: 'So it seems that other creatures have appeared here!' And this ten-thousandfold world-system shook and quaked and trembled; and there too a great measureless light surpassing the splendour of the gods appeared.

"When the Bodhisatta had descended into his mother's womb, four deities came to guard him from the four quarters, so that no human or non-human beings or anyone at all should harm him or his mother.

"When the Bodhisatta had descended into his mother's womb, she became intrinsically pure, refraining by necessity from killing living beings, from taking what is not given, from unchastity, from false speech, and from indulgence in wine, liquour and fermented brews.

"When the Bodhisatta had descended into his mother's womb, no thought of man associated with the five strands of sensual desires came to her at all, and she was inaccessible to any man with lustful mind.

"When the Bodhisatta had descended into his mother's womb, she at the same time possessed the five strands of sensual desires; and being endowed and furnished with them, she was gratified in them.

"When the Bodhisatta had descended into his mother's womb, no kind of affliction arose in her: she was blissful in the absence of all bodily fatigue. As though a blue, yellow, red, white, or brown thread were strung through a fine beryl gem of purest water, eight-faceted and well cut, so that a man with sound eyes, taking it in his hand, might review it thus—'This is a fine beryl gem of purest water, eight-faceted and well cut, and through it is strung a blue, yellow, red, white, or brown thread'—so too the Bodhisatta's mother saw him within her womb with all his limbs, lacking no faculty.

"Seven days after the Bodhisatta was born, his mother died and was reborn in the Heaven of the Contented.

"Other women give birth after carrying the child in the womb for nine or ten months; but not so the Bodhisatta's mother. She gave birth to him after carrying him in her womb for exactly ten months.

"Other women give birth seated or lying down; but not so the Bodhisatta's mother. She gave birth to him standing up.

"When the Bodhisatta came forth from his mother's womb, first deities received him, then human beings.

"When the Bodhisatta came forth from his mother's womb, he did not touch the earth. The four deities received him and set him before his mother, saying: 'Rejoice, O queen, a son of great power has been born to you.'

"When the Bodhisatta came forth from his mother's womb, just as if a gem were placed on Benares cloth, the gem would not smear the cloth or the cloth the gem—why not?—because both are pure, so too the Bodhisatta came forth from his mother's womb unsullied, unsmeared by water or humours or blood or any sort of impurity, clean and unsullied.

"When the Bodhisatta came forth from his mother's womb, two jets of water appeared to pour from the sky, one cool and one warm, for bathing the Bodhisatta and his mother.

"As soon as the Bodhisatta was born, he stood firmly with his feet on the ground; then he took seven steps to the north, and, with a white sunshade held over him, he surveyed each quarter. He uttered the words of the Leader of the Herd: 'I am the Highest in the world, I am the Best in the world, I am the Foremost in the world; this is the last birth; now there is no more renewal of being in future lives.'

"When the Bodhisatta came forth from his mother's womb, a great measureless light surpassing the splendour of the gods appeared in the world with its deities, its Māras, and its Brahmā divinities, in this generation with its monks and brahmans, with its princes and men. And even in those abysmal world interspaces of vacancy, gloom and utter darkness, where the moon and sun, powerful and mighty as they are, cannot make their light prevail—there too a great measureless light surpassing the splendour of the gods appeared; and the creatures born there perceived each other by that light: 'So it seems that other creatures have appeared here!' And this ten-thousandfold world-system shook and quaked and trembled; and there too a great measureless light surpassing the splendour of the gods appeared.

"All these things I heard and learned from the Blessed One's own lips. And I remember them as wonderful and marvellous qualities of the Blessed One."

"That being so, Ānanda, remember also this as a wonderful and marvellous quality of a Perfect One: A Perfect One's feelings of pleasure, pain or equanimity are known to him as they arise, known to him as they are present, and known to him as they subside; his perceptions are known to him as they arise, known to him as they are present, and known to him as they subside; his thoughts are known to him as they arise, known to him as they are present, and known to him as they subside."

"And that also I remember, Lord, as a wonderful and marvellous quality of the Blessed One."

That is what the venerable Ānanda said. The Master approved. The bhikkhus were satisfied, and they delighted in the venerable Ānanda's words.

M. 123; cf. D. 14

NARRATOR ONE. How a brahman seer—a seer of the "divine" or priestly caste—foretold the coming enlightenment is told in a song.

CHANTER.

The Sage Asita, in his daytime meditation,
Saw that the gods, those of the Company of Thirty,
Were happy and gay, all brightly clad, waving flags
The while their ruler Sakka they were wildly cheering.
Now when he saw the gods so happy and elated,
Respectfully he greeted them and asked them this:

"Why is the Company of Gods so joyful?
Why have they brought out flags to brandish thus?
There was no celebration such as this
Even after the battle with the demons
Wherein the gods won and the demons lost;
What marvel have they heard that so delights them?
See how they sing and shout and strum guitars,
Clapping their hands and dancing all about.
O you that dwell on Meru's airy peaks,
I beg you, leave me not in doubt, good sirs."

"At a Sakyan city in the Land of Lumbinī
A Being To Be Enlightened, a Priceless Jewel,
Is born in the world of men for welfare and weal;
Because of that we are extravagantly gay.
The Unique Being, the Personality Sublime,
The Lord of all men and Foremost among mankind,
Will turn the Wheel in the Grove of the Ancient Seers
With the roar of the lion, the monarch of all beasts."

On hearing this, the Sage in haste
Went to Suddhodana's abode.
There he sat down: "Where is the boy?"
He asked the Sakyans, "Show him to me."

Now when the Sakyans showed the child to Asita,
His colour was as pure
As beams of brilliant gold wrought in a crucible,
Shining and clear.

The joy of rapture flooded Asita's heart
On seeing the boy bright as a flame and pure
As the Lord of the stars' herd riding in the sky,
Dazzling as the cloudless autumn sun;
While gods in the heavenly vault held over him
A many-ribbed sunshade with a thousand circles,
Brandishing gold-sticked chowries, though none saw
The holders of the sunshade and the chowries.

The sage with matted hair, called Kaṇhasiri,[5]
Seeing the boy, like a gold jewel upon brocade,
With the white sunshade held above his head,
Received him full of joy and happiness.
As soon as he received the Sakyans' Lord
The adept in construing marks and signs
Exclaimed with ready confidence of heart:
"Among the biped race he is unique."
Then he remembered: seeing his own lot,
In very sadness tears came to his eyes.
The Sakyans saw him weeping, and they asked:
"Will some misfortune then befall our prince?"
But to the anxious Sakyans he replied:
"As I foresee, no harm will touch the boy,
Nor is there any danger that awaits him.
Be sure he is not of the second rank;
For he will reach the summit of true knowledge.
A seer of the peerless purity,
Through pity for the many he will set
The Dhamma Wheel turning and spread his life of holiness.
But little of my life-span now remains,
And I shall die meanwhile. I shall not hear
The matchless Hero teaching the Good Dhamma.
That saddens me; that loss distresses me."

He that lived the holy life left the inner palace chamber
After he had filled the Sakyans with an all-abounding joy.
To his sister's son he went, moved by feelings of compassion,
Telling him the Peerless Hero's future finding of the Dhamma.

"When news shall reach you that he is enlightened
And living out the Dhamma he has found,

Then go to him and ask about his teaching
And live with that Blessed One the holy life."

So Nālaka, who had laid up a store of merit,
Forewarned by one who wished him well, who had foreseen
The Being to come, attained to utter purity,
Waited with guarded senses, expecting the Victor.

On hearing that the Noble Victor
Had rolled the Wheel, he went to him;
He saw the Lord of all the Seers,
And trusted in him when he saw.
Fulfilling Asita's behest,
He questioned then the Perfect Sage
About the Silentness Supreme.

Sn. 3:11

NARRATOR ONE. Though literature of a later date supplies many details of the early years, the Tipiṭaka itself has very little to say about them. There is, in fact, only reference to two incidents: firstly, the reminiscence of the meditation under the rose-apple tree while the Bodhisatta's father was working—doing the ceremonial ploughing at the opening of the sowing season, the Commentary says—, which we shall come to later; and secondly there is the account of the "three considerations," which correspond to three of the "messengers" (the old, the sick and the dead) seen by the former Buddha Vipassī (D. 14).

FIRST VOICE. "I was delicate, most delicate, supremely delicate.[6] Lily pools were made for me at my father's house solely for my benefit. Blue lilies flowered in one, white lilies in another, red lilies in a third. I used no sandalwood that was not from Benares. My turban, tunic, lower garments and cloak were all made of Benares cloth. A white sunshade was held over me day and night so that no cold or heat or dust or grit or dew might inconvenience me.

"I had three palaces; one for the winter, one for the summer and one for the rains. In the rains palace I was entertained by minstrels with no men among them. For the four months of the rains I never went down to the lower palace. Though meals of broken rice with lentil soup are given to the servants and retainers in other people's houses, in my father's house white rice and meat was given to them.

"Whilst I had such power and good fortune, yet I thought: 'When an untaught ordinary man, who is subject to ageing, not safe from ageing, sees another who is aged, he is shocked, humiliated and disgusted; for he forgets that he himself is no exception. But I too am subject to ageing, not safe from ageing, and so it cannot befit me to be shocked, humiliated and disgusted on seeing another who is aged.' When I considered this, the vanity of youth entirely left me.

"I thought: 'When an untaught ordinary man, who is subject to sickness, not safe from sickness, sees another who is sick, he is shocked, humiliated and disgusted; for he forgets that he himself is no exception. But I too am subject to sickness, not safe from sickness, and so it cannot befit me to be shocked, humiliated and disgusted on seeing another who is sick.' When I considered this, the vanity of health entirely left me.

"I thought: 'When an untaught ordinary man, who is subject to death, not safe from death, sees another who is dead, he is shocked, humiliated and disgusted, for he forgets that he himself is no exception. But I too am subject to death, not safe from death, and so it cannot befit me to be shocked, humiliated and disgusted on seeing another who is dead.' When I considered this, the vanity of life entirely left me."

A. 3:38

2
THE STRUGGLE FOR ENLIGHTENMENT

NARRATOR ONE. The account of the Renunciation given in the Piṭakas is striking in its bare simplicity. The elaborate details of the later versions are absent in it, as they are in this oldest version of the birth and early years. Here is the account, which is drawn from several discourses delivered to various persons.

FIRST VOICE. "Before my enlightenment, while I was still only an unenlightened Bodhisatta, being myself subject to birth, ageing, ailment, death, sorrow and defilement, I sought after what was also subject to these things. Then I thought: 'Why, being myself subject to birth, ageing, ailment, death, sorrow and defilement, do I seek after what is also subject to these things? Suppose, being myself subject to these things, seeing danger in them, I sought after the unborn, unageing, unailing, deathless, sorrowless, undefiled supreme surcease of bondage, Nibbāna?' "

M. 26

"Before my enlightenment, while I was still only an unenlightened Bodhisatta, I thought: 'House life is crowded and dusty; life gone forth is wide open. It is not easy, living in a household, to lead a holy life as utterly perfect and pure as a polished shell. Suppose I shaved off my hair and beard, put on the yellow robe, and went forth from the house life into homelessness?' "

M. 36, 100

"Later, while still young, a black-haired boy blessed with youth, in the first phase of life, I shaved off my hair and beard—though my mother and father wished otherwise and grieved with tearful faces—and I put on the yellow robe and went forth from the house life into homelessness."

M. 26, 36, 85, 100

CHANTER.

Now I will tell the going forth,
How he, the mighty Seer, went forth,
How he was questioned and described
The reason for his going forth.
The crowded life lived in a house
Exhales an atmosphere of dust;
But life gone forth is open wide:
He saw this, and he chose the going forth.
By his so doing he refused
All evil action of the body,
Rejected all wrong kinds of speech
And rectified his livelihood besides.
He went to Rājagaha town,
The castle of the Magadhans;
There he—the Buddha—went for alms,
With many a mark of excellence.
King Bimbisāra from within
His palace saw him passing by,
And when he saw the excellence
Of all the marks, "Look, sirs," he said;
"How handsome is that man, how stately,
How pure and perfect is his conduct;
With downcast eyes and mindful, looking
Only a plough-yoke's length before him;
His is no lowly lineage.
Send the royal messengers at once
To follow up the path the bhikkhu takes."
The messengers were sent at once
And followed closely in his wake:
"Now which way will the bhikkhu go?
Where has he chosen his abode?
He wanders on from house to house,
Guarding sense doors with real restraint
Fully aware and mindfully.
He soon has filled his begging bowl;
His alms round is now done.
The Sage is setting out and leaves the town,

Taking the road to Paṇḍava:
He must live on the hill of Paṇḍava."

Now when he came to his abode,
The messengers went up to him;
Though one of them turned back again
To give the king the answer to his question:
"The bhikkhu, sire, like a tiger,
Or like a bull, or like a lion,
Is seated in a mountain cave
Upon the eastern slope of Paṇḍava."

The warrior heard the runner's tale.
Then summoning a coach of state,
He drove in haste out of the town,
Out to the hill of Paṇḍava.
He drove as far as he could go,
And then descended from the coach;
The little distance that remained
He went on foot, till he drew near the Sage.

The king sat down, and he exchanged
Greetings, and asked about his health.
When this exchange of courtesy
Was done, the king then spoke to him
These words: "You are quite young, a youth,
A boy in the first phase of life.
You have the good looks of a man
Of high-born warrior-noble stock,
One fit to grace a first-rate army,
To lead the troops of elephants.
I offer you a fortune: take it.
Your birth I ask you also: tell it."

"There is a prosperous country, sire,
And vigorous, right up against
The foothills of Himalaya,
Inhabited by Kosalans
Whose race is named after the Sun,
Whose lineage is Sakyan.
But I have not gone forth to seek sense pleasures.

I have gone out to strive, seeing danger in them,
And seeing safe refuge from them in renouncing.
That is my heart's desire."

Sn. 3:1

FIRST VOICE. "Now I went forth from the house life into homelessness to seek what is good,[1] seeking the supreme state of sublime peace. Therefore, I went to Āḷāra Kālāma, and I said to him: 'Friend Kālāma, I want to lead the holy life in this Dhamma and Discipline.'

"When this was said, Āḷāra Kālāma told me: 'The venerable one may stay here. This teaching is such that in no long time a wise man can enter upon and dwell in it, himself realizing through direct knowledge what his own teacher knows.'

"I soon learned the teaching. I claimed that as far as mere lip reciting and rehearsal of his teaching went I could speak with knowledge and assurance, and that I knew and saw—and there were others who did likewise.

"I thought: 'It is not through mere faith alone that Āḷāra Kālāma declares his teaching; it is because he has entered upon and dwelt in it, himself realizing it through direct knowledge. It is certain that he dwells in this teaching knowing and seeing.'

"Then I went to Āḷāra Kālāma, and I said to him: 'Friend Kālāma, how far do you declare to have entered upon this teaching, yourself realizing it through direct knowledge?'

"When this was said, he declared the base consisting of nothingness. It occurred to me: 'It is not only Āḷāra Kālāma that has faith, energy, mindfulness, concentration and understanding, but I too have these faculties. Suppose I strove to realize the teaching that he declares to enter upon and dwell in, himself realizing it through direct knowledge?'

"I soon succeeded. Then I went to Āḷāra Kālāma and I said to him: 'Friend Kālāma, is it thus far that you declare to have entered upon and dwelt in this teaching, yourself realizing it through direct knowledge?' and he told me that it was.

" 'I too, friend, have thus far entered upon and dwelt in this teaching, myself realizing it through direct knowledge.'

" 'We are fortunate, friend, we are indeed fortunate, to have found such a venerable one for our fellow in the holy life. So the teaching that I declare to have entered upon, myself realizing it through direct knowledge, that you enter upon and dwell in, yourself realizing it through direct knowledge. And the teaching that you enter upon and dwell in, yourself realizing it through direct knowledge, that I declare to have entered upon, myself realizing it through direct knowledge. So you know the teaching that I know; I know the teaching that you know. As I am, so are you: as you are, so am I. Come, friend, let us now lead this community together.' Thus Āḷāra Kālāma, my teacher, placed me, his pupil, on an equal footing with himself, according me the highest honour.

"I thought: 'This teaching does not lead to dispassion, to fading of lust, to cessation, to peace, to direct knowledge, to enlightenment, to Nibbāna, but only to the base consisting of nothingness.' I was not satisfied with that teaching. I left it to pursue my search.

"Still in search of what is good, seeking the supreme state of sublime peace, I went to Uddaka Rāmaputta, and I said to him: 'Friend, I want to lead the holy life in this Dhamma and Discipline.' "

M. 26, 36, 85, 100

NARRATOR ONE. His experience under the guidance of Uddaka Rāmaputta is told in exactly the same words, except that he learnt from him the still higher attainment of the base consisting of neither-perception-nor-non-perception, and that Uddaka Rāmaputta offered him the sole leadership of that community. But the conclusion was the same.

FIRST VOICE. "I thought: 'This teaching does not lead to dispassion, to fading of lust, to cessation, to peace, to direct knowledge, to enlightenment, to Nibbāna, but only to the base consisting of neither-perception-nor-non-perception.' I was not satisfied with that teaching. I left it to pursue my search.

"Still in search of what is good, seeking the supreme state of sublime peace, I wandered by stages through the Magadhan country and at length arrived at Senānigāma near Uruvelā. There I saw an agreeable plot of ground, a delightful grove, a clear-flowing river with pleasant smooth banks, and nearby a village as alms resort. I thought: 'This will serve for the struggle of a clansman who seeks the struggle.' "

M. 26, 36, 85, 100

"Now before my enlightenment, while I was still only an unenlightened Bodhisatta, I thought: 'Remote jungle-thicket abodes in the forest are hard to endure, seclusion is hard to achieve, isolation is hard to enjoy; one would think the jungles must rob a bhikkhu of his mind if he has no concentration.'

"I thought: 'Suppose some monk or brahman is unpurified in bodily, verbal or mental conduct, or in his livelihood, is covetous and keenly sensitive to lust for sensual desires, or malevolent, with thoughts of hate, or a prey to lethargy and drowsiness, or agitated and uncalm in mind, or doubting and uncertain; is given to self-praise and denigrating others, is subject to fright and horror, desires gain, honour and renown; is idle and wanting in energy, forgetful and not fully aware, unconcentrated and confused in mind, devoid of understanding, and drivelling—when some such monk or brahman resorts to a remote jungle-thicket abode in the forest, then owing to those faults he evokes unwholesome[2] fear and dread. But I do not resort to a remote jungle-thicket abode in the forest as one of those. I have none of those defects. I resort to a remote jungle-thicket abode in the forest as one of the noble ones, who are free from these defects.' Seeing in myself this freedom from such defects, I find great solace in living in the forest.

"I thought: 'But there are the specially holy nights of the half moons of the fourteenth and fifteenth, and the quarter moon of the eighth; suppose I spent those nights in such awe-inspiring abodes as orchard shrines, woodland shrines and tree shrines, which make the hair stand up—perhaps I should encounter that fear and dread?'

"And later, on such specially holy nights as the half moons of the fourteenth and fifteenth, and the quarter moon of the eighth, I dwelt in such awe-inspiring abodes as orchard shrines, woodland shrines and tree shrines, which make the hair stand up. And while I dwelt there, a deer would approach me, or a peacock would knock off a branch, or the wind would rustle the leaves. Then I thought: 'Surely this is the fear and dread coming.'

"I thought: 'Why do I dwell in constant expectation of the fear and dread? Why not subdue that fear and dread while maintaining the posture I am in when it comes to me?'

"And while I walked, the fear and dread came upon me; but I neither stood nor sat nor lay down till I had subdued that fear and dread. While I stood, the fear and dread came upon me; but I neither walked nor sat nor lay down till I had subdued that fear and dread. While I sat, the fear and dread came upon me; but I neither walked nor stood nor lay down till I had subdued that fear and dread. While I lay, the fear and dread came upon me; but I neither walked nor stood nor sat till I had subdued that fear and dread."

M. 4

"Now three similes occurred to me spontaneously, never heard before.

"Suppose there were a wet, sappy piece of wood lying in water, and a man came with an upper fire-stick, thinking: 'I shall light a fire, I shall produce heat,' how do you conceive this, would the man light a fire and produce heat by taking the upper fire-stick and rubbing the wet, sappy piece of wood lying in water with it?"—"No, Lord. Why not? Because it is a wet, sappy piece of wood; and besides it is lying in water. So the man would reap weariness and disappointment."—"So too, while a monk or brahman lives still bodily and mentally not withdrawn from sensual desires, and while his lust, affection, passion, thirst and fever for sensual desires are still not quite abandoned and quieted within him, then, whether the good monk or brahman feels painful, racking, piercing feelings imposed by striving, or whether he does not, he is in either case incapable of knowledge and vision and supreme enlightenment. This was the first simile that occurred to me spontaneously, never heard before.

"Again, suppose there were a wet, sappy piece of wood lying on dry land far from water, and a man came with an upper fire-stick, thinking: 'I shall light a fire, I shall produce heat,' how do you conceive this, would the man light a fire and produce heat by taking the upper fire-stick and rubbing the wet, sappy piece of wood lying on dry land far from water with it?"—"No, Lord. Why not? Because it is a wet, sappy piece of wood, though it is lying on dry land far from water. So the man would reap weariness and disappointment."—"So too, while a monk or brahman lives still only bodily withdrawn from sensual desires, and while his lust, affection, passion, thirst and fever for sensual desires are not quite abandoned and quieted within him, then, whether the good monk or brahman feels painful, racking, piercing feelings imposed by striving, or whether he does not, he is in either case incapable of knowledge and vision and supreme enlightenment. This was the second simile that occurred to me spontaneously, never heard before.

"Again, suppose there were a dry, sapless piece of wood lying on dry land far from water, and a man came with an upper fire-stick, thinking: 'I shall light a fire, I shall produce heat,' how do you conceive this, would the man light a fire and produce heat by taking the upper fire-stick and rubbing the dry, sapless piece of wood lying on dry land far from water with it?"—"Yes, Lord. Why so? Because it is a dry, sapless piece of wood, and besides, it is lying on dry land far from water."—"So too, while a monk or brahman lives both bodily and mentally withdrawn from sensual desires, and while his lust, affection, passion, thirst and fever for sensual desires are quite abandoned and quieted within him, then, whether the good monk or brahman feels painful, racking, piercing feelings imposed by striving, or whether he does not, he is in either case capable of knowledge and vision and supreme enlightenment. This was the third simile that occurred to me spontaneously, never heard before.

"I thought: 'Suppose, with my teeth clenched and my tongue pressed against the roof of my mouth, I beat down, constrain and crush my mind with my mind?' Then, as a strong man might seize a weaker by the head or shoulders and beat him down, constrain him and crush him, so with my teeth clenched and my tongue pressed against the roof of my mouth, I beat down, constrained and crushed my mind with my mind. Sweat ran from my armpits while I did so.

"Though tireless energy was aroused in me, and unremitting mindfulness established, yet my body was overwrought and uncalm because I was exhausted by the painful effort. But such painful feelings as arose in me gained no power over my mind.

"I thought: 'Suppose I practise the meditation that is without breathing?' I stopped the in-breaths and out-breaths in my mouth and nose. When I did so, there was a loud sound of winds coming from my ear holes, as there is a loud sound when a smith's bellows are blown.

"I stopped the in-breaths and out-breaths in my mouth and nose and ears. When I did so, violent winds racked my head, as if a strong man were splitting my head open with a sharp sword. And then there were violent pains in my head, as if a strong man were tightening a tough leather strap round my head, as a head-band.

And then violent winds carved up my belly, as a clever butcher or his apprentice carves up an ox's belly with a sharp knife. And then there was a violent burning in my belly, as if two strong men had seized a weaker man by both arms and were roasting him over a pit of live coals.

"And each time, though tireless energy was aroused in me and unremitting mindfulness established, yet my body was over-wrought and uncalm because I was exhausted by the painful effort. But such painful feeling as arose in me gained no power over my mind.

"Now when deities saw me, they said: 'The monk Gotama is dead.' Other deities said: 'The monk Gotama is not dead, he is dying.' Other deities said: 'The monk Gotama is neither dead nor dying; the monk Gotama is an Arahant, a saint; for such is the way of saints.'

"I thought: 'Suppose I entirely cut off food?' Then deities came to me and said: 'Good sir, do not entirely cut off food. If you do so, we shall inject divine food into your pores and you will live on that.' I thought: 'If I claim to be completely fasting, and these deities inject divine food into my pores and I live on that, then I shall be lying.' I dismissed them, saying 'There is no need.'

"I thought: 'Suppose I take very little food, say, a handful each time, whether it is bean soup or lentil soup or pea soup?' I did so. And as I did so, my body reached a state of extreme emaciation; my limbs became like the jointed segments of vine stems or bamboo stems, because of eating so little. My backside became like a camel's hoof; the projections on my spine stood forth like corded beads; my ribs jutted out as gaunt as the crazy rafters of an old roofless barn; the gleam of my eyes sunk far down in their sockets looked like the gleam of water sunk far down in a deep well; my scalp shrivelled and withered as a green gourd shrivels and withers in the wind and sun. If I touched my belly skin, I encountered my backbone too; and if I touched my backbone, I encountered my belly skin too; for my belly skin cleaved to my backbone. If I made water or evacuated my bowels, I fell over on my face there. If I tried to ease my body by rubbing my limbs with my hands, the hair, rotted at its roots, fell away from my body as I rubbed, because of eating so little.

"When human beings saw me now, they said: 'The monk Gotama is a black man.' Other human beings said: 'The monk Gotama is not a black man, he is a brown man.' Other human beings said:

'The monk Gotama is neither a black man nor a brown man; he is fair-skinned.' So much had the clear bright colour of my skin deteriorated through eating so little."

M. 36, 85, 100

CHANTER.

"As I strove to subdue myself
Beside the broad Nerañjarā
Absorbed unflinchingly to gain
The true surcease of bondage here,
Namucī came and spoke to me
With words all garbed in pity thus:

'O you are thin and you are pale,
And you are in death's presence too;
A thousand parts are pledged to death,
But life still holds one part of you.
Live, sir! Life is the better way;
You can gain merit if you live;
Come, live the holy life and pour
Libations on the holy fires,
And thus a world of merit gain.
What can you do by struggling now?
The path of struggling too is rough
And difficult and hard to bear.' "

Now Māra, as he spoke these lines,
Drew near until he stood close by.
The Blessed One replied to him
As he stood thus: "O Evil One,
O Cousin of the Negligent,
You have come here for your own ends.
Now merit I need not at all;
Let Māra talk of merit then
To those that stand in need of it.
For I have faith and energy,
And I have understanding too.
So while I thus subdue myself
Why do you speak to me of life?
There is this wind that blows can dry

Even the rivers' running streams;
So while I thus subdue myself
Why should it not dry up my blood?
And as the blood dries up, then bile
And phlegm run dry, the wasting flesh
Becalms the mind: I shall have more
Of mindfulness, of understanding,
I shall have greater concentration.
For living thus I come to know
The limits to which feeling goes.
My mind looks not to sense desires:
You see a being's purity.
Your first squadron is Sense-Desires,
Your second is called Boredom, then
Hunger and Thirst compose the third,
And Craving is the fourth in rank,
The fifth is Sloth and Accidy,
While Cowardice lines up as sixth,
Uncertainty is seventh, the eighth
Is Malice paired with Obstinacy;
Gain, Honour and Renown, besides,
And ill-won Notoriety,
Self-praise and Denigrating Others—
These are your squadrons, Namucī;
These are the Black One's fighting squadrons;
None but the brave will conquer them
To gain bliss by the victory.
I fly the ribbon that denies
Retreat. Shame on life here, I say.
Better I die in battle now
Than choose to live on in defeat.
There are ascetics and brahmans
That have surrendered here, and they
Are seen no more: they do not know
The paths the pilgrim travels by.
So, seeing Māra's squadrons now
Arrayed all round, with elephants,
I sally forth to fight, that I
May not be driven from my post.

Your serried squadrons, which the world
With all its gods cannot defeat,
I shall now break with understanding,
As with a stone a raw clay pot."[3]

Sn. 3:2

FIRST VOICE. "I thought: 'Whenever a monk or brahman has felt in the past, or will feel in the future, or feels now, painful, racking, piercing feeling due to striving, it can equal this but not exceed it. But by this gruelling penance I have attained no distinction higher than the human state, worthy of the noble one's knowledge and vision. Might there be another way to enlightenment?'

"I thought of a time when my Sakyan father was working and I was sitting in the cool shade of a rose-apple tree: quite secluded from sensual desires, secluded from unwholesome things I had entered upon and abode in the first meditation, which is accompanied by thinking and exploring, with happiness and pleasure born of seclusion. I thought: 'Might that be the way to enlightenment?' Then, following up that memory, there came the recognition that this was the way to enlightenment.

"Then I thought: 'Why am I afraid of such pleasure? It is pleasure that has nothing to do with sensual desires and unwholesome things.' Then I thought: 'I am not afraid of such pleasure for it has nothing to do with sensual desires and unwholesome things.'

"I thought: 'It is not possible to attain that pleasure with a body so excessively emaciated. Suppose I ate some solid food some boiled rice and bread?'[4]

"Now at that time five bhikkhus were waiting on me, thinking: 'If the monk Gotama achieves something, he will tell us.' As soon as I ate the solid food, the boiled rice and bread, the five bhikkhus were disgusted and left me, thinking: 'The monk Gotama has become self-indulgent, he has given up the struggle and reverted to luxury.'

M. 36, 85, 100

NARRATOR ONE. Five dreams now appeared to the Bodhi-satta.

NARRATOR TWO. It was the night before his attainment of enlightenment; and the dreams were a premonition that he was about to attain his goal.

FIRST VOICE. Just before the Perfect One, accomplished and fully enlightened, attained enlightenment, five momentous dreams appeared to him. What five? While he was still only an unenlightened Bodhisatta, the great earth was his couch; Himalaya, king of mountains, was his pillow; his left hand lay in the Eastern Ocean, his right hand lay in the Western Ocean, his feet lay in the Southern Ocean. This was the first dream that appeared to him, and it foretold his discovery of the supreme full enlightenment. While he was still only an unenlightened Bodhisatta, a creeper grew up out of his navel and stood touching the clouds. This was the second dream that appeared to him, and it foretold his discovery of the Noble Eightfold Path. While he was still only an unenlightened Bodhisatta, white grubs with black heads crawled from his feet to his knees and covered them. This was the third dream that appeared to him, and it foretold that many white-clothed laymen would go for refuge to the Perfect One during his life. While he was only an unenlightened Bodhisatta, four birds of different colours came from the four quarters, and, as they alighted at his feet, they all became white. This was the fourth dream that appeared to him, and it foretold that the four castes, the warrior-nobles, the brahman priests, the burgesses, and the plebeians would realize the supreme deliverance when the Dhamma and the Discipline had been proclaimed by the Perfect One. While he was still only an unenlightened Bodhisatta, he walked upon a huge mountain of dirt without being fouled by the dirt. This was the fifth dream that appeared to him, and it foretold that although the Perfect One would obtain the requisites of robes, alms food, abode, and medicine, yet he would use them without greed or delusion or clinging, perceiving their dangers and understanding their purpose.

A. 5:196

NARRATOR ONE. The enlightenment itself is described in a number of discourses and from several different angles, as though one were to describe a tree from above, from below and from various sides, or a journey by land, by water and by air.[5]

NARRATOR TWO. There is the description of it as the attainment of the three true knowledges told as following upon the development of meditation. Then there are descriptions of it in terms of the discovery of the structure of conditionality in the impermanent process of being, and in terms of the search for the undeceiving interpretation, the true scale of value, in the problematic world of ideas, acts and things, probabilities and certainties. Here is the description in terms of meditation leading up to the discovery of the Four Noble Truths.

FIRST VOICE. "Now when I had eaten solid food and had regained strength, then quite secluded from sensual desires, secluded from unwholesome states I entered upon and abode in the first meditation, which is accompanied by thinking and exploring, with happiness and pleasure born of seclusion. But I allowed no such pleasant feeling as arose in me to gain power over my mind. With the stilling of thinking and exploring I entered upon and abode in the second meditation, which has internal confidence and singleness of mind without thinking and exploring, with happiness and pleasure born of concentration. But I allowed no such pleasant feeling as arose in me to gain power over my mind. With the fading as well of happiness, I abode in onlooking equanimity, mindful and fully aware; still feeling pleasure with the body, I entered upon and abode in the third meditation, referring to which the noble ones announce: 'He has a pleasant abiding who looks on with equanimity and is mindful.' But I allowed no such pleasant feeling as arose in me to gain power over my mind. With the abandoning of bodily pleasure and pain and with the previous disappearance of mental joy and grief, I entered upon and abode in the fourth meditation, which has neither pain nor pleasure and the purity of whose mindfulness is due to onlooking equanimity. But I allowed no such pleasure as arose in me to gain power over my mind.

"When my concentrated mind was thus purified, bright, unblemished and rid of imperfection, when it had become malleable, wieldy, steady and attained to imperturbability, I directed, I inclined my mind to the knowledge of recollection of past lives. I recollected my manifold past lives, that is to say, one birth, two, three, four, five births, ten, twenty, thirty, forty, fifty births, a hundred births, a thousand births, a hundred thousand births, many ages of world contraction, many ages of world expansion, many ages of world contraction and expansion: 'I was there so-named, of such a race, with such an appearance, such food, such experience of pleasure and pain, such a life term; and passing away thence, I reappeared elsewhere, and there too I was so-named, of such a race, with such an appearance, such experience of pleasure and pain, such a life term; passing away thence I reappeared here'—thus with details and particulars I recollected my manifold past life. This was the first true knowledge attained by me in the first watch of the night. Ignorance was banished and true knowledge arose, darkness was banished and light arose, as happens in one who is diligent, ardent and self-controlled. But I allowed no such pleasant feeling as arose in me to gain power over my mind.

"When my concentrated mind was thus purified … I directed, I inclined my mind to the knowledge of the passing away and reappearance of beings. With the divine eye, which is purified and surpasses the human, I saw beings passing away and reappearing, inferior and superior, fair and ugly, happy and unhappy in their destinations. I understood how beings pass on according to their actions: 'These worthy beings who were ill-conducted in body, speech and mind, revilers of noble ones, wrong in their views, giving effect to wrong view in their actions, on the dissolution of the body, after death, have reappeared in states of privation, in an unhappy destination, in perdition, even in hell; but these worthy beings, who were well-conducted in body, speech and mind, not revilers of noble ones, right in their views, giving effect to right view in their actions, on the dissolution of the body, after death, have reappeared in a happy destination, even in a heavenly world.' Thus with the divine eye, which is purified and surpasses the human, I saw beings passing away and reappearing, inferior and superior, fair and ugly, happy and unhappy in their destinations. I understood how beings pass on according to their actions. This was the second true knowledge attained by me in the second watch of the night. Ignorance was banished and true knowledge arose, darkness was banished and light arose, as happens in one who is diligent, ardent and self-controlled. But I allowed no such pleasant feeling as arose in me to gain power over my mind.

"When my concentrated mind was thus purified … I directed, I inclined my mind to the knowledge of exhaustion of taints. I had direct knowledge, as it actually is, that 'This is suffering,' that 'This is the origin of suffering,' that 'This is the cessation of suffering,' and that 'This is the way leading to the cessation of suffering'; I had direct knowledge, as it actually is, that 'These are taints,' that 'This is the origin of taints,' that 'This is the cessation of taints,' and that 'This is the way leading to the cessation of taints.' Knowing thus and seeing thus, my heart was liberated from the taint of sensual desire, from the taint of being, and from the taint of ignorance. When liberated, there came the knowledge: 'It is liberated.' I had direct knowledge: 'Birth is exhausted, the holy life has been lived out, what was to be done is done, there is no more of this to come.' This was the third true knowledge attained by me in the third watch of the night. Ignorance was banished and true knowledge arose, darkness was banished and light arose, as happens in one who is diligent, ardent and self-controlled. But I allowed no such pleasant feeling as arose in me to gain power over my mind."

M. 36

NARRATOR TWO. Now here is the description in terms of the structure of conditionality, in other words, dependent arising.[6] We shall return later to this subject.

FIRST VOICE. "Before my enlightenment, while I was still only an unenlightened Bodhisatta, I thought: 'This world has fallen into a slough; for it is born, ages and dies, it passes away and reappears, and yet it knows no escape from this suffering. When will an escape from this suffering be described?'

"I thought: 'What is there when ageing and death come to be? What is their necessary condition?' Then with ordered attention[7] I came to understand: 'Birth is there when ageing and death come to be; birth is a necessary condition for them.'

"I thought: 'What is there when birth comes to be? What is its necessary condition?' Then with ordered attention I came to understand: 'Being is there when birth comes to be; being is a necessary condition for that.'

"I thought: 'What is there when being comes to be? What is its necessary condition?' Then with ordered attention I came to understand: 'Clinging is there when being comes to be; clinging is a necessary condition for that.'

"… Craving is there when clinging comes to be ….

"… Feeling (of pleasure, pain or neither) is there when craving comes to be ….

"… Contact is there when feeling comes to be….

"… The sixfold base for contact is there when contact comes to be ….

"I thought: 'What is there when the sixfold base comes to be? What is its necessary condition?' Then with ordered attention I came to understand: 'Name-and-form is there when the sixfold base comes to be; name-and-form is a necessary condition for that.'

"I thought: 'What is there when name-and-form comes to be? What is its necessary condition?' Then with ordered attention I came to understand: 'Consciousness is there when name-and-form comes to be; consciousness is a necessary condition for that.'

"I thought: 'What is there when consciousness comes to be? What is its necessary condition?' Then with ordered attention I came to understand: 'Name-and-form is there when consciousness comes to be; name-and-form is a necessary condition for that.'

"I thought: 'This consciousness turns back upon itself; it does not extend beyond name-and-form. And this is how it happens whether one is being born, ageing or dying, passing away or reappearing. That is to say: It is with name-and-form as condition that consciousness comes to be; with consciousness as condition, name-and-form; with name-and-form as condition, the sixfold base for contact; with the sixfold base as condition, contact; with contact as condition, feeling; with feeling as condition, craving; with craving as condition, clinging; with clinging as condition, being; with being as condition, birth; with birth as condition, ageing and death come to be, and also sorrow and lamentation, pain, grief and despair; that is how there is an origin to this whole aggregate mass of suffering.' The origin, the origin: such was the insight, the knowledge, the understanding, the vision, the light, that arose in me about things not heard before.

"I thought: 'What is not there when no ageing and death come to be? With the cessation of what is there cessation of ageing and death?' Then with ordered attention I came to understand: 'When there is no birth, no ageing and death come to be; with cessation of birth there is cessation of ageing and death.'

"... When there is no being, no birth comes to be ....
"... When there is no clinging, no being comes to be ....
"... When there is no craving, no clinging comes to be ....
"... When there is no feeling, no craving comes to be ....
"... When there is no contact, no feeling comes to be ....
"... When there is no sixfold base, no contact comes to be ....
"... When there is no name-and-form, no sixfold base comes to be ....

"... When there is no consciousness, no name-and-form comes to be ....

"I thought: 'What is not there when no consciousness comes to be? With cessation of what is there cessation of consciousness?' Then with ordered attention I came to understand: 'When there is no name-and-form, no consciousness comes to be; with cessation of name-and-form there is cessation of consciousness.'

"I thought: 'This is the path to enlightenment that I have now reached, that is to say: With cessation of name-and-form there is cessation of consciousness; with cessation of consciousness, cessation of name-and-form; with cessation of name-and-form, cessation of the sixfold base; with cessation of the sixfold base, cessation of contact; with cessation of contact, cessation of feeling; with cessation of feeling, cessation of craving; with cessation of craving, cessation of clinging; with cessation of clinging, cessation of being; with cessation of being, cessation of birth; with cessation of birth, ageing and death cease, and also sorrow and lamentation, pain, grief and despair; that is how there is a cessation to this whole aggregate mass of suffering.' The cessation, the cessation: such was the insight, the knowledge, the understanding, the vision, the light, that arose in me about things not heard before.

"Suppose a man wandering in a forest wilderness found an ancient path, an ancient trail, travelled by men of old, and he followed it up, and by doing so he discovered an ancient city, an ancient royal capital, where men of old had lived, with parks and groves and lakes, walled round and beautiful to see, so I too found the ancient path, the ancient trail, travelled by the Fully Enlightened Ones of old.

"And what was that ancient path, that ancient trail? It was this Noble Eightfold Path, that is to say: right view, right intention, right speech, right action, right livelihood, right effort, right mindfulness, right concentration.

"I followed it up. By doing so I directly knew ageing and death, their origin, their cessation, and the way leading to their cessation. I directly knew birth, its origin, its cessation, and the way leading to its cessation. I directly knew being ... clinging ... craving ... feeling ... contact ... the sixfold base ... name-and-form ... consciousness ... I directly knew formations, their origin, their cessation, and the way leading to their cessation."

S. 12:65; cf. D. 14

NARRATOR TWO. Now finally here is the description in terms of the right judgement of the world of conditioned acts and ideas, classified in this discourse into the five aggregates, within which all conditioned experience, when analysed, can be classified.

FIRST VOICE. "Before my enlightenment, while I was still only an unenlightened Bodhisatta, I thought: 'In the case of material form, of feeling (of pleasure, pain or neither), of perception, of formations, of consciousness, what is the gratification, what the danger, what the escape?' Then I thought: 'In the case of each the bodily pleasure and mental joy that arise in dependence on these things (the five aggregates) are the gratification; the fact that these things are all impermanent, painful, and subject to change, is the danger; the disciplining and abandoning of desire and lust for them is the escape.'

"As long as I did not know by direct knowledge, as it actually is, that such was the gratification, such the danger, and such the escape, in the case of these five aggregates affected by clinging, so long did I make no claim to have discovered the enlightenment that is supreme in the world with its deities, its Māras and its Brahmā divinities, in this generation with its monks and brahmans, with its princes and men. But as soon as I knew by direct knowledge, as it actually is, that such is the gratification, such the danger, and such the escape, in the case of these five aggregates affected by clinging, then I claimed to have discovered the enlightenment that is supreme in the world with its deities, its Māras and its Brahmā divinities, in this generation with its monks and brahmans, with its princes and men."

S. 22:26

"Being myself subject to birth, ageing, ailment, death, sorrow, and defilement, seeing danger in what is subject to those things and seeking the unborn, unageing, unailing, deathless, sorrowless, undefiled supreme surcease of bondage, Nibbāna, I attained it. The knowledge and vision arose in me: 'My deliverance is unassailable; this is my last birth; there is now no renewal of being.' "

M. 26

NARRATOR TWO. Enlightenment has now been gained. And tradition has it that the first words that came to the Buddha—now no longer the Bodhisatta—were these.

CHANTER.

Seeking but not finding the house builder,
I travelled through the round of countless births:
Oh painful is birth ever and again.

House builder, you have now been seen;
You shall not build the house again.
Your rafters have been broken down;
Your ridge pole is demolished too.

My mind has now attained the unformed Nibbāna
And reached the end of every kind of craving.

Dh. 153-54

NARRATOR TWO. Those were the newly Enlightened One's first words, though according to tradition they were not spoken aloud; the first words spoken aloud were those in the first of the three stanzas beginning "When things are fully manifest ..." (see beginning of next chapter).

3
AFTER THE ENLIGHTENMENT

FIRST VOICE. Thus I heard. On one occasion, when the Blessed One was newly enlightened, he was living at Uruvelā by the banks of the River Nerañjarā at the root of the Bodhi Tree, the Tree of Enlightenment. Then the Blessed One sat at the root of the Bodhi Tree for seven days in one session, feeling the bliss of deliverance.

At the end of the seven days he emerged from that concentration, and in the first watch of the night his mind was occupied with dependent arising in forward order thus: "That comes to be when there is this; that arises with the arising of this; that is to say: It is with ignorance as condition that formations come to be; with formations as condition, consciousness; with consciousness as condition, name-and-form; with name-and-form as condition, the sixfold base; with the sixfold base as condition, contact; with contact as condition, feeling; with feeling as condition, craving; with craving as condition, clinging; with clinging as condition, being; with being as condition, birth; with birth as condition ageing and death come to be, and also sorrow and lamentation, pain, grief and despair; that is how there is an origin to this whole aggregate mass of suffering."

Knowing the meaning of this, the Blessed One uttered this exclamation:

> When things are fully manifest
> To the ardent meditating brahman,[1]
> His doubts all vanish, for he knows
> That each thing has to have its cause.

In the second watch of the night his mind was occupied with dependent arising in reverse order thus: "That does not come to be when there is not this; that ceases with the cessation of this; that is to say: With cessation of ignorance there is cessation of formations; with cessation of formations, cessation of consciousness; with cessation of consciousness, cessation of name-and-form; with cessation of name-and-form, cessation of the sixfold base; with cessation of the sixfold base, cessation of contact; with cessation of contact, cessation of feeling; with cessation of feeling, cessation of craving; with cessation of craving, cessation of clinging; with cessation of clinging, cessation of being; with cessation of being, cessation of birth; with cessation of birth, ageing and death cease, and also sorrow and lamentation, pain, grief and despair; that is how there is a cessation to this whole aggregate mass of suffering."

Knowing the meaning of this, the Blessed One then uttered this exclamation:

> When things are fully manifest
> To the ardent meditating brahman,
> His doubts all end, for he perceives
> How the conditions come to end.

In the third watch of the night his mind was occupied with dependent arising in forward and reverse order thus: "That comes to be when there is this, that arises with the arising of this. That does not come to be when there is not this; that ceases with the cessation of this; that is to say: It is with ignorance as condition that formations come to be; with formations as condition, consciousness … with birth as condition ageing and death come to be, and also sorrow and lamentation, pain, grief and despair; that is how there is an origin to this whole aggregate mass of suffering. With cessation of ignorance there is cessation of formations; with cessation of formations, cessation of consciousness … with cessation of birth, ageing and death cease, and also sorrow and lamentation, pain, grief and despair; that is how there is a cessation to this whole aggregate mass of suffering."

Knowing the meaning of this, the Blessed One then uttered this exclamation:

> When things are fully manifest
> To the ardent meditating brahman,
> There, like the sun who lights the sky,
> He stands repelling Māra's hosts.

Ud. 1:1-3; cf. Vin. Mv. 1:1

At the end of seven days,[2] after emerging from that concentration, the Blessed One surveyed the world with the eye of an Enlightened One. As he did so he saw beings burning with the many fires and consumed with the many fevers born of lust, of hate, and of delusion. Knowing the meaning of this, he then uttered this exclamation:

This world is anguished, being exposed to contact,
Even what the world calls self is in fact ill;
For no matter upon what it conceives (its conceits of self),
The fact is ever other than that (which it conceives).
The world, whose being is to become other,
Is committed to being, is exposed to being, relishes
only being,
Yet what it relishes brings fear, and what it fears is pain.
Now this holy life is lived to abandon suffering.[3]

"Whatever monks or brahmans have described liberation from being to come about through (love of) being, none, I say, are liberated from being. And whatever monks or brahmans have described escape from being to come about through (love of) non-being, none, I say, have escaped from being. Through the essentials of existence, suffering is; with all clinging exhausted, suffering is no more."

See this broad world:
Beings exposed to ignorance relishing what is,
Never freed from being.
Whatever the kinds of being, in any way, anywhere,
All are impermanent, pain-haunted, and subject to change.
So a man who sees this as it is,
Abandons craving for being, without relishing non-being.
The remainderless fading, ceasing, the Extinction,[4]
Comes with the utter ending of all craving.
When a bhikkhu reaches Nibbāna thus through not clinging,
Then he will have no renewal of being;
Māra has been vanquished and the battle gained,
Since one such as he has outstripped all being.

Ud. 3:10

SECOND VOICE. The occasion was this too when at the end of seven days the Blessed One rose from that concentration and went from the root of the Bodhi Tree to the root of the Ajapāla Nigrodha, the Goatherds' Banyan Tree. He sat at the root of the Ajapāla Nigrodha Tree for seven days in one session, feeling the bliss of deliverance.

Then one of the brahman caste—of the haughty haw-haw-ing kind[5]—went to the Blessed One and exchanged greetings with him. When this courteous formal talk was finished he stood at one side and said: "What is a brahman, Master Gotama? And what are the things that make a brahman?"

Knowing the meaning of this, the Blessed One then uttered this exclamation:

> The brahman who is rid of evil things,
> Not haughty, undefiled and self-controlled,
> Perfect in knowledge, and living the brahma-life,
> Can rightly employ the word "brahman,"
> If he is proud of nothing in the world.

Vin. Mv. 1:2; cf. Ud. 1:4

There was an occasion then when at the end of seven days the Blessed One rose from that concentration and went from the root of the Ajapāla Nigrodha to the root of the Mucalinda Tree.

Now on that occasion a great storm arose out of season with seven days of rain, cold winds and gloom. Then Mucalinda, the royal nāga serpent, came out from his realm. He wrapped the Blessed One's body seven times in his coils, and he stayed there with his great hood spread out above the Blessed One's head, thinking: "Let the Blessed One feel no cold or heat or touch of gadflies, gnats, wind, sun and creeping things."

At the end of the seven days Mucalinda saw the sky bright and cloudless. He unwrapped his coils from the Blessed One's body. Then he made his own form vanish, and assuming the form of a brahman youth, he stood before the Blessed One with his hands raised palms together towards him in reverence.

Knowing the meaning of this, the Blessed One then uttered this exclamation:

Seclusion is happiness for one contented,
By whom Dhamma is learnt, and who has seen,
And friendliness towards the world is happiness
For him who is forbearing with living beings.
Disinterest in the world is happiness
For him that has surmounted sense desires.
But to be rid of the conceit "I am"—
That is the greatest happiness of all.

Vin. Mv. 1:3; cf. Ud. 2:1

There was an occasion when the Blessed One rose from that concentration and went from the root of the Mucalinda Tree to the Rājāyatana Tree. He sat at the root of the Rājāyatana Tree for seven days in one session, feeling the bliss of deliverance.

Now on that occasion two merchants, Tapussa and Bhalluka, were travelling by the road from Ukkalā. A deity, who had been a relative of theirs in a former life, told them: "Good sirs, there is this Blessed One living at the root of the Rājāyatana Tree newly enlightened. Go and do honour to him with an offering of rice cake and honey. That will be long for your welfare and happiness."

So they took rice cake and honey to the Blessed One, and after paying homage to him, they stood at one side. Then they said: "Lord let the Blessed One accept this rice cake and honey, so that it may be long for our welfare and happiness."

The Blessed One thought: "Perfect Ones do not accept in their hands. In what should I accept the rice cake and honey?" Then the Four Divine Kings, aware in their minds of the thought in the Blessed One's mind, brought four crystal bowls from the four quarters: "Lord, let the Blessed One accept the rice cake and honey in these."

The Blessed One accepted the rice cake and honey in a new crystal bowl, and, having done so, he ate them. Then the merchants, Tapussa and Bhalluka, said: "We go for refuge to the Blessed One, and to the Dhamma. Beginning from today let the Blessed One count us as followers who have gone to him for refuge for as long as breath lasts."

Since they were the first followers in the world, they took only two refuges.

Vin. Mv. 1:4

There was an occasion then when at the end of seven days the Blessed One rose from that concentration and went from the root of the Rājāyatana Tree to the Ajapāla Nigrodha, the Goatherds' Banyan Tree.

FIRST VOICE. Now while the Blessed One was alone in retreat this thought arose in him: "There are five spiritual faculties that, when maintained in being and developed, merge in the deathless, reach to the deathless and end in the deathless. What five? They are the faculties of faith, energy, mindfulness, concentration, and understanding."

Then Brahmā Sahampati became aware in his mind of the thought in the Blessed One's mind, and as soon as a strong man might extend his flexed arm or flex his extended arm, he vanished in the Brahma-world and appeared before him. He arranged his upper robe on one shoulder, and raising his hands palms together towards the Blessed One, he said: "So it is, Blessed One; so it is, Sublime One. When these five faculties are maintained in being and developed, they merge in the deathless, reach to the deathless and end in the deathless. There was once a time, Lord, when I lived the holy life under the Buddha Kassapa. There I was known as the bhikkhu Sahaka. It was by maintaining in being and developing these five faculties that my lust for sensual desires faded away, and that on the dissolution of the body, after death, I reappeared in a happy destination, in the Brahma-world. There I am known as the Brahmā Sahampati. So it is, Blessed One, so it is, Sublime One. I know and I see how these five faculties, when maintained in being and developed, merge in the deathless, reach to the deathless and end in the deathless."

S. 48:57

Now while the Blessed One was alone in retreat this thought arose in him: "This path, namely the four foundations of mindfulness, is a path that goes in one way only:[6] to the purification of beings, to the surmounting of sorrow and lamentation, to the disappearance of pain and grief, to the attainment of the true goal, to the realization of Nibbāna. What are the four? A bhikkhu should abide contemplating the body as a body, ardent, fully aware and mindful, having put away covetousness and grief for the world. Or he should abide contemplating feelings as feelings, ardent, fully aware and mindful, having put away covetousness and grief for the world. Or he should abide contemplating consciousness as consciousness, ardent, fully aware and mindful, having put away covetousness and grief for the world. Or he should abide contemplating mental objects as mental objects, ardent, fully aware and mindful, having put away covetousness and grief for the world."

Then Brahmā Sahampati came and expressed his approval as before.

S. 47:18, 43

Now while the Blessed One was alone in retreat the thought arose in him: "I am freed from that penance; I am quite freed from that useless penance. Absolutely sure and mindful, I have attained enlightenment."

Then Māra the Evil One became aware in his mind of the thought in the Blessed One's mind, and he went to him and spoke these stanzas:

You have forsaken the ascetic path
By means of which men purify themselves;
You are not pure, you fancy you are pure.
The path of purity is far from you.

Then the Blessed One recognized Māra the Evil One, and he answered him in stanzas:

I know these penances to gain the deathless—
Whatever kind they are—to be as vain
As a ship's oars and rudder on dry land.
But it is owing to development
Of virtue, concentration, understanding,
That I have reached enlightenment; and you,
Exterminator, have been vanquished now.

Then Māra the Evil One knew: "The Blessed One knows me, the Sublime One knows me." Sad and disappointed, he vanished at once.

S. 4:1

Now while the Blessed One was alone in retreat this thought arose in him: "He lives unhappily who has nothing to venerate and obey.

But what monk or brahman is there under whom I could live, honouring and respecting him?"

Then he thought: "I could live under another monk or brahman and respecting him in order to perfect an unperfected code of virtue or code of concentration or code of understanding or code of deliverance or code of knowledge and vision of deliverance. But I do not see in this world with its deities, its Māras and its divinities, in this generation with its monks and brahmans, with its princes and men, any monk or brahman in whom these things are more perfected than in myself under whom I could live, honouring and respecting him. But there is this Dhamma discovered by me—suppose I lived under that, honouring and respecting that?"

Then Brahmā Sahampati became aware in his mind of the thought in the Blessed One's mind. He appeared before the Blessed One: "Lord, it is good. The Blessed Ones in past ages, accomplished and fully enlightened, lived under the Dhamma honouring and respecting that. And those in future ages will do so too."

S. 6:2; A. 4:21

SECOND VOICE. Now while the Blessed One was alone in retreat this thought arose in him: "This Dhamma that I have attained to is profound and hard to see, hard to discover; it is the most peaceful and superior goal of all, not attainable by mere ratiocination, subtle, for the wise to experience. But this generation relies on attachment, relishes attachment, delights in attachment. It is hard for such a generation to see this truth, that is to say, specific conditionality, dependent arising. And it is hard to see this truth, that is to say, stilling of all formations, relinquishing of the essentials of existence, exhaustion of craving, fading of lust, cessation, Nibbāna. And if I taught the Dhamma others would not understand me, and that would be wearying and troublesome for me."

Thereupon there came to him spontaneously these stanzas never heard before:

Enough of teaching of the Dhamma
That even I found hard to reach;
For it will never be perceived
By those that live in lust and hate.

Men dyed in lust, and whom a cloud
Of darkness laps, will never see
What goes against the stream, is subtle,
Deep and hard to see, abstruse.

Considering thus, his mind favoured inaction and not teaching the Dhamma.

Then it occured to Brahmā Sahampati, who became aware in his mind of the thought in the Blessed One's mind: "The world will be lost, the world will be utterly lost; for the mind of the Perfect One, accomplished and fully enlightened, favours inaction and not teaching the Dhamma."

Then as soon as a strong man might extend his flexed arm or flex his extended arm, Brahmā Sahampati vanished in the Brahma-world and appeared before the Blessed One. He arranged his robe on one shoulder, and putting his right knee on the ground and raising his hands palms together towards the Blessed One, he said: "Lord, let the Blessed One teach the Dhamma. Let the Sublime One teach the Dhamma. There are beings with little dust on their eyes who are wasting through not hearing the Dhamma. Some of them will gain final knowledge of the Dhamma."

When Brahmā Sahampati had said this, he said further:

In Magadha there has appeared till now
Impure Dhamma thought out by men still stained:
Open the Deathless Gateway: let them hear
The Dhamma the Immaculate has found.
Ascend, O Sage, the tower of the Dhamma;
And, just as one sees all the folk around
Who stand upon a solid pile of rock,
Survey, O Sorrowless All-seeing Sage,
This human breed engulfed in sorrowing
That birth has at its mercy and old age.
Arise, O Hero, Victor, Knowledge-bringer,
Free From All Debt, and wander in the world.

Proclaim the Dhamma; for some,
O Blessed One, will understand.

The Blessed One listened to Brahmā Sahampati's pleading. Out of compassion for beings he surveyed the world with the eye of a

Buddha. Just as in a pond of blue, red or white lotuses, some lotuses that are born and grow in the water thrive immersed in the water without coming up out of it, and some other lotuses that are born and grow in the water rest on the water's surface, and some other lotuses that are born and grow in the water come right up out of the water and stand clear, unwetted by it, so too he saw beings with little dust on their eyes and with much dust on their eyes, with keen faculties and dull faculties, with good qualities and bad qualities, easy to teach and hard to teach, and some who dwelt seeing fear in the other world and blame as well. When he had seen this, he replied:

> Wide open are the portals of the Deathless.
> Let those who hear show faith.[7] If I was minded
> To tell not the sublime Dhamma I know,
> It was that I saw vexation in the telling.

Then Brahmā Sahampati thought: "I have made it possible for the Dhamma to be taught by the Blessed One." And after he had paid homage to him, keeping him on his right, he vanished at once.

Vin. Mv. 1:5; cf. M. 26 & 85; S. 6:1

The Blessed One thought: "To whom shall I first teach the Dhamma? Who will soon understand this Dhamma?" Then he thought: "Aḷārā Kālāma is wise, learned and discerning. He has had little dust on his eyes for a long time. Suppose I taught the Dhamma first to him? He will soon understand it."

Then invisible deities told the Blessed One: "Lord, Āḷāra Kālāma died seven days ago." And the knowledge and vision arose in him: "Āḷāra Kālāma died seven days ago." He thought: "Āḷāra Kālāma's loss is a great one. If he had heard this Dhamma, he would soon have understood it."

The Blessed One thought: "Uddaka Rāmaputta is wise, learned and discerning. He has had little dust on his eyes for a long time. Suppose I taught the Dhamma first to him? He will soon understand it."

Then invisible deities told the Blessed One: "Lord, Uddaka Rāmaputta died last night." And the knowledge and vision arose in him: "Uddaka Rāmaputta died last night." He thought: "Uddaka

Rāmaputta's loss is a great one. If he had heard this Dhamma he would soon have understood it."

The Blessed One thought: "To whom shall I first teach the Dhamma? Who will soon understand this Dhamma?" Then he thought: "The bhikkhus of the group of five who attended me while I was engaged in my struggle were very helpful. Suppose I taught the Dhamma first to them?" Then he thought: "Where are the bhikkhus of the group of five living now?" And with the divine eye, which is purified and surpasses the human, he saw that they were living at Benares in the Deer Park at Isipatana, the Resort of the Seers.

The Blessed One stayed on at Uruvelā as long as he chose, and then he set out to go by stages to Benares.

Between the Place of Enlightenment and Gayā the monk Upaka saw him on the road. He said: "Your faculties are serene, friend; the colour of your skin is clear and bright. Under whom have you gone forth? Or who is your teacher? Or whose Dhamma do you confess?"

When this was said, the Blessed One addressed the monk Upaka in stanzas:

I am an All-transcender,[8] an All-knower,
Unsullied by all things, renouncing all,
By craving's ceasing freed. And this I owe
To my own wisdom. To whom should I concede it?

I have no teacher, and my like
Exists nowhere in all the world
With all its gods, because I have
No person for my counterpart.
I am the Teacher in the world
Without a peer, accomplished, too,
And I alone am quite enlightened,
Quenched, whose fires are all extinct.
I go to Kāsi's city now
To set the Wheel of Dhamma
In motion: in a blindfold world
I go to beat the Deathless Drum.

"By your claims, friend, you are a Universal Victor."

The victors like me, Upaka,
Are those whose taints are quite exhausted;
I have vanquished all states of evil:
It is for that I am a Victor.

When this was said, the monk Upaka remarked: "May it be so, friend"; shaking his head, he took a side track and departed.

Then wandering by stages, the Blessed One came at length to Benares, to the Deer Park at Isipatana, where the bhikkhus of the group of five were. They saw him coming in the distance. Then they agreed among themselves: "Friends, here comes the monk Gotama who became self-indulgent, gave up the struggle and reverted to luxury. We ought not to pay homage to him or rise up for him or receive his bowl and outer robe. Still a seat can be prepared. Let him sit down if he likes."

But as soon as the Blessed One approached, they found themselves unable to keep their pact. One went to meet him and took his bowl and outer robe; another prepared a seat; another set out water, footstool and towel. The Blessed One sat down on the seat prepared and washed his feet. They addressed him by name and as "friend."

When this was said, he told them: "Bhikkhus, do not address the Perfect One by name and as 'friend': the Perfect One is accomplished and fully enlightened. Listen, bhikkhus, the Deathless has been attained. I shall instruct you. I shall teach you the Dhamma. By practising as you are instructed you will, by realizing it yourselves here and now through direct knowledge, enter upon and abide in that supreme goal of the holy life for the sake of which clansmen rightly go forth from the house life into homelessness."

Then the bhikkhus of the group of five said: "Friend Gotama, even with the hardship, privation and mortification that you practised you achieved no distinction higher than the human state worthy of the noble ones' knowledge and vision. Since you are now self-indulgent and have given up the struggle and reverted to luxury, how will you have achieved any such distinction?"

Then the Blessed One told the bhikkhus of the group of five: "The Perfect One is not self-indulgent, he has not given up the struggle, he has not reverted to luxury. The Perfect One is accomplished and fully enlightened. Listen, bhikkhus, the Deathless has been attained. I shall instruct you. I shall teach you the Dhamma. By practising as you are instructed you will, by realizing it yourselves here and now through direct knowledge, enter upon and abide in that supreme goal of the holy life for the sake of which clansmen rightly go forth from the house life into homelessness."

A second time the bhikkhus of the group of five said the same thing to him; and a second time he gave them the same answer. A third time they said the same thing. When this was said, he asked them: "Bhikkhus, have you ever known me speak like this before?"

"No, Lord."

"The Perfect One is accomplished and fully enlightened. Listen, bhikkhus, the Deathless has been attained. I shall instruct you. I shall teach you the Dhamma. By practising as you are instructed you will, by realizing it yourselves here and now through direct knowledge, enter upon and dwell in that supreme goal of the holy life for the sake of which clansmen rightly go forth from the house life into homelessness."

Vin. Mv.l:6; cf. M. 26 & 85

The Blessed One was able to convince them. They heard the Blessed One; they listened and opened their hearts to knowledge. Then the Blessed One addressed the bhikkhus of the group of five thus:

(*Setting Rolling the Wheel of the Dhamma*)

"Bhikkhus, there are these two extremes that ought not to be cultivated by one who has gone forth. What two? There is devotion to pursuit of pleasure in sensual desires, which is low, coarse, vulgar, ignoble and harmful; and there is devotion to self-mortification, which is painful, ignoble and harmful. The middle way discovered by the Perfect One avoids both these extremes; it gives vision, gives knowledge, and leads to peace, to direct knowledge, to enlightenment, to Nibbāna. And what is that middle way? It is this Noble Eightfold Path, that is to say: right view, right intention, right speech, right action, right livelihood, right effort, right mindfulness, and right concentration. That is the middle way discovered by the Perfect One, which gives vision, gives knowledge, and leads to peace, to direct knowledge, to enlightenment, to Nibbāna.

"There is this noble truth of suffering: birth is suffering, ageing is suffering, sickness is suffering, death is suffering, sorrow and lamentation, pain, grief and despair are suffering, association with the loathed is suffering, dissociation from the loved is suffering, not to get what one wants is suffering—in short, the five aggregates affected by clinging[9] are suffering.

"There is this noble truth of the origin of suffering: it is craving, which produces renewal of being, is accompanied by relish and lust, relishing this and that; in other words, craving for sensual desires, craving for being, craving for non-being.

"There is this noble truth of the cessation of suffering: it is the remainderless fading and ceasing, the giving up, relinquishing, letting go and rejecting of that same craving.

"There is this noble truth of the way leading to the cessation of suffering: it is this Noble Eightfold Path, that is to say, right view, right intention, right speech, right action, right livelihood, right effort, right mindfulness, and right concentration.

" 'There is this noble truth of suffering': such was the insight, the knowledge, the understanding, the vision, the light, that arose in me about things not heard before. 'This noble truth must be penetrated to by fully knowing suffering': such was the insight, the knowledge, the understanding, the vision, the light, that arose in me about things not heard before. 'This noble truth has been penetrated to by fully knowing suffering': such was the insight, the knowledge, the understanding, the vision, the light, that arose in me about things not heard before.

" 'There is this noble truth of the origin of suffering': such was the insight, the knowledge, the understanding, the vision, the light, that arose in me about things not heard before. 'This noble truth must be penetrated to by abandoning the origin of suffering': such was the insight, the knowledge, the understanding, the vision, the light, that arose in me about things not heard before. 'This noble truth has been penetrated to by abandoning the origin of suffering': such was the insight, the knowledge, the understanding, the vision, the light, that arose in me about things not heard before.

" 'There is this noble truth of the cessation of suffering': such was the insight, the knowledge, the understanding, the vision, the light, that arose in me about things not heard before. 'This noble truth must be penetrated to by realizing the cessation of suffering': such was the insight, the knowledge, the understanding, the vision, the light, that arose in me about things not heard before. 'This noble truth has been penetrated to by realizing the cessation of suffering': such was the insight, the knowledge, the understanding, the vision, the light, that arose in me about things not heard before.

" 'There is this noble truth of the way leading to the cessation of suffering': such was the insight, the knowledge, the understanding, the vision, the light, that arose in me about things not heard before. 'This noble truth must be penetrated to by maintaining in being[10] the way leading to the cessation of suffering': such was the insight, the knowledge, the understanding, the vision, the light, that arose in me about things not heard before. 'This noble truth has been penetrated to by maintaining in being the way leading to the cessation of suffering': such was the insight, the knowledge, the understanding, the vision, the light, that arose in me about things not heard before.

"As long as my correct knowledge and vision in these twelve aspects in these three phases of penetration to each of the Four Noble Truths—was not quite purified, I did not claim to have discovered the full enlightenment that is supreme in the world with its deities, its Māras and its divinities, in this generation with its monks and brahmans, with its princes and men. But as soon as my correct knowledge and vision in these twelve aspects—in the three phases of each of the Four Noble Truths—was quite purified, then I claimed to have discovered the full enlightenment that is supreme in the world with its deities, its Māras and its divinities, in this generation with its monks and brahmans, with its princes and men.

"The knowledge and vision arose in me: 'My heart's deliverance is unassailable; this is the last birth; there is no more renewal of being.' "

Vin. Mv. 1:6; S. 56:11

Now while this discourse was being delivered the spotless, immaculate vision of the Dhamma arose in the venerable Kondañña thus: All that is subject to arising is subject to cessation.

And when the Wheel of the Dhamma had been set rolling by the Blessed One, the earth deities cried out: "At Benares, in the Deer Park at Isipatana, the Perfect One, accomplished and fully enlightened, has set rolling the Matchless Wheel of the Dhamma which cannot be stopped by monk or brahman or deity or Māra or divinity or anyone in the world." And hearing the earth deities' cry, the deities of the Four Kings' Heaven cried out: "At Benares ..." The deities of Tāvatiṃsa (the Thirty-three) ... the deities of Tusita (the Contented) ... the deities of Yāma (those who have Gone to Bliss) ... the deities of Nimmānarati (those who Delight in Creating) ... the deities of Paranimmitavasavatti (those who Wield Power over Others' Creations) ... the deities of Brahmā's Retinue cried out: "At Benares ..."

So at that minute, at that moment, at that instant, the news travelled right up to the Brahma-world. And this ten-thousandfold world-element shook and quaked and trembled while a great measureless light surpassing the splendour of the gods appeared in the world.

Then the Blessed One exclaimed: "Kondañña knows, Kondañña knows!" And that is how that venerable one acquired the name Aññāta Kondañña—Kondañña who knows.

Then Aññāta Kondañña, who had seen and reached and found and penetrated the Dhamma, whose uncertainties were left behind, whose doubts had vanished, who had gained perfect confidence and become independent of others in the Teacher's Dispensation, said to the Blessed One: "Lord, I wish to go forth under the Blessed One and to receive the full admission."

"Come, bhikkhu," the Blessed One said: "The Dhamma is well proclaimed. Live the holy life for the complete ending of suffering." And that was his full admission.

Then the Blessed One taught and instructed the rest of the bhikkhus with talk on the Dhamma. As he did so, there arose in the venerable Vappa and the venerable Bhaddiya, the spotless, immaculate vision of the Dhamma: All that is subject to arising is subject to cessation. They too asked for and received the full admission.

Then, living on the food they brought to him, the Blessed One taught and instructed the rest of the bhikkhus with talk on the Dhamma. All six lived on the food brought back by three of them. Then there arose in the venerable Mahānāma and the venerable Assaji the spotless, immaculate vision of the Dhamma, and they too asked for and received the full admission.

Then the Blessed One addressed the bhikkhus thus:

Vin. Mv. 1:6

(*The Discourse on the Not-Self Characteristic*)

"Bhikkhus, material form is not self. If material form were self, this material form would not lead to affliction, and it could be had of material form: 'Let my material form be thus; let my material form be not thus.' And it is because material form is not self that it therefore leads to affliction, and that it cannot be had of material form: 'Let my material form be thus; let my material form be not thus.'

"Feeling is not self....

"Perception is not self....

"Formations are not self....

"Consciousness is not self. If consciousness were self, this consciousness would not lead to affliction and it could be had of consciousness: 'Let my consciousness be thus; let my consciousness be not thus.' And it is because consciousness is not self that it therefore leads to affliction, and that it cannot be had of consciousness: 'Let my consciousness be thus; let my consciousness be not thus.'

"How do you conceive this, bhikkhus, is material form permanent or impermanent?"—"Impermanent, Lord."—"But is what is impermanent unpleasant or pleasant?"—"Unpleasant, Lord."—"But is it fitting to regard what is impermanent, unpleasant and subject to change as: 'This is mine, this is what I am, this is my self?' "—"No, Lord."

"How do you conceive this, is feeling permanent .... "How do you conceive this, is perception permanent .... "How do you conceive this, are formations permanent ....

"How do you conceive this, is consciousness permanent or impermanent?"—"Impermanent, Lord."—"But is what is impermanent unpleasant or pleasant?"—"Unpleasant, Lord."—"But is it fitting to regard what is impermanent, unpleasant and subject to change as: 'This is mine, this is what I am, this is my self?"—"No, Lord."

"Therefore, bhikkhus, any material form whatsoever, whether past, future or present, in oneself or external, coarse or fine, inferior or superior, far or near, should all be regarded as it actually is by right understanding thus: 'This is not mine, this is not what I am, this is not my self.'

"Any feeling whatsoever ....

"Any perception whatsoever....

"Any formations whatsoever....

"Any consciousness whatsoever, whether past, future or present, in oneself or external, coarse or fine, inferior or superior, far or near, should all be regarded as it actually is by right understanding thus: 'This is not mine, this is not what I am, this is not my self.'

"Seeing thus, bhikkhus, a wise noble disciple becomes dispassionate towards material form, becomes dispassionate towards feeling, becomes dispassionate towards perception, becomes dispassionate towards formations, becomes dispassionate towards consciousness. Becoming dispassionate, his lust fades away; with the fading of lust his heart is liberated; when liberated, there comes the knowledge: 'It is liberated.' He understands: 'Birth is exhausted, the holy life has been lived out, what was to be done is done, there is no more of this to come.' "

That is what the Blessed One said. The bhikkhus of the group of five were glad, and they delighted in his words. Now while this discourse was being delivered the hearts of the bhikkhus of the group of five were liberated from taints through not clinging.

And there were then six Arahants, six accomplished ones, in the world.

Vin. Mv. 1:6; cf. S. 22:59

4
THE SPREADING OF THE DHAMMA

SECOND VOICE. The occasion was this. There was a clansman named Yasa. He was a rich merchant's son and delicately brought up. He had three palaces, one for the winter, one for the summer, and one for the rains. In the rains palace he was entertained by minstrels with no men among them. For the four months of the rains he never went down to the lower palace.

Now while Yasa was amusing himself, enjoying the five kinds of sensual pleasures with which he was furnished, he fell asleep, though it was still early; and his attendants fell asleep too. But an all-night lamp was burning; and when Yasa woke up early, he saw his attendants sleeping. There was one with her lute under her arm, another with her tabor under her chin, another with her drum under her arm. The hair of one had come unfastened, another was dribbling, others were muttering. It seemed like a charnel ground. When he saw it, when its squalor squarely struck him, he was sick at heart, and he exclaimed: "It is fearful, it is horrible!"[1]

Then he put on his gold slippers and went to the door of his house, and non-human beings opened the door so that none might stop his going forth from the house life into homelessness. Then he went to the city gate, and non-human beings opened the gate so that none might stop his going forth from the house life into homelessness.

He walked to the Deer Park at Isipatana. Now the occasion was one on which the Blessed One had risen early in the night towards dawn and was pacing up and down in the open. When he saw Yasa coming in the distance, he left his walk and sat down on a seat made ready for him. When Yasa was not far from the Blessed One, he exclaimed: "It is fearful, it is horrible!"

Then the Blessed One said: "This is not fearful, this is not horrible. Come, Yasa, sit down. I shall teach you the Dhamma."

He thought: "This is not fearful, it seems, this is not horrible," and he was happy and hopeful. He took off his gold slippers and went to where the Blessed One was. After paying homage to him he sat down at one side. When he had done so, the Blessed One gave him progressive instruction, that is to say, talk on giving, on virtue, on the heavens; he explained the dangers, the vanity and the defilement in sensual pleasures and the blessings in renunciation. When he saw that Yasa's mind was ready, receptive, free from hindrance, eager and trustful, he expounded to him the teaching peculiar to the Buddhas:[2] suffering, its origin, its cessation, and the path to its cessation. Just as a clean cloth with all marks removed would take dye evenly, so too while Yasa sat there the spotless, immaculate vision of the Dhamma arose in him: All that is subject to arising is subject to cessation.

Now Yasa's mother went up into his palace. Not seeing Yasa, she went to the merchant and said: "Your son Yasa cannot be found."

Then he sent messengers in all the four directions, and he himself went to the Deer Park at Isipatana. Seeing the prints of the gold slippers, he followed them. The Blessed One saw him coming. He thought: "Suppose I use my supernormal power so that while the merchant is sitting here he will not see Yasa sitting here?" He did so. Then the merchant came to the Blessed One and asked him: "Lord, might the Blessed One have seen Yasa?"

"Now sit down; and perhaps while you are sitting here you may see Yasa sitting here too."

He was glad when he heard this, and he paid homage to the Blessed One and sat down at one side. When he had done so, the Blessed One talked to him as he had done to Yasa. Then the merchant saw and reached and found and penetrated the Dhamma; he left uncertainty behind him, his doubts vanished, he gained perfect confidence and became independent of others in the Teacher's Dispensation. He said: "Magnificent, Lord, magnificent, Lord! The Dhamma has been made clear in many ways by the Blessed One, as though he were righting the overthrown, revealing the hidden, showing the way to one who is lost, holding up a lamp in the dark for those with eyes to see visible forms. I go to the Blessed One for refuge and to the Dhamma and to the Sangha of bhikkhus. Beginning from today, Lord, let the Blessed One receive me as his follower who has gone to him for refuge as long as breath lasts." And he was the first adherent in the world to take the Triple Refuge.

While the Dhamma was being taught to his father Yasa reviewed the plane of knowledge that he had seen and experienced, and through not clinging his heart was liberated from taints. Then the Blessed One thought: "After this achievement Yasa is no longer capable of reverting to what he has left behind and enjoying sensual pleasures in the house life as he used to do. Suppose I now stop using the supernormal power?"

He did so. The merchant saw his son sitting there. He said to him: "Yasa, my son, your mother is sorrowing and grieving. Give life to your mother."

Yasa looked at the Blessed One. The Blessed One said to the merchant: "How do you conceive this? If Yasa had seen the Dhamma with the learner's[3] knowledge and the learner's eyes as you have done, and if he had then reviewed the plane of knowledge that he had seen and experienced, and if through not clinging his heart had been liberated from taints, would he be capable of reverting to what he had left behind and enjoying sensual pleasures in the house life as he used to do?"

"No, Lord."

"But that is what Yasa has done. Now he is no longer capable of reverting to what he has left behind and enjoying sensual pleasures in the house life as he used to do."

"It is a gain, Lord, it is a great gain for Yasa that through not clinging his heart is liberated from taints. Lord, let the Blessed One with Yasa as his attendant monk consent to accept today's meal from me." The Blessed One consented in silence. Then when the merchant knew that the Blessed One had consented, he rose from his seat, and after paying homage to the Blessed One, he departed keeping him on his right.

Soon after he had gone Yasa said to the Blessed One: "Lord, I wish to receive the going forth and the full admission from the Blessed One."

"Come, bhikkhu," the Blessed One said, "the Dhamma is well proclaimed. Lead the holy life for the complete ending of suffering." And that was the venerable Yasa's full admission.

And then there were seven Arahants in the world.

It now being morning, the Blessed One dressed, and taking his bowl and outer robe, he went with the venerable Yasa as his attendant monk to the merchant's house, and he sat down on the appointed seat.

Then the venerable Yasa's mother and his former wife went to the Blessed One, and after paying homage to him, they sat down at one side. He talked to them as he had talked to Yasa and his father. The spotless, immaculate vision of the Dhamma arose in them too: All that is subject to arising is subject to cessation. They saw the Dhamma as the merchant had done, and they took the Triple Refuge: "Beginning from today, Lord, let the Blessed One receive us as his followers who have gone to him for refuge as long as breath lasts." And they were the first women adherents in the world to take the Triple Refuge.

Then the venerable Yasa's mother and father and his former wife served the Blessed One and the venerable Yasa with their own hands, and they satisfied them with different kinds of good food. When the Blessed One had eaten and no longer had the bowl in his hand, they sat down at one side. Then after the Blessed One had instructed, urged, roused and encouraged them with talk on the Dhamma, he rose from his seat and went away.

Now four of the venerable Yasa's friends belonging to the leading merchant families in Benares, whose names were Vimala, Sabāhu, Puṇṇaji and Gavampati, heard: "Yasa the clansman has shaved off his hair and beard, it seems, and put on the yellow robe, and he has gone forth from the house life into homelessness." When they heard this, they thought: "It can be no ordinary Dhamma and Discipline, it can be no ordinary going forth, for Yasa to have done this."

They went to the venerable Yasa, and after paying homage to him, they stood at one side. Then the venerable Yasa took them to the Blessed One. After presenting them to the Blessed One, he said: "Lord, let the Blessed One advise and instruct them." Then the Blessed One talked to them as he had done to the others, and they too became independent in the Teacher's Dispensation. They said: "Lord, we wish to receive the going forth and the full admission from the Blessed One."

"Come, bhikkhus, "the Blessed One said: "The Dhamma is well proclaimed; lead the holy life for the complete ending of suffering." And that was those venerable ones' admission. Then the Blessed One advised and instructed those bhikkhus in the Dhamma, and while they were being thus advised and instructed, their hearts through not clinging were liberated from taints.

And then there were eleven Arahants in the world.

Now fifty of the venerable Yasa's friends in the countryside, sons of leading and secondary families, heard likewise that he had gone forth into homelessness. They went to the venerable Yasa, who took them to the Blessed One. And when the Blessed One had talked to them, they too asked for the going forth and the full admission. After they had been advised and instructed by the Blessed One, their hearts through not clinging were liberated from taints. And then there were sixty-one Arahants in the world.

Then the Blessed One addressed the bhikkhus: "Bhikkhus, I am free from all shackles whether human or divine. You too are free from all shackles whether human or divine. Go now and wander for the welfare and happiness of many, out of compassion for the world, for the benefit, welfare and happiness of gods and men. Teach the Dhamma that is good in the beginning, good in the middle and good in the end, with the meaning and the letter. Explain a holy life that is utterly perfect and pure. There are beings with little dust on their eyes who will be lost through not hearing the Dhamma. Some will understand the Dhamma. I shall go to Uruvelā, to Senānigāma, to teach the Dhamma."

Then Māra the Evil One came to the Blessed One and spoke to him in stanzas:

"You are bound by every shackle
Whether human or divine;
The bonds that tie you down are strong,
And you shall not escape me, monk."

"I am free from all the shackles
Whether human or divine;
Freed from the strongest bonds, and you
Are vanquished now, Exterminator."

"The shackle in the air that has
Its hold upon the mind, with that
I hold you bound for evermore,
So you shall not escape me, monk."

"I am without desire for sights,
Sounds, tastes, and smells, and things to touch,
However good they seem, and you
Are vanquished now, Exterminator."

Then Māra the Evil One understood: "The Blessed One knows me; the Sublime One knows me." Sad and disappointed, he vanished at once.

By now the bhikkhus who had set out to wander were bringing in from various quarters and from various countries men who wanted the going forth and the admission, so that they should be given to them by the Blessed One. This was troublesome for both the bhikkhus and those who wanted the going forth and the admission. The Blessed One considered this matter, and when it was evening, he summoned the Sangha of bhikkhus on this account, for this reason. After giving a discourse on the Dhamma, he addressed them thus:

"Bhikkhus, while I was alone in retreat this thought arose in my mind: 'Bhikkhus are now bringing in from various quarters and from various countries men who want the going forth and the admission, so that these should be given to them by me. This is troublesome for both the bhikkhus and those who want the going forth and the admission. Why should I not now authorize bhikkhus to give the going forth and the admission there in whatever quarter, in whatever country they happen to be?' This in fact I allow you to do. And it should be done in this way: first the hair and beard should be shaved off. Then after putting on the yellow robe the upper robe should be arranged on one shoulder and homage should be paid at the bhikkhu's feet. Then kneeling with the hands held out palms together, this should be said: 'I go for refuge to the Buddha, I go for refuge to the Dhamma, I go for refuge to the Sangha. For the second time .... For the third time .... ' I allow the going forth and the admission to be given by the Triple Refuge."

Now when the Blessed One had spent the rains at Benares, he addressed the bhikkhus thus:

"Bhikkhus, it is with ordered attention, with ordered effort, that I have reached and have realized the supreme deliverance. It is with ordered attention, with ordered effort, that you also, bhikkhus, have reached and have realized the supreme deliverance."

Then Māra the Evil One came to the Blessed One and spoke to him in stanzas:

> "You are bound by Māra's shackles
> Whether human or divine;
> You are bound by Māra's bonds,
> And you shall not escape me, monk."

"I am free from Māra's shackles,
Whether human or divine;
Free from Māra's bonds; and you
Are vanquished now, Exterminator."

Then Māra the Evil One understood: "The Blessed One knows me, the Sublime One knows me." Sad and disappointed he vanished at once.

When the Blessed One had lived at Benares as long as he chose, he set out to wander by stages to Uruvelā. On the way he left the road to go into a wood, and there he sat down at the root of a tree. Now at that time a special party of thirty friends together with their wives were amusing themselves in the wood. One of them had no wife, so a harlot had been brought for him. While they were carelessly enjoying themselves the harlot stole his property and ran away. Then in order to help him his friends went in search of the woman. As they were wandering about in the wood they saw the Blessed One sitting at the root of a tree. They went up to him and asked: "Lord, has the Blessed One seen a woman?" "Boys, what have you to do with a woman?" They told him what had happened.

"How do you conceive this, then; which is better for you, that you should seek a woman or that you should seek yourselves?"[4]

"Lord, it is better for us that we seek ourselves."

"Then sit down, and I will teach you the Dhamma."

"Even so, Lord," they replied. And after paying homage to him, they sat down at one side.

The Blessed One gave them progressive instruction. In due course the spotless, immaculate vision of the Dhamma arose in them. And in the end they became independent of others in the Teacher's Dispensation. Then they said: "We wish to receive the going forth and the full admission from the Blessed One."

"Come, bhikkhus," the Blessed One said, "the Dhamma is well proclaimed. Lead the holy life for the complete ending of suffering." And that was those venerable ones' admission.

The Blessed One journeyed on by stages till he at length arrived at Uruvelā. Now at that time three matted-hair ascetics were living at Uruvelā called Kassapa of Uruvelā, Kassapa of the River, and Kassapa of Gayā. Kassapa of Uruvelā was the leader, guide, chief, head and principal of five hundred matted-hair ascetics, Kassapa of the River of three hundred, and Kassapa of Gayā of two hundred.

The Blessed One went to the hermitage of Kassapa of Uruvelā, and he said: "Kassapa, if you have no objection, I should like to spend one night in your fire chamber."

"I have no objection, Great Monk. But there is a savage royal nāga serpent there. He has supernormal powers. He is venomous, fearfully poisonous, and capable of killing you."

The Blessed One asked a second time and a third time and received the same reply. He said: "Perhaps he will not destroy me, Kassapa. So grant me the fire chamber."

"Then stay there as long as you like, Great Monk."

So the Blessed One went into the fire chamber. He spread out a rush mat and sat down, folding his legs crosswise, setting his body erect and establishing mindfulness in front of him. When the nāga saw the Blessed One come in, he was angry, and he produced smoke. Then the Blessed One thought: "Suppose I counter his fire by fire without injuring his outer skin or inner skin or flesh or sinews or bones or marrow?" He did so, and he produced smoke. Then the nāga, no longer restraining his fury, produced flames. The Blessed One entered upon the fire element and produced flames too. The fire chamber seemed to burn and blaze and glow with their flames. The matted-hair ascetics gathered round, and they said: "The Great Monk who is so beautiful is being destroyed by the nāga."

When the night was over and the Blessed One had countered the nāga's fire by fire without injuring him, he put him into his bowl and showed him to Uruvelā Kassapa: "This is your nāga, Kassapa. His fire has been countered by fire." Then Uruvelā Kassapa thought: "The Great Monk is very mighty and powerful since he is able to counter by fire the fire of the savage royal nāga serpent with supernormal powers who is venomous, fearfully poisonous. But he is not an Arahant like me."

The Blessed One then went to live in a wood not far from Kassapa's hermitage. When the night was well advanced the Four Divine Kings, marvellous to see and illuminating the whole wood, went to the Blessed One, and after paying homage to him they stood at the four quarters, like pillars of fire. When the night was over, the matted-hair ascetic Uruvelā Kassapa went to the Blessed One and said: "It is time, Great Monk, the meal is ready. Who were those that came to you in the night?"

"They were the Divine Kings of the Four Quarters, Kassapa. They came to me to hear the Dhamma."

Then Kassapa thought: "The Great Monk is very mighty and powerful since the Divine Kings come to him to hear the Dhamma. But he is not an Arahant like me."

On subsequent nights Sakka, Ruler of Gods, and Brahmā Sahampati came to the Blessed One. They were seen by Kassapa, and the sequel was the same.

It was at this time that Uruvelā Kassapa's great sacrificial ceremony fell due, and people from all Anga and Magadha came eagerly bringing large quantities of various kinds of food. Then Kassapa thought: "Now my great sacrificial ceremony falls due, and people from all Anga and Magadha are coming eagerly bringing large quantities of various kinds of food. If the Great Monk works a marvel before all these people, his gain and renown will increase and mine will diminish. If only the Great Monk were not to come tomorrow."

The Blessed One became aware in his mind of the thought in Kassapa's mind. So he went to the northern continent of Uttarakuru and gathered almsfood there. Then he took the almsfood to the Himalayan lake of Anotatta where he ate it and passed the day. When the night was over, Kassapa went to the Blessed One and said; "It is time, Great Monk, the meal is ready. Why did the Great Monk not come yesterday? We wondered why you did not come. Your portion of food was laid out." The Blessed One told him. Then Kassapa thought: "The Great Monk is very mighty and powerful since he was aware in his mind of the thought in my mind. But he is not an Arahant like me."

When the Blessed One had eaten Uruvelā Kassapa's meal, he went back to live in the same wood. Now at that time a refuse rag came into the Blessed One's possession. He thought: "Where shall I wash the refuse rag?" Then Sakka, Ruler of Gods, became aware in his mind of the thought in the Blessed One's mind. He scooped out a pond with his hand, and he told the Blessed One: "Lord, let the Blessed One wash the refuse rag here."

Next the Blessed One thought: "What shall I beat the refuse rag on?" Then Sakka, Ruler of Gods, aware in his mind of the thought in the Blessed One's mind, set down a large stone: "Lord, let the Blessed One beat the refuse rag here."

Next the Blessed One thought: "What shall I hang the refuse rag on?" Then a deity living in a kakudha tree bent down a branch: "Lord, let the Blessed One hang the refuse rag here."

Next the Blessed One thought: "What shall I smooth the refuse rag on?" Then Sakka, Ruler of Gods, set down a large stone: "Lord, let the Blessed One smooth the refuse rag here."

When the night was over, Kassapa went to the Blessed One and said: "It is time, Great Monk, the meal is ready. But, Great Monk, how does this pond come to be here that was not here before? Who set down this stone that was not here before? How is this kakudha branch bent down that was not bent down before?"

The Blessed One told him what had occurred. Then Kassapa thought: "The Great Monk is very mighty and powerful since Sakka, Ruler of Gods, waits on him. But he is not an Arahant like me."

Again when the night was over, Kassapa went to the Blessed One and told him: "It is time, Great Monk, the meal is ready." The Blessed One dismissed him, saying: "Go, Kassapa; I shall follow." He went to the rose-apple tree, after which the Rose-apple Continent of India is called, and he secured a fruit. Then he arrived first and sat down in the fire chamber. Kassapa saw him sitting there, and he asked: "Great Monk, what road did you come by? I left before you, but you have arrived before me and are here sitting in the fire chamber." The Blessed One told him where he had been, and he added: "Here is a rose-apple. It is coloured and has scent and taste. Eat it if you like."

"No, Great Monk, you brought it. You should eat it."

Then Kassapa thought: "The Great Monk is very mighty and powerful since he sends me off first and then goes to the rose-apple tree, secures a fruit, arrives here before me and is here sitting in the fire chamber. But he is not an Arahant like me." Afterwards the Blessed One returned to the wood.

Again on like occasions the Blessed One went to the rose-apple tree and secured a mango from a tree nearby ... secured a gall-nut from a tree nearby ... secured a yellow gall-nut from a tree nearby ... went to the Heaven of the Thirty-three and secured a flower from the Păricchattaka Tree. Each time Kassapa had the same thoughts as before.

It was at this time that the matted-hair ascetics, wanting to maintain their fires, found themselves unable to split logs. Then they thought: "It must be because of the Great Monk's supernormal power that we cannot split the logs."

The Blessed One asked Kassapa: "Should the logs be split, Kassapa? .... They should be split, Great Monk."

At once the five hundred logs were split. Then Kassapa thought: "The Great Monk is very mighty and powerful since the logs could not be split. But he is not an Arahant like me."

And again on like occasions the matted-hair ascetics, wanting to maintain their fire, could likewise not light their fires ... could likewise not put out their fires. And each time Kassapa had the same thoughts as before.

At that time too on those cold wintry nights during the "eight days of frost" the matted-hair ascetics were immersing themselves in the River Nerañjarā and emerging from it, constantly immersing and emerging. Then the Blessed One created five hundred braziers for the matted-hair ascetics to warm themselves at when they came up out of the water. They thought: "These braziers must have been created by the Great Monk's supernormal power." Then Kassapa thought: "The Great Monk is very mighty and powerful since he has created so many braziers. But he is not an Arahant like me."

About that time too a great rainstorm burst out of season and produced a huge inundation. The place where the Blessed One was living was all under water. Then he thought: "Suppose I made the waters stand back all round so that I could walk in between on dry ground?" And he did so.

Kassapa thought: "I hope the Great Monk has not been carried away by the water." And he went by boat with a number of matted-hair ascetics to the place where the Blessed One was living. He saw that the Blessed One had made the waters stand back all round and was walking in between on dry ground. When he saw, he said:

"Is that you, Great Monk?"

"It is I, Kassapa."

The Blessed One rose up into the air and came to rest on the boat. Then Kassapa thought: "The Great Monk is very mighty and powerful since even the water has not overcome him. But he is not an Arahant like me."

Then the Blessed One thought: "This misguided man will go on forever thinking 'But he is not an Arahant like me.' Suppose I give him a shock?" He told Uruvelā Kassapa: "Kassapa, you are neither an Arahant nor are you on the way to becoming one. There is nothing that you do by which you might become an Arahant or enter into the way to becoming one."

Thereupon the matted-hair ascetic prostrated himself with his head at the Blessed One's feet, and he said to him: "Lord, I wish to receive the going forth and the admission from the Blessed One."

"But, Kassapa, you are the leader, guide, chief, head and principal of five hundred matted-hair ascetics. You must consult them first so that they may do as they think fit."

So Uruvelā Kassapa went to the other matted-hair ascetics and told them: "I want to lead the holy life under the Great Monk. You may do as you think fit."

"We have long had faith in the Great Monk. If you lead the holy life under him, all of us will do likewise."

Then the matted hair ascetics took their hair, their matted locks, and their belongings and the furniture of the fire sacrifice, and they dropped them into the water to be carried away. They then went to the Blessed One, and prostrating themselves with their heads at his feet, they said: "Lord we wish to receive the going forth and the admission from the Blessed One."

"Come, bhikkhus," the Blessed One said, "The Dhamma is well proclaimed; lead the holy life for the complete ending of suffering." And that was those venerable ones' full admission.

The matted-hair ascetic Kassapa of the River saw the hair, the matted locks, and the belongings and the furniture of the fire sacrifice being carried along by the water. He thought: "I hope no disaster has befallen my brother." He sent matted-hair ascetics: "Go and find out about my brother," and he went himself with his three hundred matted-hair ascetics to the venerable Uruvelā Kassapa, and he asked him: "Is this better, Kassapa?"

"Yes, friend, this is better."

Then those matted-hair ascetics took their hair, their matted locks, and their belongings and the furniture of the fire sacrifice, and they dropped them into the water to be carried away. Then they went to the Blessed One, and prostrating themselves with their heads at his feet, they asked for and received the going forth and the admission. And the matted-hair ascetic Kassapa of Gayā with his two hundred matted-hair ascetics did just as Kassapa of the River had done.

Vin. Mv. 1:7-20

FIRST VOICE. Thus I heard. At one time the Blessed One was living at Uruvelā by the Ajapāla Nigrodha Tree on the banks of the River Nerañjarā. By that time Māra the Evil One had been following the Blessed One for seven years, looking for an opportunity but finding none. Then he went to the Blessed One and addressed him in stanzas:

"Do you now dream in woods, immersed in sorrow?
Have you lost wealth, or are you pining for it?
Is there some crime done by you in the town?
Why do you make no friends among the people?
And is there none that you can call a friend?"

"The root of sorrow is dug out of me.
Unsorrowing, I meditate in innocence
And free of taints, O Cousin of the Careless,
As one rid of all hankering for being."

"The things of which men say 'It is mine'
And men who utter the word 'mine'—
If you have thoughts allied to these,
You cannot then escape me, monk."

"Things they call 'mine' I call not so;
I am not one of those so saying.
Hear this, Then, Evil One, the path
I know you cannot even see."

"If you have truly found a path
That leads in safety to the Deathless,
Depart. But go by it alone.
What need to let another know?"

"People who seek to cross beyond
Ask me where death cannot prevail;
Thus asked, I tell the End of All,
Where is no substance for rebirth."

"Suppose, Lord, not far from a town or a village there were a pond with a crab in it; and then a party of boys or girls went out from the town or village to the pond; and they went into the pond and pulled the crab out of the water and set it on dry land; and whenever the crab extended a leg they cut it off, broke it and smashed it with sticks and stones so that the crab with all its legs cut off, broken and smashed would be unable to get back to the pond as before—so too all Māra's distorting, parodying and travestying have been cut off, broken and smashed by the Blessed One; and now I cannot get near the Blessed One any more when I seek an opportunity."

Then Māra uttered these stanzas of disappointment in the Blessed One's presence:

S. 4:24

Step by step for seven years
I have followed the Blessed One.
The Fully Enlightened One, possessed
Of mindfulness, gave me no chance.

Sn. 3.2

A crow there was who walked around
A stone that seemed a lump of fat:
"Shall I find something soft in this?
And is there something tasty here?"
He, finding nothing tasty there,
Made off: and we from Gotama
Depart in disappointment, too,
Like to the crow that tried the stone.

Full of sorrow he let his lute slip from under his arm; and then the unhappy demon vanished.

Sn. 3:2; S. 4:24

Now when Māra the Evil One had spoken these stanzas of disappointment in the Blessed One's presence, he left that place and sat down cross-legged on the ground not far from the Blessed One, silent, dismayed, with shoulders drooping and head down, glum and with nothing to say, scraping the ground with a stick.

Then Taṇhā, Aratī and Ragā (or Craving, Boredom and Lechery), Māra's three daughters, went to him and spoke to him in stanzas:

"O Father, why are you disconsolate?
Whom are you brooding over?
We can catch him,
Setting a snare of lust, we'll tie him up
Just as they catch a forest elephant,
And bring him back again into your power."

"An Arahant sublime is in the world;
And when a man escapes from Māra's sphere
There are no wiles to lure him back again
By lust, and that is why I grieve so much."

Then, Taṇhā, Aratī and Ragā, Māra's daughters, went to the Blessed One, and they said to him: "O Monk, we worship your feet." But the Blessed One took no notice since he was liberated by the utter ending of the essentials of existence.

They withdrew to one side and consulted together: "Men's tastes vary. Suppose we each create the forms of a hundred young girls?" They did so, and they went to the Blessed One and said: "O Monk, we worship your feet." Again, for the same reason, the Blessed One took no notice.

Then they withdrew to one side and consulted together: "Men's tastes vary. Suppose we each create the forms of a hundred virgin women … women that have borne once … women that have borne twice … mature women … old women?" In each case they did so, and they went to the Blessed One and said: "O Monk, we worship your feet." And again, for the same reason, the Blessed One took no notice.

Then they withdrew to one side, and they said: "It seems that our father was right; for if we had so tempted any monk or brahman who was not free from lust, his heart would have burst, or hot blood would have gushed from his mouth, or he would have gone mad or crazy, or he would have shrivelled, dried up and withered like a cut green rush." They went to the Blessed One and stood at one side. Taṇhā spoke to him in stanzas:

"Do you now dream in woods, immersed in sorrow?
Have you lost wealth or are you pining for it?
Is there some crime committed by you in the town?
Why do you make no friends among the people?
And is there none that you can call a friend?"

"I have defeated all the serried hosts
Of pleasant luring forms. I have found bliss
Pondering alone—bliss of the goal attained,
The bliss that lies in the quiet of the heart.
So I do not seek friends among the people;
For there is none with whom I need make friends."

Then Aratī spoke to him in stanzas:

"What abiding does a bhikkhu practise here
That, having crossed over five of the floods,[5]
The sixth he may cross too? What meditation
Practised forbids sense pleasures access to him?"

"Tranquil in body, with liberated mind,
Contriving nothing, mindful and detached,
Knowing Dhamma, absorbed without thought-roving,
Unangry and unanxious, unperplexed—
Such abiding does a bhikkhu practise here
That, having crossed over five of the floods,
The sixth he may cross too; such meditation
Practised forbids sense pleasures access to him."

Then Ragā uttered these stanzas in the Blessed One's presence:

"With craving severed he goes in company:
Numbers of beings will follow him, alas!
And there are multitudes the Unattached
Will filch from the realm of Death and lead ashore.
The Great Heroes, the Perfect Ones,
Lead men away by the Good Dhamma.
What jealous spite of ours avails
Against the Good Dhamma's guiding power?"

Then Taṇhā, Aratī and Ragā, Māra's daughters, went to Māra the Evil One. Seeing them coming, he uttered these stanzas:

"Fools! You have tried to split a rock
By poking it with lily stems,
To dig a hill out with your nails,
To chew up iron with your teeth,
To find a footing on a cliff
With a great stone upon your head,

To push a tree down with your chest—
And so you come from Gotama frustrated."

S. 4:24-25

SECOND VOICE. Now after staying at Uruvelā for as long as he chose, the Blessed One set out for Gayāsīsa with a large following of bhikkhus, with a thousand bhikkhus, with all the former matted-hair ascetics. The Blessed One stopped at Gayāsīsa near Gayā together with the thousand bhikkhus. There he addressed the bhikkhus thus:

(*The Fire Sermon*)

"Bhikkhus, all is burning. And what is all that is burning?

"The eye is burning. Visible forms are burning. Eye-conscious-ness is burning. Eye-contact is burning. Also feeling, whether pleasant or painful or neither-painful-nor-pleasant, that arises with eye-contact as its condition, that too is burning. Burning with what? Burning with the fire of lust, with the fire of hate, with the fire of delusion; it is burning with birth, ageing and death, with sorrow, lamentation, pain, grief and despair, I say.

"The ear is burning. Sounds are burning ....

"The nose is burning. Odours are burning ....

"The tongue is burning. Flavours are burning ....

"The body is burning. Tangibles are burning ....

"The mind is burning. Mental objects are burning. Mind-consciousness is burning. Mind-contact is burning. Also the feeling, whether pleasant, painful or neither-painful-nor-pleasant, that arises with mind-contact as its condition, that too is burning. Burning with what? Burning with the fire of lust, with the fire of hate, with the fire of delusion; it is burning with birth, ageing and death, with sorrow, lamentation, pain, grief and despair, I say.

"Seeing thus, bhikkhus, the wise noble disciple becomes dispassionate towards the eye, towards visible forms, towards eye-consciousness, towards eye-contact. Also he becomes dispassionate towards the feeling, whether pleasant, painful or neither-painful-nor-pleasant, that arises with eye-contact as its condition.

"He becomes dispassionate towards the ear, towards sounds ....

"He becomes dispassionate towards the nose, towards odours ....

"He becomes dispassionate towards the tongue, towards flavours ....

"He becomes dispassionate towards the body, towards tangibles....

"He becomes dispassionate towards the mind, towards mental objects, towards mind-consciousness, towards mind-contact. Also he becomes dispassionate towards the feeling, whether pleasant, painful or neither-painful-nor-pleasant, that arises with mind-contact as its condition.

"Becoming dispassionate, his lust fades away; with the fading of lust his heart is liberated; when his heart is liberated, there comes the knowledge: 'It is liberated.' He understands: 'Birth is exhausted, the holy life has been lived out, what was to be done is done, there is no more of this to come.' "

And while this discourse was being delivered the hearts of the thousand bhikkhus were delivered from taints through not clinging.

Vin. Mv. 1:21; S. 35:28

Now when the Blessed One had lived at Gayāsīsa as long as he chose, he set out to wander by stages to Rājagaha with a large following of bhikkhus, with a thousand bhikkhus, with all the former matted-hair ascetics. Wandering by stages, he at length reached Rājagaha, and there he stayed in the Sapling Grove at the Supaṭṭhita Shrine.

Seniya Bimbisāra, King of Magadha, heard: "It seems that the monk Gotama, the son of the Sakyans who went forth into homelessness from a Sakyan clan, has come to Rājagaha and is living in the Sapling Grove of the Supaṭṭhita Shrine. Now the good name of Master Gotama has been spread thus: 'That Blessed One is such since he is accomplished, fully enlightened, perfect in knowledge and conduct, sublime, the knower of worlds, the incomparable leader of men to be tamed, the teacher of gods and men, enlightened, blessed. He makes known this world with its deities, its Māras and its divinities, this generation with its monks and brahmans, with its princes and men, which he has himself realized through direct knowledge. He teaches the Dhamma that is good in the beginning, good in the middle and good in the end, with the meaning and the letter, and he explains a holy life that is utterly perfect and pure.' It is good to go and see such accomplished ones."

Then, accompanied by twelve hosts—by a hundred and twenty thousand—of Magadhan brahman householders, Seniya Bimbisāra,

King of Magadha, went to the Blessed One, and after paying homage to him, he sat down at one side. But of the twelve hosts of brahman householders some paid homage to the Blessed One and sat down at one side; some exchanged greetings with him and, when this courteous and formal talk was finished, sat down at one side; some raised their hands palms together in salutation to the Blessed One and sat down at one side; some pronounced their name and clan in the Blessed One's presence and sat down at one side; some kept silence and sat down at one side.

They wondered: "Does the Great Monk lead the holy life under Uruvelā Kassapa or does Uruvelā Kassapa lead the holy life under the Great Monk?" But the Blessed One became aware in his mind of the thought in their minds, and he addressed the venerable Uruvelā Kassapa in stanzas:

> "What did he see, the lean teacher who dwells
> At Uruvelā, that he left the fires?
> I ask of you this question, Kassapa:
> How did you come to leave fire worshipping?"
>
> "Sights and sounds and tastes and concubines
> Are the rewards promised for sacrifice.
> Of worldly things I saw they are a stain;
> Then worship and sacrifice gave joy no more."
>
> "But if your heart finds no delight in these,
> Kassapa," said the Blessed One,
> "In sights, and sounds, even in tastes as well,
> What then delights your hearts here in this world
> Of gods and men, Kassapa? Tell me that."
>
> "I saw the state of peace, not of this world,
> Where is no owning, and no sensual being,
> No otherness, no being led by others.
> Then worship and sacrifice gave no more joy."

Then the venerable Uruvelā Kassapa rose from his seat, and arranging his robe on one shoulder, he prostrated himself with his head at the Blessed One's feet, saying: "Lord, the Blessed One is my guide; I am a disciple. The Blessed One is my guide; I am a disciple."

Then the twelve hosts of Magadhan brahman householders

thought: "Uruvelā Kassapa lives the holy life under the Blessed One." The Blessed One, aware in his mind of the thought in their minds, then gave them progressive instruction. At length the spotless, immaculate vision of the Dhamma arose then and there in eleven of the twelve hosts of the Magadhan brahman householders: All that is subject to arising is subject to cessation. And one host became adherents.

Then Seniya Bimbisāra, King of Magadha, saw and reached and found and penetrated the Dhamma; he left uncertainty behind him; his doubts vanished, he acquired perfect confidence and he became independent of others in the Teacher's Dispensation.

He said to the Blessed One: "Lord, once when I was a boy I made five aspirations. Now they are fulfilled. Once when I was a boy I thought: 'If only I might be anointed on a throne.' That was the first aspiration I made and it has been fulfilled. The second was: 'If only I might encounter during my life a fully enlightened Arahant.' And that has been fulfilled. The third was: 'If only I might be able to do honour to that Blessed One.' And that has been fulfilled. The fourth was: 'If only the Blessed One would teach me the Dhamma.' And that has been fulfilled. The fifth was: 'If only I might understand the Blessed One's Dhamma.' And that too has been fulfilled. Magnificent, Lord, magnificent, Lord! The Dhamma has been made clear in many ways .... Lord, let the Blessed One receive me as his follower who has gone to him for refuge for as long as breath lasts. Now, Lord, let the Blessed One together with the Sangha of bhikkhus accept tomorrow's meal from me."

The Blessed One accepted in silence. When the king saw that he had consented, he rose from his seat, and after paying homage to him, he departed, keeping him on his right.

Then when the night was ended he had good food of various kinds prepared and he had the time announced: "It is time, Lord, the meal is ready."

Since it was now morning the Blessed One dressed, and taking his bowl and outer robe, he went into Rājagaha with a large following of bhikkhus, with a thousand bhikkhus, with all the former matted-hair ascetics. Now as they went Sakka, Ruler of Gods, assumed the form of a brahman youth, and he stood before the Blessed One with his hands raised palms together facing the Sangha headed by the Blessed One, singing these stanzas:

To Rājagaha he came, controlled and free,
And with him former matted-hair ascetics
Controlled and free. Bright as a golden jewel
The Blessed One went into Rājagaha.

To Rājagaha he came, quieted and free ....

To Rājagaha he came, released and free ....

To Rājagaha he came, attained and free ....

He with ten ways of life[6] and with ten powers,
Seeing ten things, possessor of ten factors,
And with a following ten hundred strong,
The Blessed One went into Rājagaha.

When people saw Sakka, Ruler of Gods, they said: "The young brahman is handsome, beautiful and graceful. Who is he?" When this was said, he addressed them in stanzas:

He is a saint, controlled always,
And purified, without a peer
In all the world, sublime, accomplished;
And I am one that follows him.

Then the Blessed One went to King Bimbisāra's dwelling, and he sat down on the seat made ready, surrounded by the Sangha of bhikkhus. With his own hands the king served and satisfied the Sangha headed by the Buddha. When the Blessed One had eaten and no longer had the bowl in his hand, the king sat down at one side. When he had done so, he thought: "Where could the Blessed One live that is neither too far from the town nor too near, with a way in and a way out, accessible to people who seek him, unfrequented by day and quiet by night, undisturbed by voices, with an atmosphere of aloofness, where one can lie hidden from people, favourable for retreat?" Then he thought: "This park of ours, the Bamboo Grove, has all these qualities. Suppose I present the Bamboo Grove to the Sangha headed by the Buddha?"

Then he took a gold jug, and he dedicated the Bamboo Grove to the Blessed One with the washing of hands, saying: "Lord, I give this Bamboo Grove to the Sangha of bhikkhus headed by the Buddha."

The Blessed One accepted the park. Then when he had instructed, incited, roused, and encouraged Seniya Bimbisāra, King of Magadha, with talk on the Dhamma, he rose from his seat and departed.

Vin. Mv. 1:22

5
THE TWO CHIEF DISCIPLES

SECOND VOICE. The occasion was this. The wanderer Sañjaya was living at Rājagaha with a large following of wanderers, with two hundred and fifty wanderers. And Sāriputta and Moggallāna were living the holy life under the wanderer Sañjaya. They had made a pact that whichever of them first reached the Deathless should inform the other. Now, it being morning, the venerable Assaji dressed, and taking his bowl and outer robe, he went into Rājagaha for alms. His manner as he went inspired confidence, whether in moving forwards or backwards, looking ahead or aside, bending or stretching, his eyes were downcast and he moved with grace. The wanderer Sāriputta saw him thus as he was begging for alms in Rājagaha, and he thought: "There are Arahants in the world, those who possess the Arahant path, and this bhikkhu is one of them. Suppose I approach him and ask under whom he has gone forth, or who is his teacher, or whose Dhamma he confesses." But then he thought: "It is not the time to ask this bhikkhu while he is wandering for alms among houses. Suppose I follow behind him to trace what the seekers have discovered?"

When the venerable Assaji had finished his round he left Rājagaha with his alms food. Then the wanderer Sāriputta went up to him and greeted him. When this courteous formal talk was finished, he stood at one side, and he said to him: "Friend, your faculties are serene, the colour of your skin is clear and bright. Under whom have you gone forth? Or who is your teacher? Or whose Dhamma do you confess?"

"There is the Great Monk, friend, the son of the Sakyans, who went forth from a Sakyan clan. I have gone forth under that Blessed One. He is my teacher. It is that Blessed One's Dhamma that I confess."

"But what does the venerable one's teacher say, what does he tell?"

"I have only recently gone forth, friend, I have only just come to this Dhamma and Discipline. I cannot teach you the Dhamma in detail. Still I will tell you its meaning in brief."

Then Sāriputta said: "So be it, friend.

"Say much or little as it suits you;
Tell me but the meaning now.
For I need no more than the meaning
With no thought of details yet."

The venerable Assaji told the wanderer Sāriputta this sketch of the Dhamma:

The Perfect One has told the cause
Of causally arisen things;
And what brings their cessation, too:
Such is the doctrine preached by the Great Monk.

Now when the wanderer Sāriputta heard this statement of the Dhamma, the spotless, immaculate vision of the Dhamma arose in him: All that is subject to arising is subject to cessation.

This is the truth: even if that were all,
You have attained the state where is no sorrow
That we for many times ten thousand ages
Have let pass by unseen.

Sāriputta the wanderer went to Moggallāna the wanderer. Moggallāna the wanderer saw him coming. He said: "Your faculties are serene, friend, the colour of your skin is clear and bright. Is it possible that you have found the Deathless?" "Yes, friend, I have found the Deathless." "But how did you find it, friend?"

Sāriputta the wanderer told what had happened. When Moggallāna the wanderer heard that statement of the Dhamma—

The Perfect One has told the cause
Of causally arisen things;
And what brings their cessation too:
Such is the doctrine preached by the Great Monk—

then the spotless, immaculate vision of the Dhamma arose in him: All that is subject to arising is subject to cessation.

This is the truth: even if that were all,
You have attained the state where is no sorrow
That we for many times ten thousand ages
Have let pass by unseen.

Then Moggallāna said: "Friend, let us go to the Blessed One. The Blessed One is our teacher."

"But, friend, these two hundred and fifty wanderers are living here depending on us, looking to us. They ought to be consulted first. They will do as they think fit."

They went together to the wanderers and told them: "Friends, we are going to the Blessed One. The Blessed One is our teacher."

"We live depending on the venerable ones, looking to them. If they go to lead the holy life under the Great Monk, then we too will do the same."

So Sāriputta and Moggallana went to Sañjaya the wanderer and told him what they were going to do.

"Enough, friends, do not go. Let us three guide this community together."

For the second and for the third time they told him the same thing and received the same answer.

Then Sāriputta and Moggallāna went with the two hundred and fifty wanderers to the Bamboo Grove. But hot blood gushed from Sañjaya the wanderer's mouth.

The Blessed One saw Sāriputta and Moggallāna coming in the distance. When he saw them, he told the bhikkhus: "Here come these two friends, Kolita and Upatissa. These two will be my chief disciples, an auspicious pair."

Then it was that the Master announced them—
They who were already liberated
In the domain of profound knowledge,
In the supreme destruction of the stuff of existence,
Before they had yet reached the Bamboo Grove—
Saying: "Here come these two friends,
Kolita and Upatissa.
These two will be my chief disciples,
An auspicious pair."

Sāriputta and Moggallāna went up to the Blessed One and prostrated themselves at his feet. They said to him: "Lord, we wish to have the going forth under the Blessed One, and the admission."

"Come bhikkhus," the Blessed One said, "the Dhamma is well proclaimed; lead the holy life for the complete ending of suffering." And that was those venerable ones' admission.

Now at that time a number of well-known Magadhan clansmen were leading the holy life under the Blessed One. People disapproved, they murmured and protested: "The monk Gotama is creating childlessness and widowhood, he is obliterating the clans. Already a thousand matted-hair ascetics have gone forth under him, and these two hundred and fifty wanderers and now these well-known clansmen have gone to lead the holy life under the monk Gotama!" When they saw bhikkhus, they mocked them with these stanzas:

Gotama the monk did come
To the Fort of Magadha;
He led away all Sañjaya's band;
Whom will he lead away today?

Bhikkhus heard this, and they went to the Blessed One and told him. He said: "This affair will not last long. It will only last seven days. At the end of seven days it will subside. So when people mock you with that stanza, you can reprove them in return with this stanza:

'They lead by Dhamma who are
Great Heroes too, and Perfect Ones;
And when they thus lead by Dhamma,
Where is the ground for jealousy?' "

So when the people mocked them, they reproved the people in return. Then people began to think: "Monks who are sons of the Sakyans lead by Dhamma, it seems, not against Dhamma." And the affair lasted seven days, and at the end of seven days it subsided.

Vin. Mv.1:23-24

NARRATOR TWO. The Elder Moggallāna attained Arahant-ship seven days after going to the Buddha. But the Elder Sāriputta passed a fortnight in reviewing and analysing with insight all levels of consciousness. How he became an Arahant is told as follows.

FIRST VOICE. Thus I heard. While the Blessed One was living at Rājagaha in the Sūkarakhatā Cave the wanderer Dīhanakha went to him and exchanged greetings. Then he said: "My theory and my view is this, Master Gotama: 'I have no liking for any.' "

"This view of yours, Aggivessana, 'I have no liking for any': have you no liking for that, too?"

"Even if I had a liking for this view of mine, it would be all the same, Master Gotama, it would be all the same."

"Well, there are plenty in the world who say 'It would be all the same' who not only fail to abandon that view but cling to some other view as well. And there are few in the world who say 'It would be all the same' who do abandon that view without clinging to some other view.

"Some monks and brahmans hold this theory and view: 'I have a liking for all'; and some this: 'I have no liking for any'; and some this: 'I have a liking for some, I have no liking for some.' Now the view of those whose theory and view is 'I have a liking for all' is close to lust, to bondage, to relishing, to acceptance, to clinging. But the view of those whose theory and view is 'I have no liking for any' is close to non-lust, to non-bondage, to non-relishing, to non-acceptance, to non-clinging."

Here the wanderer Dīghanakha remarked: "Master Gotama commends my view; Master Gotama recommends my view."

"And the view of those whose theory and view is 'I have a liking for some, I have no liking for some' is, in what they have a liking for, close to lust, to bondage, to relishing, to acceptance, to clinging, while, in what they have no liking for, it is close to non-lust, to non-relishing, to non-acceptance, to non-clinging.

"A wise man among those monks and brahmans whose theory and view is 'I have a liking for all' considers thus: 'My view is that I have a liking for all. But if I obstinately misapprehend and insist on it, saying "only this is true; everything else is wrong," then I shall clash with both the others: with the monk or brahman whose theory and view is "I have no liking for any" and with the monk or brahman whose theory or view is "I have a liking for some, I have no liking for some." I shall clash with these two. And when there is a clash, there are disputes. And when there are disputes, there are quarrels. And when there are quarrels, there is harm.'

"When he foresees that, he abandons that view without clinging to some other view. That is how these views are abandoned and relinquished."

NARRATOR TWO. The same paragraph is repeated for the "wise men" whose view is "I have no liking for any" and "I have a liking for some, I have no liking for some."

FIRST VOICE. "Now, Aggivessana, this body that has material form consists of the four great entities (of earth, water, fire, and air); it is procreated by a mother and father and built up out of rice and bread; it is subject to impermanence, to anointing and rubbing, to dissolution and disintegration. It must be regarded as impermanent, as suffering, as a boil, as a dart, as a calamity, as an affliction, as alien, as disintegrating, as void, as not self. When he regards it so, he abandons his desire and affection for it and his habit of treating it as the necessary basis for all his inferences.[1]

"Now there are three kinds of feeling: pleasant feeling, painful feeling, and neither-painful-nor-pleasant feeling. When a man feels any one of these three, he does not feel the other two. Pleasant feeling is impermanent, formed, dependently originated, subject to exhaustion, fall, fading, and ceasing. And so too is painful feeling and neutral feeling.

"When a well-taught noble disciple sees thus, he becomes dispassionate towards pleasant feeling and painful feeling and neutral feeling. Being dispassionate, his lust fades away. With the fading of lust he is liberated. When his heart is liberated, there comes the knowledge: 'It is liberated.' He understands: 'Birth is exhausted, the holy life has been lived out, what was to be done is done, there is no more of this to come.' A bhikkhu whose heart is thus liberated sides with none, disputes with none, and he employs, though without misapprehension, the speech current in the world."

During this time the venerable Sāriputta was standing behind the Blessed One fanning him. Then he thought: "The Blessed One, the Sublime One, speaks, it seems, by direct knowledge of the abandoning and relinquishing of these things." And as he considered thus, his heart was liberated from taints through not clinging.

Meanwhile the spotless, immaculate vision of the Dhamma arose in the wanderer Dīghanakha.... He said: "... I go to Master Gotama for refuge, and to the Dhamma and to the Sangha.'

M. 74

NARRATOR TWO. During this time King Suddhodana sent Kāludāyī, the son of one of his ministers, to Rājagaha in order to persuade his son, the Buddha, to visit Kapilavatthu. Before he announced his mission, Kāludāyī first became a bhikkhu. However, at the end of the winter—it was the first after the Enlightenment—he announced his mission with these verses intended to persuade the Buddha to make the journey.

CHANTER.

Lord, there are trees that now like embers burn;
Hoping for fruit, they have let their green veils drop
And blaze out boldly with a scarlet flame:
It is the hour, Great Hero, Taster of Truth.
Trees in high bloom that are a mind's delight,
Wafting odours to the four winds of space,
Their leaves they have let fall, expecting fruit;
It is time, O Hero, to set out from here.
Now is a pleasant season, Lord, for travel,
For it is not too cold or over-warm.
Let the Sakyans and the Koliyans see you
Facing the west, crossing the Rohinī River.[2]

Fields are ploughed in hope,
Seeds are sown in hope,
Traders sail in hope
Across the sea for wealth:
O may the hope I nurse
Come to success!

Again and again the planting of the seed;
Again and again the Divine King sends the rain;
Again and again the ploughmen till the fields;
Again and again the kingdom reaps the corn;
Again and again the mendicants go their rounds;
Again and again the generous give their gifts;
Again and again this giving of their gifts
Again and again finds them a place in heaven.

Into whatever lineage he is born,
A Hero, possessor of true understanding,
Ennobles it back seven generations—

You, greater than gods, I feel, can do far more;
For the word "Perfect" has now come true in you.
Thag. 527-33

SECOND VOICE. When the Blessed One had stayed at Rājagaha as long as he chose, he set out for Kapilavatthu. Wandering by stages, he eventually arrived there, and he stayed in Nigrodha's Park. Now when it was morning, the Blessed One dressed, and taking his bowl and outer robe, he went to the residence of Suddhodana the Sakyan, and there he sat down on a seat made ready.
Vin. Mv. 1:54

NARRATOR ONE. The account of this visit given in the Canon is brief to the point of abruptness. So before proceeding with it a few details from the Commentary will make the situation clearer.

NARRATOR TWO. When the Buddha arrived at Kapilavatthu, the Sakyan clansmen, well known for their pride, were disinclined to pay homage to him. Thereupon he displayed the Twin Marvel, causing the simultaneous appearance of jets of fire and water from all his limbs. This was followed by the preaching of the Vessantara Birth Story. After the first ceremonial meal had been given to him in his father's palace, he preached the Dhammapāla Birth Story, and the king attained to the third, or penultimate, stage of realization (he died an Arahant some four years later). At the same time the queen, Mahāpajāpatī, mother of Prince Nanda and aunt of the Buddha, attained the first stage of realization. That same day had been chosen for the celebration to mark the forthcoming marriage of Prince Nanda, Queen Mahāpajāpati's only son. Now when the Buddha rose to go, he gave Prince Nanda his bowl to hold and departed. Not knowing what to do, Prince Nanda followed him with the bowl, and as he left, his bride-to-be called to him: "Come back soon, Prince." When they arrived at the Buddha's dwelling the Buddha asked him if he would leave the house life. Out of reverence rather than inclination he agreed. On the seventh day the Buddha again took his meal in his father's palace.

NARRATOR ONE. Now the canonical account continues.

SECOND VOICE. Prince Rāhula's mother then said to Prince Rāhula: "That is your father, Rāhula. Go and ask for your inheritance."

So Prince Rāhula went to the Blessed One and stood before him: "Your shadow is pleasant, monk."

Then the Blessed One got up from his seat and went away. Prince Rāhula followed behind the Blessed One, saying: "Give me my inheritance, monk; give me my inheritance, monk."

Then the Blessed One told the venerable Sāriputta: "Then, Sāriputta, give him the going forth.[3]

"How am I to give Prince Rāhula the going forth, Lord?" The Blessed One then made this the reason and the occasion to give a talk on the Dhamma and he addressed the bhikkhus thus: 'I allow the going forth to be given by means of the Three Refuges. But it should be given in this way. First the hair and beard must be shaved off and the yellow robe put on. Then he who is to go forth should arrange his robe on one shoulder, and after paying homage at the bhikkhus' feet, he should kneel, and, with his hands raised palms together, he should say this: 'I go to the Buddha for refuge. I go to the Dhamma for refuge. I go to the Sangha for refuge. For the second time … For the third time …' "

Then the venerable Sāriputta gave Prince Rāhula the going forth. Now Suddhodana the Sakyan went to the Blessed One, and after paying homage to him, he sat down at one side. He said: "I ask one favour of the Blessed One."

"Perfect Ones have left favours behind, Gotama."

"It is permissible, Lord, and blameless."

"Tell it, then, Gotama."

"Lord, I suffered no little pain when the Blessed One went forth. Then there was Nanda. Rāhula is too much. Love for our children, Lord, cuts into the outer skin; having cut into the outer skin, it cuts into the inner skin; having cut into the inner skin, it cuts into the flesh; having cut into the flesh, it cuts into the sinews; having cut into the sinews, it cuts into the bones; having cut into the bones, it reaches the marrow and stays there. Lord, it would be good if the venerable ones did not give the going forth without the parents' consent."

The Blessed One instructed, urged, roused and encouraged Suddhodana the Sakyan with talk on the Dhamma. Then Suddhodana the Sakyan got up from his seat, and after paying homage to the Blessed One, he left, keeping him on his right.

The Blessed One then made this the reason and the occasion to give a talk on the Dhamma and he addressed the bhikkhus thus: "Bhikkhus, you should not give the going forth to children without their parents' consent. If anyone does this, he commits an offence of wrongdoing."

Vin. Mv. Kh. 1:54

NARRATOR ONE. Tradition claims that the decision of the Buddha's cousin Ānanda and others to leave the house life was made at the time of this visit. The Buddha had already gone away from Kapilavatthu but was still in the northern parts of Kosala. Meanwhile the two following incidents may have occurred about now, though there is no definite indication where to place them.

FIRST VOICE. Thus I heard. At one time the Blessed One was journeying through the Kosalan country with the venerable Nāgasamāla as his attendant monk. On the way the venerable Nāgasamāla saw a fork in the road. He said to the Blessed One: "Lord, that is the way; let us go that way."

When this was said, the Blessed One replied: "This is the way, Nāgasamāla. Let us go this way."

A second and a third time the venerable Nāgasamāla said the same thing and received the same answer. Then he put the Blessed One's bowl and outer robe down on the ground and departed. As he went along that road robbers appeared, and they beat him with cuffs and kicks and broke his bowl and tore his cloak of patches. Afterwards he came to the Blessed One with his bowl broken and his cloak of patches torn, and he told him what had happened. Knowing the meaning of this, the Blessed One then uttered this exclamation:

> A wise man and a foolish one
> Walked and lived in company.
> Milk-drinking cranes leave marsh water:
> The wise leave what they know is bad.

Ud. 8:7

Now while the Blessed One was staying in the Kosalan country at Araññakuṭika on the slopes of the Himalayas, this thought arose in his mind while he was alone in retreat: "Is it possible to govern without killing and ordering execution, without confiscating and sequestrating, without sorrowing and inflicting sorrow, in other words, righteously?" Then Māra the Evil One became aware in his mind of the thought in the Blessed One's mind, and he went to him and said: "Let the Blessed One govern, let the Sublime One govern, without killing and ordering execution, without confiscating and sequestrating, without sorrowing and inflicting sorrow, in other words, righteously."

"Evil One, what end have you in view that you address me thus?"

"Lord, the four bases for success[4] have been constantly maintained in being by the Blessed One, constantly practised, made the vehicle, made the basis, established, consolidated and properly undertaken. And so, Lord, if the Blessed One were willing to resolve: 'Let Himalaya, king of mountains, be made of gold,' it would become a gold mountain."

And were that mountain all of yellow gold,
Twice that is not enough for one man's wants;
To know this is to act accordingly.
How should a man who has seen suffering,
And whence its source, turn to sense desires?
For when he knows this substance of rebirth
Is that which binds him to the world, a man
Cannot but train to rid himself of it.

Then Māra the Evil One understood: "The Blessed One knows me, the Sublime One knows me." Sad and disappointed, he vanished at once.

S. 4:20

SECOND VOICE. The occasion was this. The Blessed One was staying at Anupiyā—there is a town of the Mallians' called Anupiyā—and by that time many well-known Sakyan princes had gone forth under the Blessed One. But there were two brothers, Mahānāma the Sakyan and Anuruddha the Sakyan. Anuruddha had been delicately brought up. He had three palaces, one for the summer, one for the rains and one for the winter. For four months he would be entertained in the rains palace by minstrels with no men among them and never come down to the lower palace.

It occured to Mahānāma: "Now many well-known Sakyan princes have gone forth under the Blessed One. But no one in our family has gone forth from the house life into homelessness. Suppose I went forth, or Anuruddha?"

Then he went to Anuruddha and told him what had occurred to him. Anuruddha said: "But I have been delicately brought up. I cannot go forth from the home life into homelessness. You go forth."

"Come then, Anuruddha, I shall instruct you in the household life. Now first a field must be ploughed, then it must be sown, then water must be led into it, then the water must be drained, then the field must be weeded, then the crop must be cut, then it must be gathered in, then it must be stacked, then it must be threshed, then the straw must be removed, then the chaff must be winnowed off, then it must be sifted, then it must be stored away. Now when that is done, it must all be done again next year, and the year after. The work never finishes; there is no end to the work."

"Then when will there be an end to the work? When shall we have the leisure to gratify the five strands of the sensual desires we are provided and furnished with?"

"My dear Anuruddha, the work never finishes; there is no end to the work. Our father and our grandfather both died while their work was still unfinished. So now it is for you to learn about this household life. I shall go forth from the home life into homelessness."

Anuruddha went to his mother and told her: "Mother, I want to go forth from the home life into homelessness. Please give me your permission."

When this was said, she told him: "You two sons of mine are dear and precious to me, not repugnant. In case of your death we should lose you against our will; but why should I give you my permission to go forth from the house life into homelessness while you are still living?" He asked a second and a third time. Then his mother said: "My dear Anuruddha, if Bhaddiya the royal Sakyan who is governing the Sakyans goes forth, you may do so too."[5]

Now Bhaddiya the royal Sakyan who was governing the Sakyans at the time was a friend of Anuruddha's and his mother had thought: "This Bhaddiya is a friend of Anuruddha's. He is not anxious to go forth from the home life," which is why she had spoken as she did.

Then Anuruddha went to Bhaddiya and said: "My going forth depends on yours."

"If your going forth depends on mine, then let it no longer be so. You and I will ... well, you go forth when you like."

"Come, let us both go forth together from the house life into homelessness."

"I cannot. I will do anything else for you that I can. You go forth."

"My mother has said: 'My dear Anuruddha, if Bhaddiya the royal Sakyan who is governing the Sakyans goes forth, you may go forth too.' And your words were these: 'If your going forth depends on mine, then let it no longer be so. You and I will … well, you go forth when you like.' Come, let us both go forth from the home life into homelessness."

At that time people used to speak the truth, used to keep their word. Bhaddiya told Anuruddha: "Wait seven years. At the end of seven years both of us shall go forth."

"Seven years is too long. I cannot wait seven years."

"Wait six years. At the end of six years both of us shall go forth."

"Six years is too long. I cannot wait six years."

"Wait five years … four … three … two years … one year … seven months … two months … one month …. Wait half a month. At the end of half a month both of us shall go forth."

"Half a month is too long. I cannot wait half a month."

"Wait seven days. At the end of seven days both of us shall go forth. And so I can hand over the kingdom to my children and my brothers."

"Seven days is not too long. I shall wait."

Then Bhaddiya the royal Sakyan and Anuruddha and Ānanda and Bhagu and Kimbila and Devadatta, with Upāli the barber as seventh, set out leading a four-constituent army as though to the parade ground in the pleasure park as they were used to do. When they had gone some distance, they dismissed the army. Then they went across the border to another realm where they took off their insignia. They rolled them in an upper robe, and they told Upāli the barber: "Upāli, you had better go back. There is enough here for you to live on."

Now on his way Upāli thought: "These Sakyans are fierce. With this they might even have me put to death as an abettor in the princes' going forth. So these Sakyan princes are now going forth; but how about me?" He opened the bundle and hung the things on a tree, saying: "Let him who sees these take them as given." Then he went back to the Sakyan princes. They saw him coming, and they asked him: "Why have you returned?"

He told them what had happened, and he added: "And so I have come back again."

"You did well not to go home, Upāli; for the Sakyans are fierce. With this they might even have had you put to death as an abettor in the Sakyan princes' going forth."

Then the Sakyan princes went with Upāli the barber to the Blessed One, and after paying homage to him, they sat down at one side. When they had done so, they said to the Blessed One: "Lord, we are proud Sakyans. This Upāli the barber has long attended on us. Let the Blessed One give him the going forth first so that we can pay homage to him and rise up for him and give him reverential salutation and honour. Thus the Sakyan pride will be humbled in us Sakyans." Then the Blessed One gave the going forth first to Upāli the barber and afterwards to the Sakyan princes.

It was in the course of that rainy season that the venerable Bhaddiya realized the three true knowledges. The venerable Anuruddha aroused the divine eye. The venerable Ānanda realized the fruition of stream-entry. Devadatta produced the ordinary man's supernormal powers.

At this time whenever the venerable Bhaddiya went into the forest or to the root of a tree or to a room that was void, he was constantly exclaiming: "Oh bliss! Oh bliss!"

A number of bhikkhus went to the Blessed One and told him about it, adding: "There seems no doubt, Lord, that the venerable Bhaddiya is leading the holy life dissatisfied. Or he is remembering his former position as ruler."

Then the Blessed One sent for him and asked him if it was true.

"It is so, Lord."

"But, Bhaddiya, what good do you see in doing this?" "Formerly, Lord, when I had royal status there was a well-posted guard both inside and outside the palace, and also both inside and outside the city, and also both inside and outside the district. Even though I was so guarded and protected, I was fearful, anxious, suspicious and worried. But now, Lord, when I am gone to the forest or to the root of a tree or to a room that is void, I am not fearful or anxious or suspicious or worried. I live at ease, in quiet, dependent on others' gifts, with a mind like a wild deer. This is the good that I see in doing this."

Knowing the meaning of this, the Blessed One then uttered this exclamation:

> Who has no longer conflict lurking in him
> Will have surmounted all the kinds of being;
> For he is fearless, blissful, free from sorrow.
> No deity can vie with him in glory.

Vin. Cv. 7:1; cf. Ud. 2:10

FIRST VOICE. Now the venerable Nanda, the Blessed One's half-brother, put on pressed and ironed robes, and he anointed his eyes and took a glazed bowl. Then he went to the Blessed One, and after paying homage to him, he sat down at one side. When he had done so, the Blessed One told him: "Nanda, it is not proper that you, a clansman who has gone forth out of faith from the house life into homelessness, should put on pressed and ironed robes, anoint your eyes and take a glazed bowl. What is proper for you, a clansman who has gone forth out of faith from the house life into homelessness, is to be a forest dweller, an eater only of almsfood got by begging, a wearer of refuse-rag robes, and to dwell without regard for sensual desires."

S. 2I:8

NARRATOR TWO. Meanwhile the novice Rāhula, now eleven years old, was living under the Elder Sāriputta's care at Ambalaṭṭhikā. near Rājagaha where the Buddha returned in due course.

FIRST VOICE. Thus I heard. At one time the Blessed One was living at Rājagaha in the Bamboo Grove, the Squirrels' Sanctuary, and the venerable Rāhula was living at Ambalaṭṭhikā. When it was evening the Blessed One rose from retreat, and he went to the venerable Rāhula at Ambalaṭṭhikā. The venerable Rāhula saw him coming, and he prepared a seat for him and water for washing his feet. The Blessed One sat down on the seat prepared and washed his feet. The venerable Rāhula then paid homage to him and sat down at one side. The Blessed One poured a small quantity of water into the water-dipper, and he addressed the venerable Rāhula thus: "Rāhula, do you see this small quantity of water in the water-dipper?"

"Yes, Lord."

"Unless people are careful to avoid knowingly telling lies, there is as little good in them as this."

Then the Blessed One threw the small amount of water away, and he asked: "Rāhula, did you see that small amount of water I threw away?"

"Yes, Lord."

"Unless people are careful to avoid knowingly telling lies, the good there is in them is thrown away like this."

Then the Blessed One turned the water-dipper upside-down and he asked: "Rāhula, do you see this water-dipper turned upside-down?'

"Yes, Lord."

"Unless people are careful to avoid knowingly telling lies, the good there is in them is treated like this."

Then the Blessed One turned the water-dipper right way up again, and he asked: "Rāhula, do you see this water-dipper now quite empty?"

"Yes, Lord."

"Unless people are careful to avoid knowingly telling lies, they are quite as empty of good as this. Now, Rāhula, suppose there were a royal tusker elephant with tusks as long as chariot poles, full-grown in stature, highly bred and well used to battles, and in battle he used his forefeet and his hind feet and his forequarters and his hind quarters and his head and his ears and his tusks and his tail, and yet he kept his trunk back, then the man on his back would think: 'Though he uses all his limbs, he keeps his trunk back, and so he has not yet devoted his life to the king.' But as soon as he used all his limbs and his trunk as well, then the man on his back would think: 'He uses all his limbs and also his trunk, and so he has now devoted his life to the king; he needs no more training.' So too, Rāhula, unless people are careful to avoid knowingly telling lies, I do not say of them that they need no more training. So, Rāhula, you must train yourself never to speak a falsehood even for a joke. What do you think a looking-glass is for, Rāhula?"

"To look at oneself in, Lord."

"In just the same way you should keep on looking at your acts of body, acts of speech and acts of mind."

M. 61

NARRATOR TWO. The Buddha then went on to give him detailed instructions how to review every action before, during and after its performance, judging it to be unwholesome if he found it to lead to his own harm or to that of others or to that of both, judging it to be wholesome if it did not, and shaping future action accordingly.

6
ANĀTHAPIṆḌIKA

NARRATOR TWO. The first rains after his enlightenment was spent by the Buddha at Benares. The second and third were spent at Rājagaha in the Bamboo Grove. It is after the third rains that Anāthapiṇḍika , the Feeder of the Poor, makes his appearance.

SECOND VOICE. The occasion was this. The Buddha, the Blessed One, was living at that time at Rājagaha in the Bamboo Grove, and there had been no pronouncement made by him about dwellings for bhikkhus. They were living here and there in the woods, at the roots of trees, under overhanging rocks, in ravines, in hillside caves, in charnel grounds, in jungle thickets, in the open, on heaps of straw. As they left such places in the early morning they inspired confidence, whether in moving forwards or returning, looking ahead or aside, bending or stretching; their eyes were downcast and they moved with grace.

During that time a rich merchant of Rājagaha visited the park. He saw them as they went about thus, and in his heart he trusted them. He approached them and asked: "Lords, if I had dwellings built, would you live in them?"

"The Blessed One has not allowed dwellings."

"Then, Lords, ask the Blessed One and tell me what he says." They told this to the Blessed One. He gave his permission; and when he had done so, they told the merchant. In a single day he had sixty dwellings built. Then he invited the Blessed One and the Sangha for the following day's meal. At the end of the meal he formally presented the dwellings to the Sangha.

The merchant's sister was the wife of Anāthapiṇḍika , who chose at the time to come to Rājagaha on some business or other—at the very time, in fact, when the Sangha of bhikkhus headed by the Buddha had been invited by the merchant for the following day. The merchant was directing his servants and retainers: "Now get up early. Cook gruel and rice and sauces. Make dessert sweets."

Anāthapiṇḍika thought: "Formerly when I came this householder used to lay aside all his engagements to welcome me. Now he seems distracted with ordering his servants about. Is there a taking in marriage or a giving in marriage? Or is there some great sacrifice? Or has he invited Seniya Bimbisāra, King of Magadha, for tomorrow with a full retinue?"

When the merchant had finished directing his servants, he went to Anāthapiṇḍika and welcomed him. Then when he had sat down beside him, Anāthapiṇḍika told him his thoughts. He replied: "There is no marriage, nor has the king been invited for tomorrow with a full retinue. But I have a great sacrifice: I have invited for tomorrow the Sangha of bhikkhus headed by the Buddha, the Enlightened One."

"Do you say 'the Buddha'?"

"I say 'the Buddha.' "

"Do you say 'the Buddha'?"

"I say 'the Buddha.' "

"Do you say 'the Buddha'?"

"I say 'the Buddha.' "

"This news 'the Buddha, the Buddha' is hard to come by in the world. Is it possible to go and see this Blessed One, accomplished and fully enlightened, now at this time?"

"This is not the time to go and see him. You can see him early tomorrow."

Then Anāthapiṇḍika thought: "Early tomorrow I shall be able to see a Blessed One, accomplished and fully enlightened."

He lay down thinking of the Buddha. Three times in the night he got up, fancying it was dawn. Then he went to the Sīvaka Gate. Non-human beings opened the gate. As soon as he was out of the city, light left him and darkness was before him. Fear, awe and horror arose in him. He wanted to turn back; but the invisible spirit Sīvaka made himself heard:

> "A hundred elephants, a hundred horses,
> A hundred chariots drawn by she-mules,
> A hundred thousand maidens decked with gems
> And earrings—all these are not even worth
> A sixteenth part of one step forward now.

Go forward, householder, go forward. Better go forward than turn back."

When the spirit had said this for the third time, darkness left him and light was before him. The fear, awe and horror subsided in him. Then he went to the Cool Grove where the Buddha was. Now on that occasion the Blessed One had risen early towards dawn and was pacing up and down in the open. He saw Anāthapiṇḍika coming. When he saw him, he left his walk and sat down on a seat made ready for him. When he had done so, he said to Anāthapiṇḍika : "Come, Sudatta."

Anāthapiṇḍika thought: "He addresses me by name!" and he was happy and hopeful. He went to the Blessed One and prostrated himself at his feet, and he said: "I trust that the Blessed One has slept well."

> A brahman true[1] sleeps ever well—
> Who has attained to full Nibbāna,
> Whom sense desires leave intact,
> Cooled, without substance of existence.
> He has rejected all attachments,
> There is no conflict in his heart;
> He sleeps in bliss who is at peace—
> The peace established in the mind.

Then the Blessed One gave Anāthapiṇḍika progressive instruction. While Anāthapiṇḍika sat there, the spotless, immaculate vision of the Dhamma arose in him: All that is subject to arising is subject to cessation. Then he became independent of others in the Teacher's Dispensation. He said, "Magnificent, Lord! ... Beginning from today let the Blessed One receive me as his follower who has gone to him for refuge for as long as breath lasts. Lord, let the Blessed One with the Sangha of bhikkhus accept tomorrow's meal from me."

The Blessed One accepted in silence. Then, knowing that the Blessed One had accepted, he rose from his seat, and after paying homage to the Blessed One, he departed, keeping him on his right.

The rich merchant of Rājagaha heard: "It seems that the Sangha of bhikkhus headed by the Buddha has been invited by Anāthapiṇḍika." So he said to Anāthapiṇḍika : "The Sangha of bhikkhus headed by the Buddha has been invited by you for tomorrow. But you are a guest. I will give you money to provide the food for the Sangha of bhikkhus headed by the Buddha."

"There is no need. I have money to provide food for the Sangha of bhikkhus headed by the Buddha."

A citizen of Rājagaha heard of it, and he offered to provide the money, but Anāthapiṇḍika refused. And Seniya Bimbisāra, King of Magadha, offered likewise and was refused.

Then, when that night was over, Anāthapiṇḍika had good food of various kinds prepared at the merchant's house, and he had the time announced to the Blessed One: "It is time, Lord, the meal is ready."

It now being morning, the Blessed One dressed, and taking his bowl and outer robe, he went accompanied by the Sangha of bhikkhus to the merchant's house, and he sat down on the seat made ready there. Then the householder Anāthapiṇḍika served with his own hands the Sangha headed by the Buddha and satisfied them with different kinds of good food. When the Blessed One had eaten and no longer had the bowl in his hand, Anāthapiṇḍika sat down at one side. He said to the Blessed One: "Lord, let the Blessed One with the Sangha of bhikkhus consent to dwell with me at Sāvatthī for the Rains."

"Perfect Ones delight in rooms that are void, householder."

"I know, Blessed One; I know, Sublime One."

Then, when the Blessed One had instructed and urged and roused and encouraged Anāthapiṇḍika with talk on the Dhamma, he rose from his seat and went away.

At that time Anāthapiṇḍika had many friends and acquaintances to welcome him. When he had finished his business in Rājagaha, he set out for Sāvatthī. On the way he directed people: "Sirs, make gardens, build dwellings, arrange gifts of food. A Buddha has appeared in the world. He has been invited by me. He will come by this road."

Then those people did as he had directed them.

When Anāthapiṇḍika arrived at Sāvatthī, he looked all round the city for a suitable place, a suitable retreat until he saw Prince Jeta's pleasure park, which had all the requisite qualities. He went to Prince Jeta and said: "Sir, give me your park to use."

"The park is not to be given without the sum of a hundred thousand spread over it."

"The park is taken, sir."

"The park is not taken, householder."

They asked arbitrating officers whether it was taken or not. The arbitrators said: "As soon as you set a value on it, sir, it was taken."

Then Anāthapiṇḍika had gold brought in carts, and he had Jeta's Grove covered with a hundred thousand (gold coins) spread over it. The gold they brought at first was not enough to complete it and there was a small space near the gate that was left uncovered. Anāthapiṇḍika ordered people to go and fetch gold to cover the space. Then it occured to Prince Jeta: "This can be no ordinary matter since Anāthapiṇḍika is spending so much gold." He told Anāthapiṇḍika : "Enough, householder, do not cover that space. Leave me that space. It shall be my gift."

Anāthapiṇḍika thought: "This Prince Jeta is a prominent well-known person. It will be very good if such well-known people acquire confidence in the Dhamma and Discipline." So he left that space for Prince Jeta, who had a gate-house built on it. Then Anāthapiṇḍika had dwellings erected in Jeta's Grove; he had open terraces laid out; he had gates made, waiting halls put up, fire rooms, store houses and closets built, walks levelled, well rooms prepared, baths constructed, bath-rooms arranged, ponds excavated and pavilions raised.

Vin. Cv. 6:4; S. 10:8

FIRST VOICE. Thus I heard.[2] While the Blessed One was living at Rājagaha in the Bamboo Grove, he was sitting in the open on one occasion in the blackness of the night, and it was lightly drizzling. Then Māra the Evil One, who wanted to frighten him and make his hair stand up, assumed the form of a huge royal nāga serpent and approached the Blessed One. His body was as big as a boat made of a single tree trunk; his hood was as broad as a brewer's mat; his eyes were as big as Kosalan brass plates; his tongue flickered in and out of his mouth like forked lightning in and out of a thunder cloud; the sound of his breathing was like the sound of a smith's bellows blowing.

Then the Blessed One recognized Māra the Evil One and spoke to him in stanzas:

A hermit perfect in restraint
Lives out his life in lonely haunts;
There he should live who has renounced;
For that is right for him and for his like.

Many are the wild beasts, many the terrors,
Many the biting flies and crawling things;
Yet when a sage is trained in the wilderness,
Nothing of that can make his hair stand up.
Though sky may split, though earth may quake,
Though beings all feel affright, though men
May drive a dagger in his breast,
No Wakened One will ever turn for help
To worldly things, the essentials of existence.

Then Māra the Evil One understood: "The Blessed One knows me, the Sublime One knows me." Sad and disappointed, he vanished at once.

S. 4:6

SECOND VOICE. Now when the Blessed One had stayed at Rājagaha as long as he chose, he set out to wander by stages to Vesālī. When he at length arrived there, he went to live in the Hall with the Pointed Roof in the Great Wood. People were eagerly getting building work done at that time, and bhikkhus who were overseeing the work were being liberally supplied with robes, almsfood, lodging and the requisite of medicine as cure for the sick.

There was a poor tailor who thought: "This can be no ordinary matter with these people eagerly getting building work done and the bhikkhus overseeing the work being liberally supplied with robes, almsfood, lodging and medicines. Suppose I did some building too?"

Then the poor tailor himself puddled some clay and made up some bricks, and then he set up a scaffold. But for want of skill he built his wall crooked and it fell down. The same thing happened a second and a third time. Then the poor tailor was annoyed, and he murmured and protested: "The sons of the Sakyans advise and instruct people who give them robes and almsfood and lodging and medicine. But I am poor. No one advises and instructs me or oversees my building."

Bhikkhus heard about this, and they told the Blessed One. Then he made this the reason for a talk on the Dhamma and he addressed the bhikkhus thus: "Bhikkhus, I allow building work to be formally allotted. A bhikkhu who oversees such building work shall take care to see that the dwelling is expeditiously completed, and he shall have what is damaged and broken repaired."

When the Blessed One had stayed at Vesālī as long as he chose, he set out to wander by stages to Sāvatthī. Now on that occasion the followers of the bhikkhus belonging to a certain clique of six went ahead of the Sangha of bhikkhus headed by the Buddha, and they took over lodgings and beds thus: "This will be for our preceptors, this will be for our teachers, this will be for us." When the venerable Sāriputta arrived after the Sangha of bhikkhus headed by the Buddha, the lodgings and beds had all been taken over. Finding no bed, he went and sat down at the root of a tree. When the night was ending and it was near dawn, the Blessed One got up, and he coughed. The venerable Sāriputta also coughed.

"Who is there?"

"It is I, Sāriputta, Blessed One."

"Why are you sitting there, Sāriputta?"

Then the venerable Sāriputta told what had happened. The Blessed One made this the reason to call the bhikkhus together, and he asked them if it was true. They said that it was. He administered a rebuke: "Bhikkhus, this does not rouse faith in the faithless or increase faith in the faithful; rather it keeps the faithless without faith and harms some of the faithful."

After he had administered the rebuke and given a talk on the Dhamma, he addressed the bhikkhus thus: "Bhikkhus, who is worthy of the best seat, the best water, the best almsfood?"

Some bhikkhus said that it was one gone forth from a warrior-noble family; others that it was one gone forth from a brahman family … from a householder family; others that it was one who specialized in recitation of Discourses, in recitation of the Discipline, who preached the Dhamma … who had obtained the first meditation … the second meditation … the third meditation … the fourth meditation … that it was a stream-enterer … a once-returner … a non-returner … an accomplished Arahant … that it was one who had the three true knowledges; still others said that it was one who had the six kinds of direct knowledge. Then the Blessed One addressed the bhikkhus:

"Once, bhikkhus, somewhere in the Himalayas there was a huge banyan tree, under which three companions lived. They were a partridge, a monkey and an elephant. They were often rude and disrespectful, and they lived without consideration for one another. They thought: 'If only we could find out which of us is the oldest, then we could honour, respect, revere and venerate him and follow his advice.'

"The partridge and the monkey asked the elephant: 'How far back can you remember?'

" 'When I was a calf, I used to walk over this banyan tree so that it passed between my legs and its topmost branch scratched my stomach.'

"Then the partridge and the elephant asked the monkey: 'How far back can you remember?'

" 'When I was a baby, I used to sit on the ground and nibble the topmost shoots of this banyan tree.'

"Then the monkey and the elephant asked the partridge: 'How far back can you remember?'

" 'In a certain place there was a big banyan tree. I ate one of its seeds and voided it in this place, and this banyan tree grew from that seed. So I am older than you.'

"Then the monkey and the elephant said to the partridge: 'You are older than us. We will honour, respect, revere and venerate you and follow your advice.' After that the partridge made the monkey and the elephant undertake the five precepts of virtue, and he undertook them himself. And they were courteous and respectful to one another and lived with mutual consideration. On the dissolution of the body, after death, they appeared in a happy destination, in the heavenly world. So that came to be called 'the partridge's holy life.'

> Those that reverence an elder
> Are reckoned skillful in the Dhamma,
> For they have both praise here and now
> And a happy destiny beyond.

"Now, bhikkhus, these animals could be courteous and respectful to each other and live with mutual consideration. Try and copy them. That you should be rude and disrespectful and live without mutual consideration under a Dhamma and Discipline as well proclaimed as this, does not rouse faith in the faithless or increase faith in the faithful; rather it keeps the faithless without faith and harms some of the faithful."

Wandering by stages the Blessed One at length arrived at Sāvatthī. There he went to stay in Jeta's Grove, Anāthapiṇḍika's Park. Then

Anāthapiṇḍika went to the Blessed One and invited him for the following day's meal, which the Blessed One accepted in silence. When the meal was over and the Blessed One no longer had the bowl in his hand, Anāthapiṇḍika sat down at one side, and he asked: "Lord, how shall I act about this Jeta's Grove?"

"Then, householder, you may present it to the Sangha of bhikkhus of the four quarters—past, future and present."

"Even so, Lord," he replied, and he did so. Then the Blessed One addressed him with these stanzas:

> It keeps out cold and heat,
> Wild animals besides,
> And creeping things and flies,
> And chills and rain as well.
> And it affords protection
> When sun and wind are fierce.
> The aim is to be sheltered and at ease
> In order to concentrate and practise insight.
> Gifts of dwellings to the Order
> Are praised most highly by the Buddha,
> So let a man possessed of wisdom,
> Who sees wherein his own good lies,
> Have comfortable dwellings made
> And have the learned live in them.
> He can give food to them and drink
> And clothing and a resting place,
> Letting his heart repose its trust
> In those who walk in righteousness;
> And they will teach the Dhamma to him
> For freedom from all suffering,
> Knowing which Dhamma, he here attains
> Nibbāna and is free from taints.

Then when he had given his blessing, he got up from his seat and went away.

Vin. Cv. 6:5-9

NARRATOR ONE. The Buddha, who was now staying at Sāvatthī, capital of Kosala, had come from the country of Magadha, whose capital was Rājagaha. Magadha was one of the two most powerful states in central India at that time. It lay south of the

Ganges with its northern border on the river. Its king was Bimbisāra, who had already declared himself an adherent of the Buddha. Bimbisāra's brother-in-law, King Pasenadi, governed the other great kingdom, called Kosala, which stretched north from the north bank of the Ganges to the foothills of the Himalayas. King Pasenadi had, it seems, not so far met the Buddha.

FIRST VOICE. Thus I heard. It was when the Blessed One was living at Sāvatthī that a dearly beloved only son of a citizen of Sāvatthī had died. The father went to the Blessed One, who asked him: "Householder, your faculties seem those of one out of his mind; your faculties seem in no normal state."

"How should my faculties seem in their normal state, Lord? My dearly beloved only son is dead. Since his death I have given no more thought to my work or my meals. I keep going to the charnel ground and crying: 'My only child, where are you? My only child, where are you?' "

"So it is, householder, so it is. Dear ones who endear themselves bring sorrow and lamentation, pain, grief and despair."

"Who would ever think that, Lord? Dear ones, Lord, who endear themselves bring happiness and joy."

He got up dissenting and disapproving of the Blessed One's words and went away. Now on that occasion some gamblers were playing with dice not far from the Blessed One. The householder went to them and related his conversation. They said: "So it is, householder, so it is. Dear ones who endear themselves bring happiness and joy."

Then, thinking "I agree with the gamblers," he got up and went on his way.

This story eventually reached the royal palace. King Pasenadi of Kosala told the queen: "Mallikā, what is this that the monk Gotama has said: 'Dear ones who endear themselves bring sorrow and lamentation, pain, grief and despair'?"

"Sire, if that has been said by the Blessed One, then that is so."

"No matter what the monk Gotama says, this Mallikā, applauds it: 'If that has been said by the Blessed One, then that is so.' She speaks just like a pupil who applauds, no matter what the teacher says: 'So it is, teacher, so it is.' Be off, Mallikā, away with you!"

Then Queen Mallikā told Nāḷijangha of the brahman caste: "Go to the Blessed One and pay homage to him in my name. And ask this: 'Lord, have these words been spoken by the Blessed One: "Dear ones who endear themselves bring sorrow and lamentation, pain, grief and despair"?' Take note of his reply and tell me; for Perfect Ones speak nothing untrue."

He did as he had been asked. The Blessed One said: "So it is, brahman, so it is. Dear ones who endear themselves bring sorrow and lamentation, pain, grief and despair. And how that is so can be understood from this: Once in this same Sāvatthī there was a woman whose mother died, owing to which she lost her mind and wandered mad from street to street and from crossing to crossing, asking 'Have you seen my mother? Have you seen my mother?' "

NARRATOR TWO. The Buddha then went on to relate a large number of stories to the same effect, concluding as follows:

FIRST VOICE. "And there was once in this same Sāvatthī a woman who was married and lived with her husband's family. But her own relatives wanted to divorce her from her husband and give her to another whom she did not like. She told her husband of this. He stabbed her to death and killed himself, thinking 'In death we shall be together.' It can be understood from this too how dear ones who endear themselves bring sorrow and lamentation, pain, grief and despair."

Nāḷijangha returned to the queen and told her what had been said. She thereupon went to King Pasenadi and asked him: "Sire,

what is your opinion? Is Princess Vajirī dear to you?"

"Yes, Mallikā, she is dear to me."

"Sire, what is your opinion? If a change, an alteration, took place in Princess Vajirī, would that bring sorrow and lamentation, pain, grief and despair?"

"Any change, any alteration, in Princess Vajirī would mean an alteration in my life. How could sorrow and lamentation, pain, grief and despair not arise in me?"

"Sire, it was with reference to this that the Blessed One who knows and sees, accomplished and fully enlightened, said: 'Dear ones who endear themselves bring sorrow and lamentation, pain, grief and despair.' "

NARRATOR TWO. The queen pressed the point with the examples of Queen Vāsabhā, the king's son Viḍūḍabha, herself, and his kingdoms of Kāsi and Kosala, in the same manner. Then the king said:

FIRST VOICE. "Mallikā, it is wonderful, it is marvellous, how far the Blessed One penetrates and sees with understanding. Come, give me the ablution water."

Then King Pasenadi got up from his seat, and arranging his upper robe on one shoulder, he raised his hands palms together towards where the Blessed One was, and he uttered this exclamation three times: "Honour to the Blessed One accomplished and fully enlightened!"

M. 87

NARRATOR ONE. The next incident perhaps records how the king first met the Buddha.

FIRST VOICE. Thus I heard. At one time when the Blessed One was living at Sāvatthī, King Pasenadi of Kosala went to him. He exchanged greetings with him, and when this courteous formal talk was finished, he sat down at one side. When he had done so, he said: "Does Master Gotama claim to have discovered the supreme full enlightenment?"

"If, great king, it can rightly speaking be said of anyone that he has discovered the supreme full enlightenment, then it is of me that that can rightly speaking be said."

"But, Master Gotama, there are these monks and brahmans too, each with his order, with his group, leading a group, each a renowned and famous philosopher reckoned by many as a saint—I mean Pūraṇa Kassapa, Makkhali Gosāla, the Nigaṇṭha Nāthaputta, Sañjaya Belaṭṭhiputta, Pakudha Kaccāyana, and Ajita Kesakambali. Now when I asked them if they claimed to have discovered the supreme full enlightenment, they did not claim it. But how is this? For Master Gotama is both young in years and newly gone forth into homelessness."

"Great king, there are four things that should not be looked down upon and despised because they are young. What are the four? They are a warrior noble, a serpent, a fire, and a bhikkhu."

So the Blessed One said. The Sublime One having said this, the Master said further:

Let a man not despise and not contemn
A warrior youth born in a famous line
For being young. Perhaps that warrior youth
May gain despotic rule and be vindictive,

Visiting the royal vengeance on him.
Let him avoid it, then, and save his life.

Let a man not despise and not contemn
The writhing snake he sees in town or wood
For being young. A serpent travels fast
In many a guise; he may attack and bite
A heedless man or woman any time.
Let him avoid it, then, and save his life.

Let a man not despise and not contemn
The black-trailed fire that blazes hungrily
For being young.
If it should find the fuel
To grow and spread, it may attack and burn
A heedless man or woman any time.
Let him avoid it, then, and save his life.

Though black-trailed conflagrations burn up woods,
Yet shoots appear when a few days have passed;
But he whom virtuous bhikkhu's fire shall burn[3]
Will lack offspring, no heirs will have his wealth:
Such have, like palm stumps, neither child nor heir.

So the wise man, perceiving his own good,
Will treat the serpent rightly, and the fire,
The warrior noble, and the virtuous bhikkhu.

When this was said, King Pasenadi said to the Blessed One: "Magnificent, Lord! … Let the Blessed One receive me as a follower who has gone to him for refuge for as long as breath lasts."

S. 3:1

SECOND VOICE. The occasion was this. The Blessed One was living at Rājagaha in the Bamboo Grove, the Squirrels' Sanctuary, at a time when residence in one place during the rains had not yet been made obligatory by the Blessed One. Bhikkhus went wandering in the cold season, in the hot season and in the rainy season. People were annoyed, and they murmured and protested: "How can these monks, these sons of the Sakyans, go wandering in all three seasons, trampling down the green grass, harassing one-facultied life, and bringing harm to many little creatures? Even these other sectarians with their ill-proclaimed teaching do at least keep to their residence during the rains; and even these vultures that make their nests on the tree tops do at least keep to their residence during the rains. But these Sakyan monks go wandering in all three seasons, trampling down the green grass, harassing one-facultied life and bringing harm to many little creatures."

Bhikkhus heard this. They told the Blessed One. He made this the occasion for a talk on the Dhamma and he addressed the bhikkhus thus: "Bhikkhus, I allow a fixed residence for the rains."

Vin. Mv. 3:1

NARRATOR ONE. Although Anāthapiṇḍika's death occurred much later (when, is uncertain), still an account of it is perhaps most appropriate here.

NARRATOR TWO. Anāthapiṇḍika in his last illness sent a message to the Elder Sāriputta asking him to visit him. Accordingly the two elders, Sāriputta and Ānanda, went to him. He told them how his sickness was worsening, and then the elder Sāriputta instructed him as follows.

FIRST VOICE. "Then householder, you should train thus: 'I will not cling to the eye; there shall be no consciousness of mine based on the eye.' You should train thus."

NARRATOR TWO. Then he went on to instruct him likewise about the other four senses and the mind, about the objects of those five senses and the mind, about these six kinds of consciousness and contact and feeling, about the elements of earth, water, fire, air, space and consciousness, about the five aggregates, about the four formless states, about this world and the world beyond, and finally about all that is seen, heard, sensed (by nose, tongue and body), and cognized, sought after and accessible to the mind.

FIRST VOICE. When this was said, Anāthapiṇḍika wept and tears ran down his face. Then the venerable Ānanda asked him: "Are you holding back, householder? Are you failing?"—"I am not holding back, venerable Ānanda, I am not failing. Though I have long waited on the Master and the meditative bhikkhus, yet I have never before heard such a talk on the Dhamma as that."—"Such talks on the Dhamma are not given to the white-clothed laity, householder, they are given to those gone forth from the house life."—"Nevertheless, venerable Sāriputta, let such talks on the Dhamma be given to them. There are some with little dust on their eyes who are wasting through not hearing such talks on the Dhamma. Some of them will gain final knowledge of the Dhamma."

M. 143

Narrator Two. Anāthapiṇḍika expired on the same day, and it is told how he was reborn in heaven as a stream-enterer, with consequently not more than seven rebirths before him.

7
FORMATION OF THE ORDER OF NUNS

NARRATOR ONE. The account just given has shown how the Buddha agreed to spend the rains at Sāvatthī[1]. So if the traditional reckoning of the first three rains after the Enlightenment is correct, the fourth was spent in Jeta's Grove. Here is a story that might belong to this period.

FIRST VOICE. Thus I heard. On an occasion when the Blessed One was living at Sāvatthī in Jeta's Grove, Anāthapiṇḍika's Park, the venerable Nanda, the son of the Blessed One's maternal aunt, told a number of bhikkhus: "Friends, I am leading the holy life dissatisfied. I cannot carry on with the holy life. I shall renounce the training and return to what I abandoned."

Then those bhikkhus went to the Blessed One and told him this. The Blessed One said to a bhikkhu: "Come, bhikkhu, tell the bhikkhu Nanda in my name 'The Teacher calls you, friend.' "

"Even so, Lord," the bhikkhu replied. And he went to the venerable Nanda and gave him the message. The venerable Nanda went to the Blessed One, who asked him: "Nanda, is it true, as it seems, that you are leading the holy life dissatisfied, that you cannot carry on the holy life, and that you will renounce the training and go back to what you abandoned?"

"Yes, Lord."

"But, Nanda, why is this?"

"Lord, when I left to renounce the house life, the Sakyan beauty Janapadakalyāṇī gazed after me with her hair partly held back and she said: 'Come back soon, prince.' When I remember that, I lead the holy life dissatisfied."

Then the Blessed One took the venerable Nanda by the arm, and as quickly as a strong man might extend his flexed arm or flex his extended arm, they vanished in Jeta's Grove and appeared among the deities of the Thirty-three. Now on that occasion five hundred nymphs with dove's feet had come to wait upon Sakka, Ruler of

Gods. The Blessed One asked the venerable Nanda: "Nanda, do you see those five hundred nymphs with dove's feet?"

"Yes, Lord."

"What is your opinion, Nanda, which is more lovely, more beautiful, more alluring, the Sakyan beauty Janapadakalyāṇī or these five hundred nymphs with dove's feet?"

"Lord, the Sakyan beauty Janapadakalyāṇī is like a scalded she-monkey with her nose and ears lopped off compared to these five hundred nymphs with dove's feet. She does not count at all; she is nothing like them; there is no comparison whatever. These five hundred nymphs are infinitely more lovely and beautiful and alluring."

"Then enjoy the holy life, Nanda; enjoy it and I guarantee your obtaining five hundred nymphs with dove's feet."

"Lord, if the Blessed One guarantees my obtaining that, then I shall enjoy the holy life."

Then the Blessed One took the venerable Nanda by the arm and as before they vanished in the Heaven of the Thirty-three and reappeared in Jeta's Grove.

Bhikkhus heard: "It seems that the venerable Nanda is living the holy life for the sake of nymphs; for it seems that the Blessed One has guaranteed his obtaining five hundred nymphs with dove's feet." Then his friends among the bhikkhus treated him as a hireling who had sold himself: "The venerable Nanda is a hireling, it seems, who has sold himself, since he leads the holy life for the sake of nymphs. The Blessed One, it seems, has guaranteed his obtaining five hundred nymphs with dove's feet."

He became humiliated, ashamed and dismayed at his companions' words. So he went to dwell alone and withdrawn, diligent, ardent and self-controlled, till by realization himself with direct knowledge, he here and now entered upon and abode in that supreme goal of the holy life for the sake of which clansmen rightly go forth from the house life into homelessness. He knew directly: "Birth is exhausted, the holy life has been lived out, what was to be done has been done, there is no more of this to come." And the venerable Nanda became one of the Arahants.

When the night was well advanced, a deity of outstanding beauty, illuminating the whole of Jeta's Grove, went to the Blessed One, and after paying homage, stood at one side. The deity said:

"Lord, the venerable Nanda, the Blessed One's half-brother, his mother's sister's son, has, by realization himself with direct knowledge, here and now entered upon and dwells in the deliverance of mind and deliverance by understanding that are taintless with exhaustion of taints." And the knowledge of that fact was in the Blessed One too.

At the end of the night the venerable Nanda went to the Blessed One. He said: "Lord, in so far as the Blessed One guaranteed my obtaining five hundred nymphs with dove's feet, I release him from that promise."

"I had already read your mind with my mind, Nanda. Also deities had told me this. So when your heart was freed from taints, I was already then released from my promise." And knowing the meaning of this, the Blessed One uttered this exclamation:

> When a bhikkhu has crossed the slough,
> And crushed the thorn of sense desires,
> And reached destruction of delusion,
> Pleasures and pains will shake him not.

Ud. 3:2

NARRATOR ONE. The next rains—the fifth was spent at Vesālī, the capital of Videha, a country on the southeast flank of Kosala and on the north bank of the Ganges. It was a confederacy ruled by an oligarchy, not a monarchy.

NARRATOR TWO. In the months that followed, King Suddhodana fell sick, and he died an Arahant. The Buddha again visited his native city.

SECOND VOICE. The occasion was this. The Buddha, the Blessed One, was living among the Sakyans in Nigrodha's Park at Kapilavatthu. Mahāpajāpatī Gotamī went to him. She paid homage and stood at one side. Then she said: "Lord, it would be good if women could obtain the going forth from the house life into homelessness in the Dhamma and Discipline declared by the Perfect One."

"Enough, Gotamī, do not ask for the going forth from the house life into homelessness for women in the Dhamma and Discipline declared by the Perfect One."

She asked a second and a third time and was refused. Then she thought: "The Blessed One does not allow it," and she was sad and unhappy. She paid homage to the Blessed One and departed, keeping him on her right.

Now when the Blessed One had stayed at Kapilavatthu as long as he chose, he set out to wander by stages to Vesālī. When he eventually arrived there, he went to live in the Hall with the Pointed Roof in the Great Wood.

Meanwhile Mahāpajāpatī Gotamī had her hair cut off and put on the yellow robe. With a number of Sakyan women she set out for Vesālī. On arrival there she went to the Hall with the Pointed Roof in the Great Wood, and she stood there outside the porch. Her feet were swollen, her limbs covered with dust, and she was sad and unhappy, with tears on her face and sobbing. As she stood thus, the venerable Ānanda saw her. He asked her: "Gotamī, why are you standing outside the porch like this?"

"Lord Ānanda, it is because the Blessed One does not allow the going forth for women in the Dhamma and Discipline declared by the Perfect One."

"Then, Gotamī, wait here till I ask the Blessed One about this." The venerable Ānanda went to the Blessed One and told him what had happened and he said: "Lord, it would be good if women might obtain the going forth from the house life into homelessness in the Dhamma and Discipline declared by the Perfect One."

"Enough, Ānanda, do not ask for the going forth from the house life into homelessness for women in the Dhamma and Discipline declared by the Perfect One."

He asked a second and a third time and was refused. Then he thought: "The Blessed One does not allow it. But suppose I asked the Blessed One in another way?" Then he said: "Lord, are women capable, after going forth from the house life into homelessness in the Dhamma and Discipline declared by the Perfect One, of realizing the fruit of stream-entry or once-return or non-return or Arahantship?"

"They are, Ānanda."[2]

"If that is so, Lord, then since Mahāpajāpatī Gotamī has been exceedingly helpful to the Blessed One when as his mother's sister she was his nurse, his foster mother, his giver of milk—she suckled the Blessed One when his own mother died—since that is so, Lord, it would be good if women could obtain the going forth."

"Ānanda, if Mahāpajāpatī Gotamī accepts eight capital points, that will count as her full admission. These are the eight points. A bhikkhuni who has been admitted even a hundred years must pay homage to, get up for, reverentially salute, and respectfully greet, a bhikkhu admitted that day. A bhikkhuni must not spend the rains in a place where there are no bhikkhus. Every half-month a bhikkhuni should expect two things from the Sangha of bhikkhus; the appointment of the Uposatha day of observance each half-month, and a visit for exhortation. At the end of the rains a bhikkhuni must invite criticism of both Sanghas in the three instances, that is, whether anything improper in her conduct has been seen, heard or suspected. When a bhikkhuni has committed a grave offence, she must do the penance before both Sanghas. A probationer who seeks admission must do so from both Sanghas and after training in the six things for two years. A bhikkhuni must not find fault with or abuse a bhikkhu in any manner at all. From today onwards it is not allowed for bhikkhunis to address discourses to bhikkhus, but it is allowed for bhikkhus to address bhikkhunis. These eight things are to be honoured, respected, revered and venerated, and they are not to be transgressed as long as life lasts. If Mahāpajāpatī Gotamī accepts these eight capital points, that will count as her full admission.'

When the venerable Ānanda had learned these eight capital points from the Blessed One, he went to Mahāpajāpatī Gotamī and told her what the Blessed One had said.

"Lord Ānanda, suppose a woman—-or a man—young, youthful, fond of ornaments, with head washed, had got a garland of lotuses or jasmine or roses,[3] she would accept it with both hands and place it on her head; so too do I accept these eight capital points not to be transgressed as long as life lasts."

Then the venerable Ānanda returned to the Blessed One and told him: "Lord, Mahāpajāpatī Gotamī has accepted the eight capital points. She is now fully admitted."

"Ānanda, if women had not obtained the going forth from the house life into homelessness in the Dhamma and Discipline declared by the Perfect One, the holy life would have lasted long, the holy life would have lasted a thousand years. But now, since women have obtained it, the holy life will not last long, the holy life will last only five hundred years.

"Just as clans with many women and few men are easily ruined by robbers and bandits, so too in the Dhamma and Discipline in which women obtain the going forth the holy life does not last long. Just as when the blight called gray mildew falls on a field of ripening rice, that field of ripening rice does not last long—just as when the blight called red rust falls on a field of ripening sugarcane, that field of ripening sugarcane does not last long—so too in the Dhamma and Discipline in which women obtain the going forth the holy life does not last long. As a man might construct in advance an embankment so that the waters of a great reservoir should not cause a flood, so I too have made known in advance these eight capital points for bhikkhunis not to be transgressed as long as life lasts."

Vin. Cv. 10:1; A. 8:51

NARRATOR TWO. When she asked later for instructions about the Sakyan women who had accompanied her, the Buddha directed that the bhikkhus should give them the full admission as bhikkhunis. The bhikkhunis thus fully admitted then claimed that unlike themselves Mahāpajāpatī was not fully admitted. She appealed through the Elder Ānanda to the Buddha, who settled the dispute by repeating that her acceptance of the eight points was the full admission in her case. Later still she went to the Elder Ānanda asking him for the Buddha to allow bhikkhus and bhikkhunis to pay homage to seniors regardless of which of the two communities they belonged to. The Buddha's answer was that no bhikkhu should pay homage to a bhikkhuni.

SECOND VOICE. At another time Mahāpajāpatī Gotamī went to the Blessed One. After paying homage to him she stood at one side, and she said: "Lord, it would be good if the Blessed One would instruct me briefly, so that, having heard the Dhamma from the Blessed One, I may dwell alone, withdrawn, diligent, ardent and self-controlled."

"Gotamī, those things of which you know: 'These things lead to passion, not to dispassion; to attachment, not to detachment; to amassing, not to dispersal; to ambition, not to modesty; to discontent, not to content; to association, not to seclusion; to idleness, not to energy; to luxury, not to frugality,' of them you can quite certainly decide: 'This is not the Dhamma, this is not the Discipline, this is not the Master's teaching.' But those things of which you know: 'These things lead to dispassion, not to passion; to detachment, not to attachment; to dispersal, not to amassing; to modesty, not to ambition; to content, not to discontent; to seclusion, not to association; to energy, not to idleness; to frugality, not to luxury,' of them you can quite certainly decide: 'This is the Dhamma, this is the Discipline, this is the Master's teaching.' "

Vin. Cv. 10:5; A. 8:53

8
THE QUARREL AT KOSAMBĪ

NARRATOR TWO. Tradition has it that the sixth rains was spent on the Makula Mountain and that during the following year the Twin Marvel was displayed again at Sāvatthī, after which the Buddha ascended to the Heaven of the Thirty-three. There he spent the seventh rains expounding the Abhidhamma to deities including the deity who had formerly been his mother. At the end of that rainy season the "descent of the gods" took place when the Buddha returned to earth. He spent the eighth rains at Suṃsumāragira and the ninth at Kosambī.

NARRATOR ONE. Kosambī was the capital of the small kingdom of Vaṃsa wedged between the Ganges and the Jumna. Its king, Udena, is hardly mentioned in the Canon. Most of the events placed in these years by the later tradition, including the visit to the Heaven of the Thirty-three and the descent of the gods, are not mentioned in the Canon at all.

NARRATOR TWO. Here to start with is the account of the petty circumstance that led to the first great quarrel, which threatened to produce a schism in the Sangha. It seems that there were two bhikkhus in one monastery, one an expert in Discipline and the other a teacher of Discourses. The latter went to the latrine one day and left a vessel there with some unused washing water in it. The other went in later and found it there. He asked the teacher of Discourses: "Did you leave that vessel with water in it there?"—"Yes."—"You did not know it was an offence?"—"No, I did not."—"It constitutes an offence, friend."—"Then I will acknowledge it."—"But if you did it unintentionally and out of forgetfulness, there was no offence." The teacher of Discourses went away under the impression that he had done no wrong. However, the expert in Discipline told his pupils: "This teacher of Discourses does not know when he has committed an offence." They told the other's pupils: "Your preceptor has committed an offence, though he is under the impression that he has not." When they told their preceptor of this, he said: "This Discipline expert said first that there was no offence, and now he says that there was one. He is a liar." They told the pupils of the expert in Discipline: "Your preceptor is a liar." His answer was to convene a chapter and suspend the teacher of Discourses.

NARRATOR ONE. Now here is the canonical account of what followed.

SECOND VOICE. The occasion was this. While the Buddha, the Blessed One, was living at Kosambī in Ghosita's Park a certain bhikkhu became involved in an offence. He saw the offence as an offence, but other bhikkhus saw the offence as no offence. Later he himself saw the offence as no offence, but other bhikkhus saw the offence as an offence. Those bhikkhus then said to him: "Friend, you have committed an offence. Do you see the offence?"

"Friends, I have committed no offence that I should see."

Those bhikkhus then agreed to suspend that bhikkhu though he still did not see his offence. But that bhikkhu was learned. He knew the Canon and was expert in the Dhamma and the Discipline and the Codes. He was wise, sagacious, understanding, modest, scrupulous and desirous of training. He went to his intimate associates and said: "This is no offence, this is not an offence, I have not offended ... I am not suspended, I have been suspended by a wrongful act that is invalid and groundless. Let the venerable ones side with me in the Dhamma and Discipline."

He got them on his side, and he sent messengers to his friends and associates in the country. Then the bhikkhus who supported the suspended one went to those who had suspended him and stated their case. When this was done, the others reaffirmed the validity of their act of suspension, and they said: "Let the venerable ones not support and follow a suspended bhikkhu." But though the bhikkhus who supported the suspended bhikkhu were spoken to thus by those who had suspended him, they continued to support and follow him.

Then a certain bhikkhu went to the Blessed One and told him about this. The Blessed One said: "There will be schism in the Sangha, there will be schism in the Sangha." He got up from his seat and went to the bhikkhus who had done the suspending. He sat down on a seat made ready, and he said to them: "Bhikkhus, do not imagine that such and such a bhikkhu should be suspended simply for this reason: 'We think thus.' Take the case of a bhikkhu who has committed an offence, and though he does not see it as such, other bhikkhus do see it as such. Now bhikkhus who know the gravity of schism in the Sangha should not suspend that bhikkhu as long as he does not see his offence, if they judge thus: 'He is learned and desirous of training; if we suspend him without his seeing his offence, we shall not be able to keep the holy day Uposatha observance with him, or the Pavāraṇā ceremony (Invitation to Criticise) at the end of the rains, or carry out acts of the Sangha, or sit on the same seat, or share gruel, or share the refectory, or live under the same roof, or perform acts of respect to elders, with him; we shall do these things without him, and because of that there will be quarrelling, brawling, wrangling, disputing and eventually schism, division and dissenting acts in the Sangha.' "

When he had said this, he got up and went to the bhikkhus who followed the suspended bhikkhu. He sat down on a seat made ready, and he said to them: "Bhikkhus, do not imagine that an offence having been committed, it should not be made amends for simply because you think: 'We have not committed it.' Take the case of a bhikkhu who has committed an offence, and though he does not see it as such, other bhikkhus do see it as such. Now a bhikkhu who knows the gravity of schism in the Sangha should acknowledge the offence out of faith in the others, if he judges thus: 'They are learned and desirous of training; it is absurd to go astray through zeal, hate, delusion and fear on my account or on these others' account; if these bhikkhus suspend me for an offence that I do not see, they will not keep the holy day Uposatha observance with me, or the Pavāraṇā ceremony, or carry out acts of the Sangha, or sit on the same seat, or share gruel, or share the refectory, or live under the same roof, or perform acts of respect to elders, with me; they will do these things without me, and because of that there will be quarrelling, brawling, wrangling, disputing and eventually schism, division and dissenting acts in the Sangha.' "

When the Blessed One had said this, he got up and went away.

Vin. Mv. 10:1

FIRST VOICE. But now quarrels, brawls and disputes broke out in the midst of the Sangha, and bhikkhus wounded each other with verbal arrows. They could not settle their litigation. A bhikkhu then went to the Blessed One, and after paying homage to him, he stood at one side. He recounted what was taking place, and he added; "Lord, it would be good if the Blessed One went to those bhikkhus out of compassion."

The Blessed One consented in silence. Then he went to those bhikkhus and said to them: "Enough, bhikkhus, no quarrelling, no brawling, no wrangling, no disputing."

When this was said, a certain bhikkhu replied: "Lord, let the Blessed One, the Master of the Dhamma wait; let the Blessed One live devoted to a pleasant abiding here and now and not concern himself with this. It is we who shall be known on account of this quarrelling, brawling, wrangling and disputing."

A second and a third time the Blessed One said the same thing and received the same answer. Then he thought: "These misguided men seem obsessed. It is impossible to make them see." He got up and went away.

When it was morning he dressed, and taking his bowl and outer robe, he went into Kosambī for alms. When he had wandered for alms and had returned from his alms round after the meal, he set his resting place in order and took up his bowl and outer robe. Then he uttered these stanzas.

M.128; cf. Vin. Mv. 10:2-3

When many voices shout at once,
There is none thinks himself a fool;
The Order being split, none thinks:
'I too took part, I helped in this.'
They have forgot wise speech, they talk
With minds obsessed by words alone;
Uncurbed their mouths, they bawl at will;
None knows what leads him so to do.

M.128; Jā. 3:488; Ud. 5:9;
Thag. 275; Vin. Mv. 10:3

"It is he abused me, he that beat me,
He that worsted me, that robbed me!"
Hate never is appeased in those
Who cherish suchlike enmity.

"It is he abused me, he that beat me,
He that worsted me, that robbed me!"
Hate surely is appeased in those
Who cherish no such enmity.
For enmity by enmity
Is never in this world appeased;
It is appeased by amity—
That is an ancient principle.
Those others do not recognize
That here we should restrain ourselves.[1]
Still there are some who are aware,
And so their quarrels are appeased.

M.128; Dh. 3-6; Jā. 3:212, 488; Vin. Mv. 10:3

Breakers of bones and murderers,
Stealers of cattle, horses, wealth—
While bent on pillaging the realm,
Even these can act in concord;
So why can you not do so too?

M.128; Jā. 3:488; Vin. Mv. 10:3

If you can find a trustworthy companion
With whom to walk, both virtuous and steadfast,
Then walk with him content and mindfully,
Overcoming any threat of danger.
If you can find no trustworthy companion
With whom to walk, both virtuous and steadfast,
Then, as a king who leaves a vanquished kingdom,
Walk like a tusker in the woods alone.
Better it is to walk alone:
There is no fellowship with fools.
Walk alone, harm none, and know no conflict;
Be like a tusker in the woods alone.

M. 128: Jā. 3:488; Vin. Mv. 10:3
Dh. 328-30; cf. Sn. 45-46

Now when the Blessed One had spoken these stanzas, he went away to Bālakaloṇakāragāma. The venerable Bhagu was living there at that time. When he saw the Blessed One coming in the distance, he prepared a seat and set out water for washing the feet and a footstool and a foot-towel. Then he went out to meet him and took his bowl and outer robe. The Blessed One sat down on the seat made ready, and he washed his feet. The venerable Bhagu paid homage to him and sat down at one side. Then the Blessed One said to him: "Bhikkhu, I hope that you are well, that you are comfortable and that you have no trouble on account of almsfood?"

"I am well, Blessed One, I am comfortable and I have no trouble on account of almsfood."

Then the Blessed One instructed, urged, roused and encouraged the venerable Bhagu with talk on the Dhamma after which he got up from his seat and left for the Eastern Bamboo Park. The venerable Anuruddha, the venerable Nandiya and the venerable Kimbila were living there at that time. The park keeper saw the Blessed One coming. He told him: "Do not go into this park, monk; there are three clansmen living there, seeking their own good. Do not disturb them."

The venerable Anuruddha heard the park keeper speaking to the Blessed One. He told the park keeper: "Friend park keeper, do not keep the Blessed One out. It is our own teacher, the Blessed One, who has come."

The venerable Anuruddha went to the venerable Nandiya and the venerable Kimbila and said: "Come out, venerable sirs, come out; our teacher has come."

Then all three went to meet the Blessed One. One took his bowl and outer robe, one prepared a seat and one placed water for washing his feet. The Blessed One sat down on the seat made ready and washed his feet. Then they paid homage to him and sat down at one side. The Blessed One said: "I hope that all of you are well, Anuruddha, that you are comfortable and that you have no trouble on account of almsfood."

"We are well, Blessed One, we are comfortable and we have no trouble on account of almsfood."

"I hope that you all live in concord, Anuruddha, as friendly and undisputing as milk with water, viewing each other with kindly eyes?"

"Surely we do so, Lord."

"But, Anuruddha, how do you live thus?"

The venerable Anuruddha replied: "Lord, as to that, I think that it is gain and good fortune for me here that I am living with such companions in the holy life. I maintain acts and words and thoughts of loving-kindness towards these venerable ones both in public and in private. I think: 'Why should I not set aside what I am minded to do and do only what they are minded to do?' and I act accordingly. We are different in body, Lord, but only one in mind, I think."

The other two each said the same thing. They added: "Lord, that is how we live in concord, as friendly and undisputing as milk and water, viewing each other with kindly eyes."

"Good, good, Anuruddha. I hope you all dwell diligent, ardent and self-controlled?"

"Surely we do so, Lord."

"But, Anuruddha, how do you dwell thus?"

"Lord, as to that, whichever of us returns first from the village with almsfood gets the seats ready, sets out the water for drinking and for washing and puts the refuse bucket in its place. Whichever of us returns last eats any food left over if he wishes; otherwise he throws it away where there is no grass or drops it into water where there is no life. He puts away the seats and the water for drinking and for washing. He puts away the refuse bucket after washing it, and he sweeps out the refectory. Whoever notices that the pots of drinking water or washing water or water for the privy are low or empty sees to them. If any are too heavy for him, he beckons someone else by a sign of the hand and they move it by joining hands. We do not speak for that purpose. But every five days we sit out the night together in talk on the Dhamma. It is in this way that we dwell diligent, ardent and self-controlled."

M. 128; Vin. Mv. 10:4

SECOND VOICE. Now when the Blessed One had instructed, urged, roused and encouraged them with talk on the Dhamma, he rose from his seat. He set out to wander by stages to Pārileyyaka. At length in the course of wandering he arrived there, and he went to live in the Rakkhita jungle at the root of an auspicious sāla tree. While he was alone in retreat this thought arose in his mind: "Formerly I lived in discomfort, pestered by those Kosambī bhikkhus who quarrel, brawl, wrangle, harangue and litigate in the midst of the Sangha. Now I am alone and companionless, living at ease and in comfort, away from all of them."

There was also a certain tusker elephant who had been living pestered by elephants and cow elephants and calf elephants and sucking elephants and he had been eating grass with bruised ends, and broken-up bits of branches, and he had been drinking dirty water, and his body had been jostled by cow elephants as he came up out of the bathing place. He had considered all this and he thought: "Why should I not live alone, withdrawn from the crowd?" And so he had left the herd and had gone to Pārileyyaka, to the Rakkhita jungle, to the root of the auspicious sāla tree where the Blessed One was. He looked after the Blessed One, providing food and drink for him, and with his trunk he cleared the leaves away. He thought: "Formerly I lived pestered by elephants .... Now, alone and withdrawn from the herd, I live at ease and in comfort away from all those elephants."

The Blessed One, relishing his own seclusion, became aware in his mind of the thought in the tusker elephant's mind. He uttered this exclamation:

> Tusker agrees with tusker here;
> The elephant with tusks as long
> As shafts delights alone in woods:
> Their hearts are thus in harmony.

Vin. Mv. 10:4; cf. Ud. 4:5

FIRST VOICE. Soon after the Blessed One had left Kosambī a certain bhikkhu went to the venerable Ānanda and said: "Friend Ānanda, the Blessed One has put his resting place in order, and he has taken his bowl and outer robe and set out to wander alone and unaccompanied without informing his attendants or taking leave of the Sangha of bhikkhus."

"Friend, when the Blessed One does that, then he wants to live alone, and he must not be followed by anyone."

Some time later a number of bhikkhus went to the venerable Ānanda and said: "Friend Ānanda, it is long since we heard a talk on the Dhamma from the Blessed One's own lips. We should like to hear that."

So the venerable Ānanda went with those bhikkhus to the Blessed One at the root of the auspicious sāla tree at Pārileyyaka, and after paying homage they sat down at one side. Then the Blessed One encouraged them with talk on the Dhamma.

S. 22:81

SECOND VOICE. When the Blessed One had stayed at Pārileyyaka as long as he chose, he set out to wander by stages to Sāvatthī. In the course of his wandering he at length arrived there, and he went to live in Jeta's Grove, Anāthapiṇḍika 's Park.

Meanwhile the lay followers of Kosambī thought: "These venerable Kosambī bhikkhus are doing us great harm. They have plagued the Blessed One till he has gone away. Let us no longer pay homage to them or rise up for them or give them reverential salutation or treat them with courtesy, let us not honour, respect, revere or venerate them, let us give them no more almsfood even when they come for it. So when they get no honour, respect, reverence or veneration from us, when they are regularly ignored, they will either go elsewhere or leave the Sangha or make amends to the Blessed One."

They acted accordingly. In consequence the Kosambī bhikkhus decided: "Let us go to Sāvatthī, friends, and settle this litigation in the Blessed One's presence." So they put their resting places in order, took their bowls and outer robes and set out for Sāvatthī.

The venerable Sāriputta heard that they were coming. He went to the Blessed One and asked: "Lord, it seems that those Kosambī bhikkhus who quarrel, brawl, dispute, wrangle and litigate in the midst of the Sangha are coming here to Sāvatthī. How am I to treat them, Lord?"

"Keep to the Dhamma, Sāriputta."

"Lord, how am I to know what is Dhamma—and what is not?"

"There are eighteen instances in which one who says what is not Dhamma can be recognized. Here a bhikkhu shows what is not Dhamma as Dhamma and what is Dhamma as not Dhamma; he shows what is not the Discipline as the Discipline and what is the Discipline as not the Discipline; he shows what has not been stated by the Perfect One as so stated and what has been stated by the Perfect One as not so stated; he shows what is not practised by the Perfect One as so practised, and he shows the opposite; he shows what has not been made known by the Perfect One as so made known and he shows the opposite; he shows what is not an offence as an offence and what is an offence as not an offence; he shows a slight offence as a grave one and a grave offence as a slight one; he shows an offence with remainder as one without and an offence without remainder as one with; he shows a serious offence as not serious and one not serious as serious. One who says what is Dhamma can be known in the opposite way."

The venerable Mahā-Moggallāna, the venerable Mahā-Kassapa, the venerable Mahā-Kaccāna, the venerable Mahā-Koṭṭhita, the venerable Mahā-Kappina, the venerable Mahā-Cunda, the venerable Anuruddha, the venerable Revata, the venerable Upāli, the venerable Ānanda and the venerable Rāhula heard that they were coming. They each went to the Blessed One and received the same instructions.

Mahāpajāpatī Gotamī heard about it, and she went to the Blessed One and asked him how she was to treat them.

"Hear the Dhamma from both sides, Gotamī. When you have done so, approve the views, the liking, the opinions and judgements of those who say what is Dhamma. What the Sangha of bhikkhunis has to expect from the Sangha of bhikkhus should be expected from those who speak according to Dhamma."

Anāthapiṇḍika and Visākhā, Migāra's Mother, heard about it, and they went to the Blessed One for advice. He told them: "Give gifts to both sides. Approve the views of those who speak according to Dhamma."

Eventually the Kosambī bhikkhus arrived at Sāvatthī. The venerable Sāriputta went to the Blessed One and asked: "Lord, it seems that those Kosambī bhikkhus have arrived at Sāvatthī. How should they be accommodated for lodging?"

"Lodge them secluded from each other."

"But if there are no secluded lodgings, Lord, what is to be done?"

"Then allot them after having had them made secluded, Sāriputta. I say, however, that in no circumstances should a resting place be denied to a senior bhikkhu—Whoever does so commits an offence of wrongdoing."

"But, Lord, what is to be done about food and so on?"

"Food and so on must be shared out equally with all."

Now while the suspended bhikkhu was reflecting on the Discipline, it occurred to him: "That was an offence, not no offence, I have offended ... I am suspended. I have been suspended by a lawful act that cannot be quashed and is fit to stand." Then he went to his supporters and told them this, and he said: "So the venerable ones may reinstate me."

His followers then took him to the Blessed One, and after paying homage they sat down at one side. They recounted what the suspended bhikkhu had said, and they asked: "Lord how should we act?"

"Bhikkhus, that was an offence and not no offence, he has offended ... he is suspended. He has been suspended by a lawful act that cannot be quashed and is fit to stand. Since that bhikkhu, who has committed that offence and has been suspended, has seen it, you can reinstate him."

Then after the followers of the suspended bhikkhu had reinstated him they went to the bhikkhus who had suspended him, and they said: "Friends, about that case over which there was quarrelling and disunion in the Sangha—the bhikkhu has committed an offence, he has been suspended; now he has seen it, and he has been reinstated. Let us have an act of settlement before the Sangha in order to close the matter."

Then the bhikkhus who had done the suspending went to the Blessed One and told him what had occurred. The proposed act of settlement was approved and the procedure laid down.

Vin. Mv. 10:5

9
THE END OF THE FIRST TWENTY YEARS

NARRATOR TWO. The tenth rains after the Enlightenment was spent at Pārileyyaka, while the quarrel at Kosambī was at its height. The same tradition has it that the eleventh rains was spent in the Southern Hills (the hills south of Rājagaha), and that the following event happened then.

FIRST VOICE. Thus I heard. At one time the Blessed One was living in the Magadhan country at the village of Ekanālā. It was then sowing time, and Kasi (the "ploughman") Bhāradvāja of the brahman caste had as many as five hundred ploughs at work. In the early morning the Blessed One dressed, and taking his bowl and outer robe, he went to where Kasi Bhāradvāja's work was in progress. It happened to be the occasion when the brahman was making a distribution of food. The Blessed One went to where the food was being distributed, and he stood at one side. The brahman, seeing him waiting for almsfood, said:

"I plough, monk, and I sow, and having ploughed and sown, I eat. You too, monk, should likewise plough and sow, and having ploughed and sown, you shall eat."

"I too, brahman, plough and sow, and having ploughed and sown, I eat."

"We see no yoke or plough or shoe or goad or oxen of Master Gotama's; yet Master Gotama has said 'I too, brahman, plough and sow, and having ploughed and sown, I eat.' " And then he addressed the Blessed One in stanzas:

> "You claim to be a ploughman, yet
> We see no ploughing that you do.
> Give answer therefore, sir, that we
> May recognize your ploughing."
>
> "My seed is faith, my rain control,
> My plough and yoke are understanding,

My pole is conscience, mind is my tie,
And mindfulness my shoe and goad.
Guarded in body as in speech
And modest in the use of food,
Truth is the reaping that I do,
Forbearance my unharnessing;
My harnessed ox is energy,
Which draws on to surcease of bondage,
Going to where no sorrow is
And never turning back again.
Such is the ploughing that I do;
It has the Deathless for its fruit.
Who does this ploughing will be freed
From every kind of suffering."

Then Kasi Bhāradvāja had a large bronze bowl filled with milk-rice and brought to the Blessed One: "Let Master Gotama eat the milk-rice. Master Gotama is a ploughman since he does the ploughing that has the Deathless for its fruit."

"I cannot use rewards for singing songs;
Such is the law of seers. Enlightened Ones
Will not accept rewards for singing songs;
Such is their habit while their law prevails.
When a seer is free from taints, with conflicts stilled—
As you would say, 'has reached the Absolute'.[1]—
Then give him gifts with other thoughts in mind:
He is the field for those who would reap merit."

"Then whom shall I give this milk-rice to, Master Gotama?"

"Brahman, in this world with its deities, its Māras and its divinities, in this generation with its monks and brahmans, with its princes and men, I do not see anyone who could rightly digest this milk-rice if he ate it, unless it were a Perfect One or a disciple of his. Therefore, brahman, throw the milk-rice away where there is no grass or drop it into water where there is no life."

Kasi Bhāradvāja the brahman dropped the milk-rice into water where there was no life. As soon as it was dropped into the water it hissed and boiled and fumed and steamed. Just as a plough shoe heated for a day and dropped into water would hiss and boil and fume and steam, so did that milk-rice.

Then the brahman was awestruck and his hair stood on end. He went to the Blessed One and prostrated himself at his feet and said: "Magnificent, Master Gotama! ... I wish to receive the going forth from Master Gotama and the admission." ... And not long after ... the venerable Bhāradvāja became one of the Arahants.

Sn. 1:4; S. 7:11

NARRATOR TWO. The novice Rāhula, the Buddha's son, was now eighteen. The Buddha was staying at Jeta's Grove, and he had set out one morning to the city for alms. His son was following close behind, and as he did so, his thoughts wandered, and he began to speculate on what his prospects might have been had his father become a universal monarch, as had been predicted of him if he did not renounce the house life.

FIRST VOICE. While the venerable Rāhula was following close behind, the Blessed One turned and looked at him, and he addressed him thus: "Rāhula, any kind of material form whatever, whether past, future or present, in oneself or external, coarse or fine, inferior or superior, far or near, should all be regarded as it actually is with right understanding thus: 'This is not mine, this is not what I am, this is not my self.' "

"Only material form, Blessed One? Only material form, Sublime One?"

"Material form, Rāhula, and feeling and perception and formations and consciousness."

Then the venerable Rāhula thought: "Who can go on into the town for alms now after being publicly admonished by the Blessed One?" And he turned back and sat down under a tree with his legs crossed, body held erect and mindfulness established before him. The venerable Sāriputta saw him thus, and he told him: "Rāhula, maintain mindfulness of breathing in being; if that is maintained in being and well developed, it brings great fruit and many blessings."

When it was evening, the venerable Rāhula rose from retreat and went to the Blessed One. After paying homage to him he sat down at one side. Then he said: "Lord, how should mindfulness of breathing be maintained in being and well developed in order that it may bring great fruit and many blessings?"

M. 62

NARRATOR TWO. The Buddha then first described to him in detail the four primary elements of material form—earth or hardness, water or cohesion, fire or temperature and ripening, and air or distension and motion—and also space, and how each should be regarded in the same way as material form. Then he said:

FIRST VOICE. "Try to be like the earth, Rāhula; for by so doing, when agreeable or disagreeable contacts arise, they will not invade your heart and stay there, just as when people drop clean things or filthy things or excrement or urine or spittle or pus or blood on the earth, for that the earth is not ashamed, humiliated or disgusted. Try to be like water, Rāhula; when people wash away these things with water, for that the water is not ashamed, humiliated or disgusted. Try to be like fire, Rāhula; when fire burns these things, for that the fire is not ashamed, humiliated or disgusted. Try to be like air, Rāhula; for by so doing, when agreeable or disagreeable contacts arise, they will not invade your heart and stay there, just as when air blows away clean things or filthy things or excrement or urine or spittle or pus or blood, for that the air is not ashamed, humiliated or disgusted. Try to be like space, Rāhula; for by so doing, when agreeable or disagreeable contacts arise, they will not invade your heart and stay there; for space has no standing place of its own.

"Practise loving-kindness to get rid of ill will. Practise compassion to get rid of cruelty. Practise sympathy to get rid of apathy. Practise equanimity to get rid of resentment. Practise contemplation of loathsomeness in the body to get rid of lust. Practise contemplation of impermanence to get rid of the conceit 'I am.' Practise mindfulness of breathing; for when that is maintained in being and well developed, it brings great fruit and many blessings."

M. 62

NARRATOR TWO. The Buddha then described sixteen modes in which mindfulness of breathing can be practised.

NARRATOR ONE. The novice Rāhula's attainment of Arahantship is told later.

NARRATOR TWO. The next rains, the twelfth, found the Buddha at Verañjā.

SECOND VOICE. The occasion was this. The Buddha, the Blessed One, was living at Verañjā at the root of Naḷeru's nimba tree with a large community of bhikkhus, with five hundred bhikkhus, when a brahman of Verañjā heard about the Blessed One and decided to go and see him. He went to him and exchanged greetings with him, and when this courteous formal talk was finished, he sat down at one side. He said: "Master Gotama, I have heard that the monk Gotama pays no homage to brahmans who are old, aged, burdened with years, advanced in life and come to the last stage, that he does not rise up for them or invite them to sit down. And I find that this is actually so, too; for Master Gotama does not in fact do these things. That is not good, Master Gotama."

"Brahman, in the world with its deities, its Māras and its divinities, in this generation with its monks and brahmans, with its princes and men, I see none whom I should pay homage to or rise up for or invite to sit down; for his head would burst open whom a Perfect One paid homage to or rose up for or invited to sit down."

"Master Gotama is lacking in taste."

"There is one way in which it could rightly be said that the monk Gotama is lacking in taste:[2] taste for visible forms, taste for sounds, odours, flavours and tangibles—these are rejected in a Perfect One, cut off at the roots, made like palm stumps, done away with and no more subject to future arising. But surely, brahman, you did not mean that?"

"Master Gotama has no sense of values."

"There is a way in which it could rightly be said that the monk Gotama has no sense of values: sense of value of visible forms, sense of value of sounds, odours, flavours and tangibles—these are rejected in a Perfect One … and no more subject to future arising. But surely, brahman, you did not mean that?"

"Master Gotama teaches that there is no ought-to-do."

"There is a way in which it could rightly be said that the monk Gotama teaches that there is no ought-to-do: for I do teach that no one ought to do wrong bodily or verbal or mental acts and the many sorts of evil unwholesome things. But surely, brahman, you did not mean that?"

"Master Gotama teaches nihilism."

"There is a way in which it could rightly be said that the monk Gotama teaches nihilism: for I do teach annihilation of lust and hate and delusion and the many sorts of evil unwholesome things. But surely, brahman, you did not mean that?"

"Master Gotama is fastidious."

"There is a way in which it could rightly be said that the monk Gotama is fastidious: for I am fastidious about wrong bodily, verbal and mental acts and the many sorts of evil unwholesome things. But surely, brahman, you did not mean that?"

"The monk Gotama is one to lead away."

"There is a way in which it could rightly be said that the monk Gotama is one to lead away: for I teach the Dhamma for the leading away of lust and hate and delusion and the many sorts of evil unwholesome things. But surely, brahman, you did not mean that?"

"The monk Gotama is a mortifier."

"There is a way in which it could rightly be said that the monk Gotama is a mortifier: for I say that wrong bodily, verbal and mental acts are evil unwholesome things to be mortified; and him I call a mortifier in whom evil unwholesome things to be mortified are rejected, cut off at the roots, made like palm stumps, done away with, and no more subject to future arising; and in a Perfect One these things are rejected … and no more subject to future arising. But surely, brahman, you did not mean that?"

"The monk Gotama has missed his rebirth."

"There is a way in which it could rightly be said that the monk Gotama has missed his rebirth; when a person's re-entry into a womb and his future coming to birth are rejected … and no more subject to future arising, then I say of him that he has missed his rebirth; and in the Perfect One re-entry into a womb and future rebirth are rejected … and no more subject to future arising. But surely, brahman, you did not mean that?

"Now suppose a hen had eight or ten or twelve eggs which she brooded over, incubated and hatched with care: should the first of those chickens to pierce the shell with the points of its claws and beak, the first to come out safely, be called the eldest or the youngest?"

"It should be called the eldest, Master Gotama, for it is the eldest of them."

"So too, brahman, in this generation given over to ignorance, enclosed in an egg of ignorance, sealed in by ignorance, I alone in the world have discovered the supreme full enlightenment by piercing the shell of ignorance, of nescience. So it is I who am the eldest and the foremost in the world."

Vin. Sv. Pārā. 1; A. 8:11

NARRATOR TWO. The Buddha then described how, by attaining the four meditations and the three true knowledges, he had come to know directly that birth was ended for him. The brahman was convinced, and he took the Three Refuges. He then offered lodging and support to the Buddha for the coming rains, which was accepted.

SECOND VOICE. Now almsfood was hard to get in Verañjā then. There was a famine and food tickets had been issued. It was not easy to survive even by strenuous gleaning. However, some horse dealers from the North Country with five hundred horses had taken up residence for the rains at Verañjā at that time. They let it be known that for bhikkhus there would be a measure of bran each, which could be obtained at the horse pens.

One morning bhikkhus dressed, and taking their bowls and outer robes, they wandered for alms in Verañjā. When they got no almsfood, they went to the horse pens, and each brought a measure of bran back to the monastery, where they pounded it up in a mortar and ate it. The venerable Ānanda ground up a measure of bran on a stone and then took it to the Blessed One. The Blessed One ate it.

He had heard the sound of a mortar. Now Perfect Ones know and ask, and also they know and do not ask. They ask when they judge it to be opportune, and they refrain from asking when they judge it to be inopportune. Perfect Ones ask in order to promote good, not for any other reason. The bridge to the bad is demolished in the case of Perfect Ones. Enlightened Ones, Perfect Ones, question bhikkhus for two reasons: in order to teach the Dhamma or in order to make a training precept known to disciples. On that occasion the Blessed One asked the venerable Ānanda: "Ānanda, what is that sound of a mortar?" The venerable Ānanda explained.

"Good, good, Ānanda. You have conquered, like good men. But there will be later generations who will look down upon even cooked meals of fine rice with meat."

The venerable Mahā-Moggallāna went to the Blessed One. He said: "Lord, almsfood is hard to get in Verañjā now. There is a famine and food tickets have been issued. It is not easy to survive even by strenuous gleaning. Lord, this earth's under-surface is rich and as sweet as pure honey. It would be good if I turned the earth over. Then the bhikkhus will be able to eat the humus that water plants live on."

"But, Moggallāna, what will become of the creatures that depend on the earth's surface?"

"Lord, I shall make one hand as broad as the great earth and get the creatures that depend on the earth's surface to go on to it. I shall turn the earth over with the other hand."

"Enough, Moggallāna, do not suggest turning the earth over. Creatures will be confounded."

"Lord, it would be good if the Sangha of bhikkhus went to the Northern Continent of Uttarakuru for alms."

"Enough, Moggallāna, do not suggest that the Sangha of bhikkhus should go to Uttarakuru for alms."

While the venerable Sāriputta was alone in retreat this thought arose in him: "Which Buddhas' holy life did not last long? Which Buddhas' holy life lasted long?"

When it was evening, he rose from retreat, and he went to the Blessed One and put this question to him.

"In the time of the Blessed Ones Vipassī, Sikhī and Vessabhū the holy life did not last long, Sāriputta. In the time of the Blessed Ones Kakusandha, Koṇāgamana and Kassapa the holy life lasted long."

"Lord, what was the reason why the holy life did not last long in the time of the Blessed Ones Vipassī, Sikhī and Vessabhū?"

"Those Blessed Ones were not forward in teaching the Dhamma to their disciples in detail, and they pronounced few Threads of Argument (Suttas),[3] Songs, Expositions, Stanzas, Exclamations, Sayings, Birth Stories, Marvels, and Questions. No disciples' training rule was made known. The Pātimokkha, the Monastic Code, was not laid down. Just as, when various flowers are put on a table without being held together by threads, they easily get scattered, blown away and lost—why is that? because they are not held together with threads—so too, when those Buddhas, those Blessed Ones, and the disciples enlightened by them personally, disappeared, then the disciples most recently gone forth, variously named, of various races and various clans, soon let the holy life lapse. Those Blessed Ones habitually read their disciples' minds and advised them accordingly. Once in a certain awe-inspiring jungle thicket the Blessed One Vessabhū, accomplished and fully enlightened, read the minds of the Sangha of bhikkhus a thousand strong, and this was how he advised and instructed them: 'Think thus; do not think thus. Give attention thus; do not give attention thus. Abandon this; enter upon and abide in this.' Then by following his instructions their hearts were freed from taints through not clinging. And that jungle thicket was one so awe inspiring that normally it would make a man's hair stand on end if he were not free from lust. That was the reason why those Blessed Ones' holy life did not last long."

"But, Lord, what was the reason why the holy life lasted long in the time of the Blessed Ones Kakusandha, Koṇāgamana and Kassapa?"

"Those Blessed Ones were forward in teaching the Dhamma to their disciples in detail, and they pronounced many Threads of Argument, Songs, Expositions, Stanzas, Exclamations, Sayings, Birth Stories, Marvels and Questions. The disciples' training rule was made known. The Pātimokkha, the Monastic Code, was laid down. Just as, when various flowers are put on a table well tied together with threads, they do not get scattered, blown away and lost—why is that? because they are well tied together with threads—so too, when those Buddhas, those Blessed Ones, and the disciples enlightened by them personally, disappeared, then the disciples who had gone forth most recently, variously named, of various races, of various clans, maintained the holy life for a long time. That was the reason why those Blessed Ones' holy life lasted long."

Then the venerable Sāriputta rose from his seat, and arranging his robe on one shoulder, he raised his hands palms together towards the Blessed One and said: "This is the time, Blessed One, this is the time Sublime One, for the Blessed One to make known the training rule, to lay down the Pātimokkha, so that the holy life may last long."

"Wait, Sāriputta, wait! The Perfect One will know the time for that. The Master does not make known the disciples' training rule or lay down the Pātimokkha till certain taint-producing things manifest themselves here in the Sangha. But as soon as they do, then the Teacher will see to both of these, doing so for the purpose of warding off those taint-producing things. Some taint-producing things do not manifest themselves until the Sangha has become great by long establishment and grown large: it is then that they manifest themselves and then that the Teacher makes known the disciples' training rule and lays down the Pātimokkha for the purpose of warding off those taint-producing things. Some taint-producing things do not manifest themselves till the Sangha has become great by completeness ... become great by excessive gain ... become great by learning .... But as yet the Sangha is free from infection, free from dangers, it is stainless, pure and consists of heartwood. For of these five hundred bhikkhus the most backward is a stream-enterer no more subject to perdition, certain of rightness, and destined to enlightenment."

Then the Blessed One turned to the venerable Ānanda: "Ānanda, it is a custom of Perfect Ones not to set out wandering in the country without taking leave of those who invited them for the rains. Let us go and take leave of the Verañjā brahman."

"Even so, Lord," the venerable Ānanda replied.

Then the Blessed One dressed, and taking his bowl and outer robe, he went with the venerable Ānanda as his attendant monk to the Verañjā brahman's house, where he sat down on a seat made ready.

The brahman came and paid homage to him. The Blessed One said: "We have spent the rains invited by you, brahman, and we take our leave. We wish to set out wandering in the country."

"It is true, Master Gotama. You were invited by me to spend the rains. What ought to have been given was not given; though that was not because we had not got it, or because we were unwilling to give. But how could we manage it? For the lay life is a busy one with much to be done. Let Master Gotama together with the Sangha of bhikkhus accept tomorrow's meal from me."

The Blessed One consented in silence. Then, after he had instructed the brahman with talk on the Dhamma, he got up and went away.

Next day when the meal was finished, the Verañjā brahman clothed the Blessed One with a robe, and he clothed each bhikkhu with two pieces of cloth. And when the Blessed One had instructed him with a talk on the Dhamma, he departed.

Vin. Sv. Pārā. 1

NARRATOR TWO. While the thirteenth rains was being spent at Cālikā the following episode took place.

FIRST VOICE. Thus I heard. At one time the Blessed One was living at Cālikā on the Cālikā Rock, and the venerable Meghiya was his attendant at that time. He went to the Blessed One and said: "Lord, I want to go into Jantugāma for alms."

"It is time to do as you think fit, Meghiya."

It was then morning and so the venerable Meghiya dressed, and taking his bowl and outer robe, he went into Jantugāma for alms. When he had wandered for alms and was returning from his alms round after his meal, he came to the banks of the Kimikālā River. While he was walking and wandering along the river bank for exercise he saw a charming and inviting mango grove. He thought: "This charming and inviting mango grove will serve for the struggle of a clansman who seeks the struggle. If the Blessed One allows it, I shall come to this mango grove for the struggle."

Then he went to the Blessed One and told him about it. The Blessed One said: "Wait, Meghiya; we are still alone. Wait till some other bhikkhu comes."

A second time the venerable Meghiya said: "The Blessed One has nothing more left to do, Lord. He has no need to confirm what he has already done. But we still have something left to do. We need to confirm what we have already done. If the Blessed One allows it, Lord, I should like to go to that mango grove for the struggle."

A second time the Blessed One said: "Wait, Meghiya; we are still alone. Wait till some other bhikkhu comes."

A third time the venerable Meghiya repeated his request.

"Since you say 'struggle,' Meghiya, what can we say to you? It is time for you now to do as you think fit."

Then the venerable Meghiya got up from his seat, and after paying homage to the Blessed One, keeping him on his right, he went off to the mango grove, where he sat down at the root of a tree for his daytime abiding. Now for almost all of the time that he remained in the mango grove, three kinds of evil unwholesome thoughts occupied his mind, that is to say, thoughts of sensual desires, thoughts of ill will and thoughts of cruelty. Then it occurred to him: "It is wonderful, it is marvellous! Here am I who have gone forth out of faith from the house life into homelessness and yet I am harassed by these three kinds of evil, unwholesome thoughts."

When it was evening, he rose from retreat and went to the Blessed One. He told him what had happened.

"Meghiya, while the heart's deliverance is still unripe, five things lead to its ripening. What five? Firstly, a bhikkhu has good friends and companions. Secondly, a bhikkhu is perfect in virtue, restrained with the Pātimokkha restraint, perfect in conduct and resort, and seeing fear in the slightest fault, he trains by giving effect to the precepts of training. Thirdly, he is one who finds at will with no trouble or reserve such talk as is concerned with effacement, as favours the heart's release, as leads to complete dispassion, fading, ceasing, pacification, direct knowledge, enlightenment, Nibbāna, that is to say, talk on wanting little, on contentment, seclusion, dissociation from society, energeticness, virtue, concentration, understanding, deliverance, knowledge and vision of deliverance. Fourthly, a bhikkhu is energetic in abandoning unwholesome things and in giving effect to wholesome things; he is steadfast, persistent and untiring with respect to wholesome things. Fifthly, a bhikkhu has understanding; he has the noble ones' penetrative understanding of rise and disappearance that leads to the complete ending of suffering.

"Now when a bhikkhu has good friends and good companions, it can be expected of him that he will be virtuous ... that he will be one who finds at will ... such talk as is concerned with effacement ... that he is energetic in abandoning unwholesome things and in giving effect to wholesome things ... that he has the noble ones' penetrative understanding of rise and disappearance that leads to the complete ending of suffering.

"But in order to become established in those five things a bhikkhu should, in addition, maintain in being these four things. Loathsomeness (as the repulsive aspect of the body)[4] should be maintained in being for the purpose of abandoning lust; loving-kindness for the purpose of abandoning ill will; mindfulness of breathing for the purpose of cutting off discursive thoughts; perception of impermanence for the purpose of eliminating the conceit 'I am.' For when a person perceives impermanence, perception of not-self becomes established in him; and when a person perceives not-self, he arrives at the elimination of the conceit 'I am,' and that is Nibbāna here and now."

Knowing the meaning of this, the Blessed One then uttered this exclamation:

> Mean thoughts, trivial thoughts
> Come tempting the mind and fly away;
> Not understanding these thoughts in the mind,
> The heart strays chasing them back and forth.

A man understanding these thoughts in his mind
Expels them with vigorous mindfulness.
And one enlightened has done with them all;
For no more temptation then stirs his mind.

Ud. 4:1; A. 9:3.

NARRATOR TWO. The Buddha's son was now twenty years old. He was accordingly given the full admission (not conferrable before the age of twenty). And the tradition has it that it was in that same year that the Buddha delivered the discourse which was the cause of his attaining Arahantship.

FIRST VOICE. Thus I heard. At one time the Blessed One was living at Sāvatthī in Jeta's Grove, Anāthapiṇḍika's Park. Now while he was alone in meditation this thought arose in his mind: "The things that ripen in deliverance are ripe in Rāhula's mind. Suppose I lead him on to the final exhaustion of taints?"

When it was morning the Blessed One dressed, and taking his bowl and outer robe, he went into Sāvatthī for alms. When he had wandered in Sāvatthī and had returned from his alms round after the meal, he said to the venerable Rāhula: "Rāhula, take a seat with you; let us go to the Blind Men's Grove to pass the day."

"Even so, Lord," the venerable Rāhula replied, and taking a seat, he followed behind the Blessed One. But also many thousands of deities followed behind the Blessed One on that occasion, thinking: "Today the Blessed One is going to lead the venerable Rāhula on to the final exhaustion of taints."

Then the Blessed One entered the Blind Men's Grove, and he sat down at the root of a tree on a seat made ready. And the venerable Rāhula paid homage to the Blessed One and sat down at one side. When he had done so, the Blessed One said:

(1a) "How do you conceive this, Rāhula, is the eye permanent or impermanent?"

"Impermanent, Lord."

"But is what is impermanent unpleasant or pleasant?"

"Unpleasant, Lord."

"But is it fitting to regard what is impermanent, unpleasant and subject to change as: 'This is mine, this is what I am, this is my self?' "

"No, Lord."

(lb) "How do you conceive this, Rāhula, are visible forms permanent or impermanent?" ...

(lc) "How do you conceive this, Rāhula, is eye-consciousness permanent or impermanent?" ...

(ld) "How do you conceive this, Rāhula, is eye-contact permanent or impermanent?" ...

(le) "How do you conceive this, Rāhula, are any feelings, any perceptions, any formations, any consciousness, that arise with eye-contact as their condition permanent or impermanent?" ...

NARRATOR TWO. The same five clauses (a) to (e) were repeated for (2) ear and sounds, (3) nose and odours, (4) tongue and flavours, (5) body and tangibles, (6) mind and mental objects.

FIRST VOICE. "Seeing thus, Rāhula, the wise noble disciple becomes dispassionate towards the eye, visible forms, eye-consciousness, and eye-contact, and he becomes dispassionate towards any feelings, perceptions, formations, and consciousness that arise with eye-contact as their condition.

"He becomes dispassionate towards the ear, sounds ... towards the nose, odours ... towards the tongue, flavours ... towards the body, tangibles ... towards the mind, mental objects ....

"Being dispassionate, his lust fades away; with the fading away of lust he is liberated; when his heart is liberated, there comes the knowledge: 'It is liberated.' He understands: 'Birth is exhausted, the holy life has been lived out, what has to be done is done, there is no more of this to come.' "

That is what the Blessed One said. The venerable Rāhula rejoiced at his words. And when this discourse was ended, the venerable Rāhula's heart was liberated from taints through not clinging. And in those several thousand deities the spotless, immaculate vision of the Dhamma arose: All that is subject to arising is subject to cessation.

M. 147

NARRATOR TWO. The six following rainy seasons—that is to say the fourteenth to the nineteenth—were spent in different places. The twentieth was spent at Sāvatthī in Jeta's Grove. According to the tradition of the Commentaries, the Buddha now decided to spend each rains regularly at Sāvatthī, and he appointed the Elder Ānanda as his permanent attendant. Two outstanding events related in the Piṭakas are ascribed by tradition to this year. They are the conversion of the robber Angulimāla and an attempt made by some of the Buddha's opponents to discredit him.

FIRST VOICE. Thus I heard. Once when the Blessed One was living at Sāvatthī a bandit had appeared in the realm of King Pasenadi of Kosala. He was called Angulimāla, that is to say, "Finger-necklace," and he was murderous, bloody-handed, given to blows and violence, and merciless to all living beings. Villages, towns and districts were laid waste by him. He went on murdering people, and he wore their fingers as a necklace.

One morning the Blessed One took his bowl and outer robe, and he went into Sāvatthī for alms. When he had wandered for alms in Sāvatthī, and had returned from his alms round after the meal, he set his resting place in order, and then, carrying his bowl and outer robe, he took the road to where Angulimāla then was.

Cowherds, shepherds, farmers and travellers[5] saw the Blessed One and they said: "Do not take that road, monk. On that road there is the bandit Angulimāla. Men have come by that road in bands of ten, twenty, thirty and even forty from time to time, but they have all fallen into the hands of Angulimāla."

When this was said, the Blessed One went on in silence. A second time the same thing happened, and the Blessed One went on in silence. A third time the same thing happened, and the Blessed One went on in silence.

Seeing him coming in the distance, the robber Angulimāla thought: "It is wonderful, it is marvellous indeed! Men have come along this road in bands of even forty from time to time. And now this monk comes alone and unaccompanied. One would think he had been fated to come. Why should I not take this monk's life?"

Seizing his sword and shield and buckling on his bow and quiver, he went in pursuit of the Blessed One. Then the Blessed One performed a feat of supernormal power such that Angulimāla, going as fast as he could, was unable to catch up with the Blessed One who was walking at his normal pace. Then Angulimāla thought: "It is wonderful, it is marvellous! I used to catch up with a galloping elephant and seize it, or a galloping horse or a galloping chariot or a galloping deer. But although I am going as fast as I can, I am unable to catch up with this monk who is walking at his normal pace."

He paused and called out: "Stop, monk! Stop, monk!"

"I have stopped, Angulimāla; do you stop also."

The robber thought: "These monks, sons of the Sakyans, speak truth and assert truth; but though this monk is walking, yet he says: 'I have stopped, Angulimāla; do you stop also.' Suppose I question this monk?" Then he addressed the Blessed One in stanzas:

> "While you are walking, monk, you tell me you
> have stopped;
> But now when I have stopped, you say I have not stopped.
> I ask of you, O monk, what is the meaning of it?
> How is it you have stopped and I have not?"
>
> "Angulimāla, I have stopped for ever,
> Forswearing violence to every living being,
> But you have no restraint towards anything.
> So that is why I have stopped and you have not."
>
> "Oh, at long last a sage I can revere,
> This monk has now appeared in this great forest.
> Surely I will for long renounce all evil,
> Hearing your stanza setting forth the Dhamma."
>
> So saying, the robber took his sword and weapons
> And flung them in a gaping chasm's pit.
> The robber worshipped the Sublime One's feet
> And then and there asked for the going forth.
>
> The Enlightened One, the Sage of great compassion,
> The teacher of the world with its gods,
> Addressed him with these words: "Come, bhikkhu,"
> And that was how he came to be a bhikkhu.

The Blessed One then set out to wander by stages to Sāvatthī with Angulimāla as his attendant monk. At length they arrived at Sāvatthī and the Blessed One stayed in Jeta's Grove. Now at that time great crowds of people were gathered at the gate of King Pasenadi's palace, very clamorous and noisy, demanding that the robber should be put down. At midday the king set out for the park accompanied by five hundred horsemen. He went as far as the road was passable for carriages and then dismounted and approached the Blessed One on foot. After he had paid homage he sat down at one side. The Blessed One asked: "What is wrong, great king? Is Seniya Bimbisāra, King of Magadha, attacking you? Or is it the Licchavis of Vesālī, or some other hostile rulers?"

"It is not that, Lord. A bandit has appeared in my realm. He goes on murdering people, and he wears their fingers as a necklace. I shall never succeed in putting him down, Lord."

"But, great king, if you saw that Angulimāla had shaved off his hair and beard, put on the yellow robe and gone forth from the house life into homelessness, and that he was abstaining from killing and stealing and was eating in only one half of the day, living the holy life, virtuous, with goodness for his ideal, what would you do to him?"

"Lord, we should pay homage; or we should rise up or we should invite him to sit down or we should ask him to accept robes, almsfood, lodging and medicine, or we should arrange for his protection, shelter and defence. But, Lord, he is a miscreant with evil for his ideal; how could he have such virtue and restraint?"

Just then, however, the venerable Angulimāla was sitting not far off. The Blessed One extended his right arm, and he said: "Great king, there is Angulimāla.'

The king was shocked and alarmed and his hair stood on end. The Blessed One saw this, and he said: "Do not be afraid, great king, do not be afraid. There is nothing to fear."

Then the king's alarm and fear and horror subsided. He went up to the venerable Angulimāla and said: "Lord, Angulimāla was a noble lord, was he not?"

"Yes, great king."

"What was the family of the noble lord's father? What was his mother's family?"

"My father, great king, was a Gagga. My mother was a Mantāṇī."

"Let the noble lord Gagga Mantānīputta consent to my seeing to his robes, almsfood, lodging and medicine."

At that time, however, the venerable Angulimāla was a forest dweller, an eater only of almsfood got by begging, a wearer of refuse rags, and he was restricting himself to three robes. He replied: "There is no need, great king, my triple robe is complete."

King Pasenadi returned to the Blessed One, and after paying homage he sat down at one side. He said: "It is wonderful, Lord, it is marvellous how the Blessed One subdues the unsubdued, quiets the unquieted, brings about extinguishment in the unextinguished. One whom we could not subdue with punishment and weapons the Blessed One has subdued without punishment or weapons. And now, Lord, we depart; we are busy and have much to do."

"It is time now, great king, to do as you think fit."

So King Pasenadi got up from his seat, and after paying homage, he departed, keeping the Blessed One on his right.

One morning the venerable Angulimāla took his bowl and outer robe, and he went into Sāvatthī for alms. As he was wandering for alms from house to house in Sāvatthī he saw a certain woman in travail with a deformed child. He thought: "What defilement creatures suffer! Oh, what defilement creatures suffer!" Afterwards he went to the Blessed One and told him about it.

"Then, Angulimāla, go into Sāvatthī and say to that woman: 'Sister, since I was born I have never purposely taken a living being's life. By that truth may you and the child have peace.' "

"Lord, should I not be lying in full awareness? For I have purposely taken the lives of many living beings."

"Then, Angulimāla, go into Sāvatthī and say to that woman: 'Sister, since I was born with the noble birth I have never purposely taken a living being's life. By that truth may you and the child have peace.' "

"Even so, Lord," he replied, and he went into Sāvatthī and said to the woman: "Sister, since I was born with the noble birth I have never purposely taken a living being's life. By that truth may you and the child have peace." And the woman and the child had peace.

Then, dwelling alone, withdrawn, diligent, ardent and self-controlled, the venerable Angulimāla, by realization himself with direct knowledge, here and now entered upon and dwelt in that supreme goal of the holy life for the sake of which clansmen rightly go forth from the house life into homelessness. He knew directly: "Birth is exhausted, the holy life has been lived out, what was to be done is done, there is no more of this to come." And the venerable Angulimāla became one of the Arahants.

Then one morning the venerable Angulimāla dressed, and taking his bowl and outer robe, he went into Sāvatthī for alms. Now on that occasion a clod thrown by someone fell on his body, and a stick thrown by someone fell on his body, and a potsherd thrown by someone fell on his body. Then, with his head broken with blood flowing, with his bowl in pieces and his outer robe of patches torn, he went to the Blessed One. Seeing him coming, the Blessed One said: "Bear it, brahman, bear it. You have experienced here and now in this life the ripening of deeds whose ripening you might have experienced in hell over many a year, many a century, many a millennium."

When the venerable Angulimāla was alone in retreat savouring the bliss of deliverance, he uttered this exclamation:

Who once did live in recklessness
And then is reckless nevermore
Shall light the world like the full moon
When clouds unmask it.
Who checks with wholesome deeds
The evil deeds already done
Shall light the world like the full moon
When clouds unmask it.
Who as a youthful bhikkhu shows
Devotion to the Buddha's Dhamma
Shall light the world like the full moon
When clouds unmask it.

Oh, let my enemies hear discourse on the Dhamma,
Oh, let my enemies come to the Buddha's teaching,
Oh, let my enemies wait on such persons
As serve the Dhamma because they are at peace.
Oh, let my enemies give ear from time to time
And hear the Dhamma from those who preach forbearance,
From those who speak as well in praise of kindness,
And suit the while their actions to their words.
For surely then they would not wish to harm me;
They would not try to injure other beings.
So who would guard all beings faint or bold,
Let him attain the all-surpassing peace.

Conduit makers guide the water,
Fletchers straighten out the arrow,
Joiners straighten out the timber,
Wise people seek to tame themselves.
There are some that tame with beatings,
Some with goads and some with lashes:
One who has neither rod nor weapon—
I am tamed by such as he.

Innocent is the name I bear
Who was obnoxious in the past.
The name I bear today is true:
I hurt not anyone at all.
And though I once lived as a robber
With the name of 'Finger-necklace,'
And whom the great flood swept along,
I went for refuge to the Buddha.
And though I once was bloody-handed
With the name of "Finger-necklace,"
See now the refuge I have found:
What leads to rebirth is no more.
Whilst I did many deeds that promised
Birth in unhappy destinations,
Yet their result has reached me now;
And so I eat no more in debt.

Oh, they are fools and have no wits
Who give themselves to recklessness;
But those of sense guard diligence
And treat it as their greatest good.
Oh, give not way to recklessness
Nor harbour love of sense desires,
But diligently meditate
So as to reach the highest bliss.

So welcome to that choice of mine
And let it stand, it was not ill-made;
The best I know is this alone
Of all teachings the world has known.
So welcome to that choice of mine
And let it stand, it was not ill-made;
The triple science has been gained
And what the Seer ordained is done.

M. 86

NARRATOR TWO. Now here is the story of the attempt to discredit the Buddha.

FIRST VOICE. Thus I heard. At one time when the Blessed One was living at Sāvatthī he was honoured, respected, revered, venerated and lauded. He obtained robes, almsfood, lodging and medicine and so did the Sangha of bhikkhus. But the wanderers of other sects fared otherwise. They could not stomach the honour that was accruing to the Blessed One and the Sangha of bhikkhus, so they went to the wanderer nun Sundarī and said: "Sister, try and help your cousins."

"What must I do, Lords? What can I do? My very life is pledged for my cousins' good."

"Then, sister, visit Jeta's Grove regularly."

"Even so, Lords," she replied. And she visited Jeta's Grove regularly.

When the wanderers knew that she had been seen by many people going regularly to Jeta's Grove, they killed her and buried her in a hole dug in the ditch of Jeta's Grove. Then they went to King Pasenadi of Kosala and said: "Great king, the wanderer nun Sundarī cannot be found."

"Where do you suspect she is?"

"In Jeta's Grove, great king."

"Then search Jeta's Grove."

The wanderers made a search of Jeta's Grove, and they disinterred her from the hole in the ditch where she had been buried. They placed her on a bed, and entering Sāvatthī, they went from street to street and from crossroad to crossroad protesting to people: "See, Lords, see the work of these sons of the Sakyans! These sons of the Sakyans are shameless, brazen, wicked liars, and lechers to boot! They who claim to walk in the Dhamma and in equity and purity, to speak truth, to be virtuous and good—they have nothing of the monk, nothing of the brahman; monk and brahman are travestied in them; where are the monk and brahman in them? They are far indeed from the monk or brahman; for how can a man do a man's work on a woman and then kill her?"

When people saw bhikkhus, they abused and cursed and reviled and upbraided them with rude harsh words: "These sons of the Sakyans are shameless, brazen, wicked liars, and lechers to boot!" And they repeated the whole accusation. Bhikkhus, hearing this, reported it to the Blessed One.

"This uproar will not last long, bhikkhus. It will last only seven days. At the end of seven days it will subside. So when people abuse bhikkhus thus, exhort them with this stanza:

The liar goes to hell, like him who did
And afterwards declares 'I did it not.'
They both of them on dying fare alike
In life to come, as men whose acts are vile.

The bhikkhus learned this stanza from the Blessed One. When people abused them, they exhorted them with it. People thought: "These monks, these sons of the Sakyans, did not do it. It was not done by them. They swear to that."

The uproar did not last long. It lasted only seven days. At the end of seven days it subsided. Then a number of bhikkhus went to the Blessed One and said: "It is wonderful, Lord, it is marvellous how well that was foretold by the Blessed One!"

Knowing the meaning of this, the Blessed One then uttered this exclamation:

Unguarded men provoke with words like darts
Let fly against an elephant in battle.
But when hard words are spoken to a bhikkhu,
Let him endure them with unruffled mind.

Ud. 4:8

NARRATOR ONE. We do not know when the following events told next took place; but with them we may close the first twenty years.

FIRST VOICE. Thus I heard. The Blessed One was once living at Cātumā in a myrobalan grove. Now on that occasion five hundred bhikkhus headed by the venerable Sāriputta and the venerable Mahā-Moggallāna had come to Cātumā to see the Blessed One. While the visiting bhikkhus were exchanging greetings with the resident bhikkhus and were preparing beds and putting away bowls and outer robes, they were very clamorous and noisy. Then the Blessed One addressed the venerable Ānanda: "Ānanda, who are these clamorous noisy people? One would think they were fishermen peddling fish."

When the venerable Ānanda told him, he said: "Then, Ānanda, tell those bhikkhus in my name 'The teacher calls the venerable ones.' " And the venerable Ānanda did so. They came to the Blessed One, and after paying homage to him, they sat down at one side. When they had done so, the Blessed One asked them: "Bhikkhus, why are you clamorous and noisy? One would think you were fishermen peddling fish."

"Lord, these are five hundred bhikkhus headed by the venerable Sāriputta and the venerable Mahā-Moggallāna, who have come to see the Blessed One. And it was while they were exchanging greetings with the resident bhikkhus and were preparing beds and putting away bowls and outer robes that they were very clamorous and noisy." "Go, bhikkhus. I dismiss you. You cannot live with me."

"Yes, Lord," they replied, and they rose from their seats, and after paying homage to the Blessed One, keeping him on their right, they went and packed up their beds, and then, taking their bowls and outer robes, they departed.

Now on that occasion the Sakyans of Cātumā had met together in their assembly hall for some business or other. They saw the bhikkhus coming in the distance. They went out to meet them and asked: "Where are you going, Lords?"

"Friends, the Sangha of bhikkhus has been dismissed by the Blessed One."

"Then let the venerable ones be seated a while. Perhaps we shall be able to restore the Blessed One's confidence."

So the Sakyans of Cātumā went to the Blessed One, and after paying homage to him, they sat down at one side. When they had done so, they said: "Lord, let the Blessed One forgive the Sangha of bhikkhus, let the Blessed One welcome and help them now, as he used to do in the past. Lord, there are new bhikkhus here just gone forth, but recently come to this Dhamma and Discipline. If they get no opportunity to see the Blessed One, some change and alteration may take place in their hearts. Lord, just as when young seedlings get no water some change and alteration may take place in them, or just as when a young calf does not see its mother some change and alteration may take place in its heart, so too it may be with them. Lord, let the Blessed One welcome and help the Sangha of bhikkhus as he used to do in the past."

And the Brahmā Sahampati vanished in the Brahma-world to appear before the Blessed One and make the same plea.

Between them they were able to restore the Blessed One's confidence with the figures of the seedling and the young calf.

Then the venerable Mahā-Moggallāna addressed the bhikkhus thus: "Get up, friends, take your bowls and robes. The Blessed

One's confidence has been restored by the Sakyans of Cātumā and the Brahmā Sahampati with the figures of the seedling and the young calf."

When they had returned to the Blessed One's presence, he asked the venerable Sāriputta: "What did you think, Sāriputta, when the Sangha of bhikkhus was dismissed by me?"

"Lord, then I thought: 'The Blessed One will now abide inactive devoted to a pleasant abiding here and now; and we too shall now abide inactive devoted to a pleasant abiding here and now.' "

"Stop, Sāriputta, stop! Such thoughts as those should never occur to you again." Then he addressed the venerable Mahā-Moggallāna: "What did you think, Moggallāna, when the Sangha of bhikkhus was dismissed by me?"

"Lord, then I thought: 'The Blessed One will now abide inactive devoted to a pleasant abiding here and now, while I and the venerable Sāriputta shall continue to lead the Sangha of bhikkhus now.' "

"Good, good, Moggallāna. Either I shall continue to lead the Sangha of bhikkhus or else Sāriputta and Moggallāna will do so."

M. 67

NARRATOR TWO. The Buddha told the bhikkhus of a visit made to the high heavens of the Brahma-world.

FIRST VOICE. "Bhikkhus, on one occasion when I was living at Ukkaṭṭhā in the Subhaga Grove at the root of a royal sāla tree, there had arisen in the Brahmā Baka a pernicious view (of his own permanence and absoluteness). I became aware in mind of the thought in the Brahmā's mind, and ... I appeared in that world. The Brahmā Baka saw me coming, and he said: 'Come, good sir! Welcome, good sir! It is long, good sir, since you made an occasion to come here. Now, good sir, this is permanent, this is everlasting, this is eternal, this is totality, this is not subject to passing away; for this neither is born nor ages nor dies nor passes away nor reappears, and beyond this there is no escape.'

"Then Māra the Evil One entered into a member of the Brahmā's assembly, and he told me: 'Bhikkhu, bhikkhu, do not disbelieve him, do not disbelieve him; for this Brahmā is the Great Brahmā, Transcendent Being untranscended, Sure-sighted Wielder of Mastery, Lord Maker and Creator, Most High Providence, Master and Father of those that are and ever can be. Before your time, bhikkhu, there were monks and brahmans in the world who condemned earth through disgust with earth, who condemned water … fire … air … beings … gods … Pajāpati, Lord of the Race … who condemned Brahmā through disgust with Brahmā; now on the dissolution of the body, when their breath was cut off, they became established in an inferior body. Before your time, bhikkhu, there were monks and brahmans in the world who lauded all these through love of them; now on the dissolution of the body, when their breath was cut off, they became established in a superior body. So, bhikkhu, I tell you this: Be sure, good sir, to do only as Brahmā says. Never overstep Brahmā's word; for if you do that, bhikkhu, then you will be like a man who tries to deflect a beam of light with a stick when it comes upon him, or like a man who loses his hold of the earth with his hands and feet as he slips into a deep abyss. Be sure, good sir, to do only as Brahmā says. Never overstep Brahmā's word. Do you not see the Divine Assembly seated here, bhikkhu?' And Māra the Evil One thus called the Divine Assembly to witness.

"When this was said, I told Māra the Evil One: 'I know you, Evil One; do not fancy 'He does not know me.' You are Māra the Evil One, and Brahmā and the Divine Assembly with all its members have all fallen into your hands, they have all fallen into your power. You, Evil One, think that I have fallen into your power too; but that is not so.'

"When this was said, Brahmā Baka told me: 'Good sir, I say of the permanent that it is permanent, of the everlasting that it is everlasting, of the eternal that it is eternal, of totality that it is totality, of what is not subject to passing away that it is not subject to passing away, of what neither is born nor ages nor dies nor passes away nor reappears, that it neither is born nor ages nor dies nor passes away nor reappears, and of that beyond which there is no escape, that there is no escape beyond it. Before your time, bhikkhu, there were monks and brahmans in the world whose asceticism lasted as long as your whole life. They knew, when there was an escape beyond, that there was an escape beyond, and, when there was no escape beyond, that there was no escape beyond. So, bhikkhu, I tell you this: Beyond this you will find no escape, and in trying to do so you will eventually reap weariness and disappointment. If you will believe in[6] earth … in water … in fire … in air … in beings … in gods … in Pajāpati … If you will believe in Brahmā you will be one to lie near me, to lie within my province, as you will be for me to work my will upon and punish.'

" 'I know that too, Brahmā. But I understand your reach and your sway thus: Brahmā Baka's power, his might, his following, extend thus far and no further.'

" 'Now, good sir, how far do you understand my reach and my sway to extend?'

" 'As far as moon and sun do circulate
Shining and lighting up the four directions,
Over a thousand times as wide a world
Your power can exert its influence.
And there you know the high and low as well,
And those governed by lust and free from lust,
The state of what is thus and otherwise,
And creatures' provenance and destination.

" 'Thus far do I understand your reach and sway to extend. Yet there are three other main bodies of Brahmā gods which you neither know nor see, and which I know and see. There is the body called Ābhassara (of Streaming Radiance) whence you passed away and reappeared here. But with long dwelling here your memory of it has lapsed, and so you no more know or see it, but I know and see it. Standing thus, as I do, not on the same level of direct knowledge as you, it is not less that I know, but more. And likewise with the still higher bodies of the Subhakiṇṇa (of Refulgent Glory) and the Vehapphala (of Great Fruit).

" 'Now, Brahmā, having had direct knowledge of earth as earth, and having had direct knowledge of what is not co-essential with the earthness of earth, I did not claim to be earth,[7] did not claim to be in earth, I did not claim to be apart from earth, I did not claim earth to be mine, I made no affirmation about earth. Having had direct knowledge of water as water … of fire … air … beings … gods …. Pajāpati … Brahmā … the Ābhassara … the Subhakiṇṇa … the Vehapphala … the Transcendent Being (Abhibhū) … Having had direct knowledge of all as all, and having had direct knowledge of what is not co-essential with the allness of all, I did not claim to be all, I did not claim to be in all, I did not claim to be apart from all, I did not claim all to be mine, I made no affirmation about all. Standing thus, too, as I do, it is not less that I know, but more.'

" 'Good sir, if you claim to have access to what is not coessential with the allness of all, may you not be proved vain and empty!'

> " 'The consciousness that makes no showing
> Nor has to do with finiteness,
> Claiming no being apart from all:

that is not co-essential with the earthness of earth, with the waterness of water ... with the allness of all.'

" 'Then, good sir, I will vanish from you.'

" 'Then, Brahmā, vanish from me if you can.'

"Then Brahmā Baka, thinking 'I will vanish from the monk Gotama; I will vanish from the monk Gotama,' was unable to do so. I said: 'Then, Brahmā, I will vanish from you.'

'Then, good sir, vanish from me if you can.'

"I made a determination of supernormal power thus: 'Just to the extent of Brahmā and the Assembly, let them hear the sound of my voice without seeing me,' and after I had vanished, I uttered this stanza:

> " 'I have seen fear in every mode of being
> Including being seeking for non-being;
> There is no mode of being I affirm,
> No relish whatsoever whereto I cling.'

"Then Brahmā and the Assembly and all its members wondered and marvelled at that, and they said: 'It is wonderful, sirs, it is marvellous! This monk Gotama who went forth from a Sakyan clan has such great power and might as we have never before seen in any other monk or brahman! Sirs, though living in a generation that delights in being, loves being, finds gladness in being, he has extirpated being together with its root!'

"Then Māra the Evil One entered into a member of the Assembly, and he said: 'Good sir, if that is what you know, if that is what you have discovered, do not lead your lay disciples to it or those gone forth, do not teach them your Dhamma or create in them a yearning for it. Before your time, bhikkhu, there were monks and brahmans in the world claiming to be accomplished and fully enlightened, and they did that; but on the dissolution of the body when their breath was cut off, they became established in an inferior body. Before your time, bhikkhu, there were also such monks and brahmans in the world, and they did not do that; and on the dissolution of the body, when their breath was cut off, they became established in a superior body. So, bhikkhu, I tell you this: Be sure, good sir, to abide inactive; devote yourself to a pleasant abiding here and now. This is better left undeclared, good sir, and so inform no one else of it at all.'

"When this was said, I replied: 'I know you, Evil One. It is not out of compassion or desire for my welfare that you speak thus. You are thinking that those to whom I teach this Dhamma will go beyond your reach. Those monks and brahmans of yours who claimed to be accomplished and fully enlightened were not really so; but I am, as I claim to be, accomplished and fully enlightened. A Perfect One is such whether he teaches his Dhamma to disciples or not, whether he leads his disciples to it or not. Why is that? Because such taints as defile, as renew being, as bring anxiety, as ripen in suffering, as produce future birth, ageing and death, are in him cut off at the root, made like palm tree stumps, done away with, so that they are no more subject to future arising, just as a palm tree is incapable of further growth when its crown is cut off.' So, since Māra had nothing more to say, and on account of Brahmā's invitation (to me to vanish), this discourse may be termed 'On the Invitation of a Brahmā."

M. 49

The Blessed One was once living at Nālandā in the Pāvārikā Grove. Then the householder's son Kevaḍḍha went to him, and after paying homage to him, he sat down at one side. He said: "Lord, this Nālandā is successful, prosperous, populous, crowded with human beings, and it is confident in the Blessed One. Lord, it would be good if the Blessed One appointed a bhikkhu to work a marvel of supernormal power higher than the human state, so that this Nālandā might become much more confident in the Blessed One."

The Blessed One replied: "Kevaḍḍha , I do not teach the Dhamma to bhikkhus in that way: 'Come, bhikkhus, work a marvel of supernormal power higher than the human state for the white-clothed laity.' "

NARRATOR TWO. The Buddha gave the same reply when the question was put a second time. When it was put again, he replied that he knew from his own experience three kinds of marvels: the marvel of supernormal power consisting in ability to become many and pass through walls, to fly through the air and walk on water, and even to visit the Brahma-world (see Chapter 16); the marvel of divination consisting in ability to read minds; and the marvel of guidance consisting in instructing people, in brief or in detail, what to do for their own good. The first two, if displayed for their own sake in order to impress people, are no different from the magical arts called respectively "Gandhārī" and "Maṇikā," and it could well be said that such a bhikkhu was practising those arts, which was the reason why he, the Buddha, regarded such marvels as a source of shame, humiliation and disgust. The third kind, the marvel of guidance, consisted in the teaching as given by him, which, though it included those very manifestations, had the exhaustion of taints and the ending of suffering for its goal. In order to underline the inadequacy of such attainments as the first two, the Buddha recounted the story of a bhikkhu who possessed these magical powers, and how they served him nothing in his search for an escape from suffering.

FIRST VOICE. "There was once a bhikkhu in this Sangha of bhikkhus who had this thought: 'Where do these four great entities cease without remainder, that is, the earth element, the water element, the fire element, and the air element?' Then he entered upon concentration such that, when his mind was concentrated, the path to the gods was manifest. Then he went to the deities of the Realm of Four Divine Kings and asked them: 'Friends, where do these four great entities cease without remainder?' They replied: 'We do not know that, bhikkhu; but there are these Four Divine Kings themselves who are greater than us and superior; they should know that.' So he went to them."

NARRATOR TWO. They gave him the same answer and sent him to the Tāvatiṃsā Heaven, and so he was passed on up through all the heavens of sensual existence till he was sent beyond that to the Brahma-world, the world of high divinities. He asked the gods of Brahmā's Assembly the same question. They told him:

FIRST VOICE. " 'We do not know that, bhikkhu, but there is Brahmā, the Great Brahmā, the Transcendent Being Untranscended, the Sure-sighted Wielder of Mastery, Lord Maker and Creator, Most High Providence, Master of all those that are and ever can be, who is greater than us and superior. He should know that.'—'Where is that Brahmā now, friends?'—'Bhikkhu, we do not know the where or the how or the whence of the Great Brahmā. Only that Brahmā will be manifest according as signs are seen, as a light appears, as a radiance is manifest; for that is the precursor of Brahmā's manifestation.'

"Then soon afterwards the Great Brahmā became manifest. The bhikkhu approached and asked his question. When that was said, Brahmā replied: 'Bhikkhu, I am Brahmā, the Great Brahmā, the Transcendent Being Untranscended, Sure-sighted Wielder of Mastery, Lord Maker and Creator, Most High Providence, Master of those that are and ever can be.' The bhikkhu asked a second time: 'Friend, I did not ask that. What I asked was: Where do the four great entities cease without remainder?' The Great Brahmā gave the same answer as before. When the question was put a third time, the Great Brahmā took the bhikkhu by the arm and led him aside. He said: 'Bhikkhu, the deities in Brahmā's Assembly here think thus: "There is nothing that Brahmā has not seen, known and realized." That is why I did not reply in their presence. Friend, I do not know where the four great entities cease without remainder. So you have done wrong, you have transgressed, in that you overlooked the Blessed One and sought an answer to your question away from him. Go and ask the Blessed One your question, and as he tells you, so you should remember it.'

"The bhikkhu then vanished from that world, and he came and asked me the same question. I told him: 'Bhikkhu, it happens that seafaring traders set sail with a shore-finding bird, and when their ship is out of sight of land they release the bird. It goes to the east, south, west and north, and up and in between. If it sees land to one side, it goes towards it, but if it sees none, it comes back to the ship. So too, bhikkhu, wherever you sought, even in the Brahma-world you found no answer to your question, and you came back to me. But the question should not be put like that; it should be put like this:

> " 'Tell, then, where do water, earth,
> Fire and air no footing find?
> Where likewise the long and short,
> Small and big and fair and foul?
> Where is it that name-and-form
> Do without remainder cease?'

And the answer thereto is this:

> " 'The consciousness that makes no showing
> Nor has to do with finiteness,
> Claiming no being apart from all:
> There it is that water, earth,
> Fire and air no footing find,
> And likewise the long and short,
> Small and big and fair and foul;
> There it is that name-and-form
> Do without remainder cease.' "

D.11

10
THE MIDDLE PERIOD

NARRATOR ONE. After the twentieth year following the Enlightenment—the Buddha was now fifty-five years old—all traditions abandon the attempt to trace a chronological order of events until the last year. The internal evidence of the Tipiṭaka itself took us, chronologically, only as far as the appearance of the two chief disciples in the second year; the tradition incorporated in the commentaries of Ācariya Buddhaghosa traced some very general outlines for the first twenty years, enabling us to place a good deal more Piṭaka material; the much later tradition of the *Mālāḷan-kāravatthu* allotted certain events, some non-canonical and so not included here, to each of those years. Each later tradition thus supplements the earlier. The canonical evidence is historically reliable. While there is no conflicting outside evidence, that in the Commentaries can be accepted, too. But the later tradition is probably no more than conjecture; however, this seems no reason for not following its placing of otherwise undatable canonical incidents. And most of the material in the Vinaya and Sutta Piṭakas is undatable, though sometimes a certain succession of events can be worked out. Here, then, follow a number of episodes and discourses, many of which may well have happened at any time.

NARRATOR TWO. First one event should be mentioned, which the later tradition places thirty-one years after the Enlightenment. It is the donation of the Eastern Monastery in Sāvatthī by the devoted lay-woman adherent, Visākhā. She was singled out by the Buddha himself as the foremost among his women adherents. Since she was instrumental in converting her father-in-law, Migāra, to the teaching, she became known as "Migāra's Mother" in the Dispensation.

NARRATOR ONE. Here is an episode characteristic of her.

SECOND VOICE. The occasion was this. The Blessed One had stayed as long as he chose at Benares, and he set out to wander by stages to Sāvatthī. When he eventually arrived there, he stayed in Jeta's Grove, Anāthapiṇḍika's Park. Then Visākhā, Migāra's Mother, went to the Blessed One, and after paying homage to him, she sat down at one side. After the Blessed One had instructed her with talk on the Dhamma, she said: "Lord, let the Blessed One together with the Sangha of bhikkhus accept tomorrow's meal from me."

The Blessed One accepted in silence. When she saw that the Blessed One had accepted, she rose from her seat, and after paying homage, she left, keeping him on her right.

Now on that occasion towards the end of the night a vast rain cloud was raining over all the continents. Then the Blessed One addressed the bhikkhus: "Bhikkhus, just as it is raining down on Jeta's Grove, so it is raining down on all the four continents. Let it rain on your bodies, bhikkhus; this is the last time that there will be a great rain cloud over all the four continents."

"Even so, Lord," they replied, and they put aside their robes and let it rain on their bodies.

When Visākhā had finished preparing good food of various kinds, she told a maid: "Go to the park and announce that it is time thus:

'It is time, Lord; the meal is ready.' "

"Yes, madam," she replied.

She went to the park, and there she saw the bhikkhus with their robes put aside, letting it rain on their bodies. She thought: "There are no bhikkhus in the park; there are naked ascetics letting it rain on their bodies," and she went back and told Visākhā this.

Then it occurred to Visākhā who was wise, understanding and sagacious: "Surely it will be the lords who have put aside their robes and are letting it rain on their bodies. This silly girl thought that they were not bhikkhus but only naked ascetics letting it rain on their bodies." So she sent the maid back again with the message.

By that time the bhikkhus had cooled their limbs and refreshed their bodies, and they had taken their robes and gone into their dwellings. When the maid saw no bhikkhus, she thought: "There are no bhikkhus; the park is empty," and she went back and told Visākhā this.

Then it occurred to Visākhā who was wise, understanding and sagacious: "Surely the lords have cooled their limbs and refreshed their bodies, and they must have taken their robes and gone into their dwellings. This silly girl thought that there were no bhikkhus in the park and that it was empty." So she sent the maid back again with the message.

Then the Blessed One addressed the bhikkhus thus: "Bhikkhus, take your bowls and outer robes. It is time; the meal is ready."

"Even so, Lord," they replied.

Then, it being morning, the Blessed One dressed, and taking his bowl and outer robe, as quickly as a strong man might extend his flexed arm or flex his extended arm, he vanished from Jeta's Grove and appeared at Visākhā's gate. Then the Blessed One sat down on the seat made ready, and likewise the Sangha of bhikkhus. Visākhā said: "It is wonderful, Lord, it is marvellous how mighty and powerful the Perfect One is; for though there are floods knee deep and waist deep not a single bhikkhu's feet or robes are wet!" and she was happy and elated. Then with her own hands she served the Sangha of bhikkhus headed by the Buddha and satisfied them with good food of various kinds. When the Blessed One had eaten and no longer had the bowl in his hand, she sat down at one side, and she said: "Lord, I ask eight favours of the Blessed One."

"Perfect Ones have left favours behind, Visākhā."

"They are permissible, Lord, and blameless."

"Then tell them, Visākhā."

"Lord, I should like to provide the Sangha with rains cloths for as long as I live. And I should like similarly to provide food for visiting bhikkhus, food for those setting out on a journey, food for the sick, and food for sick-attendants; and I should like similarly to provide medicine, and a constant supply of gruel; and I should like similarly to provide bathing cloths for the Sangha of bhikkhunis."

"But, Visākhā, what benefits do you foresee when you ask the Perfect One for these eight favours?"

"Lord, when I sent a maid to announce the time for the meal, she saw bhikkhus with their robes laid aside letting it rain on their bodies; she thought that there were no bhikkhus but only naked ascetics letting it rain on their bodies, and she told me this. Nakedness, Lord, is improper, it is disgusting and repulsive. This is the benefit I foresee in wanting to provide rains cloths for the Sangha for as long as I live.

"Again, Lord, a visiting bhikkhu who does not know the streets and alms resorts, gets tired wandering for alms. After eating my food for a visitor, he will get to know the streets and alms resorts without getting tired wandering for alms. This is the benefit I foresee in wanting to provide food for visitors for as long as I live.

"Again, Lord, when a bhikkhu is setting out on a journey, he may miss his caravan through having to seek food for himself, or he may arrive late at the place where he wants to stay, and he gets tired on the journey. After eating my food for those setting out on a journey, he will not suffer in that way. This is the benefit I foresee in wanting to provide food for those setting out on a journey for as long as I live.

"Again, Lord, when a sick bhikkhu does not get suitable food, his sickness can get worse and he can die. But when he eats my food for the sick, his sickness may not get worse and he may not die. This is the benefit I foresee in wanting to provide food for the sick in the Sangha for as long as I live.

"Again, Lord, when a sick-nurse bhikkhu has to seek his own food, he may bring the sick bhikkhu his food after midday, and there will be a breach of the rule not to eat after midday. But when he eats my food for sick-nurses, he can bring the sick bhikkhu his food in time, and there will be no breach of the rule. This is the benefit I foresee in wanting to provide food for sick-nurses in the Sangha for as long as I live.

"Again, Lord, when a sick bhikkhu does not get suitable medicine, his sickness can get worse and he can die. But when he uses my medicine for the sick, his sickness may not get worse and he may not die. This is the benefit I foresee in wanting to provide medicine for the sick in the Sangha for as long as I live.

"Again, Lord, gruel was allowed at Andhakavinda by the Blessed One who saw ten advantages in it. Seeing these ten advantages, I want to provide a constant supply of gruel for the Sangha for as long as I live.

"Now, Lord, the bhikkhunis are bathing naked at the same bathing place on the River Aciravatī as the harlots use. The harlots make fun of the bhikkhunis, saying: 'Why practise the holy life so young, ladies? Are not sensual desires to be enjoyed? You can live the holy life when you are old. Then you will have the benefit of both.' When harlots make fun of them thus, the bhikkhunis are put out. Nakedness for women is improper, Lord, it is disgusting and repulsive. This is the benefit I foresee in wanting to provide bathing cloths for the bhikkhunis for as long as I live."

"But, Visākhā, what benefits do you foresee for yourself in asking the Perfect One for the eight favours?"

"As to that, Lord, bhikkhus who have spent the rains in different parts will come to Sāvatthī to see the Blessed One. They will approach the Blessed One and question him thus: 'Lord, the bhikkhu named so-and-so has died; what is his destination? What is his rebirth?' The Blessed One will tell how it is that of one who has reached the fruit of stream-entry, of once-return, of non-return, or of Arahantship. I shall approach them and ask: 'Lords, did that lord ever come to Sāvatthī?' If they answer that he did, I shall conclude that surely a rains cloth will have been used by that lord or visitors' food or food for one going on a journey or food for the sick or food for a sick-nurse or medicine for the sick or the constant gruel supply.

"When I remember it, I shall be glad. When I am glad, I shall be happy. When my mind is happy, my body will be tranquil. When my body is tranquil, I shall feel pleasure. When I feel pleasure, my mind will become concentrated. That will maintain the spiritual faculties in being in me and also the spiritual powers and also the enlightenment factors. This, Lord, is the benefit I foresee for myself in asking the eight favours of the Perfect One."

"Good, good, Visākhā; it is good that you have asked the Perfect One the eight favours foreseeing these benefits. I grant you the eight favours." Then the Blessed One gave his blessing with these stanzas:

> Now when a woman disciple of a Sublime One,
> Glad in virtue, gives both food and drink,
> And, conquering avarice, bestows a gift
> That leads to heaven, quells sorrow, and brings bliss,
> She gains the holy life and by a path
> Alike unblemished and immaculate.
> So loving merit, in happiness and health,
> She long rejoices in the heavenly world.

Vin. Mv. 8:15

FIRST VOICE. Thus I heard. At one time the Blessed One was living at Sāvatthī in the Eastern Park, the palace of Migāra's Mother. Then a dear and beloved granddaughter of Visākhā's had died. In broad day Visākhā went to the Blessed One with her clothes and hair wet. After paying homage to him, she sat down at one side, and the Blessed One said to her: "Now where have you come from, Visākhā, in broad day with your clothes and hair wet?"

"Lord, a dear and beloved grandchild of mine has died. That is why I have come here in broad day with my clothes and hair wet.'

"Visākhā, would you like as many children and grandchildren as there are people in Sāvatthī?"

"Lord, I would like as many children and grandchildren as there are people in Sāvatthī."

"But, Visākhā, how many people die in Sāvatthī in a day?" "Ten people die in a day in Sāvatthī, Lord, or nine or eight or seven or six or five or four or three or two, or one person dies in a day in Sāvatthī. Sāvatthī is never without people dying."

"Then what do you think, Visākhā, would you ever be with your clothes and hair not wet?"

"No, Lord. Enough of so many children and grandchildren for me!"

"Those who have a hundred dear ones have a hundred pains. Those who have ninety dear ones have ninety pains. Those who have eighty ... twenty ... ten ... five ... four ... three ... two dear ones have two pains. Those who have one dear one have one pain. Those who have no dear ones have no pains. They are the sorrowless, the dispassionate, the undespairing, I say.

Sorrow and mourning in the world,
Or suffering of every sort,
Happen because of one beloved,
But happen not when there is none.
Happy are they and sorrowless
That have no loved one in the world.
Who seeks the sorrowless dispassion
Should have no loved one in the world.

Ud. 8:8

NARRATOR ONE. We shall now leave Visākhā.

SECOND VOICE. The occasion was this. The Blessed One was living at Rājagaha on the Vulture Peak Rock, and at that time the wanderers of other sects were in the habit of meeting together on the half moons of the fourteenth and fifteenth and the quarter moon of the eighth and preaching about their Dhamma. People went to hear about the Dhamma from them. They grew fond of the wanderers of other sects and believed in them. So the wanderers gained support.

Now while Seniya Bimbisāra, King of Magadha, was alone in retreat he considered this, and he thought: "Why should the venerable ones not meet together too on these days?"

Then he went to the Blessed One and told him what he had thought, adding: "Lord, it would be good if the venerable ones met together too on these days."

The Blessed One instructed the king with talk on the Dhamma, after which the king departed. Then the Blessed One made this the occasion for a discourse on the Dhamma and he addressed the bhikkhus thus: "Bhikkhus, I allow meetings on the half moons of the fourteenth and fifteenth and the quarter moon of the eighth."

So the bhikkhus met together on those days as allowed by the Blessed One, but they sat in silence. People went to hear the Dhamma. They were annoyed, and they murmured and protested: "How can the monks, the sons of the Sakyans, meet together on these days and sit in silence as dumb as hogs? Ought not the Dhamma to be preached when they meet?"

Bhikkhus heard this. They went to the Blessed One and told him. He made this the occasion for a discourse on the Dhamma, and he addressed the bhikkhus thus: "Bhikkhus, when there is a meeting on the half moons of the fourteenth and fifteenth and the quarter moon of the eighth, I allow preaching of the Dhamma."

Vin. Mv. 2:1-2

NARRATOR ONE. An account is given in the Vinaya Piṭaka of events that led to the constitution of the Pātimokkha (or Code of Rules). The account is very long, and so here is a summary version.

NARRATOR TWO. Sudinna was the son of a rich merchant of Kalanda, a village near Vesālī. He was married but without children. He heard the Buddha preach in Vesālī, and as a result he asked for the going forth; but he was told he must get his parents' consent. There was a protracted struggle with them, and it was only after he had refused to eat that they gave in. Later on, after he had gone into homelessness, there was a famine, and he thought: "Suppose I lived supported by my family? Relatives will provide the gifts for my support and in that way they will earn merit and the bhikkhus will benefit and I shall not go short of almsfood." His relatives at Vesālī brought him plenty of offerings.

One day he went to Kalanda with his bowl, and he came to his father's house without, however, announcing himself. A servant girl recognized him and told his father, who pressed him to come for the next day's meal. When he came the next day, his parents used all their arts to persuade him to return to the lay life. His mother told him: "Sudinna, our family is rich with vast possessions ... for this reason you must beget an heir. Do not let the Licchavis take over our heirless property." He answered: "That I can do, mother." So his mother brought his former wife to him in the Great Wood. He took her into the Wood. Seeing no harm, since no training rule had been made known, he had intercourse with her three times. As a result she conceived. Then the earth deities set up a clamour: "Good sirs, though the Sangha of bhikkhus has hitherto been free from infection and free from dangers, yet infection and danger are being sown in it by Sudinna the Kalandian." And the cry was taken up through all the heavens till it reached the Brahma-world.

The venerable Sudinna's former wife gave birth to a son. Friends called him "Bījaka," and they called his mother "Bījaka's Mother," and they called the venerable Sudinna "Bījaka's Father." Later on Bījaka and his mother both left the home life and went forth into homelessness.

SECOND VOICE. But the venerable Sudinna grew remorseful. Because of his bad conscience he became thin and wretched. When bhikkhus asked him what was wrong, he confessed. They rebuked him, and the matter was brought before the Blessed One. The Blessed One said:

"Misguided man, it is unfitting, unseemly, improper, and unworthy of a monk; it is unrighteous and must not be done. How can you not live out the holy life in complete perfection and purity after going forth into homelessness in a Dhamma and Discipline as well proclaimed as this? Misguided man, have I not taught the Dhamma in various ways for the sake of dispassion, not for the sake of passion? Have I not taught the Dhamma for the sake of unfettering, nor for the sake of fettering? Have I not taught the Dhamma for the sake of relinquishing, not for the sake of clinging? The Dhamma thus taught by me for dispassion, unfettering and relinquishment you would conceive to be for passion, fettering, and clinging. Has the Dhamma not been taught by me in many ways for dispassion, for disintoxication, for curing thirst, for abolishing attachment, for severing the round of being, for exhausting craving, for dispassion, for cessation, for Nibbāna? Have I not described in many ways the abandoning of sensual desires, the full understanding of perceptions of sensual desires, the curing of thirst for sensual desires, the eradication of thoughts of sensual desires, the allaying of the fever of sensual desires?

"Misguided man, it were better for you (as one gone forth) that your member should enter the mouth of a hideous venomous viper or cobra than that it should enter a woman. It were better for you that your member should enter a pit of coals burning, blazing and glowing than that it should enter a woman. Why is that? For the former reason you would risk death or deadly suffering, but you would not, on the dissolution of the body, after death, reappear in a state of privation, in an unhappy destination, in perdition, even in hell. But for the latter reason you would do so. Therefore, misguided man, by this act you would pursue the Dhamma's opposite, you would pursue the low, vulgar ideal that is impure and ends in ablution, that is done in secrecy by couples. You are the first to give effect to more than a few wrong ideas. This neither rouses faith in the faithless nor increases faith in the faithful; rather, it keeps the faithless without faith and harms some of the faithful."

Then, when he had rebuked the venerable Sudinna (who was not expelled since no rule had yet been made), after giving an appropriate talk on the Dhamma, he addressed the bhikkhus thus: "Bhikkhus, because of this I shall constitute a training rule for bhikkhus. I shall do so for ten reasons: for the welfare of the Sangha, for the comfort of the Sangha, for the restraint of the evil-minded, for the support of virtuous bhikkhus, for the restraint of taints in this life, for the prevention of taints in the life to come, for the benefit of unbelievers, for growth in believers, for the establishment of the Good Dhamma, and for ensuring rules for restraint. The (first) training rule should be made known thus: Any bhikkhu who indulges in sexual intercourse is defeated; he is no more in communion."

That is how this training rule was made known by the Blessed One.

Vin. Sv. Pārā. 1

Once while the Blessed One was alone in retreat this thought arose in his mind: "Suppose I allowed the training rules already made known by me to be recited by the bhikkhus as their Pātimokkha. That would be their Uposatha day observance, their holy day observance."

When it was evening, he rose from retreat, and making this the occasion for a talk on the Dhamma, he addressed the bhikkhus and told them of his decision.

Vin. Mv. 2:3

The occasion was this. The Blessed One was living at Sāvatthī in the Palace of Migāra's Mother, the Eastern Park. It was then the Uposatha day, and the Blessed One was sitting surrounded by the Sangha of bhikkhus.

Well on into the night when the first watch was ended, the venerable Ānanda rose from his seat, and arranging his robe on one shoulder, he raised his hands palms together towards the Blessed One and said: "Lord, it is now well on into the night and the first watch is ended. The Sangha of bhikkhus has been sitting long. Let the Blessed One recite the Pātimokkha to the bhikkhus."

When this was said, the Blessed One remained silent.

A second time, well on into the night when the second watch was ended, the venerable Ānanda rose from his seat, and arranging his robe on one shoulder, he raised his hands palms together towards the Blessed One and said: "Lord, it is now well on into the night and the second watch is ended. The Sangha of bhikkhus has been sitting long. Let the Blessed One recite the Pātimokkha to the bhikkhus."

A second time the Blessed One remained silent.

A third time, well on into the night when the third watch was ended with the red dawn coming up and joy on the face of the night, the venerable Ānanda rose from his seat, and arranging his robe on one shoulder, he raised his hands palms together towards the Blessed One and said: "Lord, it is now well on into the night and the third watch is ended with the dawn coming up and joy on the face of the night. The Sangha of bhikkhus has been sitting long. Let the Blessed One recite the Pātimokkha to the bhikkhus.'

"The assembly is not pure, Ānanda."

Then the venerable Mahā-Moggallāna thought: "Who is the

person referred to by the Blessed One in saying that?" He read with his mind the minds of the whole Sangha of bhikkhus. He saw that person, unvirtuous, wicked, unclean, of suspect habits, secretive of his acts, no monk but claiming to be one, nor leading the holy life but claiming to do so, rotten within, libidinous and full of corruption, sitting in the midst of the Sangha. He went up to him and said: "Get up, friend, you are seen by the Blessed One. For you there is no living in communion with the Sangha of bhikkhus."

When this was said, that person remained silent. When it was said to him a second and a third time, he remained silent. Then the venerable Mahā-Moggallāna took him by the arm and put him outside the door, which he bolted. He went to the Blessed One and said: "Lord, I have ejected that person. The assembly is now pure. Let the Blessed One recite the Pātimokkha to the Sangha of bhikkhus."

"It is wonderful, Moggallāna, it is marvellous how that misguided man waited till he was taken by the arm." Then the Blessed One addressed the bhikkhus thus: "Bhikkhus, from now on I shall not participate in the Uposatha. I shall not recite the Pātimokkha. From now on you yourselves will participate in the Uposatha and recite the Pātimokkha. It is impossible, it cannot happen, that a Perfect One should participate in the Uposatha and recite the Pātimokkha in an unpurified assembly.

"Bhikkhus, there are eight wonderful and marvellous qualities of the great ocean that the asura demons delight in whenever they see them. So too there are eight wonderful and marvellous qualities of this Dhamma and Discipline that bhikkhus delight in whenever they see them. What are the eight?

"Just as the great ocean gradually slopes and inclines and shelves without any sudden drop, so too in this Dhamma and Discipline there is gradual training and work and practice without any sudden penetration of final knowledge. Again, just as the great ocean is stable and keeps within the limits of its ebb and flow without exceeding them, so too my disciples transgress no training rules made known by me. Again, just as the great ocean will nor tolerate a dead body, but, when there is a dead body in it, soon casts it ashore, throws it up on dry land, so too the Sangha does not tolerate a person who is unvirtuous, wicked, of suspect habits, secretive of his acts, no monk but claiming to be one, not leading the holy life but claiming to do so, rotten within, libidinous and full of corruption, but when it has met together it soon throws him out; and even though he may be sitting in the midst of the Sangha, he is yet far from the Sangha and the Sangha is far from him.

"Again, just as all the great rivers, the Ganges, the Yamunā, the Aciravatī, the Sarabhū and the Mahī, give up their former names and identities when they reach the great ocean, and they come to be reckoned one with the great ocean itself, so too there are these four castes—the warrior-noble khattiyas, the brahman priests, the burgess vessas and the plebeian suddas—and when they have gone forth from the house life into homelessness in the Dhamma and Discipline declared by the Perfect One, they give up their former name and clan and come to be reckoned one with the bhikkhus who are sons of the Sakyans. Again, just as the great rivers in the world flow into the great ocean, and the rains from the sky fall into it, yet for all that the great ocean is never described as not full or full, so too, though many bhikkhus attain final Nibbāna by the Nibbāna element without result of past clinging left, yet for all that the Nibbāna element is never described as not full or full. Again, just as the great ocean has one taste, the taste of salt, so too, this Dhamma and Discipline has one taste, the taste of liberation. Again, just as the great ocean holds many and various treasures—there are such treasures in it as pearls, crystals, beryls, shells, marbles, corals, silver, gold, rubies, opals—so too this Dhamma and Discipline holds many and various treasures—there are such treasures in it as the four foundations of mindfulness, the four right endeavours, the four bases for success, the five spiritual faculties, the five powers, the seven enlightenment factors, and the Noble Eightfold Path.

"Again, just as the great ocean is the abode of great beings—there are such beings in it as whales, sea-serpents, demons, monsters and tritons—and in the great ocean there are creatures whose persons are a hundred leagues, two, three, four, five hundred leagues in size, so too this Dhamma and Discipline is the abode of great beings—there are such beings in it as the stream-enterer, and one who has entered on the way to the fruit of stream-entry; the once-returner, and one who has entered on the way to the fruit of once-return; the non-returner, and one who has entered on the way to the fruit of non-return; the Arahant, and one who has entered on the way to the fruit of Arahantship."

Knowing the meaning of this, the Blessed One then uttered this exclamation:

Rain soddens what is kept wrapped up,
But never soddens what is open;
Uncover, then, what is concealed,
Lest it be soddened by the rain.

Vin. Cv. 9:1; Ud. 5:5; A. 8:20

FIRST VOICE. Thus I heard. At one time when the Blessed One was living at Sāvatthī, the venerable Mahā-Kassapa went to him. He asked: "Lord, what is the cause, what is the reason, why formerly there were fewer training rules and more bhikkhus became established in final knowledge? What is the cause, what is the reason, why now there are more training rules and fewer bhikkhus become established in final knowledge?"

"That is how it is, Kassapa. When beings are degenerating and the Good Dhamma is disappearing, there come to be more training rules and fewer bhikkhus become established in final knowledge. The Good Dhamma does not disappear until the counterfeit of the Good Dhamma has arisen in the world, but as soon as the counterfeit of the Good Dhamma arises in the world, the Good Dhamma disappears, just as gold does not disappear from the world as long as counterfeit gold does not appear, but as soon as counterfeit gold appears in the world, gold disappears. It is not the earth element or the water element or the fire element or the air element that will bring about the disappearance of the Good Dhamma; rather, it is the misguided men that appear here who bring about the disappearance of the Good Dhamma. But the disappearance of the Good Dhamma does not happen all at once like the sinking of a ship.

"There are these five deleterious things that lead to the forgetting of the Good Dhamma and to its disappearance. What are the five? Here the bhikkhus and bhikkhunīs and men and women lay adherents become disrespectful and contemptuous about the Teacher, about the Dhamma, about the Sangha, about the training, and about concentration. There are also these five things that lead to the enduring of the Good Dhamma, to its not being forgotten and to its non-disappearance. What are the five? Here the bhikkhus and bhikkhunīs and men and women lay adherents are respectful and devout towards the Teacher, towards the Dhamma, towards the Sangha, towards the training and towards concentration."

S. 16:13; cf. A. 7:56

At one time the Blessed One was living at Vesālī in the Hall with the Pointed Roof in the Great Wood. Then a certain Vajjiputtaka bhikkhu went to the Blessed One ... and he said: "Lord, every fortnight more than a hundred and fifty rules of conduct come up for recitation. Lord, I cannot train in all those."

"Can you train in three training rules, bhikkhu? The training rule of the higher virtue, the training rule of the higher consciousness, and the training rule of the higher understanding?"

"I can train in those, Lord."

"Then, bhikkhu, train in those three training rules. As soon as you have completed that training, then, being completely trained, lust, hate and delusion will have been abandoned in you. With that you will no more do unwholesome acts or cultivate evil."

Later on that bhikkhu completed that training; then, being completely trained, lust, hate and delusion were completely abandoned in him. With that he no more did unwholesome acts or cultivated evil.

A. 3:83

SECOND VOICE. The occasion was this. When the Blessed One had lived at Rājagaha as long as he chose, he set out to wander by stages to Vesālī. Now while travelling between the two cities he saw many bhikkhus on the road loaded down with robes, with bundles of robes on their heads, on their shoulders and on their hips. He thought: "These misguided men with their robes only too easily revert to luxury. Suppose I laid down a maximum and set a limit for bhikkhus' robes?"

Then in the course of his journey the Blessed One at length arrived at Vesālī, where he stayed in the Gotamaka Shrine. At that time the Blessed One sat in the open in the night during the cold wintry nights of the "eight days of frost," and he wore only one robe, but he felt no cold. When the first watch was over, he felt cold and he put on a second robe and felt no more cold. When the middle watch was over, he felt cold and put on a third robe and felt no more cold. When the last watch was over with the red dawn coming up and joy on the face of the night, he felt cold and put on a fourth robe and felt no more cold. Then he thought: "Even clansmen sensitive to cold, afraid of cold, who have gone forth in this Dhamma and Discipline can survive with the triple robe. Why should I not lay down a maximum and set a limit for bhikkhus' robes by allowing the triple robe?"

The Blessed One then addressed the bhikkhus, and after telling them what had occurred, he announced the rule for wearing not more than the triple robe: "Bhikkhus, I allow the triple robe: an outer robe of patches and of double thickness, a single inner robe and a single waist cloth."

Vin. Mv. 8:13

Once too when the Blessed One was on his way from Rājagaha to the Southern Hills, he said to the venerable Ānanda: "Ānanda, do you see the land of Magadha, laid out in squares, laid out in strips, laid out with borders, laid out with cross-lines?'

"Yes, Lord."

"Try to arrange robes for bhikkhus like that, Ānanda."

Vin. Mv. 8:12

FIRST VOICE. Thus I heard. At one time while the Blessed One was living at Sāvatthī the venerable Mahā-Kaccāna was living in the Avanti country on the Pavatta Rock at Kururaghara, and he was being supported by a lay follower called Soṇa Kuṭikaṇṇa. Now Soṇa Kuṭikaṇṇa went to the venerable Mahā-Kaccāna, and after paying homage to him, he sat down at one side. Then he said: "Lord, according to what I know of the Dhamma taught by the Lord Mahā-Kaccāna, it is not easy for one living in a house to lead the holy life as utterly perfect and pure as a polished shell. So why should I not shave off my hair and beard, put on the yellow robe and go forth into homelessness? Will the Lord Kaccāna allow me the going forth?"

The venerable Mahā-Kaccāna told him: "Soṇa, it is hard to live the holy life for the rest of one's life, eating in only one part of the day and lying alone. Please devote yourself to the Buddha's teaching there where you are in the household life, and try to live the holy life there, at the proper times eating in only one part of the day and lying alone."

Then Soṇa Kuṭikaṇṇa's ideas of going forth subsided.

Later he made the same request again and received the same answer. Still later he made the same request a third time. Then the venerable Mahā-Kaccāna gave him the going forth. But there were few bhikkhus in the country of Avanti then, and it was only after three years that the venerable Mahā-Kaccāna was able, with trouble and difficulty, to get together a chapter of ten bhikkhus. When he had done so, he gave the venerable Soṇa the admission.

After the rains he rose one evening from retreat and went to the venerable Mahā-Kaccāna. He said: "Lord, while I was alone in retreat this thought arose in me: 'I have never seen the Blessed One face to face but I have heard that he is like this and like this. So, Lord, if my preceptor permits, I will go and see the Blessed One, accomplished and fully enlightened.' "

"Good, good, Soṇa. Go and see the Blessed One, accomplished and fully enlightened. You will see the Blessed One, who inspires trust and confidence, whose sense faculties are stilled, whose heart is stilled, who has attained the supreme control and serenity, a tusker elephant self-controlled and guarded with sense faculties restrained. When you see him, pay homage in my name with your head at his feet. Ask whether he is free from sickness, free from ailment, and is healthy, strong and living in comfort, and tell him that I asked this."

"Even so, Lord," he replied. He was glad, and rejoiced at the venerable Mahā-Kaccāna's words. He took his bowl and outer robe and set out to wander by stages to Sāvatthī where the Blessed One was. Once there, he went to Jeta's Grove and paid homage to the Blessed One. Then he sat down at one side, and he gave his preceptor's message.

"Are you well, bhikkhu? Are you happy? Have you had little trouble on the journey and no difficulty about almsfood?"

"I am well, Blessed One. I am happy. I had little trouble on the journey and no difficulty about almsfood."

The Blessed One said to the venerable Ānanda: "Ānanda, have a resting place prepared for this visiting bhikkhu."

Then the venerable Ānanda thought: "When the Blessed One tells me this, it is because he wants to be together with the visiting bhikkhu. The Blessed One wants to be together with the venerable Soṇa." So he had a resting place prepared in the dwelling in which the Blessed One was living.

The Blessed One spent much of the night sitting in the open. Then he washed his feet and entered his dwelling, and the venerable Soṇa did likewise. When the night was near dawn, the Blessed One rose, and he said to the venerable Soṇa: "You may recite something of the Dhamma, bhikkhu."

"Even so, Lord," he replied. He recited all the sixteen Octets,[1] intoning them. When he had finished, the Blessed One approved, saying: "Good, good, bhikkhu. You have learnt the sixteen Octets well; you know them and remember them well. You have a fine voice, incisive and without faults, which makes the meaning clear.How many rains have you, bhikkhu?"

"I have one rains, Lord."

"Why did you leave it so long, bhikkhu?"

"I have long seen the danger in sensual desires, Lord; but the household life is burdensome with so much to do and many duties."

Knowing the meaning of this, the Blessed One uttered this exclamation:

> Seeing the world to be unsatisfying,
> Knowing the state with no essentials for rebirth,
> The noble one takes no delight in evil;
> Evil gives no delight to the pure in heart.

Ud. 5:6; cf. Vin. Mv. 5:13

At one time the Blessed One was living at Vesālī in the Hall with the Pointed Roof in the Great Wood, together with many very experienced elder disciples: with the venerable Cāla, the venerable Upacāla, the venerable Kakkaṭa, the venerable Kalimbha, the venerable Nikaṭa, the venerable Kaṭissaha and many other very experienced elder disciples.

Now at that time many eminent Licchavis entered the Great Wood to see the Blessed One, arriving in state coaches with postilions and outriders, very clamorous and noisy. Then those venerable ones thought: "There are these many Licchavis come to see the Blessed One .... But it has been said by the Blessed One that noise is a thorn to meditation. Suppose we went to the Gosinga Sāla-tree Wood? Let us dwell there in comfort without noise and company."

So they went to the Gosinga Sāla-tree Wood, and they dwelt there in comfort without noise and company. Then the Blessed One addressed the bhikkhus thus: "Bhikkhus, where is Cāla, where are

Upacāla, Kakkaṭa, Kalimbha, Nikaṭa and Kaṭissaha? Where have those elder bhikkhus gone?"

Bhikkhus described what had happened. The Blessed One said: "Good, good, bhikkhus. They say rightly who say as those great disciples have done; for it has been said by me that noise is a thorn to meditation. There are these ten thorns. What ten? Love of company is a thorn to a lover of seclusion. Devotion to the sign of beauty is a thorn to one devoted to contemplating the sign of loathsomeness in the body. Seeing shows is a thorn to one guarding his sense doors. The vicinity of women is a thorn to one leading the holy life. Noise is a thorn to the first meditation. Thinking and exploring are a thorn to the second meditation. Happiness is a thorn to the third meditation. In-breaths and out-breaths are a thorn to the fourth meditation. Perception and feeling are a thorn to the attainment of the cessation of perception and feeling. Lust is a thorn, hate is a thorn, delusion is a thorn. Dwell without thorns, bhikkhus, dwell thornless, dwell without thorns and thornless. The Arahants are without thorns, bhikkhus, the Arahants are thornless, the Arahants are without thorns and thornless."

A. 10:72

The Blessed One was once living at Vesālī in the Hall with the Pointed Roof in the Great Wood. It was an occasion when he had talked to the bhikkhus in many ways on contemplation of loathsomeness (in the body), commending contemplation of loathsomeness and the maintenance of it in being. Then he told the bhikkhus: "Bhikkhus, I wish to go into retreat for half a month. I am not to be approached by anyone except by him who brings me almsfood.'

"Even so, Lord," they replied, and they did as they had been instructed.

Then those bhikkhus thought over what the Blessed One had said in commendation of contemplating the loathsomeness (of the body), and they dwelt devoted to the pursuit of maintaining in being that contemplation. So doing, they became humiliated, ashamed and disgusted with this body, and they sought the use of the knife (to take their lives). On a single day as many as ten, twenty or thirty bhikkhus used the knife.

At the end of the half month the Blessed One rose from retreat, and he addressed the venerable Ānanda thus: "Ānanda, why has the Sangha of bhikkhus become so thinned out?"

The venerable Ānanda told him what had happened, and he added: "Lord, let the Blessed One announce another way for this Sangha of bhikkhus to find establishment in final knowledge."

"In that case, Ānanda, summon as many bhikkhus as are living in the neighbourhood of Vesālī to meet in the assembly hall."

The venerable Ānanda did so, and when they had met, he informed the Blessed One. The Blessed One then went to the assembly hall where he sat down on a seat made ready. When he had done so, he addressed the bhikkhus thus:

"Bhikkhus, when this mindfulness of breathing is maintained in being and developed, it offers peace and a superior goal, it is unadulterated (by loathsomeness) and a pleasant abiding, and it causes evil unwholesome mental objects to vanish at once as soon as they arise, just as when dirt and dust are blown about in the last month of the hot season, a great shower out of season makes them vanish at once as soon as they arise."

S. 54:9

When the Blessed One was living at Rājagaha, a bhikkhu called Thera lived alone and recommended living alone; he went into the village for alms alone, returned alone, sat in private alone, and walked up and down alone. Then a number of bhikkhus went to the Blessed One and told him about this. The Blessed One sent for him and asked if it was true. He replied that it was. The Blessed One said: "There is that kind of living alone, Thera, I do not say that there is not. Nevertheless, hear how living alone is perfected in detail, and heed well what I shall say."

"Yes, Lord," the venerable Thera replied. The Blessed One said: "And how is living alone perfected in detail? Here, Thera, what is past is left behind, what is future is renounced, and lust and desire for the selfhood acquired in the present is quite put away. That is how living alone is perfected in detail."

So the Blessed One said. The Sublime One having said this, the Master said further:

A sagely all-transcender, an all-knower,
Unsullied in all things, renouncing all,
By craving's ceasing freed: him do I call
A man who lives alone and to perfection.

S. 21:10

SECOND VOICE. The occasion was this. The Blessed One was living on the Vulture Peak Rock at Rājagaha at a time when Seniya Bimbisāra, King of Magadha, was exercising government in the lordship and rule over eighty thousand villages. At that time too there was one of the Kolivisa clan called Soṇa living at Campā. He was the son of a magnate. He was so delicate that hair grew on the soles of his feet. Now the king, who had assembled representatives from the eighty thousand villages for some business or other, sent a message to Soṇa Kolivisa, saying: "Let Soṇa come. I want Soṇa to come."

So Soṇa's parents told him: "The king wants to see your feet, Soṇa dear. Now don't stretch your feet out towards the king; sit down in front of him cross-legged with your soles uppermost, so that he will be able to see your feet as you sit there."

They brought him in a litter, and he went to see the king. After he had paid homage to him, he sat down in front of him cross-legged, and the king saw the soles of his feet with the hair growing on them.

Then the king instructed the representatives of the eighty thousand villages in the aims of this life, after which he dismissed them, saying: "You have been instructed by me in the aims of this life. Now go and do honour to the Blessed One; he will instruct you in the aims of the lives to come."

They went to the Vulture Peak Rock. When the Blessed One had discoursed to them, they took the Three Refuges. But soon after they had gone Soṇa approached the Blessed One and asked for the going forth. He took the going forth and the admission.

Not long after he had been admitted to the Sangha, he went to live in the Cool Grove. As he walked up and down, striving for progress, his feet blistered, and the walk became all covered with blood like a shambles. The Blessed One went to the venerable Soṇa's dwelling, and he sat down on a seat made ready, and the venerable Soṇa paid homage and sat down at one side. The Blessed One said: "When you were alone in retreat, Soṇa, did it not just now occur to you: 'Whatever disciples the Blessed One has that are energetic, I am one of them. Yet my heart is not freed from taints by not clinging. Now there are still riches in my family; I could use those riches and make merit. Suppose I return to the lay life and use those riches to make merit'?"

"Even so, Lord."

"What do you think, Soṇa, were you once a good lute player as a layman?"

"Even so, Lord."

"When the strings of your lute were too taut, did your lute sound well and respond well then?"

"No, Lord."

"When the strings of your lute were too slack, did your lute sound well and respond well then?"

"No, Lord."

"When the strings of your lute were neither too taut nor too slack and were evenly tuned, did your lute sound well and respond well then?"

"Yes, Lord."

"So too, Soṇa, overstriving leads to agitation, and understriving leads to slackness. Therefore resolve upon evenness of energy, acquire evenness of the spiritual faculties, and take that as your sign."

"Even so, Lord," he replied.

Vin. Mv. 5:1; cf. A. 6:55

FIRST VOICE. Thus I heard. At one time the Blessed One was living at Rājagaha in the Bamboo Grove, the Squirrels' Sanctuary. Now at that time there was a leper called Suppabuddha at Rājagaha. He was a pauper and a miserable wretch.

Once when the Blessed One was sitting expounding the Dhamma surrounded by a large gathering of people, the leper saw the great crowd in the distance. He thought: "Surely there will be something to eat being distributed there. Suppose I approach that great crowd; perhaps I might get something to eat there?" He approached the crowd, and he saw the Blessed One sitting expounding the Dhamma surrounded by a large gathering of people. He thought: "There is nothing to eat being distributed here. It is the monk Gotama expounding the Dhamma to an assembly. Suppose I listened to the Dhamma?" He sat down there at one side, thinking: "I shall hear the Dhamma." Then the Blessed One surveyed the whole assembly, reading their minds with his mind and wondering who was capable there of recognizing the Dhamma. He saw Suppabuddha the leper sitting in the assembly. Then he thought: "He is capable of recognizing the Dhamma."

For the benefit of Suppabuddha the leper he gave progressive instruction on generosity, on virtue and on the heavens, and then on the inadequacy, the vanity and the defilement in sensual pleasures and the blessings in renunciation. When he saw that his mind was ready ... he expounded the teaching peculiar to the Buddhas: suffering, its origin, its cessation, and the path to its cessation ....

The spotless, immaculate vision of the Dhamma arose in him: All that is subject to arising is subject to cessation. He said: "Magnificent, Lord! ... Let the Blessed One remember me as one who has gone to him for refuge for as long as breath lasts."

When Suppabuddha the leper had been instructed ... he was satisfied with the Blessed One's words, and rejoicing, he paid homage to the Blessed One and departed, keeping him on his right.

Then a cow with a young calf set upon Suppabuddha the leper and killed him.

Afterwards, many bhikkhus went to the Blessed One. They said: "Lord, Suppabuddha the leper whom the Blessed One instructed ... is dead. What is his destination? What is his future life?"

"Bhikkhus, Suppabuddha the leper was wise; he entered into the way of the Dhamma, he did not trouble me with arguments about the Dhamma. With the destruction of three fetters Suppabuddha has become a stream-enterer; he is no more subject to states of privation, he is certain of rightness and is destined to enlightenment."

When this was said, a bhikkhu asked: "Lord, what was the cause, what was the reason, why Suppabuddha the leper was a pauper and such a miserable wretch?"

"Formerly, bhikkhus, Suppabuddha the leper was a rich man's son in this same Rājagaha. On his way to a pleasure park he saw the Paccekabuddha Tagarasikhī going into the city for alms[2] Then he thought: 'Who is that leper wandering there?' And he spat on him and insulted him and went away. He experienced the ripening of that deed in hell for many a year, many a century, many a millennium. With the ripening of that same deed he was now a pauper and a miserable wretch in this same Rājagaha. Through the Dhamma and Discipline proclaimed by the Perfect One he has acquired faith, virtue, wisdom, generosity and understanding. With the ripening of that he has, on the dissolution of the body, after death, reappeared in the heavenly world in the company of the Thirty-three Gods. There he outshines the other deities in appearance and fame."

Ud. 5:3

SECOND VOICE. The occasion was this. There were two bhikkhus called Yamelu and Tekula living at Sāvatthī, and they were brothers. They were of brahman stock, and they had fine voices and a fine delivery. They asked the Blessed One: "Lord, now the bhikkhus are of various names, of various races, variously born, having gone forth from various clans. They spoil the word of the Blessed One by using their own language. Let us render the words of the Buddha into classical metre."

The Buddha, the Blessed One, rebuked them: "Misguided men, how can you say 'Let us render the words of the Buddha into classical metre'? This will not rouse faith in the faithless or increase faith in the faithful; rather it will keep the faithless without faith and harm some of the faithful." Having rebuked them and given a talk on the Dhamma, he addressed the bhikkhus thus: "Bhikkhus, the word of the Buddha is not to be rendered into classical metre. Whoever does so commits an offence of wrongdoing. I allow the words of the Buddha to be learnt in one's own language."

Vin. Cv. 5:33

Once while the Blessed One was expounding the Dhamma, surrounded by a large number of bhikkhus, he sneezed. The bhikkhus made a loud noise, saying: "Long life to you, Lord; long life to you, Lord." The noise interrupted the talk on the Dhamma. Then the Blessed One addressed the bhikkhus thus: "Bhikkhus, when 'Long life to you' is said to someone who sneezes, may he live or die because of that?"

"No, Lord."

"Bhikkhus, 'Long life to you' is not to be said to someone who sneezes; whoever does so commits an offence of wrongdoing."

So then, when bhikkhus sneezed and householders said "Long life to you, Lord," they were embarrassed and did not answer. People disapproved, and they murmured and protested: "How can these monks, these sons of the Sakyans, not answer when 'Long life to you' is said to them?"

Bhikkhus told this to the Blessed One. He said: "Bhikkhus, householders are accustomed to such superstitions. I allow you, when they say 'Long life to you,' to reply 'May you live long.' "

Vin. Cv. 5:33

FIRST VOICE. Thus I heard. At one time the Blessed One was living at Sāvatthī in the Eastern Park, the Palace of Migāra's Mother. On that occasion he had risen from retreat in the evening, and he was sitting outside the gatehouse in the porch. Then King Pasenadi of Kosala came up to him, and after paying homage, he sat down at one side.

But just then seven matted-hair ascetics, seven Nigaṇṭhas, seven naked ascetics, seven single-garment ascetics, and seven wanderers, all with long hair and nails and carrying a variety of monks' outfits, went by not far from the Blessed One. King Pasenadi got up from his seat, and after arranging his robe on one shoulder, he knelt down with his right knee on the ground. Then raising his hands palms together towards the ascetics, he pronounced his own name, "Lords, I am Pasenadi, King of Kosala," three times.

Soon after they had passed, he went back to the Blessed One, and after paying homage to him, he sat down at one side. He said: "Lord, are any of these among the world's Arahants, or among those on the way to Arahantship?"

"Great king, as a layman you enjoy sense pleasures; you live amid the encumbrance of children, you employ Benares sandalwood, you wear garlands, scents and unguents, you use gold and silver. It is hard for you to know if people are Arahants or are on the way to Arahantship. A man's virtue is to be known by living with him, and then only if we attend not a little over a long period, if we neither fail in attention nor lack understanding. A man's purity is to be known by talking with him .... A man's fortitude is to be known in times of adversity .... A man's understanding is to be known by discussing with him, and then only if we attend not a little over a long period, if we neither fail in attention nor lack understanding."

"It is wonderful, Lord, it is marvellous how well the Blessed One has expressed that! There are men, agents of mine, who come to me still disguised as common robbers after they have been spying in the countryside. At first I am deceived by them and only afterwards I realize who they are. But once they have cleaned off all that dirt and dust and are well bathed and anointed, with their hair and beards trimmed, and dressed in white clothes, they enjoy themselves surrounded by all the five kinds of sensual desires."

Knowing the meaning of this, the Blessed One uttered this exclamation:

It is hard to know a man by his appearance,
Nor can you judge him on a passing glance.
The unrestrained can go about this world
Wearing the guise of men that are restrained;
For there are some who, hidden by a mask,
Glitter without and are corrupt within,
Like jewels counterfeited out of clay
Or copper farthings with a plate of gilt.

S. 3:11; Ud. 6:2

(*The Kālāma Sutta*)

The Blessed One was once wandering by stages in the Kosala country with a large number of bhikkhus. He arrived at a town belonging to the Kālāmans called Kesaputta. When the Kesaputtians heard that the Blessed One had arrived, they went to him and they asked him: "Lord, some monks and brahmans come to Kesaputta, and they expound only their own tenets while they abuse and rend and censure and rail at the tenets of others. And other monks and brahmans come to Kesaputta, and they too expound only their own tenets while they abuse and rend and censure and rail at the tenets of others. We are puzzled and in doubt about them, Lord. Which of these reverend monks has spoken truly and which falsely?"

"You may well be puzzled, Kālāmans. You may well be in doubt. For your doubt has arisen precisely about what ought to be doubted. Come, Kālāmans, do not be satisfied with hearsay or with tradition[3] or with legendary lore or with what has come down in your scriptures or with conjecture or with logical inference or with weighing evidence or with liking for a view after pondering over it or with someone else's ability or with the thought 'The monk is our teacher.' When you know in yourselves: 'These ideas are unwholesome, liable to censure, condemned by the wise, being adopted and put into effect they lead to harm and suffering,' then you should abandon them. How do you conceive this, Kālāmans: when lust arises in a person, is it for good or evil?"—"For evil, Lord."—"Now it is when a person is lustful and he is overcome by lust, with his mind obsessed by lust, that he kills breathing things, takes what is not given, commits adultery, speaks falsehood, and gets others to do likewise, which will be long for his harm and suffering."—"Even so, Lord."—"How do you conceive this, Kālāmans; when hate arises in a person ... ? When delusion arises in a person ... ? "—"Even so, Lord."—"How do you conceive this, Kālāmans: are these things wholesome or unwholesome?"—"Unwholesome, Lord."—"Censurable or blameless?"—"Censurable, Lord."—"Condemned or commended by the wise?"—"Condemned by the wise, Lord."—"Being adopted and put into effect, do they lead to harm and suffering, or do they not, or how does it appear to you in this case?"—"Being adopted and put into effect, Lord, they lead to harm and suffering. So it appears to us in this case."—"So, Kālāmans, those are the reasons why I told you: 'Come, Kālāmans, do not be satisfied with hearsay ... or with the thought "The monk is our teacher." When you know in yourselves: "These things are unwholesome ... " then you should abandon them.'

"Come, Kālāmans, do not be satisfied with hearsay ... or with the thought 'The monk is our teacher.' When you know in yourselves: 'These things are wholesome, blameless, commended by the wise, being adopted and put into effect they lead to welfare and happiness,' then you should practise them and abide in them. How do you conceive this, Kālāmans: when non-lust arises in a person, is it for good or evil?"—"For good, Lord."—"Now it is when a person is not lustful and he is not overcome by lust, and his mind is not obsessed by lust, that he does not kill breathing things, or take what is not given, or commit adultery, or speak falsehood, and gets others to do likewise, which will be long for his welfare and happiness."—"Even so, Lord."—"How do you conceive this, Kālāmans: when non-hate arises in a person ... ? When non-delusion arises in a person ... ?"—"Even so, Lord."—"How do you conceive this, Kālāmans: are these things wholesome or unwholesome?"—"Wholesome, Lord."—"Censurable or blameless?"—"Blameless, Lord."—"Condemned or commended by the wise?"—"Commended by the wise, Lord."—"Being adopted and put into effect, do they lead to welfare and happiness, or do they not, or how does it appear to you in this case?"—"Being adopted and put into effect, Lord, they lead to welfare and happiness, so it appears to us in this case."—"So, Kālāmans, those are the reasons why I told you: 'Come, Kālāmans, do not be satisfied with hearsay ... or with the thought "The monk is our teacher." When you know in yourselves: "These things are wholesome ... " then you should practise them and abide in them.'

"Now when a noble disciple is in this way free from covetousness free from ill will, and undeluded, then, fully aware and mindful, he abides with a heart endued with loving-kindness extending to one quarter; likewise to the second quarter, likewise to the third quarter, likewise to the fourth quarter; so above, below, around, and everywhere, and to all as to himself; he abides with a heart endued with abundant, exalted, measureless loving-kindness, unhostile and unafflicted by ill will, extending to the entire world. He abides with a heart endued with compassion .... He abides with a heart endued with gladness .... He abides with a heart endued with equanimity ... extending to the entire world.

"With his heart thus unhostile and unafflicted by ill will, thus undefiled and unified, a noble disciple here and now acquires these four comforts. He thinks: 'If there is another world and there is fruit and ripening of actions well done and ill done, then it is possible that on the dissolution of the body, after death, I might be reborn in a heavenly world.' This is the first comfort acquired. 'But if there is no other world and there is no fruit and ripening of actions well done and ill done, then here and now in this life I shall be free from hostility, affliction and anxiety, and I shall live happily.' This is the second comfort acquired. 'If evil befalls one who does evil, then since I have no evil thought of anyone, how shall evil deeds bring suffering to me, doing no evil?' This is the third comfort acquired. 'But if no evil befalls one who does evil, then I know myself to be pure in this life on both these counts.' This is the fourth comfort acquired."

A. 3:65

Now a certain bhikkhu was once sick with dysentery, and he lay fouled in his own urine and excrement. As the Blessed One was going the round of the lodgings with the venerable Ānanda as his attendant monk, he came to that bhikkhu's dwelling. When he saw him lying where he was, he went up to him and said: "What is your sickness, bhikkhu?"

"It is dysentery, Blessed One."

"But, bhikkhu, have you no attendant?"

"No, Blessed One."

"Why do the bhikkhus not look after you, bhikkhu?"

"I am of no use to the bhikkhus, Lord; that is why they do not look after me."

Then the Blessed One said to the venerable Ānanda: "Ānanda, go and fetch some water. Let us wash this bhikkhu."

"Even so, Lord," the venerable Ānanda replied, and he brought some water. The Blessed One poured out the water and the venerable Ānanda washed the bhikkhu. Then the Blessed One took him by the head and the venerable Ānanda took him by the feet, and they raised him up and put him on a bed.

With this as the occasion and this as the reason, the Blessed One summoned the bhikkhus and asked them: "Bhikkhus, is there a bhikkhu sick in a certain dwelling?"

"There is, Blessed One."

"What is that bhikkhu's illness?"

"He has dysentery, Lord."

"Has he anyone to look after him?"

"No, Blessed One."

"Why do the bhikkhus not look after him?"

"Lord, that bhikkhu is of no use to the bhikkhus; that is why they do not look after him."

"Bhikkhus, you have neither mother nor father to look after you. If you do not look after each other, who will look after you? Let him who would look after me look after one who is sick. If he has a preceptor, his preceptor should as long as he lives look after him until his recovery. His teacher, if he has one, should do likewise. Or his co-resident, or his pupil, or one who has the same preceptor, or one who has the same teacher. If he has none of these, the Sangha should look after him. Not to do so is an offence of wrongdoing.[4]

"When a sick man has five qualities, he is hard to look after: he does what is unsuitable; he does not know the measure of what is suitable; he does not take medicine; he does not disclose his illness to his sick-nurse who seeks his welfare, or tell him that it is better when it is so, or worse when it is so, or the same when it is so; he is of a type unable to endure arisen bodily feelings that are painful, harsh, racking, piercing, disagreeable, unwelcome and menacing to life. When a sick man has the five opposite qualities, he is easy to look after."

Vin. Mv. 8:26

"When a sick-nurse has five qualities, he is unfit to look after the sick: he is not clever at preparing medicine; he does not know what is and what is not suitable, so he brings what is unsuitable and takes away what is suitable; he looks after the sick for mercenary reasons rather than with thoughts of loving-kindness; he is squeamish about removing excrement, urine, spittle or vomit; he is not clever at instructing, urging, rousing and encouraging the sick with timely talk on the Dhamma. When a sick-nurse has the five opposite qualities, he is fit to look after the sick."

Vin. Mv. 8:26; A. 5:123-24

FIRST VOICE. The Blessed One was once sitting outside in the blackness of the night, and oil lamps were burning. Now numbers of moths were meeting ruin, calamity and disaster on that occasion by falling into the oil lamps. Knowing the meaning of this, the Blessed One then uttered this exclamation:

> Though some may court extremes, they find
> No essence, but renew their bonds,
> For they dwell in the seen and sensed
> Like moths that fall into a flame.

Ud. 6:9

One morning the Blessed One dressed, and taking his bowl and outer robe, he went to Sāvatthī for alms. Between Jeta's Grove and Sāvatthī he saw a party of boys ill-treating fishes. He went up to them and asked: "Boys, are you afraid of pain? Do you dislike pain?"

"Yes, Lord, we are afraid of pain; we dislike pain."

Knowing the meaning of this, the Blessed One then uttered this exclamation:

> Who does not want to suffer
> Should do no evil deeds
> Openly or in secret.
> Do evil now, then later,
> Try though you may to flee it,
> Yet surely you will suffer.

Ud. 5:4

CHANTER:[5]

This should be done by one with skill in good
In order to attain the state of peace.

Let him be able, upright, straight,
And meek and gentle and not proud;
Contented, easy to support,
Unbusy, frugal, and serene;
In faculties, prudent and modest,
Ungrasping among families;
And let him do no slightest thing
That other wise men might deplore.

(Then let him think:) "In joy and safety
Let every being's heart rejoice.
Whatever breathing beings there are,
No matter whether faint or bold,
With none excepted, long or big
Or middle-sized or short or thin
Or thick or those seen or unseen
Or whether dwelling far or near,
That are or that yet seek to be,
Let every being's heart rejoice.
Let none betray another's trust
Or offer any slight at all,
Or ever let them wish in wrath
Or in revenge each other's ill."

Thus as a mother with her life
Will guard her son, her only child,
Let him extend unboundedly
His heart to every living being.
And so with love for all the world
Let him extend unboundedly
His heart, above, below, around,
Unchecked, with no ill will or hate.

Whether he stands, or sits, or walks,
Or lies down (while yet not asleep),

Let him such mindfulness pursue:
This is Holy Abiding here, they say.

But he that traffics not with views,
Is virtuous, with perfected vision,
And longs no more for sense desires:
He is not born again in any womb.

Sn. 1:8

11
THE PERSON

NARRATOR ONE. Now that the stream of events is no longer traceable for a period, a pause can be made here in order to see what is said in the Canon about the personal qualities of the Buddha: to see both what the Buddha had to say of himself, and what other people of the time who encountered him said of him, in the oldest reports that have come down to us.

FIRST VOICE. Thus I heard. Once when the Blessed One was living at Sāvatthī in Jeta's Grove, Anāthapiṇḍika's Park, he sat reviewing the many evil unwholesome things abandoned, and the many wholesome things perfected by development in himself. Knowing the meaning of this, he then uttered this exclamation:

What earlier was, later was not;
What earlier was not, later was;
What had not been both will not be
And is not at the present time.[1]

Ud. 6:3

Again the Blessed One sat reviewing the abandonment of the varieties of diversification[2] in himself. Knowing the meaning of this, he then uttered this exclamation:

Who, with no basis for diversifying,
Has set aside the tie and block as well,
And lives on as a seer released from craving,
Him the world with its gods will not despise.

Ud. 7:7

"Bhikkhus, there are these Four Noble Truths: the noble truth of suffering, the noble truth of the origin of suffering, the noble truth of the cessation of suffering, and the noble truth of the way leading to the cessation of suffering. A Perfect One, accomplished and fully enlightened, is so called because of his discovery of these Four Noble Truths according as they actually are.

S. 56:23

NARRATOR TWO. The Buddha names the six Buddhas that preceded him.

FIRST VOICE. "It is ninety-one ages ago, bhikkhus, that the Blessed One Vipassī, accomplished and fully enlightened, appeared in the world. It is thirty-one ages ago that the Blessed One Sikhī, accomplished and fully enlightened, appeared in the world. In that same thirty-first age the Blessed One Vessabhū, accomplished and fully enlightened, appeared in the world. In this auspicious age the Blessed One Kakusandha, accomplished and fully enlightened, has appeared in the world. In this same auspicious age the Blessed One Koṇāgamana, accomplished and fully enlightened, has appeared in the world. In this same auspicious age the Blessed One Kassapa, accomplished and fully enlightened, has appeared in the world. In this same auspicious age I now, accomplished and fully enlightened, have appeared in the world."

D. 14 (condensed)

NARRATOR ONE. After describing the others, here is what he says about himself.

FIRST VOICE. "I am of khattiya, warrior-noble stock. I was reborn into a khattiya family. I am a Gotama by clan. My life's span is of short length, it is brief and soon over; one who lives long now completes the century or a little more. I was enlightened at the root of an assattha banyan as my Enlightenment Tree. My chief disciples are Sāriputta and Moggallāna. I have had one convocation consisting of twelve hundred and fifty disciples, all of them Arahants. My attendant, my chief attendant, is the bhikkhu Ānanda. A king, Suddhodana by name, was my father. A queen, Māyā by name, was the mother that bore me. The royal capital was the city of Kapilavatthu."

D. 14 (condensed)

This was said by the Blessed One, said by the Accomplished One, so I heard:

"Bhikkhus, the world has been discovered by the Perfect One, the Tathāgata: the Perfect One is dissociated from the world. The origin of the world has been discovered by the Perfect One: the Perfect One has abandoned the origin of the world. The cessation of the world has been discovered by the Perfect One: the Perfect One has realized the cessation of the world. The way leading to the cessation of the world has been discovered by the Perfect One: the Perfect One has maintained in being the way leading to the cessation of the world.

"In the world with its deities ... whatever can be seen, heard, sensed (by nose, tongue or body), and cognized, or reached, sought out and encompassed by the mind, has been discovered by the Perfect One: that is why he is called a Perfect One (Tathāgata). All that he says, all that he utters, between the night when he discovers the supreme full enlightenment and the night when he attains final Nibbāna, the element of Nibbāna without result of former clinging left, is true (*tatha*), not other than that: that is why he is called a Perfect One (Tathāgata). As he says, so (*tathā*) he does; as he does, so (*tathā*) he says: that is why he is called a Perfect One (Tathāgata). In the world with its deities ... it is the Perfect One who is the Transcendent Being Untranscended, All-seer and Wielder of Powers: that is why he is called a Perfect One."

Iti. 112; A. 4:23

"Whatever in this world with its deities ... is to be seen, heard, sensed, and cognized, or reached, sought out and encompassed by the mind, that I know, that I have directly known. Now while that is recognized by a Perfect One, he nevertheless does not use it as a basis (for conceits). Were I to say of all that, that I know it not, that would be falsely spoken by me; and were I to say of it that I know it and know it not, that would be the same; and were I to say of it that I neither know it nor know it not, that would be incorrect on my part. So, having seen what can be seen, a Perfect One conceives no conceit[3] of what is seen, he conceives no conceit of what is unseen, he conceives no conceit of what could be seen, he conceives no conceit of any seer. Having heard what can be heard ... Having sensed what can be sensed ... Having cognized what can be cognized ... he conceives no conceit of any cognizer. A Perfect One thus equipoised towards things seen, heard, sensed, or cognized, remains thus equipoised; and there is no other equipoise that is beyond or superior to that equipoise, I say."

A. 4:24

King Pasenadi of Kosala asked the Blessed One: "Lord, I have heard this: 'The monk Gotama says: "There is no monk or brahman who can claim to have complete knowledge and vision as one who is omniscient and all seeing: that is not possible." ' Lord, do those who say that, perhaps say what has been said by the Blessed One and not misrepresent the Blessed One with what is not the fact, and do they express ideas in accordance with the Dhamma with nothing legitimately deducible from their assertions that would provide grounds for condemning them?"

"Great king, those who say that say what has not been said by me and misrepresent me."

"Then, Lord, could it have been said with reference to something else that the Blessed One said that, and the person believed it was otherwise? At any rate, Lord, in what way does the Blessed One know the utterance to have been made?"

"I know an utterance to have been made in this way, great king: 'There is no monk or brahman who knows all, sees all, in one single moment.' "

"What the Blessed One says appears reasonable."

M. 90

"A Perfect One has these ten Perfect One's powers, possessing which he claims the leader's place in the herd, makes his lion's roar in the assemblies, and sets the matchless Wheel of Brahmā turning. What ten?

"A Perfect One understands, according as it actually is, the possible as possible and the impossible as impossible.

"He understands, according as it actually is, with its possibilities and reasons, the past, future and present liability to ripening of actions that have been effected.

"He understands likewise whither all ways lead.

"He understands likewise the world with its many elements and various elements.

"He understands likewise the differing inclinations of beings.

"He understands likewise the dispositions of the spiritual faculties in other beings, other persons.

"He understands likewise the corruption, purification, and emergence, in the meditations, liberations, concentrations, and attainments.

"He recollects his manifold past life ....

"With the divine eye, which is purified and surpasses the human, he sees beings passing away and reappearing .... He understands how beings pass on according to their actions.

"By realization himself with direct knowledge he here and now enters and abides in the deliverance of mind and the deliverance by understanding that are taintless with the exhaustion of taints."

M. 12; cf. A. 10:21

"A Perfect One has these four kinds of intrepidity[4] possessing which he claims the leader's place in the herd ...:

"I see no sign that any monk or brahman or deity or Māra or Brahmā in the world will justly accuse me thus: 'By you who claim to be fully enlightened, these things are still undiscovered,' or thus: 'In you who claim to have exhausted taints, these taints are still not exhausted,' or thus: 'Those things which are said by you to be obstructive are not in fact obstructive to one who practises them,' or thus: 'When your Dhamma is taught for someone's benefit, it does not lead to the complete exhaustion of suffering in one who practises it.' Seeing no sign of that, I dwell secure, unanxious and fearless."

M. 12

This was said by the Blessed One, said by the Accomplished One, so I heard:

"Two thoughts often occur to a Perfect One, accomplished and fully enlightened: The thought of harmlessness and the thought of seclusion. A Perfect One takes pleasure and delights in non-affliction, and with that it often occurs to him: 'By such behaviour I afflict none, timid or bold.' A Perfect One takes pleasure and delight in seclusion, and with that it often occurs to him: 'What is unwholesome has been abandoned.' "

Iti. 38

"Bhikkhus, do not fear merit. Merit is a term for pleasure, for the wanted, the desired, the agreeable and the loved. I have had direct knowledge by experience for a long period of what is wanted, desired, agreeable and loved as the ripening of merit made over a long period. After maintaining in being the meditation of loving-kindness for seven years, I did not return to this world for seven ages of world contraction and expansion. In the age when the world was contracting I went to the Heaven of the Brahmas of Streaming Radiance. In the age when the world was expanding I was reborn in an empty Brahmā mansion. There I was a Brahmā, a Great Brahmā, a Transcendent Being Untranscended, an All-seer, a Wielder of Powers. I have been Sakka, Ruler of (sensual) Gods, thirty-six times. I have been a king many hundred times as a righteous Universal Monarch turning the wheel, victorious in all four quarters, with my realm stabilized and in possession of the seven treasures. What need I say of local kingship? I thought: 'Of what action of mine is this the fruit, is this the ripening, that I am now so mighty and powerful?' Then it occurred to me: 'It is the fruit, the ripening of three kinds of actions of mine that I am now so mighty and powerful, that is to say, of giving, of control, and of restraint.' "

Iti. 22

At one time the Blessed One was travelling by the road between Ukkaṭṭhā and Setavyā; and the brahman Doṇa was travelling by that road too. He saw in the Blessed One's footprints wheels with a thousand spokes and with rims and hubs all complete. Then he thought: "It is wonderful, it is marvellous! Surely this can never be the footprint of a human being."

Then the Blessed One left the road and sat down at the root of a tree, crosslegged, with his body held erect and mindfulness established before him. Then the brahman Doṇa, who was following up the footprints, saw him sitting at the root of the tree. The Blessed One inspired trust and confidence, his faculties being stilled, his mind quiet and attained to supreme control and serenity: a tusker elephant self-controlled and guarded by restraint of sense faculties. The brahman went up to him and asked: "Sir, will you be a god?"

"No, brahman."

"Sir, will you be a heavenly angel?"

"No, brahman."

"Sir, will you be a spirit?"

"No, brahman."

"Sir, will you be a human being?"

"No, brahman."

"Then, sir, what indeed will you be?"

"Brahman, the taints by means of which, through my not having abandoned them, I might be a god or a heavenly angel or a spirit or a human being have been abandoned by me, cut off at the root, made like a palm stump, done away with, and are no more subject to future arising. Just as a blue or red or white lotus is born in water, grows in water and stands up above the water untouched by it, so too I, who was born in the world and grew up in the world, have transcended the world, and I live untouched by the world. Remember me as one who is enlightened."

A. 4:36

Again the Blessed One was wandering at one time in the country of the Videhans with a large community of bhikkhus, with five hundred bhikkhus. Now at that time the brahman Brahmāyu was living at Mithilā. He was old, aged, burdened with years, advanced in life and come to the last stage; he was in his hundred and twentieth year. He was expert in the three Vedas, he knew the text and context of the Itihāsas, the fifth of the brahmanical authorities, with their invocations, liturgy and word-analysis, and he was fully versed in natural science and that of the marks of the Great Man.

He had heard of the Blessed One's qualities and that he was wandering in the country of the Videhans. He had a pupil, a young brahman student named Uttara, who was as expert as his teacher and as fully versed too in the science of the marks of the Great Man. The brahman said to his pupil: "Come, my dear Uttara; go to the monk Gotama and find out whether the report of him that has been spread abroad is true or not, and whether he is one such as that or not. We shall see the monk Gotama through you."

"But how shall I find out, sir?"

"My dear Uttara, the thirty-two marks of the Great Man have been handed down in our scriptures, and the Great Man who is endowed with them has only two possible destinies and no other. If he lives the house life, he becomes a righteous Universal Monarch, a conqueror of the four quarters, all-victorious, who stabilizes his country and possesses the seven treasures: the wheel treasure, the elephant treasure, the horse treasure, the jewel treasure, the woman treasure, the householder treasure, and the steward treasure as the seventh; his children who exceed a thousand are brave and heroic and crush others' armies; over this earth bounded by the ocean he rules without a rod, without a weapon and in righteousness. But if he goes forth from the house life into homelessness, he becomes an Accomplished One, a Fully Enlightened One, who draws aside the veil in the world. But I, my dear Uttara, am the giver of the scriptures; you are the receiver of them."

"Even so, sir," he replied.

He rose from his seat, and after paying homage to the brahman, keeping him on his right, he left for where the Blessed One was wandering in the country of the Videhans. Travelling by stages, he came to where the Blessed One was. He exchanged greetings with him, and when this courteous formal talk was finished, he sat down at one side. When he had done so, he looked for the thirty-two marks of the Great Man on the Blessed One's body. He saw, more or less, the thirty-two marks there except for two; he was doubtful and uncertain about two of the marks, and he could not decide and make up his mind about them—about what should be hidden by cloth being enclosed in a sheath, and about the largeness of the tongue.

Then it occurred to the Blessed One that he was doubtful about these two marks. He worked a feat of supernormal power such that the brahman student Uttara saw that in the Blessed One what should be hidden by cloth was enclosed by a sheath. Then the Blessed One extruded his tongue, and he repeatedly touched both ear holes, and he repeatedly touched both nostril holes, and he hid the whole of his forehead with his tongue. Then the brahman thought: "The monk Gotama is endowed with the thirty-two marks of the Great Man. Suppose I follow him and observe his behaviour?"

Then he followed him for seven months like a shadow, never leaving him. At the end of seven months in the country of the Videhans he set out to return to Mithilā.

He went to Brahmāyu the brahman, paid homage and sat down at one side. Then the brahman asked him: "Well, my dear Uttara, is the report of the monk Gotama that has been spread about true, or not true? And is Master Gotama one such as that, or not?"

"The report is true, sir, not incorrect; Master Gotama is one such as that and no other. Now Master Gotama sets his foot down squarely—this is a mark of the Great Man in him. On the soles of his feet there are wheels with a thousand spokes and with rims and hubs complete .... He has projecting heels .... He has long fingers and toes... His hands and feet are soft and tender .... He has netted hands .... His feet are arched .... His legs are like an antelope's .... When he stands without stooping, the palms of both his hands touch and rub against his knees .... That in him which should be covered by cloth is enclosed in a sheath .... He is the colour of gold .... His skin has a golden sheen, but he is fine-skinned; because of the fineness of his skin, dust and dirt do not stick to his body .... His body-hairs grow singly, each hair growing alone in its pore .... The tips of his body-hairs turn up; the up-turned hairs are blue-black, the colour of jet, curled, and turned to the right .... He has the straight limbs of a Brahmā .... He has seven convexities ... He has the upper torso of a lion.... The furrow between his shoulders is filled in .... He has the proportions of a banyan tree; the spread of his arms equals the height of his body, and the height of his body equals the spread of his arms .... His neck and shoulders are even .... His sense of taste is supremely acute .... He is lion-jawed .... He has forty teeth .... His teeth are even .... His teeth have no gaps between .... His teeth are quite white .... He has a large tongue .... He has a divine voice, like that of the Karavīka bird .... His eyes are very black .... He has the eyelashes of an ox .... In the space between his eyebrows he has down growing, which is white with the sheen of soft cotton .... His head is shaped like a turban—this also is a mark of the Great Man in him. So Master Gotama is endowed with these thirty-two marks of the Great Man.

"When he walks, he steps out with the right foot first. He does not extend his foot too far or put it down too near. He walks neither too quickly nor too slowly. He walks without his knees knocking together. He walks without his ankles knocking together. He walks without raising or lowering his thighs or bringing them together or keeping them apart. When he walks, only the lower part of his body oscillates, and he walks with no bodily effort. When he turns to look, he does so with his whole body. He does not look vertically down. He does not look vertically up. He does not walk looking about. He looks a plough-yoke's length before him; beyond that he has the vision of unhindered knowledge.

"When he goes indoors, he does not raise or lower his body or bend it forward or back. He turns round neither too far from the seat nor too near it. He does not lean on the seat with his hand. He does not throw his body down on to the seat.

"When seated indoors, he does not fidget with his hands. He does not fidget with his feet. He does not sit with his knees crossed. He does not sit with his ankles crossed. He does not sit with his hand holding his chin. When seated indoors, he is not afraid; he does not shiver and tremble, he is not nervous; his hair does not stand up on that account, and he is intent on seclusion.

"When he receives water for the bowl, he does not raise or lower the bowl or tip it forwards or backwards. He receives neither too little nor too much water for the bowl. He washes the bowl without splashing. He washes the bowl without turning it about. He does not put the bowl on the floor to wash his hands; when his hands are washed, the bowl is washed; and when the bowl is washed, his hands are washed. He pours the water for the bowl away neither too far nor too near, and he does not pour it about.

"When he receives rice, he does not raise or lower the bowl or tip it forwards or backwards. He receives neither too little nor too much rice. He adds sauces in the right proportion; he does not exceed the right amount of sauce in the mouthful. He turns the mouthful over three or four times in his mouth and then swallows it; and no rice grain enters his body unmasticated nor does any remain in his mouth; then he takes another mouthful. He takes his food experiencing the taste without experiencing greed for the taste. The food he takes has five factors: it is neither for amusement nor for intoxication nor for smartening nor for embellishing but only for the endurance and continuance of this body, for the ending of discomfort, and for assisting the holy life: 'Thus I shall terminate old feelings without arousing new feelings, and I shall live in comfort, healthy and blameless.'

"When he has eaten and receives water for the bowl, he does not raise or lower the bowl or tip it forwards or backwards. He receives neither too little nor too much water for the bowl. He washes the bowl without making a splashing noise. He washes the bowl without turning it about. He does not put the bowl on the floor to wash his hands; when his hands are washed, the bowl is washed; when the bowl is washed, his hands are washed. He pours the water for the bowl neither too far nor too near, and he does not pour it about.

"When he has eaten, he puts the bowl on the floor neither too far nor too near; and he is neither careless of the bowl nor over-solicitous about it.

"When he has eaten, he sits in silence for a while, but he does not let the time for the blessing go by. When he gives the blessing after eating, he does not do so criticizing that meal or expecting another meal; he instructs, urges, rouses and encourages that audience with talk purely on the Dhamma. When he has finished that, he rises from his seat and departs.

"He walks neither too fast nor too slow, and he does not go as one does who wants to get away.

"His robe is worn neither too high nor too low on his body, nor tight against his body nor loose on his body, nor does the wind blow his robe away from his body. Dust and dirt do not soil his body.

"When he has gone to the forest, he sits down on a seat made ready. Having sat down, he washes his feet. He does not concern himself with pedicure. After washing his feet he seats himself crosslegged, sets his body erect and establishes mindfulness in front of him. He does not occupy his mind with self-affliction or affliction of others or affliction of both; he sits with his mind set on his own welfare, on others' welfare and on the welfare of both; in fact, on the welfare of the whole world.

"When he goes to the monastery, he teaches the Dhamma to an audience. He neither flatters nor berates that audience; he instructs, urges, rouses and encourages that audience with talk purely on the Dhamma. The speech issuing from his mouth has eight qualities: it is distinct, intelligible, melodious, audible, ringing, incisive, deep, and sonorous; but while his voice is intelligible as far as the confines of the audience, his speech does not extend beyond that audience. When the people have been instructed, urged, roused and encouraged by him, they rise from their seats and depart, looking only to him and concerned with nothing else.

"Sir, we have seen Master Gotama walking, we have seen him standing, we have seen him indoors seated in silence, we have seen him indoors eating, we have seen him indoors sitting in silence after eating, we have seen him giving the blessing after eating, we have seen him going to the monastery, we have seen him sitting in the monastery in silence, we have seen him in the monastery teaching the Dhamma to an audience. Such is Master Gotama. Such he is and more than that."

When this was said, the Brahman Brahmāyu rose from his seat, and arranging his upper robe on one shoulder, he raised his hands palms together towards where the Blessed One was, and he uttered this exclamation three times: "Honour to the Blessed One, accomplished and fully enlightened! Honour to the Blessed One, accomplished and fully enlightened! Honour to the Blessed One, accomplished and fully enlightened! Now suppose some time or other we were to meet Master Gotama. Suppose we had some conversation together."

M. 91

At one time the Blessed One was living at Campā on the banks of the Gaggarā Lake. Then one midday the householder Vajjiyamāhita went out from Campā to see the Blessed One. But on the way he thought: "It is not yet time to see the Blessed One; he is in retreat. And it is not yet time to see the meditative bhikkhus; they are in retreat. Suppose I went to the park belonging to the wanderers of other sects?"

He went there. At that time the wanderers of other sects had met together, and they were sitting talking all kinds of low talk, shouting with a loud noisy clamour. Seeing the householder Vajjiyamāhita coming in the distance, they quieted each other, saying: "Sirs, let there be no noise. Do not make a noise. The householder Vajjiyamāhita is coming, and he is a follower of the monk Gotama. If there are any white-clothed laymen living in Campā who are followers of the monk Gotama, he is one of them. Those worthy people like little noise and are trained to make little noise, and they recommend making little noise. Perhaps, if he finds that ours is a congregation little given to noise, he will think it one worth his while to approach."

Then the wanderers were silent. The householder Vajjiyamāhita went up to them and exchanged greetings. Then he sat down at one side. They asked him: "Householder, is it true, as it seems, that the monk Gotama disapproves of austerity and condemns and censures without qualification everyone who leads the hard life of austerity?"

"That is not so, Lords. The Blessed One disapproves of what should be disapproved of and recommends what should be recommended. But in doing so he is one who speaks with discrimination, he is not one who makes one-sided utterances."

Then a certain wanderer said to him: "Wait a moment, householder, this monk Gotama whom you praise is a nihilist (one to lead away): he does not describe anything, according to what you say of him."

"On the contrary, Lords, I say with justification to the venerable ones that the Blessed One has described how certain things are wholesome and how certain things are unwholesome. So since he describes that he is one who does describe something, not one who does not."

When this was said, the wanderers were silent.

A. 10:94

NARRATOR TWO. Saccaka, a Nigaṇṭha's son, came to dispute with the Buddha at Vesālī. The Buddha described how his struggle before the Enlightenment led to his discovery that mortification led nowhere. He said:

FIRST VOICE. "I have had experience of teaching the Dhamma to an assembly of many hundreds. Perhaps someone has fancied: 'The monk Gotama is preaching the Dhamma on my personal account.' But it should not be regarded so. A Perfect One preaches the Dhamma to others in order to give them knowledge. When the talk is over, then I steady my mind in myself, quiet it, bring it to singleness and concentrate it on that same object of consciousness on which I was concentrating before."

"That is to be expected since Master Gotama is accomplished and fully enlightened. But has Master Gotama ever slept by day?"

"In the last month of the hot season, on returning from the alms round after the meal, I have had experience of laying out my outer robe of patches folded in four and lying down on my right side, falling asleep mindful and fully aware."

"Some monks and brahmans call that a deluded man's abiding."

"It is not in that way that a man is either deluded or not deluded. Him I call deluded in whom the taints that defile, that renew being, ripen in future suffering and lead to birth, ageing and death, are unabandoned; for it is with the non-abandoning of taints that a man is deluded. Him I call undeluded in whom these taints are abandoned; for it is with the abandoning of taints that a man is undeluded. Just as a palm tree with its crown cut off is incapable of growing, so too in a Perfect One these taints are abandoned, cut off, severed at the root, made like a palm stump, done away with and not subject to future arising."

When this was said, Saccaka observed: "It is wonderful, Master Gotama, it is marvellous how, when Master Gotama is attacked again and again with personal remarks, the colour of his skin brightens, the colour of his face clears, as happens in one who is accomplished and fully enlightened! I have had experience of engaging Pūraṇa Kassapa in argument, and then he prevaricated and diverted the talk and even showed anger, hate and surliness. And likewise with Makkhali Gosāla and the rest. And now, Master Gotama, we depart; we are busy and have much to do."

M. 36

NARRATOR TWO. Saccaka, however, was unconvinced and retained his own views.

NARRATOR ONE. There is an incident which shows that the Buddha was not immune from illness.

FIRST VOICE. At one time the Blessed One was living in Nigrodha's Park at Kapilavatthu in the Sakyan country. He had only just recovered from a sickness. Then Mahānāma the Sakyan went to him and said: "Lord, I have long known the Dhamma to be taught by the Blessed One thus: 'Knowledge is for one who is concentrated, not for one who is unconcentrated.' Does concentration come first, Lord, and knowledge afterwards, or knowledge first and concentration afterwards?"

The venerable Ānanda thought: "The Blessed One has only just recovered from a sickness, and this Sakyan Mahānāma asks him a very profound question. Suppose I take Mahānāma aside and teach him the Dhamma?"

He did so, and he said: "The Blessed One has declared the learner's virtue, concentration and understanding, and he has declared the adept's virtue, concentration and understanding. The learner's virtue is that of a bhikkhu who is virtuous, restrained with the Pātimokkha restraint, perfect in conduct and resort, and who, seeing fear in the slightest fault, trains by giving effect to the precepts of virtue. His concentration is that of a bhikkhu who enters upon and dwells in one of the four meditations. His understanding is that of a bhikkhu who understands as it actually is: 'This is suffering, this is the origin of suffering, this is the cessation of suffering, this is the way leading to the cessation of suffering.' Now in the case of the adept, the noble disciple who already has such virtue, concentration and understanding, by realization himself with direct knowledge here and now enters upon and dwells in the deliverance of mind and the deliverance by understanding[5] that are taintless because of exhaustion of taints."

A. 3:73

NARRATOR ONE. The Buddha was of normal height. This may be presumed from the story of his exchange of robes with the Elder Mahā-Kassapa, which will be given later, and from the following incident.

SECOND VOICE. The occasion was this. The Blessed One was living at Sāvatthī in Jeta's Grove, Anāthapiṇḍika's Park, and at that time the venerable Nanda, the son of the Blessed One's aunt, was there. He was handsome, inspiring faith and confidence; and he was four finger-breadths shorter than the Blessed One. He used to wear a robe of the same measurement as the Sublime One's robe, and when the elder bhikkhus saw the venerable Nanda coming in the distance, they mistook him for the Blessed One, and so they rose from their seats. But when he arrived they found out their mistake. They disapproved, and they murmured and protested: "How can the venerable Nanda wear a robe of the same measurement as the Sublime One's robe?"

They told the Blessed One. He rebuked the venerable Nanda, and he made this training rule: "Any bhikkhu who should wear a robe of the measurement of the Sublime One's robe commits an offence involving expiation. The measurements of the Sublime One's robe are: nine spans long and six spans across, of the Sublime One's span."

Vin. Sv. Pāc. 92

NARRATOR ONE. The story of the Elder Vakkali is appropriate here because it illustrates the Buddha's attitude to bodily presence.

FIRST VOICE. Thus I heard. Once when the Blessed One was living at Rājagaha in the Bamboo Grove, the Squirrels' Sanctuary, the venerable Vakkali was living in a potter's house. He was afflicted, suffering and gravely ill. He told his attendants: "Friends, go to the Blessed One and pay homage to him on my behalf with your heads at his feet, and say: 'Lord, the bhikkhu Vakkali is afflicted, suffering and gravely ill; he pays homage with his head at the Blessed One's feet.' And say this: 'Lord, it would be good if the Blessed One went to the bhikkhu Vakkali out of compassion.' "

"Yes, friend," the bhikkhus replied. They went to the Blessed One, and they gave him the message and the request. The Blessed One consented in silence. Then he dressed, and taking his bowl and outer robe, he went to the venerable Vakkali. The venerable Vakkali saw him coming and tried to get up from his bed. The Blessed One said: "Enough, Vakkali. Do not get up from your bed. There are seats ready; I shall sit down there." He sat down on one of the seats made ready. Then he said: "I hope it goes well with you, Vakkali; I hope you are comfortable, that your pains are departing, not increasing, that they seem to be getting less, not more."

"Lord, it is not going well with me. I have no comfort. My pains are increasing, not departing; they seem to be getting more, not less."

"I hope you have no worry and remorse, Vakkali?"

"Surely, Lord, I have no little worry and remorse."

"I hope, then, you have nothing to reproach yourself with on account of virtuous conduct?"

"I have nothing to reproach myself with on account of virtuous conduct, Lord."

"If not, Vakkali, then what is your worry and remorse about?"

"Lord, I have long wanted to come and see the Blessed One, but I have never had bodily strength enough to do so."

"Enough, Vakkali; why do you want to see this filthy body? He who sees the Dhamma sees me; he who sees me sees the Dhamma. For it is when he sees the Dhamma that he sees me; and it is when he sees me that he sees the Dhamma. How do you conceive this, Vakkali, is material form permanent or impermanent?"

NARRATOR TWO. The Buddha went on to repeat the discourse as he had given it to the bhikkhus of the group of five after the Enlightenment.

FIRST VOICE. Now when the Blessed One had given the venerable Vakkali this instruction, he rose from his seat and went to the Vulture Peak Rock.

Soon after he had gone the venerable Vakkali told his attendants: "Come, friends, put me on a bed and take me to the Black Rock on the slopes of Isigili. How can one like me think of dying in a house?"

"Yes, friend," they replied, and they did so.

The Blessed One passed the rest of that day and that night on the Vulture Peak Rock. When the night was over, he addressed the bhikkhus: "Come, bhikkhus, go to the bhikkhu Vakkali and tell him this: 'Friend Vakkali, hear what deities have told the Blessed One. Last night two deities of marvellous appearance, who illuminated the whole of the Vulture Peak Rock, went to the Blessed One, and after paying homage to him, one deity said: "Lord, the bhikkhu Vakkali has his heart set on liberation." And the other deity said: "Lord, he will certainly be completely liberated." And the Blessed One tells you this, friend, "Do not be afraid, Vakkali, do not be afraid. Your death will be innocent of evil; the completion of your time will be innocent of evil." ' "

"Even so, Lord," they replied. Then they went to the venerable Vakkali and told him: "Friend, hear a message from the Blessed One and from two deities."

The venerable Vakkali told his attendants: "Come, friends, take me down from the bed; for how can one like me think of hearing the Blessed One's message sitting on a high seat?"

"Yes, friend," they replied, and they did as he had asked. Then the message was given him.

He said: "Now, friends, pay homage on my behalf to the Blessed One with your heads at his feet, and say: 'Lord, the bhikkhu Vakkali is afflicted, suffering and gravely ill; he pays homage with his head at the Blessed One's feet, and he says this: "Lord, I do not doubt that material form, feeling, perception, formations, and consciousness are impermanent. I have no uncertainty that what is impermanent is suffering. I have no desire or lust or affection for what is impermanent, painful and subject to change; of that too I have no uncertainty." ' "

"Yes, friend," they replied. Then they departed. Soon after they had gone the venerable Vakkali took his own life.

When the bhikkhus had gone to the Blessed One and told him the venerable Vakkali's words, he said: "Let us go to the Black Rock on the slopes of Isigili, bhikkhus, where clansman Vakkali has taken his own life."

"Even so, Lord," they replied. Then the Blessed One went to the Black Rock on the slopes of Isigili with a number of bhikkhus. He saw from a distance the venerable Vakkali's senseless body lying on a bed. But at the same time a smoky haze, a sombre shadow, was moving to the east and to the west and to the north and to the south and to all the intermediate directions. Then the Blessed One said to the bhikkhus: "Bhikkhus, do you see that smoky haze, that sombre shadow?"

"Yes, Lord."

"Bhikkhus, that is Māra the Evil One. He is searching for the clansman Vakkali's consciousness: 'Where has the clansman Vakkali's consciousness established itself?' But, bhikkhus, the clansman Vakkali has attained final Nibbāna without his consciousness becoming established anywhere at all."

S. 22:87

NARRATOR ONE. There are several instances related in the Piṭakas of bhikkhus taking their own lives. This was pronounced by the Buddha to be blameless only on one condition: that the bhikkhu was already an Arahant, without lust, hate or delusion, or would certainly become one before his death, and that the taking of his own life subject to that condition was merely the terminating of an incurable disease. Otherwise, the taking of human life, or the recommendation of death, constitutes one of the four Defeats, or capital offences which entail permanent expulsion from the Sangha (the other three being theft, sexual intercourse, and knowingly making false claims to spiritual attainments), though attempted suicide is a minor wrongdoing.

NARRATOR TWO. It was related earlier how the Buddha named the six Buddhas that preceded him. He also named the Buddha who will next succeed him in the future, which will be after his own teaching and all memory of him have completely vanished from the world.

FIRST VOICE. "When the human life span shall have increased to eighty thousand years, the Blessed One Metteyya, accomplished and fully enlightened, will arise in the world, perfect in knowledge and conduct, sublime, a knower of worlds, an incomparable leader of men to be tamed, a teacher of gods and men, enlightened, blessed, just as I am now. He will himself realize with direct knowledge, and declare, this world with its deities, its Māras and its Brahmā divinities, this generation with its monks and brahmans, with its princes and men, just as I have done now. He will teach the Dhamma that is good in the beginning, good in the middle and good in the end, with the meaning and the letter, and will explain the holy life that is utterly perfect and pure, just as I have done now."

D. 26

This was said by the Blessed One, said by the Accomplished One, so I heard: "Bhikkhus, I am a brahman, used to liberality and open-handed; I bear my last body; I am the supreme physician. You are the children of my breast, born of my lips, born of the Dhamma, heirs in the Dhamma, not in material things. There are two kinds of gifts: the gift of material things and the gift of the Dhamma. The greater of these is the gift of the Dhamma."

Iti. 100

"Now, bhikkhus, if others should ask a bhikkhu: 'What are the evidences and certainties owing to which you, venerable sir, say: "The Blessed One is fully enlightened, the Dhamma is well proclaimed, the Sangha has entered upon the good way"?' then, answering rightly, you would answer thus: 'Here, friends, I approached the Blessed One for the sake of hearing the Dhamma. The teacher showed me the Dhamma at each successively higher stage, at each superior level, with dark and bright counterparts. According as he did so, by arriving at direct knowledge here of a certain teaching (namely, one of the four stages in the path of realization) among the teachings taught in the Dhamma, I reached my goal: then I had confidence in the teacher thus: "The Blessed One is fully enlightened, the Dhamma is well proclaimed, the Sangha has entered upon the good way." ' When anyone's faith in the Perfect One is planted and rooted and established with these evidences, these phrases and these syllables, then his faith is called supported by evidence, rooted in vision, sound, and invincible by monk or brahman or Māra or Brahmā or anyone in the world."

M. 47

"When Master Gotama's disciples are advised and instructed by him, do they all attain the supreme goal of Nibbāna, or do some not attain it?"

"Some do, brahman, and some do not."

"Why is that, Master Gotama, since there is Nibbāna, and the way leading to it, and Master Gotama as guide?"

"Now as to that, brahman, I shall ask you a question in return. Answer it as you like. How do you conceive this: are you familiar with the road that leads to Rājagaha?'

"Yes, Master Gotama, I am."

"How do you conceive this: suppose a man came who wanted to go to Rājagaha, and he approached you and said, 'Sir, show me the road to Rājagaha,' and then you told him: 'Now, good man, this road goes to Rājagaha. Follow it for a while and you will see a certain village, then a certain town, then Rājagaha with its gardens and groves and lands and lakes'; then, having been thus advised and instructed by you, he took a wrong road and went on to the west. And then a second man appeared, and after asking the same question and receiving the same advice and instruction from you, he got safely to Rājagaha. Now since there is Rājagaha, and the way leading to it, and yourself as guide, why is it that of these two men, advised and instructed by you, one takes a wrong road and goes on to the west and one gets safely to Rājagaha?"

"What have I to do with that, Master Gotama? I am simply one who shows the way."

"So too, brahman, there is Nibbāna, and the way leading to it, and myself as guide, yet when my disciples are advised and instructed by me, some attain Nibbāna and some do not. What have I to do with that, brahman? A Perfect One is simply one who shows the way."

M. 107 (condensed)

Once some wanderers of other sects went to the venerable Anurādha and asked him: "Friend Anurādha, one who is a Perfect One, highest of men, the supreme among men, one attained to the supreme attainment, when a Perfect One is describing him, in which of the four following instances does he describe him: After death a Perfect One is; or after death a Perfect One is not; or after death a Perfect One both is and is not; or after death a Perfect One neither is nor is not?'[6]

"Friends, a Perfect One in describing him describes him apart from these four instances."

When this was said they remarked: "This will be a new bhikkhu or an Elder not long gone forth who is foolish and inexperienced." Then, having no confidence in the venerable Anurādha and thinking him newly gone forth and foolish, they got up from their seats and went away. Then, soon after they had gone he wondered: "If they had questioned me further, how should I have answered them so that I might say what the Blessed One says without misrepresenting him with what is not fact and might express ideas in accordance with the Dhamma with nothing legitimately deducible from my assertions that would provide grounds for condemning me?" So he went to the Blessed One and told him about this.

"How do you conceive this, Anurādha, is material form permanent or impermanent?"—"Impermanent, Lord."

NARRATOR TWO. The Buddha then continued as he had done in the Second Sermon preached to the bhikkhus of the group of five, after which he asked:

"How do you conceive this, Anurādha: do you see material form as the Perfect One?"—"No, Lord."—"Do you see feeling ... perception ... formations ... consciousness as the Perfect One?"—"No, Lord."

"How do you conceive this, Anurādha: do you see the Perfect One as in material form?"—"No, Lord."—"Do you see the Perfect One as apart from material form?"—"No, Lord."—"Do you see the Perfect One as in feeling ... as apart from feeling ... as in perception ... as apart from perception ... as in formations ... as apart from formations ... as in consciousness ... as apart from consciousness?"—"No, Lord."

"How do you conceive this, Anurādha: do you see the Perfect One as material form, feeling, perception, formations and consciousness?"—"No, Lord."

"How do you conceive this, Anurādha: do you see this Perfect One as having no material form, no feeling, no perception, no formations, no consciousness?"—"No, Lord."

"Anurādha, when a Perfect One is here and now unapprehendable by you as true and established, is it fitting to say of him: 'Friends, one who is a Perfect One, highest of men, the supreme among men, one attained to the supreme attainment, when a Perfect One is describing him, he describes him apart from the following four instances: After death a Perfect One is; or after death a Perfect One is not; or after death a Perfect One both is and is not; or after death a Perfect One neither is nor is not?' "

"No, Lord."

"Good, good, Anurādha. What I describe, now as formerly, is suffering and the cessation of suffering."

S. 44:2

"Why are these questions not answered by a Perfect One? Because they all treat of a Perfect One after death in terms of form (and the rest)" (S. 44:3). "Because they are asked by one who is not free from desire, love, thirst, fever, and craving for form (and the rest)" (S. 44:5). "Because they are asked by one who relishes form (and the rest) and also being and clinging and craving, and who does not know how these things cease" (S. 44:6). "Such questions belong to the thicket of views ... the fetter of views: they are connected with suffering, anguish, despair and fever, and they do not lead to dispassion, fading, stilling, direct knowledge, enlightenment, Nibbāna"

(M. 72).

"One who is Thus-gone (Tathāgata, a Perfect One)[7] is here and now unknowable, I say. So saying, so proclaiming, I have been baselessly, vainly, falsely, and wrongly misrepresented by certain monks and brahmans thus: 'The monk Gotama is one who leads away (to annihilation); for he describes the annihilation, the loss, the non-being, of an existing creature.' "

M. 22

"There are these three types of acquisition of self: the gross, the mind-constituted, and the formless.... The first has (material) form, consists of the four great entities and consumes physical food. The second has form and is constituted by mind with all the limbs and lacking no faculty. The third is formless and consists in perception .... I teach the Dhamma for the abandoning of acquisitions of self in order that in you, who put the teaching into practice, defiling qualities may be abandoned and cleansing qualities increased, and that you may, by realisation yourselves here and now with direct knowledge, enter upon and abide in the fullness of understanding's perfection.... If it is thought that to do that is a painful abiding, that is not so; on the contrary, by doing that there is gladness, happiness, tranquillity, mindfulness, full awareness, and a pleasant abiding."

NARRATOR TWO. The Buddha went on to say that from one

rebirth to another any one of these three kinds of acquisition of self can succeed another. That being so, it cannot be successfully argued that only one of them is true and the others wrong; one can only say that the term for any one does not fit the other two; just as, with milk from a cow, curd from milk, butter from curd, ghee from butter, and fine-extract of ghee from ghee, the term of each fits only that and none of the others, yet they are not disconnected. The Buddha concluded:

FIRST VOICE. "These are worldly usages, worldly language, worldly terms of communication, worldly descriptions, by which a Perfect One communicates without misapprehending them."

D. 9 (condensed)

12
The Doctrine

CONTENTS

Various Questions 206

There is No First Beginning 212

The Four Noble Truths 212

The Truth of Suffering 214

The Truth of the Origin of Suffering 219

The Truth of the Cessation of Suffering 222

The Truth of the Way 224

1. Right View 224
2. Right Intention 237
3. Right Speech 238
4. Right Action 238
5. Right Livelihood 239
6. Right Effort 239
7. Right Mindfulness 240
8. Right Concentration 246

The Noble Eightfold Path in Practice 251

The Means 255

The End 256

12
THE DOCTRINE

NARRATOR ONE. What is the "Dhamma" that was "well proclaimed" by the "Supreme Physician"? Is it an attempt to make a complete description of the world? Is it a metaphysical system?

FIRST VOICE. The Blessed One was once living at Sāvatthī in Jeta's Grove. A deity called Rohitassa came to him late in the night, paid homage to him and asked: "Lord, the world's end where one neither is born nor ages nor dies nor passes away nor reappears: is it possible to know or see or reach that by travelling there?"

"Friend, that there is a world's end where one neither is born nor ages nor dies nor passes away nor reappears, which is to be known or seen or reached by travelling there—that I do not say. Yet I do not say that there is ending of suffering without reaching the world's end. Rather it is in this fathom-long carcase with its perceptions and its mind that I describe the world, the origin of the world, the cessation of the world, and the way leading to the cessation of the world.

"It is utterly impossible
To reach by walking the world's end;
But none escape from suffering
Unless the world's end has been reached.

"It is a Sage, a knower of the world,
Who gets to the world's end, and it is he
By whom the holy life has been lived out;
In knowing the world's end he is at peace
And hopes for neither this world nor the next."

S. 2:36; A. 4:46

The Blessed One was once living at Kosambī in a wood of siṃsapa trees. He picked up a few leaves in his hand, and he asked the bhikkhus: "How do you conceive this, bhikkhus, which is more, the few leaves that I have picked up in my hand or those on the trees in the wood?"

"The leaves that the Blessed One has picked up in his hand are few, Lord; those in the wood are far more."

"So too, bhikkhus, the things that I have known by direct knowledge are more: the things that I have told you are only a few. Why have I not told them? Because they bring no benefit, no advancement in the holy life, and because they do not lead to dispassion, to fading, to ceasing, to stilling, to direct knowledge, to enlightenment, to Nibbāna. That is why I have not told them. And what have I told you? 'This is suffering; this is the origin of suffering; this is the cessation of suffering; this is the way leading to the cessation of suffering.' That is what I have told you. Why have I told it? Because it brings benefit, and advancement in the holy life, and because it leads to dispassion, to fading, to ceasing, to stilling, to direct knowledge, to enlightenment, to Nibbāna. So, bhikkhus, let your task be this: This is suffering, this is the origin of suffering, this is the cessation of suffering, this is the way leading to the cessation of suffering."

S. 56:31

NARRATOR ONE. It is not, then, an attempt to make some complete description of the world, either internal or external. Is it a metaphysical system—a consistent logical construction—and if so, what premise is it based on?

FIRST VOICE. Once when the Blessed One had gone into Rājagaha for alms the naked ascetic Kassapa went up to him, and after greeting him, he said: "We would ask Master Gotama something, if Master Gotama would consent to give an answer."—"It is not the time for questions, Kassapa; we are among houses." He asked a second and a third time and received the same reply. Then he said: "It is not much we want to ask, Master Gotama."—"Ask, then, Kassapa, whatever you like."

"How is it, Master Gotama, is suffering of one's own making?" "Do not put it like that, Kassapa."—"Then is suffering of another's making?"—"Do not put it like that, Kassapa."—"Then is suffering both of one's own and another's making?"—"Do not put it like that, Kassapa."—"Then is suffering neither of one's own nor another's making but fortuitous?"—"Do not put it like that, Kassapa."—"Then is there no suffering?"—"It is not a fact that there is no suffering: there is suffering, Kassapa."—"Then does Master Gotama neither know nor see suffering?"—"It is not a fact that I neither know nor see suffering: I both know and see suffering, Kassapa."

S. 12:17

Once too the wanderer Uttiya went to the Blessed One, and after greeting him, he sat down at one side. Then he asked: "How is it, Master Gotama, the world is eternal: is only that the truth and everything else wrong?"—"That is not answered by me, Uttiya."—"Then the world is not eternal: is only that the truth and everything else wrong?"—"That too is not answered by me, Uttiya."—"The world is finite: is only that the truth and everything else wrong?"—"That too is not answered by me, Uttiya."—"Then the world is infinite: is only that the truth and everything else wrong?"—"That too is not answered by me, Uttiya."—"The soul is the same as the body: is only that the truth and everything else wrong?"—"That too is not answered by me, Uttiya."—"Then the soul is one and the body another: is only that the truth and everything else wrong?"—"That too is not answered by me, Uttiya."—"After death a Perfect One is: is only that the truth and everything else wrong?"—"That too is not answered by me, Uttiya."—"Then after death a Perfect One is not: is only that the truth and everything else wrong?"—"That too is not answered by me, Uttiya."—"Then after death a Perfect One both is and is not: is only that the truth and everything else wrong?"—"That too is not answered by me, Uttiya."—"Then after death a Perfect One neither is nor is not: is only that the truth and everything else wrong?"—"That too is not answered by me, Uttiya."

"But why does Master Gotama decline to answer when I ask him these questions? What then is answered by Master Gotama?"

"I teach the Dhamma to disciples from direct knowledge, Uttiya, for purification of beings, for surmounting sorrow and lamentation, for ending pain and grief, for attainment of the true goal, for realizing Nibbāna."

"Master Gotama, does that Dhamma provide an outlet from suffering for all the world, or for half, or for a third?"

When this was said, the Blessed One remained silent.

Then the venerable Ānanda thought: "The wanderer Uttiya must not conceive any such pernicious view as 'When the monk Gotama is asked a question peculiar to me and to no one else and he founders and does not answer, is it because he is unable?' That would be long for his harm and suffering." So he said to him: "Friend Uttiya, I shall give you a simile; for some wise men here get to know through a simile the meaning of what is said. Suppose a king had a city with strong ditches, ramparts and bastions, and a single gate, and he had a wise, clever, sagacious gate-keeper there who stopped those whom he did not know and admitted only those whom he knew; and since he had himself gone round the path encircling the city and had seen no gaps in the ramparts or any hole even big enough for a cat to pass through, he might conclude that living beings above a certain size must go in and out through the gate—so too, friend Uttiya, a Perfect One's concern is not that 'All the world shall find an outlet by this, or a half, or a third,' but rather that 'Whoever has found or finds or will find an outlet from the world of suffering, that is always done by abandoning the five hindrances (of desire for sensuality, ill will, lethargy-and-drowsiness, agitation-and-worry, and uncertainty), defilements that weaken understanding, and by maintaining in being the seven factors of enlightenment with minds well established on the four foundations of mindfulness.' Your question which you put to the Blessed One was framed in the wrong way; that was why the Blessed One did not answer it."

A. 10:95

On another occasion the wanderer Vacchagotta went to the Blessed One and exchanged greetings with him. Then he asked: "How is it, Master Gotama, does self exist?" When this was said, the Blessed One was silent. "How is it, then, Master Gotama, does self not exist?" And for a second time the Blessed One was silent. Then the wanderer Vacchagotta got up from his seat and went away. Not long after he had gone the venerable Ānanda asked the Blessed One: "Lord, how is it that when the Blessed One was questioned he did nor answer?"

"If, when I was asked 'Does self exist?' I had answered 'Self exists,' that would have been the belief of those who hold the theory of eternalism. And if, when I was asked 'Does self not exist?'

I had answered 'Self does not exist,' that would have been the belief of those who hold the theory of annihilationism. Again, if, when asked 'Does self exist?' I had answered 'Self exists,' would that have been in conformity with my knowledge that all things are not-self? And if, when asked 'Does self not exist?' I had answered 'Self does not exist,' then confused as he already is, Ānanda, the wanderer Vacchagotta would have become still more confused, assuming: 'Surely then I had a self before and now have none.' "

S. 44:10

At one time the Blessed One was living at Sāvatthī, and at that time a number of wandering monks and brahmans of various sects had gone into Sāvatthī for alms. They had differing views, opinions and notions, and they relied for support on their differing views. There were some monks and brahmans who asserted and believed that "The world is eternal: only this is true, everything else is wrong," and some who asserted and believed each of the other nine views. They quarreled, brawled, wrangled and wounded each other with verbal darts: "The Dhamma is like this; the Dhamma is not like this! The Dhamma is not like this; the Dhamma is like this!"

Then a number of bhikkhus, on their return from their alms round, told the Blessed One about it. The Blessed One said:

"Bhikkhus, there was once a certain king in Sāvatthī. He told a man: 'Come, man, get together all the men in Sāvatthī who have been born blind.'—'Yes, sire,' he replied. And when he had done so, he told the king, who said, 'Then show them an elephant.' He did so, saying, 'You men blind from birth, an elephant is like this,' and he showed the elephant's head to some and its ear to others and its tusk to others and its trunk to others and its body to others and its foot to others and its rump to others and its tail to others and the tuft at the end of its tail to others. Then he went to the king and told him what he had done. So the king went to the men blind from birth, and he asked them: 'Has an elephant been shown to you?'—'Yes, sire.'—'Then describe what the elephant is like.' Now those who had been shown the head said 'Sire, the elephant is like a jar,' and those shown the ear said 'It is like a winnowing basket,' and those shown the tusk said 'It is like a post,' and those shown the trunk said 'It is like a plough's pole,' and those-shown the body said 'It is like a granary,' and those shown the foot said 'It is like the base of a column,' and those shown the rump said 'It is like a mortar,' and those shown the tail said 'It is like a pestle,' and those shown the tuft at the end of the tail said 'It is like a broom.' They fought among themselves with their fists, crying: 'The elephant is like this; it is not like this! The elephant is not like this; it is like this!' But the king was pleased. So too the wanderers of other sects are blind and eyeless. That is why they quarrel, brawl, wrangle and wound each other with verbal darts: 'The Dhamma is like this; the Dhamma is not like this! The Dhamma is not like this; the Dhamma is like this!' "

Ud. 6:4

NARRATOR ONE. So it would appear to be a mistake to call the Buddha's teaching either an attempt to describe the world completely or a metaphysical system built up by logic. Is it, then, an ethical commandment, a revealed religion of faith, or simply a stoical code of behaviour? Before an attempt can be made to find answers to those questions, some sort of a survey of the doctrines taught is needed. The material contained in the Discourses seems, in fact, to be rather in the nature of material for a map, for each to make his own map, but all oriented alike. These oriented descriptions of facets of experience, in fact, enable a person to estimate his position and judge for himself what he had better do. The Discourses offer not so much a description as a set of overlapping descriptions. Close examination of existence finds always something of the qualities of the mirage and of the paradox behind the appearance. The ends can never be made quite to meet. The innumerable different facets presented in the Suttas with countless repetitions of certain of these facets in varying combinations and contexts remind one of a collection of air photographs from which maps are to be made. The facets in the Discourses are all oriented to cessation of suffering, the four points of their compass being the Four Noble Truths. Let us try and make a specimen map out of some of this material. In this case, since a start has to be made somewhere, we can start for our baseline with birth, which, like death, is to the ordinary man an everyday fact and at the same time an insoluble mystery.

THERE IS NO FIRST BEGINNING

NARRATOR TWO. Is consciousness conceivable without a past? Can it be said to have a beginning?

FIRST VOICE. "Bhikkhus, the round is beginningless. Of the beings that travel and trudge through this round, shut in as they are by ignorance and fettered by craving, no first beginning is describable."

S. 15:1

"That both I and you have had to travel and trudge through this long round is owing to our not discovering, not penetrating, four truths. What four? They are: (I) the noble truth of suffering, (II) the noble truth of the origin of suffering, (III) the noble truth of the cessation of suffering, and (IV) the noble truth of the way leading to the cessation of suffering."

D. 16

THE FOUR NOBLE TRUTHS

NARRATOR TWO. Now here is a description of the Four Noble Truths.

FIRST VOICE. I "What is the noble truth of suffering? Birth is suffering, ageing is suffering, sickness is suffering, death is suffering; sorrow and lamentation, pain, grief and despair are suffering; association with the loathed is suffering, dissociation from the loved is suffering, not to get what one wants is suffering; in short, the five aggregates affected by clinging are suffering."[1]

S. 56:11

II. "What is the noble truth of the origin of suffering? It is craving, which renews being, and is accompanied by relish and lust, relishing this and that: in other words, craving for sensual desires, craving for being, craving for non-being. But whereon does this craving arise and flourish? Wherever there is that which seems lovable and gratifying, thereon it arises and flourishes."

D. 22

"It is with ignorance as condition that formations come to be; with formations as condition, consciousness; with consciousness as condition, name-and-form; with name-and-form as condition, the sixfold base for contact; with the sixfold base as condition, contact; with contact as condition, feeling; with feeling as condition, craving; with craving as condition, clinging; with clinging as condition, being; with being as condition, birth; with birth as condition, ageing and death come to be, and also sorrow and lamentation, pain, grief and despair; that is how there is an origin to this whole aggregate mass of suffering. This is called the noble truth of the origin of suffering."

A. 3:61

III. "What is the noble truth of the cessation of suffering? It is the remainderless fading and cessation of that same craving, the rejecting, relinquishing, leaving and renouncing of it. But whereon is this craving abandoned and made to cease? Wherever there is that which seems lovable and gratifying, thereon it is abandoned and made to cease."

D. 22

With the remainderless fading and cessation of ignorance there is cessation of formations; with cessation of formations, cessation of consciousness ... with cessation of birth, ageing and death cease, and also sorrow and lamentation, pain, grief and despair; that is how there is a cessation to this whole aggregate mass of suffering. This is called the noble truth of the cessation of suffering."

A. 3:61

IV. "What is the noble truth of the way leading to the cessation of suffering? It is this Noble Eightfold Path, that is to say: right view, right intention, right speech, right action, right livelihood, right effort, right mindfulness, and right concentration."

D. 22

"Of these Four Noble Truths, the noble truth of suffering must be penetrated to by full knowledge of suffering; the noble truth of the origin of suffering must be penetrated to by abandoning craving; the noble truth of the cessation of suffering must be penetrated to by realizing cessation of craving; the noble truth of the way leading to the cessation of suffering must be penetrated to by maintaining in being the Noble Eightfold Path."

S. 56:11 and 29 (adapted)

"These Four Noble Truths (Actualities) are real, not unreal, not other than they seem."

S. 56:27

NARRATOR ONE. The Four Noble Truths are each analysed and defined in detail.

I THE TRUTH OF SUFFERING

NARRATOR TWO. It was said that the truth of suffering was "in short, the five aggregates affected by clinging." Here are definitions of them.

FIRST VOICE. "What are the five aggregates affected by clinging? They are the (material) form aggregate affected by clinging, the feeling aggregate affected by clinging, the perception aggregate affected by clinging, the formations aggregate affected by clinging, and the consciousness aggregate affected by clinging."

D. 22

"Why does one say 'form'? It is deformed (*ruppati*), that is why it is called 'form' (*rūpa*). Deformed by what? By cold and heat and hunger and thirst, by contact with gadflies, gnats, wind, sunburn and creeping things."

S. 22:79

"What is form? The four great entities and any form derived upon them by clinging are called form."

S. 22:56

"Whatever in oneself, belonging to oneself, is solid, solidified, and clung to (organic), such as head-hairs, body-hairs, nails, teeth, skin; flesh, sinews, bones, bone-marrow, kidneys; heart, liver, midriff, spleen, lights; bowels, entrails, gorge, dung, or whatever else in oneself, belonging to oneself, is solid, solidified, and clung to: that is called earth element[2] in oneself. Now earth element in oneself and external earth element are only earth element.

"Whatever in oneself ... is water, watery, and clung to, such as bile, phlegm, pus, blood, sweat, fat; tears, grease, spittle, snot, oil of the joints, urine, or whatever else in oneself... is water, watery, and clung to: that is called water element in oneself. Now water element in oneself and external water element are only water element.

"Whatever in oneself ... is fire, fiery, and clung to, such as that whereby one is warmed, ages, and is consumed, and whereby what is eaten, drunk, chewed and tasted gets digested and assimilated, or whatever else in oneself ... is fire, fiery, and clung to: that is called fire element in oneself. Now fire element in oneself and external fire element are only fire element.

"Whatever in oneself ... is air, airy, and clung to, such as up-going winds (forces), down-going winds (forces), winds (forces) in the belly and in the bowels, winds (forces) that pervade all the limbs, in-breath and out-breath, or whatever else in oneself ... is air, airy, and clung to: that is called air element in oneself. Now air element in oneself and external air element are only air element.

"Also whatever in oneself ... is space, spatial, and clung to, such as ear-hole, nose-hole, mouth-hole, mouth-door, and that (aperture) whereby what is eaten, drunk, chewed and tasted is swallowed, and that wherein it is contained, and that whereby it passes out below, or whatever else in oneself ... is space, spatial, and clung to: that is called space element. Now space element in oneself and external space element are only space element ... And space element has nowhere any standing of its own."

M. 62

"Any form whatever, whether past, future, or present, in oneself or external, coarse or fine, inferior or superior, far or near, that is affected by taints and provocative of clinging: that is called the form aggregate affected by clinging."

S. 22:48

"Why does one say 'feeling'? It is felt, that is why it is called feeling. Felt as what? Felt as pleasure, as pain, or as neither-pain-nor-pleasure."

S. 22:79; cf. M. 43

"Whatever is felt bodily or mentally as pleasant and gratifying is pleasant feeling. Whatever is felt bodily or mentally as painful and hurting is painful feeling. Whatever is felt bodily or mentally as neither gratifying nor hurting is neither-painful-nor-pleasant feeling .... Pleasant feeling is pleasant in virtue of presence and painful in virtue of change. Painful feeling is painful in virtue of presence and pleasant in virtue of change. Neither-painful-nor-pleasant feeling is pleasant in virtue of knowledge and painful in virtue of want of knowledge."

M. 44

"There are these six bodies of (such) feeling: feeling born of eye-contact, of ear-contact, of nose-contact, of tongue-contact, of body-contact, and of mind-contact."

S. 22:56

"Any feeling whatever ... that is affected by taints and provocative of clinging: that is called the feeling aggregate affected by clinging."

S. 22:48

"Why does one say 'perception'? It perceives, that is why it is called perception. Perceives what? It perceives, for example, blue and yellow and red and white."

S. 22:79

"There are these six bodies of perception: perception of (visible) forms, of sounds, of odours, of flavours, of tangibles, and of ideas."

S. 22:56

"Any perception whatever ... that is affected by taints and provocative of clinging: that is called the perception aggregate affected by clinging."

S. 22:48

"Why does one say 'formations'? They form the formed, that is why they are called formations. What is the formed that they form? (Material) form as the state (essence) of form is the formed (compounded) that they form (compound); feeling as the state of feeling is the formed that they form; perception as the state of perception is the formed that they form; formations as the state of formations is the formed that they form; consciousness as the state of consciousness is the formed that they form." [3]

S. 22:79

"Three kinds of formations: formation of merit (as action which ripens in pleasure), formation of demerit (as action which ripens in pain), and formation of imperturbability (as action, namely, meditation, which ripens in the formless states, which for as long as they last are unperturbed by perception of form, resistance or difference)."

D. 33

"Three formations: in-breaths and out-breaths belong to a body, these are things bound up with a body, that is why they are a bodily formation. Having previously thought and explored, one breaks into speech, that is why thinking and exploring are a verbal formation. Perception and feeling belong to consciousness, these are things bound up with consciousness, that is why they are a mental formation."

M. 44; cf. M. 9

"What are formations? There are six bodies of choice:[4] choice among visible forms, sounds, odours, flavours, tangibles, and mental objects."

S. 22:56

"Choice I call action."

A. 6:63

"Any formations whatever ... that are affected by taints and provocative of clinging: these are called the formations aggregate affected by clinging."

S. 22:48

"Why does one say 'consciousness'? It cognizes, that is why it is called consciousness. Cognizes what? It cognizes, for example, the sour, bitter, pungent, sweet, alkaline, unalkaline, salty, and unsalty."

S. 22:79

"What does that consciousness cognize? It cognizes, for example, that there is pleasure, that there is pain, that there is neither-pain-nor-pleasure."

M. 43, 140

"There are these six bodies of consciousness: eye-consciousness, ear-, nose-, tongue-, body-, and mind-consciousness."

S. 22:56

"Consciousness is called after the conditions due to which it arises. When consciousness arises due to eye and forms, it is called eye-consciousness; due to ear and sounds, ear-consciousness; ... due to mind and ideas, mind-consciousness."

M. 38

"Feeling, perception and consciousness are conjoined, not disjoined, and it is impossible to separate each from each in order to describe their different potentialities; for what one feels, that one perceives, and what one perceives, that one cognizes. By bare mind-consciousness disjoined from the five sense-faculties the (external) base consisting of infiniteness of space can be known thus 'infinite space'; the (external) base consisting of infiniteness of consciousness can be known thus 'infinite consciousness'; and the (external) base consisting of nothingness can be known thus 'there is nothing at all.' A knowable idea is understood by the eye of understanding."

M. 43

"Consciousness depends for its being upon a duality (the duality of the in-oneself and the external bases for contact)."

S. 35:93

"Any consciousness whatever, whether past, future or present, in oneself or external, coarse or fine, inferior or superior, far or near, that is affected by taints and provocative of clinging: that is called the consciousness aggregate affected by clinging."

S. 22:48

"These five aggregates affected by clinging have desire for their root .... The four great entities (of earth, water, fire, and air) are the cause and condition for describing the form aggregate. Contact is the cause and condition for describing the aggregates of feeling, perception and formations. Name-and-form is the cause and condition for describing the consciousness aggregate."

M. 109

"Whatever monks or brahmans recollect their past life in its various modes, they all recollect the five aggregates affected by clinging or one or another of them."

S. 22:79

II THE TRUTH OF THE ORIGIN OF SUFFERING

NARRATOR TWO. Here are detailed definitions of the second noble truth.

FIRST VOICE. "These five aggregates affected by clinging have desire for their root .... The clinging is neither the same as the five aggregates affected by clinging, nor is it something apart from them. It is the desire and lust comprised in them that is the clinging there."

M. 109

"That comes to be when there is this; that arises with the arising of this."[5]

M. 38

"(In the statement of dependent arising:)[6] What is *ageing*? In the various orders of beings, it is any being's ageing, old age, brokenness of teeth, greyness of hair and wrinkledness, decline of life and weakening of sense-faculties. What is *death*? In the various orders of beings, it is any being's passing, passing away, dissolution, disappearance, dying, completion of time, dissolution of aggregates, laying down of the carcase. What is *birth*? In the various orders of beings, it is any being's birth, coming to birth, precipitation in a womb, generation, manifestation of aggregates, acquisition of bases for contact. What is *being*? Three kinds of being are: being in the mode of sensual desire, being in the mode of form, being in the mode of the formless. What is *clinging*? There are four varieties of clinging: clinging as the habit of sensual desire, clinging as the habit of wrong view, clinging as the habit of (misapprehension of) virtue and duty,[7] and clinging as the habit of self-theories. What is *craving*? There are six bodies of craving: craving for visible forms, sounds, odours, flavours, tangibles, and ideas. What is *feeling*? There are six bodies of (the three sorts of) feeling: feeling born of eye-contact, of ear-contact, of nose-contact, of tongue-contact, of body-contact, and of mind-contact. What is *contact*?[8] There are six bodies of contact: eye-contact, ear-contact, nose-contact, tongue-contact, body-contact, mind-contact. What is *the sixfold base*? It is the eye-base, ear-base, nose-base, tongue-base, body-base, and mind-base. What is *name-and-form*?[9] What is called *name* comprises feeling, perception, choice,[10] contact, and attention; what is called *form* comprises the four great entities and any forms derived upon them by clinging; so this name and this form are what is called name-and-form. What is *consciousness*? There are six bodies of consciousness: eye-consciousness, ear-consciousness, nose-consciousness, tongue-consciousness, body-consciousness, and mind-consciousness. What are *formations*? Three formations are: the bodily formation, verbal formation, and mental formation. What is *ignorance*? It is nescience about suffering, about the origin of suffering, about the cessation of suffering, and about the way leading to the cessation of suffering."

S. 12:2

"Dependent on eye and visible forms, eye-consciousness arises; the coincidence of the three is contact; with contact as condition, feeling; with feeling as condition, craving; that is how there is an origin to suffering (and so with ear ... mind)."

S. 12:43

"Inflamed by lust, incensed by hate, confused by delusion, transcended by them and his mind obsessed, a man chooses for his own affliction, for others' affliction, and for the affliction of both, and experiences pain and grief."

A. 3:55

"Beings are owners of actions, heirs of actions, they have actions as their progenitor, actions as their kin (and responsibility), actions as their home-refuge; it is actions that differentiate beings into the inferior and superior."

M. 135

"What is old action? Eye, ear, nose, tongue, body, mind, are old action (already) determined and chosen that must be experienced to be seen. What is new action? It is whatever action one does now, whether by body, speech or mind."

S. 35:145

"This body is not yours or another's, but is past action (already) determined and chosen that must be experienced to be seen."

S. 12:37

"It is choice that I call action; it is in choosing that a man acts by body, speech and mind. There are actions whose ripening will be experienced in hell, in the animal womb, in the realm of ghosts, among human beings, and in heavenly worlds. Actions ripen in three ways: they can ripen here and now, on reappearance, or in some life-process beyond that."

A. 6:63

"Actions done out of lust or hate or delusion ripen wherever an individual selfhood is generated, and wherever those actions ripen, there their ripening is experienced, whether here and now or on next reappearance or in some life-process beyond that."

A. 3:33

"There are four incalculables, which cannot be calculated, an attempt to calculate which would lead to frustration and madness. What four? They are the objective field of the Buddhas, the objective field of one who has acquired the meditations, the ripening of action, and the calculation of the world."

A. 4:77

"The world is led by mind."

S. 1:72

III THE TRUTH OF THE CESSATION OF SUFFERING

NARRATOR TWO. Here are detailed definitions of the third noble truth.

FIRST VOICE. "That does not come to be when there is not this; that ceases with the cessation of this."

M. 38

"Dependent on eye and visible forms, eye-consciousness arises; the coincidence of the three is contact; with contact as condition, there arises what is felt as pleasant or as painful or as neither-painful-nor-pleasant. If, on experiencing the contact of pleasant feeling, one does not relish it or welcome it or accept it, and if no underlying tendency in one to lust for it any longer underlies it—if, on experiencing the contact of painful feeling, one does not sorrow or lament or beat one's breast, weep and become distraught, and if no underlying tendency in one to resistance to it any longer underlies it—if, on experiencing the contact of neither-painful-nor-pleasant feeling, one understands, as it actually is, the arising, disappearance, gratification, dangerous inadequacy, and escape, in the case of that feeling, and if no underlying tendency in one to ignorance any longer underlies it—then, indeed, that one shall make an end of suffering by abandoning the underlying tendency to lust for pleasant feeling, by eliminating the underlying tendency to resist painful feeling, and by abolishing the underlying tendency to ignore neither-painful-nor-pleasant feeling: that is possible."

M. 148

"When lust, hate and delusion are abandoned, a man does not choose for his own affliction or for others' affliction or for the affliction of both. In that way there comes to be extinction here and now, without delay, inviting inspection, onward-leading, and experienceable by the wise."

A. 3:55

"Actions done out of non-lust, non-hate and non-delusion, done when lust, hate and delusion have disappeared, are abandoned, cut off at the root, made like a palm stump, done away with, and are no more subject to future arising."

A. 3:33

"Formless states are more peaceful than states of form; cessation is more peaceful than formless states."[11]

Iti. 73

"There is that (external) base where no earth (is), or water or fire or air or base consisting of infinity of space or base consisting of infinity of consciousness or base consisting of nothingness or base consisting of neither-perception-nor-non-perception or this world or the other world or moon or sun; and that I call neither a coming nor a going nor a staying nor a dying nor a reappearance; it has no basis, no evolution, no support; it is the end of suffering.

"The Unaffected is hard to see;
It is not easy to see Truth.
To know is to uncover craving;
To see is to have done with owning.

"There is an unborn, an un-brought-to-being, an unmade, an unformed. If there were not, there would be no escape made known here for one who is born, brought to being, made, formed. But since there is an unborn, an un-brought-to-being, an unmade, an unformed, an escape is therefore described for one who is born, brought to being, made, formed."

Ud. 8:1-3

"There are two elements of Nibbāna. What two? There is the element of Nibbāna with result of past clinging still left, and the element of Nibbāna without result of past clinging left. What is the element of Nibbāna with result of past clinging still left? Here a bhikkhu is an Arahant with taints exhausted, who has lived out the life, done what was to be done, laid down the burden, reached the highest goal, destroyed the fetters of being, and who is completely liberated through final knowledge. His five sense-faculties remain, owing to the presence of which he still encounters the agreeable and disagreeable, still experiences the pleasant and painful. It is the exhaustion of lust, of hate, and of delusion in him that is called the element of Nibbāna with result of past clinging still left. And what is the element of Nibbāna without result of past clinging left? Here a bhikkhu is an Arahant who has lived out the life ... and is completely liberated through final knowledge. All in him that is felt will, since he does not relish it, become cool here in this very life: this is called the element of Nibbāna without result of past clinging left."

Iti. 44

"That which is the exhaustion of lust, of hate, and of delusion, is called Nibbāna."

S. 38:1

"Just as a flame blown by the wind's force,
Upasīva," said the Blessed One,
"Goes out, and designation applies to it no more,
So too the Silent Sage, being freed from the name-body,
Goes out, and designation applies to him no more."

"Then when he has thus gone out, does he exist no more?
Or is he made immortal for eternity?
So may it please the Sage to make this plain to me,
Because it is a state that he has understood."

"There is no measuring of one who has gone out,
Upasīva,' said the Blessed One,
"And nothing of him whereby one could say aught of him;
For when all ideas have been abolished,
All ways of saying, too, have been abolished."

Sn. 5:7

IV THE TRUTH OF THE WAY

NARRATOR TWO. The fourth noble truth is the Noble Eightfold Path. Each of its eight components needs a separate definition.

(1) RIGHT VIEW

FIRST VOICE. "Just as the dawn heralds and foretells the rising of the sun, so right view heralds and foretells the penetration to the Four Noble Truths according as they really are."

S. 56:37

NARRATOR TWO. Right view has many facets. Let us take them one by one, beginning with "ripening of action," which, in certain forms and with some reservations, is also shared by other teachings.

FIRST VOICE. "Right view comes first.[12] How? One understands wrong view as wrong view, and one understands right view as right view. What is wrong view? The view that there is nothing given, offered or sacrificed,[13] no fruit or ripening of good and bad actions, no this world, no other world, no mother, no father, no apparitional beings, no good and virtuous monks and brahmans who have themselves realized by direct knowledge and declare this world and the other world: this is wrong view.

"What is right view? There are two kinds of right view: there is that affected by taints, which brings merit and ripens in the essentials of existence; and there is the noble ones' right view without taints, which is supramundane and a factor of the path. What is right view affected by taints? The view that there is what is given, offered and sacrificed, and that there is fruit and ripening of good and bad actions, and there is this world and the other world and mother and father and apparitional beings and good and virtuous monks and brahmans who have themselves realized by direct knowledge and declare this world and the other world: this is right view affected by taints which brings merit and ripens in the essentials of existence. And what is the noble ones' right view? Any understanding, understanding faculty, understanding power, investigation-of-states enlightenment factor, right view as path factor, in one whose mind is ennobled and taintless, who possesses the path, and who maintains it in being: this is the noble ones' right view without taints, which is supramundane and a factor of the path."

M. 117

NARRATOR TWO. Again, it is right view of dependent arising—the basic structure of the "teaching peculiar to Buddhas" and the first of the new discoveries made by the Buddha. Nothing can arise alone without the support of other things on which its existence depends.

SECOND VOICE.

The Perfect One has told the cause
Of causally arisen things;
And what brings their cessation too:
Such is the doctrine preached by the Great Monk.

"The spotless, immaculate vision of the Dhamma arose in him: All that is subject to arising is subject to cessation."

Vin. Mv. 1:23

FIRST VOICE. "That comes to be when there is this; that arises with the arising of this. That does not come to be when there is not this; that ceases with the cessation of this."

M. 38

"He who sees dependent arising sees the Dhamma; he who sees the Dhamma sees dependent arising."

M. 28

"Whether Perfect Ones appear or not, there remains this element, this structure of things (phenomena), this certainty in things, namely: specific conditionality. A Perfect One discovers it."

S. 12:20

"If there were no birth altogether in any way of anything anywhere ... there being no birth, with the cessation of birth, could ageing and death be described?"—"No, Lord."—"Consequently this is a reason, a source, an origin, a condition, for ageing and death." (And so on with the other pairs in the formula of dependent arising.)

D. 15

"Lord, 'right view, right view' is said. What does 'right view' refer to?"—"Usually, Kaccāyana, this world depends upon the dualism of existence and non-existence. But when one sees the world's origin as it actually is with right understanding, there is for him none of (what is called) non-existence in the world; and when he sees the world's cessation as it actually is with right understanding, there is for him none of (what is called) existence in the world.

"Usually the world is shackled by bias, clinging and insistence; but one such as this (who has right view), instead of allowing bias, instead of clinging, and instead of deciding about 'my self,' with such bias, such clinging, and such mental decision in the guise of underlying tendency to insist, he has no doubt or uncertainty that what arises is only arising suffering, and what ceases is only ceasing suffering, and in this his knowledge is independent of others. That is what 'right view' refers to. '(An) all exists' is one extreme; '(an) all does not exist' is the other extreme. Instead of resorting to either extreme, a Perfect One expounds the Dhamma by the middle way: 'It is with ignorance as condition that formations come to be; with formations as condition, consciousness; with consciousness ...' (And so on with both arising and cessation.)"

S. 12:15

"If one asserts: 'He who makes (suffering) feels (it): being one existent from the beginning, his suffering is of his own making,' then one arrives at eternalism. But if one asserts: 'One makes (suffering), another feels (it): being one existent crushed out by feeling, his suffering is of another's making,' then one arrives at annihilationism. Instead of resorting to either of these extremes, a Perfect One expounds the Dhamma by the middle way: ... (that is, by dependent arising and cessation)."

S. 12:17

"All beings are maintained by nutriment."

D. 33; A. 10:27, 28; Khp. 2

"What is nutriment? There are these four kinds of nutriment for the maintenance of beings that already are, and for the assistance of those seeking renewal of being: they are physical food as nutriment, gross or subtle, contact as the second, choice as the third, and consciousness as the fourth."

S. 12:63; M. 38

NARRATOR TWO. The very essence of right view is, however, understanding of the Four Noble Truths, which embrace dependent arising and constitute the "teaching peculiar to Buddhas." They formed the subject of the First Sermon.

FIRST VOICE. "What is right view? It is knowledge of suffering, of the origin of suffering, of the cessation of suffering, and of the way leading to the cessation of suffering: this is called right view."

S. 45:8; D. 22

(I) " 'Four venomous snakes' is a name for the four great entities (of earth, water, fire, and air)."

S. 35:197

Form is like a lump of froth,
Feelings like a water bubble,
Perception too is like a mirage,
Formations like a plaintain trunk.[14]
And consciousness, the Sun's Kinsman shows,
Seems nothing but a conjuring trick.

S. 22:95

"The six bases in oneself can be termed an empty village; for whether a wise man investigates them as to the eye, ear, nose, tongue, body, or mind, they appear alike hollow, empty and void. The six external bases can be termed village-raiding robbers; for the eye is harassed among agreeable and disagreeable forms, the ear among such sounds, the nose among such odours, the tongue among such flavours, the body among such tangibles, and the mind among such mental objects."

S. 35:197

(II) In the world I see this generation racked by
craving for being
Wretched men gibbering in the face of Death,
Still craving, hoping, for some kind of being.
See how they tremble over what they claim as "mine,"
Like fishes in the puddles of a failing stream.

Sn. 4:2

(III) "This is (the most) peaceful, this is (the goal) superior (to all), that is to say, the stilling of all formations, the relinquishing of all essentials of existence, the exhaustion of craving, cessation, Nibbāna."

A. 10:60

(IV) The greatest of (worldly) gains is health;
Nibbāna is the greatest bliss;
The eightfold path is the best of paths,
To lead in safety to the Deathless.

M. 75

NARRATOR TWO. Again it is right view of the three general characteristics of impermanence, suffering (or insecurity), and not-self, which express comprehensively what dependent arising expresses structurally. They were the subject of the Second Sermon.

FIRST VOICE. "There are three formed characteristics of what is formed:[15] arising is evident, fall is evident, and alteration of what is present is evident. There are three unformed characteristics of what is unformed: no arising is evident, no fall is evident, and no alteration of what is present is evident."

A. 3:47

"When one understands how form, feeling, perception, formations, and consciousness (and how the eye, etc.) are impermanent, one therein possesses right view."

S. 22:51; 35:155

"All is impermanent. And what is the all that is impermanent? The eye is impermanent, forms are impermanent, eye-consciousness ... eye-contact, whatever is felt as pleasant, painful or neither-painful-nor-pleasant born of eye-contact is impermanent. The ear, etc .... The nose, etc .... The tongue, etc .... The body, etc .... The mind is impermanent, mental objects ... mind-consciousness ... mind-contact ... whatever is felt ... born of mind-contact is impermanent."

S. 35:43

"What is impermanent is suffering, what is suffering is not-self."

S. 35:1; 22:46

"Whether Perfect Ones appear or not, there remains this element, this structure of things (phenomena), this certainty in things: All formations are impermanent; all formations are suffering; all things are not-self."

A. 3:134

"Bhikkhus, I do not dispute with the world: the world disputes with me. One who proclaims the Dhamma disputes with no one in the world. What wise men in the world say there is not, that I too say there is not; and what wise men in the world say there is, that I too say there is. Wise men in the world say there is no permanent, everlasting, eternal form which is not subject to change, and I too say that there is none. (And so too of the other four aggregates.) Wise men in the world say that there is impermanent form, which is suffering and subject to change, and I too say that there is. (And so with the other four.)"

S. 22:94

"This body is impermanent, it is formed and it is dependently arisen."

S. 36:7

"It would be better for an untaught ordinary man to treat as self this body, which is constructed upon the four great entities, than mentality.[16] Why? Because this body can last one year, two years ... a hundred years; but what is called 'mentality' and 'mind' and 'consciousness' arises and ceases differently through night and day, just as a monkey ranging through a forest seizes a branch, and, letting that go, seizes another."

S. 12:61

"Fruitful as the act of giving is ... yet it is still more fruitful to go with confident heart for refuge to the Buddha, the Dhamma and the Sangha and undertake the five precepts of virtue .... Fruitful as that is ... yet it is still more fruitful to maintain loving-kindness in being for only as long as the milking of a cow ... fruitful as that is ... yet it is still more fruitful to maintain perception of impermanence in being only for as long as the snapping of a finger."

A. 9:20 (condensed)

"Whosoever relishes the eye, etc., relishes suffering, and he will not be freed from suffering, I say."

S. 35:19

"What is the ripening of suffering? When someone is overcome, and his mind is obsessed by suffering, either he sorrows and laments, and beating his breast, he weeps and becomes distraught, or else he undertakes a search externally: 'Who is there that knows one word, two words, for the cessation of suffering?' I say that suffering either ripens in confusion or in search."

A. 6:63

"That anyone should see formations as pleasure ... or Nibbāna as suffering, and have a liking that is in conformity (with truth) is not possible. (But the opposite) is possible."

A. 6:99

"All form, feeling, perception, formations, and consciousness, of whatever kind, whether past, future or present, in oneself or external, coarse or fine, inferior or superior, far or near, should be regarded as it actually is thus: 'This is not mine, this is not what I am, this is not my self.' "

S. 22:59

"That in the world by which one perceives the world and conceives conceits about the world is called 'the world' in the Noble One's Discipline. And what is it in the world with which one does that? It is with the eye, ear, nose, tongue, body, and mind."

S. 35:116

"It is being worn away (*lujjati*), that is why it is called 'the world' (*loka*)."

S. 35:82

"Void world, void world' is said, Lord; in what way is 'void world' said?"—"It is because of what is void of self and self's property that 'void world' is said, Ānanda. And what is void of self and self's property? The eye ... forms ... eye-consciousness ... eye-contact ... any feeling ... born of eye-contact ... The ear, etc ....

The nose, etc .... The tongue, etc .... The body, etc .... The mind, etc .... any feeling whether pleasant, painful or neither-painful-nor-pleasant born of mind-contact is void of self and self's property."

S. 35:85

"When a bhikkhu abides much with his mind fortified by perception of impermanence, his mind retreats, retracts, and recoils from gain, honour and renown instead of reaching out to it, just as a cock's feather or a shred of sinew thrown on a fire retreats, retracts and recoils from it instead of reaching out to it .... When he abides much with his mind fortified by perception of suffering in impermanence, there is established in him vivid perception of fear, of laxity, indolence, idleness, negligence, and failure in devotion and reviewing, as of a murderer with poised weapon .... When he abides much with his mind fortified by perception of not-self in suffering, his mind is rid of the conceits that treat in terms of I and 'mine' this body with its consciousness and all external signs."

A. 7:46

NARRATOR TWO. The rationalized "self-theory," which is called, in whatever form it may take, "both a view and a fetter," is based upon a subtle fundamental distortion in the act of perceiving, the "conceit 'I am,' " which is "a fetter, but not a view." Now self-theories may or may not be actually formulated; but if they are, they cannot be described specifically without reference to the five aggregates. For that reason they can, when described, all be reduced to one of the types of what is called the "embodiment view,"[17] which is set out schematically. These are all given up by the stream-enterer, though the conceit "I am" is not.

FIRST VOICE. "How does there come to be the embodiment view?"—"Here the untaught ordinary man who has no regard for noble ones and is unconversant with their Dhamma and Discipline ... sees form as self, or self as possessed of form, or form as in self, or self as in form. (And so with each of the other four aggregates: feeling, perception, formations and consciousness.) A well-taught noble disciple does not do this."

M. 44; M.109

"The untaught ordinary man who has no regard for noble ones ... gives unreasoned (uncritical) attention in this way: 'Was I in the past? Was I not in the past? What was I in the past? How was I in the past? Having been what, what was I in the past? Shall I be in the future? Shall I not be in the future? What shall I be in the future? How shall I be in the future? Having been what, what shall

I be in the future?' Or else he wonders about himself now in the presently arisen period in this way: 'Am I? Am I not? What am I? How am I? Whence has this being come? Whither is it bound?'

"When he gives unreasoned attention in this way, then one of six types of view arises in him as true and established: 'My self exists' or 'My self does not exist' or 'I perceive self with self' or 'I perceive not-self with self' or 'I perceive self with not-self' or some such view as 'This is my self that speaks and feels and experiences here or there the ripening of good and bad actions; but this my self is permanent, everlasting, not subject to change, and will endure as long as eternity.' This field of views is called the thicket of views, the wilderness of views, the contortion of views, the vacillation of views, the fetter of views. The untaught ordinary man bound by the fetter of views is not freed from birth, ageing and death, sorrow and lamentation, pain, grief and despair: he is not freed from suffering, I say."

M. 2

"Bhikkhus, there are two kinds of (wrong) view, and when deities and human beings are in their grip, some hang back and some overreach; it is only those with vision that see. How do some hang back? Deities and human beings love being, delight in being, enjoy being; when the Dhamma is expounded to them for the ending of being, their hearts do not go out to it or acquire confidence, steadiness and decision. So some hang back. And how do some overreach? Some are ashamed, humiliated and disgusted by that same being, and they look forward to non-being in this way: 'Sirs, when with the dissolution of the body this self is cut off, annihilated and accordingly after death no longer is, that is the most peaceful, that is the goal superior to all, that is reality.' So some overreach. And how do those with vision see? Here a bhikkhu sees whatever has come to being as come to being. By seeing it thus he has entered upon the way to dispassion for it, to the fading and ceasing of lust for it. That is how one with vision sees."

Iti. 49

"Bhikkhus, the possession that one might possess that were permanent, everlasting ... do you see any such possession?"—"No, Lord."—"... The self-theory clinging whereby one might cling that would never arouse sorrow and ... despair in him who clung thereby; do you see any such self-theory clinging?"—"No, Lord."—"... The view as support that one might take as support that would never arouse sorrow and ... despair in him who took it as support; do you see any such view as support?"—"No, Lord."—"...Bhikkhus, there being self, would there be self's property?"—"Yes, Lord."—"And there being self's property, would there be self?."—"Yes, Lord."—"Bhikkhus, self and self's property being unapprehendable as true and established, then would not this view—'This is the world, this the self; after death I shall be permanent, everlasting, eternal, not subject to change, I shall endure as long as eternity'—be the pure perfection of a fool's idea?"—"How could it not be, Lord? It would be the pure perfection of a fool's idea."

M. 22

"Whenever any monks or brahmans see self in its various forms, they all of them see the five aggregates affected by clinging, or one or another of them. Here an untaught ordinary man who disregards noble ones ... sees form as self, or self as possessed of form, or form as in self, or self as in form (or he does likewise with the other four aggregates). So he has this (rationalized) seeing, and he has also this (fundamental) attitude 'I am'; but as long as there is the attitude 'I am' there is organization of the five faculties of eye, ear, nose, tongue, and body. Then there is mind, and there are ideas, and there is the element of ignorance. When an untaught ordinary man is touched by feeling born of the contact of ignorance, it occurs to him 'I am' and 'I am this' and 'I shall be' and 'I shall not be' and 'I shall be with form' and 'I shall be formless' and 'I shall be percipient' and 'I shall be unpercipient' and 'I shall be neither percipient nor unpercipient.' But in the case of the well-taught noble disciple, while the five sense faculties remain as they are, his ignorance about them is abandoned and true knowledge arisen. With that it no more occurs to him 'I am' or ... 'I shall be neither percipient nor unpercipient.' "

S. 22:47

NARRATOR TWO. The ordinary man is unaware of the subtle fundamental attitude, the underlying tendency or conceit 'I am.' It makes him, in perceiving a percept, automatically and simultaneously conceive in terms of 'I,' assuming an I-relationship to the percept, either as identical with it or as contained within it, or as separate from it, or as owning it. This attitude, this conceiving, is only given up with the attainment of Arahantship, not before. (See e.g. M. 1 and M. 49.)

FIRST VOICE. " 'I am' is derivative, not underivative. Derivative upon what? Derivative upon form, feeling, perception, formations, and consciousness."

S. 22:83

"When any monk or brahman, with form (and the rest) as the means, which is impermanent, suffering and subject to change, sees thus 'I am superior' or 'I am equal' or 'I am inferior,' what is that if not blindness to what actually is?"

S. 22:49

(Questioned by Elders, the Elder Khemaka said:) "I do not see in these five aggregates affected by clinging any self or self's property ... yet I am not an Arahant with taints exhausted. On the contrary, I still have the attitude 'I am' with respect to these five aggregates affected by clinging, although I do not see 'I am this' with respect to them .... I do not say 'I am form' or 'I am feeling' or 'I am perception' or 'I am formations' or 'I am consciousness,' nor do I say 'I am apart from form ... apart from consciousness'; yet I still have the attitude 'I am' with respect to the five aggregates affected by clinging although I do not see 'I am this' with respect to them. Although a noble disciple may have abandoned the five more immediate fetters (see below), still his conceit 'I am,' desire 'I am,' underlying tendency 'I am,' with respect to the five aggregates affected by clinging remains as yet unabolished. Later he abides contemplating rise and fall thus: 'Such is form, such is its origin, such its disappearance' (and so with the other four), till by so doing, his conceit 'I am' eventually comes to be abolished."

S. 22:89

NARRATOR TWO. Lastly, we come to the ten fetters, which are progressively broken by the four stages of realization.

FIRST VOICE. "An untaught ordinary man who disregards

noble ones ... lives with his heart possessed and enslaved by the embodiment view, by uncertainty, by misapprehension of virtue and duty[18] by lust for sensuality, and by ill will, and he does not see how to escape from them when they arise; these, when they are habitual and remain uneradicated in him, are called the more immediate fetters."

M. 64

"The five more remote fetters are: lust for form, lust for the formless, conceit (the conceit 'I am'), distraction, and ignorance."

D. 33

"There are bhikkhus who, with the exhaustion of (the first) three fetters, have entered the stream, are no more subject to perdition, certain of rightness, and destined to enlightenment. There are bhikkhus who, with the exhaustion of three fetters and the attenuation of lust, hate and delusion, are once-returners: returning once to this world, they will make an end of suffering. There are bhikkhus who, with the destruction of the five more immediate fetters, are destined to reappear spontaneously elsewhere and will there attain final Nibbāna, never returning meanwhile from that world. There are bhikkhus who are Arahants with taints exhausted, who have lived out the life, done what was to be done, laid down the burden, reached the highest goal, destroyed the fetters of being, and who are completely liberated through final knowledge."

M. 118

"That which is the exhaustion of lust, of hate, and of delusion is called Arahantship.'

S. 38:2

"When a bhikkhu travels in many countries, learned people of all stations will ask him questions. Learned and inquiring people will ask 'What does the venerable one's teacher tell, what does he preach?' Rightly answering you can say: 'Our teacher preaches the removal of desire and lust.' And if you are then asked 'Removal of desire and lust for what?' you can answer: 'Removal of desire and lust for form (and the rest).' And if you are then asked 'But what inadequacy (danger) do you see in those things?' you can answer:

'When a person is not without lust and desire and love and thirst and fever and craving for these things, then with their change and alteration, sorrow and lamentation, pain, grief and despair arise in him.' And if you are then asked 'And what advantage do you see in doing thus?' you can answer: 'When a person is free from lust and desire and love and thirst and fever and craving for form, feeling, perception, formations, and consciousness, then, with their change and alteration, no sorrow and lamentation, pain, grief and despair arise in him."

S. 22:2

(2) RIGHT INTENTION

NARRATOR TWO. The survey of right view is now concluded. The next factor of the Noble Eightfold Path is right intention.

FIRST VOICE. "What is right intention? It is the intention of renunciation, the intention of non-ill will, the intention of non-cruelty: this is called right intention."

S. 45:8; D. 22

"When a noble disciple has clearly seen with right understanding, as it actually is, how little gratification sensual desires provide and how much pain and despair they entail, and how great is their inadequacy, and he attains to happiness and pleasure dissociated from sensual desires and unwholesome states, or to something higher than that, then he is no more interested in sensual desires."

M. 14

"Even if bandits brutally severed him limb from limb with a two-handled saw, he who entertained hate in his heart on that account would not be one who followed my teaching."

M. 21

"He does not choose for his own affliction, or for others' affliction, or for the affliction of both."

M. 13

(3) RIGHT SPEECH

NARRATOR TWO. These two factors of right view and right intention together constitute (the group of path factors) "understanding" (*paññā*). Now the third factor, right speech.

FIRST VOICE. "What is right speech? Abstention from lying, slander, abuse, and gossip; this is called right speech."

S. 45:8; D. 22

"Here someone abandons lying: when summoned to a court or to a meeting or to his relatives' presence or to his guild or to the royal family's presence and questioned as a witness thus 'So, good man, tell what you know,' then, not knowing, he says 'I do not know,' knowing, he says 'I know,' not seeing, he says 'I do not see,' seeing, he says 'I see'; he does not in full awareness speak falsehood for his own ends or for another's ends or for some petty worldly end. He abandons slander: as one who is neither a repeater elsewhere of what is heard here for the purpose of causing division from these, nor a repeater to these of what is heard elsewhere for the purpose of causing division from those, who is thus a reuniter of the divided, a promoter of friendships, enjoying concord, rejoicing in concord, delighting in concord, he becomes a speaker of words that promote concord. He abandons abuse: he becomes a speaker of such words as are innocent, pleasing to the ear and lovable, as go to the heart, are civil, desired of many and dear to many. He abandons gossip: as one who tells that which is seasonable, factual, good, and the Dhamma and Discipline, he speaks in season speech worth recording, which is reasoned, definite, and connected with good."

M. 41

(4) RIGHT ACTION

NARRATOR TWO. And the fourth factor, right action.

FIRST VOICE. "What is right action? Abstention from killing living beings, stealing, misconduct in sensual desires: this is called right action."

S. 45:8; D. 22

"When a lay follower possesses five things, he lives with confidence in his house, and he will find himself in heaven as sure as if he had been carried off and put there. What are the five? He abstains from killing living beings, from taking what is not given, from misconduct in sensual desires, from speaking falsehood, and from indulging in liquor, wine, and fermented brews."

A. 5:172-73

(5) RIGHT LIVELIHOOD

NARRATOR TWO. And the fifth factor, right livelihood.

FIRST VOICE. "What is right livelihood? Here a noble disciple abandons wrong livelihood and gets his living by right livelihood."

S. 45:8; D. 22

"Scheming (to deceive), persuading, hinting, belittling, and pursuing gain with gain; this is called wrong livelihood (for bhikkhus)."

M. 117

There are five trades that a lay follower should not ply. What five? They are: trading in weapons, living beings, meat, liquor, and poisons."

A. 5:177

(6) RIGHT EFFORT

NARRATOR TWO. These last three factors, right speech, action and livelihood, constitute (the group of path factors) "virtue" (*sīla*). They are known as the preliminary stage of the path. Now comes the sixth factor, right effort.

FIRST VOICE. "What is right effort? Here a bhikkhu awakens desire for the non-arising of unarisen evil unwholesome states, for which he makes efforts, arouses energy, exerts his mind, and endeavours. He awakens desire for the abandoning of arisen evil unwholesome states, for which he makes efforts .... He awakens desire for the arising of unarisen wholesome states, for which he makes efforts .... He awakens desire for the continuance, non-corruption, strengthening, maintenance in being, and perfecting, of arisen wholesome states, for which he makes efforts, arouses energy, exerts his mind, and endeavours: this is called right effort."

S. 45:8; D. 22

(7) RIGHT MINDFULNESS

NARRATOR TWO. Now comes the seventh factor, right mindfulness.

FIRST VOICE. "What is right mindfulness? Here a bhikkhu abides contemplating the body as a body, ardent, fully aware and mindful, having put away covetousness and grief for the world. He abides contemplating feelings as feelings, ardent ... He abides contemplating consciousness as consciousness, ardent ... He abides contemplating mental objects as mental objects, ardent, fully aware and mindful, having put away covetousness and grief for the world. This is called right mindfulness."

S. 45:8; D. 22

"How does a bhikkhu abide contemplating the body as a body? Here a bhikkhu, gone to the forest or to the root of a tree or to a room that is void, sits down; having folded his legs crosswise, set his body erect, and established mindfulness in front of him, just mindful he breathes in, mindful he breathes out.[19] As a skilled turner or his apprentice, when making a long turn, understands 'I make a long turn,' or when making a short turn, understands 'I make a short turn,' so, breathing in long, the bhikkhu understands 'I breathe in long,' or breathing out long, he understands 'I breathe out long'; breathing in short, he understands 'I breathe in short,' or breathing out short, he understands 'I breathe out short.' He trains thus: 'I shall breathe in experiencing the whole body (of breaths)'; he trains thus: 'I shall breathe out experiencing the whole body (of breaths).' He trains thus: 'I shall breathe in tranquillizing the bodily formation (function)'; he trains thus: 'I shall breathe out tranquillizing the bodily formation (function).'"[20]

"He abides contemplating the body as a body in this way either in himself, or externally, or in himself and externally.[21]

"Or else he contemplates in the body either its factors of origination, or its factors of fall, or its factors of origination and fall.

"Or else mindfulness that 'There is a body' is established in him to the extent of bare knowledge and remembrance of it while he abides independent, not clinging to anything in the world.

"That is how a bhikkhu abides contemplating the body as a body.

"Again, when walking, a bhikkhu understands 'I am walking'; or when standing, he understands 'I am standing'; or when sitting, he understands 'I am sitting'; or when lying down, he understands 'I am lying down.' Or whatever position his body is in, he understands it to be so disposed.

"He abides contemplating the body as a body ... externally.

"Or else he contemplates ... the factors of origination and fall.

"Or else mindfulness ... not clinging to anything in the world.

"That also is how a bhikkhu abides contemplating the body as a body.

"Again, a bhikkhu is fully aware in moving to and fro, in looking ahead and away, in flexing and extending the limbs, in wearing the outer cloak of patches, the bowl and other robes, in eating, drinking, chewing, and tasting, in evacuating the bowels and making water, and he is fully aware and mindful in walking, standing, sitting, going to sleep, waking, talking, and keeping silent.

"He abides contemplating ....

"That also is how a bhikkhu abides contemplating the body as a body.

"Again, as though there were a bag with two openings full of many sorts of grain, such as hill rice, red rice, beans, peas, millet, and white rice, and a man with good sight had opened it and were reviewing it: 'This is hill rice, this is red rice, this is beans, this is peas, this is millet, this is white rice'; so too a bhikkhu reviews this body up from the soles of the feet and down from the top of the hair as full of many kinds of filth: 'There are in this body head-hairs, body-hairs, nails, teeth, skin; flesh, sinews, bones, bone-marrow, kidneys; heart, liver, midriff, spleen, lights; bowels, entrails, gorge, dung; bile, phlegm, pus, blood, sweat, fat; tears, grease, spittle, snot, oil-of-the-joints, and urine.'

"He abides contemplating ....

"That also is how a bhikkhu abides contemplating the body as a body.

"Again, as though a skilled butcher or his apprentice had slaughtered a cow and were seated at the four crossroads with it cut up into pieces; so too, in whatever position a bhikkhu finds this body, he reviews it according to the elements: 'There are in this body earth element, water element, fire element, and air element.'

"He abides contemplating ....

"That also is how a bhikkhu abides contemplating the body as a body.

"Again, a bhikkhu judges this same body as though he were looking at a corpse thrown on a charnel ground, one-day dead, two-days dead, three-days dead, bloated, livid, and oozing with matter: 'This body too is of such a nature, will be like that, is not exempt from that.'

"He abides contemplating ....

"That also is how a bhikkhu abides contemplating the body as a body.

"Again, a bhikkhu judges this same body as though he were looking at a corpse thrown on a charnel ground, being devoured by crows, kites, vultures, dogs, jackals, and the multitudinous varieties of worms: ... as though he were looking at a corpse thrown on a charnel ground, a skeleton with flesh and blood, and held together by sinews: ... a fleshless skeleton smeared with blood and held together by sinews: ... a skeleton without flesh or blood, held together by sinews: ... bones without sinews, scattered in all directions, here a hand-bone, there a foot-bone, there a shin-bone, there a thigh-bone, there a hip-bone, there a back-bone, there a skull: ... bones bleached white, the colour of shells: ... bones heaped up, more than a year old: ... bones rotted and crumbled to dust: 'This body too is of such a nature, will be like that, is not exempt from that.'

"He abides contemplating ....

"That also is how a bhikkhu abides contemplating the body as a body.

"And how does a bhikkhu abide contemplating feelings as feelings?

"Here, when feeling a pleasant feeling, a bhikkhu understands 'I feel a pleasant feeling'; when feeling a painful feeling, he understands 'I feel a painful feeling'; when feeling a neither-painful-nor-pleasant feeling, he understands 'I feel a neither-painful-nor-pleasant feeling.' When feeling a materialistic pleasant feeling,[22] he understands 'I feel a materialistic pleasant feeling'; ... (and so with the other two). When feeling an unmaterialistic pleasant feeling, he understands 'I feel an unmaterialistic pleasant feeling'; ... (and so with the other two).

"He abides contemplating feelings as feelings in this way either in himself, or externally, or in himself and externally.

"Or else he contemplates in feelings either their factors of origination, or their factors of fall, or their factors of origination and fall.

"Or else mindfulness that 'There are feelings' is established in him to the extent of bare knowledge and remembrance of it while he abides independent, not clinging to anything in the world.

"That is how a bhikkhu abides contemplating feelings as feelings.

"And how does a bhikkhu abide contemplating consciousness as consciousness ?

"Here a bhikkhu understands consciousness affected by lust as affected by lust, and that unaffected by lust as unaffected by lust. He understands consciousness affected by hate as affected by hate, and that unaffected by hate as unaffected by hate. He understands consciousness affected by delusion as affected by delusion, and that unaffected by delusion as unaffected by delusion. He understands contracted consciousness as contracted, and distracted consciousness as distracted. He understands exalted consciousness as exalted, and that unexalted as unexalted. He understands surpassed consciousness as surpassed, and that unsurpassed as unsurpassed.[23] He understands concentrated consciousness as concentrated, and that unconcentrated as unconcentrated. He understands liberated consciousness as liberated, and that unliberated as unliberated.

"He abides contemplating consciousness as consciousness in this way either in himself, or externally, or in himself and externally.

"Or else he contemplates in consciousness its factors of origination, or its factors of fall, or its factors of origination and fall.

"Or else mindfulness that 'There is consciousness' is established in him to the extent of bare knowledge and remembrance of it while he abides independent, not clinging to anything in the world.

"That is how a bhikkhu abides contemplating consciousness as consciousness.

"And how does a bhikkhu abide contemplating mental objects as mental objects?

"Here, a bhikkhu abides contemplating mental objects as mental objects in terms of the five hindrances.[24] How is that done? Here, when there is desire for sensuality in him, he understands 'There is desire for sensuality in me'; or when there is no desire for sensuality in him, he understands 'There is no desire for sensuality in me'; and also he understands how there comes to be the arising of unarisen desire for sensuality, and how there comes to be the abandoning of arisen desire for sensuality, and how there comes to be the future non-arising of abandoned desire for sensuality. When there is ill will in him ... When there is lethargy and drowsiness in him ... When there is agitation and worry in him ... When there is uncertainty in him ... he understands how there comes to be the future non-arising of abandoned uncertainty.

"He abides contemplating mental objects as mental objects in himself, or externally, or in himself and externally.

"Or else he contemplates in mental objects either their factors of origination, or their factors of fall, or their factors of origination and fall.

"Or else mindfulness that 'There are mental objects' is established in him to the extent of bare knowledge and remembrance of it, while he abides independent, not clinging to anything in the world.

"That is how a bhikkhu abides contemplating mental objects as mental objects in terms of the five hindrances.

"Again, a bhikkhu abides contemplating mental objects as mental objects in terms of the five aggregates affected by clinging. How is that done? Here a bhikkhu understands: 'Such is form, such its origin, such its disappearance; such is feeling, such its origin, such its disappearance; such is perception, such its origin, such its disappearance; such are formations, such their origin, such their disappearance; such is consciousness, such its origin, such its disappearance.'

"He abides contemplating ....

"That is how a bhikkhu abides contemplating mental objects as mental objects in terms of the five aggregates affected by clinging.

"Again, a bhikkhu abides contemplating mental objects as mental objects in terms of the six bases in oneself and external. How is that done? Here a bhikkhu understands the eye and visible forms and the fetter that arises owing to both; he understands how there comes to be the arising of the unarisen fetter, and how there comes to be the abandoning of the arisen fetter, and how there comes to be the future non-arising of the abandoned fetter. He understands the ear and sounds ... the nose and odours ... the tongue and flavours ... the body and tangibles ... the mind and mental objects and the fetter that arises owing to both; ... and he understands how there comes to be the future non-arising of the abandoned fetter.

"He abides contemplating ....

"That is how a bhikkhu abides contemplating mental objects as mental objects in terms of the six bases in oneself and external.

"Again, a bhikkhu abides contemplating mental objects as mental objects in terms of the seven enlightenment factors. How is that done? Here, when there is the mindfulness enlightenment factor in him, a bhikkhu understands 'There is the mindfulness enlightenment factor in me'; when there is no mindfulness enlightenment factor in him, he understands 'There is no mindfulness enlightenment factor in me'; and he understands how there comes to be the arising of the unarisen mindfulness enlightenment factor and how there comes to be the development and perfection of the arisen mindfulness enlightenment factor. When there is the investigation-of-states enlightenment factor in him ... the energy enlightenment factor in him ... the happiness enlightenment factor in him ... the tranquillity enlightenment factor in him ... the concentration enlightenment factor in him ... the equanimity enlightenment factor in him ... and he understands how there comes to be the arising of the unarisen equanimity enlightenment factor and how there comes to be the development and perfection of the arisen equanimity enlightenment factor.

"He abides contemplating ....

"That is how a bhikkhu abides contemplating mental objects as mental objects in terms of the seven enlightenment factors.

"Again, a bhikkhu abides contemplating mental objects as mental objects in terms of the Four Noble Truths. How is that done? Here a bhikkhu understands according as it actually is: 'This is suffering' and 'This is the origin of suffering' and 'This is the cessation of suffering' and 'This is the way leading to the cessation of suffering.'

"He abides contemplating mental objects as mental objects in himself, or externally, or in himself and externally.

"Or else he contemplates in mental objects either their factors of origination, or their factors of fall, or their factors of origination and fall.

"Or else mindfulness that 'There are mental objects' is established in him to the extent of bare knowledge and remembrance of it while he abides independent, not clinging to anything in the world.

"That is how a bhikkhu abides contemplating mental objects as mental objects in terms of the Four Noble Truths.

"Bhikkhus, were anyone to maintain in being these four foundations of mindfulness for seven years ... let alone for seven years ... for seven days, then one of two fruits could be expected of him: either final knowledge here and now, or else non-return."

D. 22; M. 10

"Bhikkhus, I shall expound to you the origin and disappearance of the four foundations of mindfulness: the body has nutriment for its origin, and it disappears with cessation of nutriment; feelings have contact for their origin, and they disappear with cessation of contact; consciousness has name-and-form for its origin, and it disappears with cessation of name-and-form; mental objects have attention for their origin, and they disappear with cessation of attention."

S. 47:42

"All things have desire for their root, attention provides their being, contact their origin, feeling their meeting-place, concentration confrontation with them, mindfulness control of them, understanding is the highest of them, and deliverance is their core."

A. 8:83

"Would one guard oneself, then the foundations of mindfulness should be cultivated; would one guard others, then the foundations of mindfulness should be cultivated. Who guards himself guards others; who guards others guards himself."

S. 47:19

(8) RIGHT CONCENTRATION

NARRATOR TWO. Now we come to the eighth and last factor, right concentration.

FIRST VOICE. "What is right concentration?

"Here, quite secluded from sensual desires, secluded from unwholesome states, a bhikkhu enters upon and abides in the first meditation, which is accompanied by thinking and exploring, with happiness and pleasure born of seclusion."

D. 2; D. 22; M. 39; S. 45:8

"Just as a skilled bath man or his apprentice heaps bath-powder in a metal basin, and sprinkling it gradually with water, kneads it up till the moisture wets his ball of bath powder, soaks it, and extends over it within and without though the ball itself does not become liquid; so too, the bhikkhu makes happiness and pleasure born of seclusion drench, steep, fill and extend throughout this body, so that there is nothing of his whole body to which it does not extend."

D. 2; M. 39

"With the stilling of thinking and exploring he enters upon and abides in the second meditation, which has self-confidence and singleness of mind without thinking and exploring, with happiness and pleasure born of concentration."

D. 2; D. 22; M. 39; S. 45:8

"Just as if there were a lake whose waters welled up from below, having no inflow from the east, west, north or south, nor yet replenished from time to time with showers from the skies, then the cool fount of water welling up from the lake would make the cool water drench, steep, fill and extend throughout the lake, and there would be nothing of the whole lake to which the cool water did not extend; so too, the bhikkhu makes happiness and pleasure born of concentration drench, steep, fill and extend throughout this body, so that there is nothing of his whole body to which they do not extend."

D. 2; M. 39

"With the fading away as well of happiness he abides in equanimity, and, mindful and fully aware, still feeling pleasure with the body, he enters upon and abides in the third meditation, on account of which the noble ones announce: 'He has a pleasant abiding who is an onlooker with equanimity and is mindful.' "

D. 2; D. 22; M. 39; S. 45:8

"Just as, in a pond of blue or white or red lotuses, some lotuses are born under the water, grow under the water, do not stand up out of the water, flourish immersed in the water, and the water drenches, steeps, fills and extends throughout them to their tips and to their roots, and there is nothing of the whole of those lotuses to which it does not extend; so too, the bhikkhu makes the pleasure divested of happiness drench, steep, fill and extend throughout this body, so that there is nothing of his whole body to which it does not extend."

D. 2; M. 39

"With the abandoning of pleasure and pain, and with the previous disappearance of joy and grief, he enters upon and abides in the fourth meditation, which has neither pain nor pleasure, and the purity of whose mindfulness is due to equanimity."

D. 2; D.22; M. 39; S. 45:8

"Just as if a man were sitting clothed from head to foot in white cloth, and there were nothing of his whole body to which the white cloth did not extend; so too the bhikkhu sits with pure bright cognizance extending over his body and there is nothing of his whole body to which it does not extend."

D. 2; M. 39

"What is the noble ones' right concentration with its causes and its equipment? It is any unifiedness of mind that is equipped with the other seven factors of the path. Right view comes first: one understands wrong view, intention, speech, action, and livelihood, as wrong; one understands right view, intention, speech, action, and livelihood, as right, each of two kinds, that is, either associated with taints and ripening in the essentials of existence, or supramundane and a factor of the path. One makes efforts to abandon wrong view and the other four, and to acquire right view and the other four: this is one's right effort. Mindfully one abandons the wrong and enters upon the way of the right: this is one's right mindfulness."

M. 117 (condensed)

NARRATOR TWO. These last three factors, right effort, mindfulness and concentration, together constitute "concentration." The eight, with right knowledge and right deliverance, are called the "ten rightnesses," which constitute the "certainty of rightness" attained with the path of stream-entry. Before leaving the subject of concentration, though, there are four more stages attainable called the four "formless states." They are extra to "right concentration," merely refinements of the fourth meditation.

FIRST VOICE. "With the complete surmounting of perceptions of form, with the disappearance of perceptions of resistance, by not giving attention to perceptions of difference, (aware of) 'infinite space,' a bhikkhu enters upon and abides in the base consisting of infinity of space.

"Again, by completely surmounting the base consisting of infinity of space, (aware of) 'infinite consciousness,' he enters upon and abides in the base consisting of infinity of consciousness.

"Again, by completely surmounting the base consisting of infinity of consciousness, (aware that) 'there is nothing at all,' he enters upon and abides in the base consisting of nothingness.

"Again, by completely surmounting the base consisting of nothingness, he enters upon and abides in the base consisting of neither-perception-nor-non-perception.

"The four meditations are not called effacement in the Noble One's Discipline; they are called in the Noble One's Discipline, a pleasant abiding here and now. The four formless states are not called effacement in the Noble One's Discipline; they are called in the Noble One's Discipline, quiet abidings."

M. 8

"This bhikkhu (who practises these eight attainments) is said to have blindfolded Māra, to have (temporarily) deprived Māra's eyesight of its object and become invisible to the Evil One."

M. 25

NARRATOR TWO. None of these eight attainments (nor the four divine abidings—see, p. 177) is claimed as peculiar to the Buddhas' teaching. The practice of them without right view leads only to heaven, but not to Nibbāna. The teaching peculiar to Buddhas is the Four Noble Truths. A ninth attainment, the "attainment of cessation," is described as reached only in the two highest stages of realization and is thus peculiar to Buddhas and their disciples.

FIRST VOICE. "By completely surmounting the base consisting of neither-perception-nor-non-perception, a bhikkhu enters upon and abides in the cessation of perception and feeling, and his taints are exhausted by his seeing with understanding. Then a bhikkhu is said to have blindfolded Māra, to have deprived Māra's eyesight of its object and become invisible to the Evil One, and, what is more, to have gone beyond all attachment to the world."

M. 25

"When a wise man, established well in virtue,
Develops consciousness and understanding,
Then as a bhikkhu, ardent and sagacious,
He succeeds in disentangling this tangle."

S. 1:23

"Bhikkhus, if one man were to travel and trudge through one age, then the heap, the pile, the mass of his bones would be as high as this Vepulla Hill, if they were collected and the store were not destroyed."

Iti. 24

"Suppose a man threw into the ocean a yoke with one hole in it, and then the east wind blew it west and the west wind blew it east and the north wind blew it south and the south wind blew it north; and suppose there were a blind turtle that came up to the surface once at the end of each century. How do you conceive this, bhikkhus, would that blind turtle eventually put his head through that yoke with the one hole in it?"

"He might, Lord, at the end of a long period."

"Bhikkhus, the blind turtle would sooner put his head through that yoke with a single hole in it than a fool, once gone to perdition, would find his way back to the human state."

M. 129

"Bhikkhus, the Dhamma well proclaimed by me thus is frank, open, evident, and stripped of padding. In this Dhamma well proclaimed by me thus, any who have simply faith in me, simply love for me, are destined for heaven."

M. 22

"What should be done for the disciples out of compassion by a teacher who seeks their welfare and is compassionate, that I have done for you. There are these roots of trees, these rooms that are void: meditate, bhikkhus, do not delay lest you regret it later. This is our instruction to you."

M. 8; M. 152

NARRATOR TWO. That concludes the survey. But how is the Way actually followed?

THE NOBLE EIGHTFOLD PATH IN PRACTICE

FIRST VOICE. One morning the venerable Ānanda dressed, and taking his bowl and outer robe, he went into Sāvatthī for alms. He saw Jānussoni the brahman driving out of Sāvatthī in a chariot drawn by four mares, all in white: white steeds, white harnesses, white chariot, white upholstery, white sandals; and he was even being fanned with a white fan. When people saw this, they said: "What a divine vehicle! Now that is like a divine vehicle!"

On his return, the venerable Ānanda told the Blessed One about it, and he asked: "Lord, can a divine vehicle be pointed to in this Dhamma and Discipline?"

"It can, Ānanda,' the Blessed One said." 'Divine vehicle' is a name for the Noble Eightfold Path; and so is 'vehicle of Dhamma,' and so is 'peerless victory in battle'; for all the components of the Noble Eightfold Path culminate in the expulsion of lust, hate and delusion."

S. 45:4

"(Once a child is conceived and with birth and the growth of youth) his sense faculties mature, then he becomes furnished and invested with the five strands of sensual desires and exploits them: forms cognizable through the eye that are wished for, desired, agreeable and likable, connected with sensual desire and provocative of lust; likewise sounds cognizable through the ear, odours cognizable through the nose, flavours cognizable through the tongue, and tangibles cognizable through the body.

"On seeing a visible form with the eye, hearing a sound with the ear, smelling an odour with the nose, tasting a flavour with the tongue, touching a tangible with the body, cognizing an idea with the mind, he lusts after it if it is likable, or has ill will towards it if it is dislikeable. He abides without mindfulness of the body established and with mind limited while he does not understand as they actually are the deliverance of mind and deliverance by understanding wherein those evil unwholesome states cease without remainder. Engaged as he is in favouring and opposing, when he feels any feeling, whether pleasant or painful or neither-painful-nor-pleasant, he relishes that feeling, affirms and accepts it. Relishing arises in him when he does that. Now any relishing of those feelings is clinging. With his clinging as condition, being; with being as condition, birth; with birth as condition, ageing and death come to be, and also sorrow and lamentation, pain, grief and despair. That is how there is an origin to this whole aggregate mass of suffering.

"Here a Perfect One appears in the world, accomplished and fully enlightened, perfect in true knowledge and conduct, knower of worlds, incomparable leader of men to be tamed, teacher of gods and men, enlightened, blessed. He declares this world with its deities, its Māras and its Brahmas, this generation with its monks and brahmans, with its princes and men, which he has himself realized by direct knowledge. He teaches a Dhamma good in the beginning, the middle and the end, with the meaning and the letter, and he announces a holy life that is utterly perfect and pure.

"Some householder, or his son, or one born in some clan, hears that Dhamma. On hearing it, he has faith in the Perfect One. Possessed of that faith, he considers: 'House life is crowded and dirty; life gone forth is wide open. It is not easy, living in a household, to lead a holy life as utterly perfect and pure as a polished shell. Suppose I shaved off hair and beard, put on the yellow robe, and went forth from the home life into homelessness?'

"And on another occasion, abandoning perhaps a small, perhaps a large fortune, abandoning perhaps a small, perhaps a large circle of relatives, he shaves off his hair and beard, puts on the yellow robe, and goes forth from the home life into homelessness.

"Being thus gone forth and possessing the bhikkhus' training and way of life, he abandons killing living beings, abstaining therefrom with rod and weapon laid aside; gentle and kindly, he abides compassionate to all beings. He abandons taking what is not given, abstaining therefrom by taking only what is given; expecting only what is given, he abides pure in himself by not stealing. He abandons incelibacy; he lives the celibate life as one who lives apart, abstaining from vulgar lechery. He abandons false speech, abstaining therefrom by speaking truth; cleaving to truth when he speaks, he is trustworthy, reliable and undeceiving of the world. He abandons slander .... He abandons abuse .... He abandons gossip ... he speaks in season speech worth recording, which is reasoned, definite, and connected with good.[25]

"He abstains from injuring seeds and plants. He eats only in one part of the day, refraining from food at night and late meals. He abstains from dancing, singing, music, and theatrical shows; from wearing garlands, smartening with scents, and embellishing with unguents; from high and large couches; from accepting gold and silver, corn, raw meat, women and girls, bondswomen and bondsmen, sheep and goats, poultry and pigs, elephants, cattle, horses and mares, fields and lands; from going on errands; from buying and selling; from false weights, false metals, and false measures; from cheating, deceiving, defrauding and trickery; from mutilating, executing, imprisoning, robbery, plunder and violence.

"He is content with robes to protect the body, with almsfood to sustain the belly, so that wherever he goes he takes everything with him, just as whenever a winged bird flies it flies using its own wings. Possessing this store of the noble ones' virtue, he feels in himself a bliss that is blameless.

"He becomes one who, on seeing a form with the eye, apprehends no signs and features through which, if he left the eye faculty unguarded, evil unwholesome states of covetousness and grief might invade him; he practises the way of its restraint, he guards the eye faculty, gives effect to restraint of the eye faculty. (Likewise, on hearing a sound with the ear, smelling an odour with the nose, tasting a flavour with the tongue, touching a tangible with the body, and cognizing an idea with the mind.) Possessing this noble ones' faculty restraint, he feels in himself an unsullied bliss.

"He comes to be fully aware when moving to and fro ... and keeping silent.[26]

"Possessing this store of the noble ones' virtue, and this noble ones' faculty restraint, and this noble ones' mindfulness and full awareness, he resorts to a secluded resting place—to the forest, a tree root, a rock, a ravine, a mountain cave, a charnel ground, a jungle thicket, an open space, a heap of straw. On returning from his alms round after the meal, he sits down, folding his legs crosswise setting his body erect, and establishing mindfulness in front of him.

"Abandoning covetousness for the world, he abides with a mind devoid of covetousness; he purifies his mind from covetousness. Abandoning ill will and hatred, he abides with no thought of ill will, compassionate for the welfare of all living beings; he purifies his mind from ill will and hatred. Abandoning lethargy and drowsiness, he abides with a mind free of lethargy and drowsiness, percipient of light, mindful and fully aware; he purifies his mind from lethargy and drowsiness. Abandoning agitation and worry, he abides unagitated with mind stilled in himself; he purifies his mind of agitation and worry. Abandoning uncertainty, he abides with a mind that has outgrown uncertainty, questioning no more about unwholesome states; he purifies his mind of uncertainty."

M. 38

"Suppose a man borrowed a loan and undertook works and the works succeeded so that he repaid all the money of the old loan and there remained over some extra for his wife and children; then on considering that, he was glad and joyful; or suppose a man was afflicted, suffering and gravely ill and his food did not sustain him and his body had no strength, but later he recovered from the affliction and his body regained strength; or suppose a man were imprisoned in a prison-house, but later he was released from imprisonment safe and sound with no loss to his property; or suppose a man were a bondsman, not self-dependent but dependent on others and unable to go where he wanted, but later he was freed from that bondage and was self-dependent, independent of others and a freeman able to go where he wanted; or suppose a man with property and goods entered on a road across a desert, but later he crossed over the desert safe and sound with no loss to his property; then on considering that, he was glad and joyful; so too, when these five hindrances are unabandoned in himself, a bhikkhu sees them respectively as a debt, a disease, a prison-house, a bondage, and a road across a desert; and when they are abandoned in himself, he sees that as unindebtedness, health, release from prison, freedom from bondage, and a land of safety."

M. 39

"Having abandoned the five hindrances, mental imperfections that weaken understanding, then quite secluded from sensual desires, secluded from unwholesome states, he enters upon and abides in the first meditation ... the second meditation ... the third meditation ... the fourth meditation.

"On seeing a form with the eye, hearing a sound with the ear, smelling an odour with the nose, tasting a flavour with the tongue, touching a tangible with the body, cognizing an idea with the mind, he does not lust after it if it is likable; and he has no ill will towards it if it is dislikable. He abides with mindfulness of the body established and a measureless state of mind while he understands as they actually are the deliverance of mind and deliverance by understanding wherein those evil unwholesome states cease without remainder. Having thus abandoned favouring and opposing, when he feels any feeling, whether pleasant or painful or neither-painful-nor-pleasant, he does not relish that feeling or affirm or accept it. When he does not do that, his relishing of those feelings ceases. With cessation of his relishing, cessation of clinging; with cessation of clinging, cessation of being; with cessation of being, cessation of birth; with cessation of birth, ageing and death cease, and also sorrow and lamentation, pain, grief and despair; that is how there is a cessation to this whole aggregate mass of suffering."

M. 38

THE MEANS

"Suppose a man wanting a snake saw a large snake, and when he wrongly grasped it by its coils or its tail, it turned back and bit him, on which account he came to death or deadly suffering—why? because of his wrong grasp of the snake—; so too, some misguided men learn the Dhamma without examining the meaning of the teachings with understanding, so they acquire no liking for meditating upon them. Learning it instead for the sake of carping and rebuttal of criticism, they fail to appreciate the purpose for which the Dhamma is learnt, and they find that the teachings being wrongly grasped by them, for long conduce to their harm and suffering. But suppose a man who wanted a snake saw a large one, and when he caught it in a forked stick and rightly grasped it by the neck, then for all it might wrap its coils about his hand or arm or limbs, still he would not on that account come to death or deadly suffering; so too some clansmen learn the Dhamma and examine the meaning of the teachings with understanding, so that they acquire a liking for meditating upon them. Not learning it for the sake of carping and rebuttal of criticism, they appreciate the purpose for which the Dhamma is learnt, and they find that those teachings being rightly grasped by them, for long conduce to their welfare and happiness.

"Bhikkhus, suppose a traveller saw a great expanse of water, whose near shore was dangerous and fearful and whose further shore was safe and free from fear, but there was no ferry or bridge. Then after considering this, he collected grass and branches and twigs and leaves and bound them together into a raft, supported by which, and making efforts with his hands and feet, he got safely across. Then, when he had got across, he thought: 'This raft has been very helpful to me since by its means I got safely across; suppose I hoist it on my head or load it on my shoulder and go where I mean to go?' Now would he be doing what should be done with a raft?"

"No, Lord."—"What should he do with it? If, when he got across, he thought: 'This raft has been very helpful to me since by its means I got safely across; suppose I haul it up on dry land or set it adrift on the water and go where I mean to go?', then that is how he is doing what should be done with the raft. So I have shown you how the Dhamma resembles a raft in being for the purpose of crossing over, not for grasping. Bhikkhus, when you know the Simile of the Raft (then even good) teachings should be abandoned by you, how much more so bad teachings."

M. 22 (condensed)

THE END

"Cessation of lust, of hate and of delusion is the Unformed (Unconditioned), the End, the Taintless, the Truth, the Other Shore, the Subtle, the Very Hard To See, the Unweakening, the Everlasting, the Undisintegrating, the Invisible, the Undiversified, Peace, the Deathless, the Superior Goal, the Blest, Safety, Exhaustion of Craving, the Wonderful, the Marvellous, Non-distress, the Naturally Non-distressed, Nibbāna, Non-affliction (Unhostility), Fading of Lust, Purity, Freedom, Independence of Reliance, the Island, the Shelter, the Harbour, the Refuge, the Beyond."

S. 43:1-44

13
DEVADATTA

NARRATOR TWO. Devadatta was the Buddha's first cousin. His attempt to usurp the Buddha's place is ascribed to the thirty-seventh year after the Enlightenment: when, in other words, the Buddha was seventy-two years old.

NARRATOR ONE. Here is the account given in the Vinaya Piṭaka.

SECOND VOICE. The occasion was this. Once when Devadatta was alone in retreat this thought arose in his mind: "Who is there whose confidence I can win over and thereby acquire much gain, honour and renown?" Then he thought: "There is Prince Ajātasattu. He is young with a glorious future. Suppose I win over his confidence? Much gain, honour and renown will accrue to me if I do so."

So Devadatta packed his bed away, and he took his bowl and outer robe and set out for Rājagaha, where he at length arrived. There he discarded his own form and assumed the form of a youth with a girdle of snakes, and in that guise he appeared on Prince Ajātasattu's lap. Then Prince Ajātasattu was fearful, anxious, suspicious and worried. Devadatta asked: "Are you afraid of me, prince?"

"Yes, I am afraid. Who are you?"

"I am Devadatta."

"If you are Devadatta, Lord, then please show yourself in your own form."

Devadatta discarded the form of the youth and stood before Prince Ajātasattu, wearing his patched outer cloak, bowl and robes. Then Prince Ajātasattu felt prodigious confidence in Devadatta owing to his supernormal powers. After that he waited on him evening and morning with five hundred carriages and five hundred offerings of milk-rice as a gift of food. Devadatta became overwhelmed with gain, honour and renown. Ambition obsessed his mind, and the wish arose in him: "I will rule the Sangha of bhikkhus." Simultaneously with the thought his supernormal powers vanished.

Vin. Cv. 7:2; cf. S. 17:36

After the Blessed One had stayed at Kosambī as long as he chose, he set out to wander by stages to Rājagaha, where he arrived in due course. He went to live in the Bamboo Grove, the Squirrels' Sanctuary. Then a number of bhikkhus went to him and told him: "Lord, Prince Ajātasattu goes to wait on Devadatta each evening and morning with five hundred carriages and five hundred offerings of milk-rice as a gift of food."

"Bhikkhus, do not begrudge Devadatta his gain, honour and renown. Just as, if one were to break a gall bladder under a fierce dog's nose, the dog would get much fiercer, so too, as long as Prince Ajātasattu keeps waiting on Devadatta as he is doing, so long may wholesome states be expected to diminish and not increase in Devadatta. Just as a plantain bears its fruit for its own destruction and its own undoing, so too, Devadatta's gain, honour and renown have arisen for his self-destruction and his own undoing."

Vin. Cv. 7:2; cf. S. 17:35-36 and A. 4:68

The occasion was this. The Blessed One was seated teaching the Dhamma and surrounded by a huge gathering, including the king. Then Devadatta got up from his seat, and arranging his upper robe on one shoulder, he raised his hands palms together towards the Blessed One: "Lord, the Blessed One is now old, aged, burdened with years, advanced in life and come to the last stage. Let the Blessed One now rest. Let him dwell in bliss in the present life. Let him hand over the Sangha of bhikkhus to me. I will govern the Sangha of bhikkhus."

"Enough, Devadatta. Do not aspire to govern the Sangha of bhikkhus."

A second time Devadatta made the same proposal and received the same answer. When he made the proposal for the third time, the Blessed One said: "I would not hand over the Sangha of bhikkhus even to Sāriputta and Moggallāna. How should I do so to such a wastrel, a clot of spittle, as you?"

Then Devadatta thought: "Before the public, including the king, the Blessed One has disgraced me with the words 'clot of spittle' and praised Sāriputta and Moggallāna." He was angry and indignant. He paid homage to the Blessed One and departed, keeping him on his right. Now this was his first grudge against the Blessed One.

The Blessed One addressed the bhikkhus: "Now, bhikkhus, let the Sangha carry out an act of public denunciation in Rājagaha against Devadatta thus: 'Formerly Devadatta had one nature; now he has another. Whatever Devadatta may do by body or speech neither the Blessed One nor the Dhamma nor the Sangha should be held as having part in it: only Devadatta himself is to be held responsible for it.' "

Then the Blessed One addressed the venerable Sāriputta: "Now, Sāriputta, you must denounce Devadatta in Rājagaha."

"Lord, hitherto, I have spoken in Devadatta's favour thus: 'The son of Godhī is mighty and powerful.' How can I denounce him in Rājagaha?"

"Were you not speaking the truth in praising Devadatta thus?"

"Yes, Lord."

"Then likewise speaking truth you must denounce him in Rājagaha."

"Even so, Lord," the venerable Sāriputta replied.

When the venerable Sāriputta had been formally authorized by the Sangha, he went into Rājagaha accompanied by a number of bhikkhus and denounced Devadatta. Then people without faith and confidence, unwise and indiscreet, said: "These monks, sons of the Sakyans, are jealous of Devadatta's gain, honour and renown." But the faithful and confident, the wise and discreet, said: "This can be no ordinary matter for the Blessed One to have had Devadatta denounced in Rājagaha."

Then Devadatta went to Prince Ajātasattu and said to him: "Formerly men were long-lived, now they are short-lived. Maybe you will die while still only a prince, so why do you not kill your father and become king? And I shall kill the Blessed One and become the Buddha."

Prince Ajātasattu thought: "The Lord Devadatta is mighty and powerful; he should know." He fastened a dagger on his thigh, and then in broad day, fearful, anxious, suspicious and worried, he tried to slip into the inner palace. The king's officers at the entry to the inner palace saw him as he did so, and they arrested him. On searching him, they found the dagger fastened to his thigh. They asked him: "What is it you want to do, prince?"

"I want to kill my father."

"Who prompted you to do this?"

"The Lord Devadatta."

Some officers were of the opinion that the prince should be killed, and Devadatta and all of the bhikkhus, too. Others were of the opinion that the bhikkhus should not be killed since they had done no wrong, but that the prince and Devadatta should be killed. Still others were of the opinion that neither the prince nor Devadatta nor the bhikkhus should be killed, but that the king should be informed and his orders carried out.

Then the officers brought Prince Ajātasattu before Seniya Bimbisāra, King of Magadha, and they told him what had happened.

"What was the officers' opinion?"

They told him.

"What have the Buddha, the Dhamma and the Sangha to do with it? Has not Devadatta been denounced in Rājagaha by the Blessed One?"

Then he stopped the pay of those officers whose opinion had been that Prince Ajātasattu and Devadatta and the bhikkhus should be killed. And he degraded those officers whose opinion had been that the bhikkhus, having done no wrong, should not be killed, but that the prince and Devadatta should be killed. And he promoted those officers whose opinion had been that neither the prince nor Devadatta nor the bhikkhus should be killed, but that the king should be informed and his orders carried out. Then King Bimbisāra asked: "Why do you want to kill me, prince?"

"I want the kingdom, sire."

"If you want the kingdom, prince, the kingdom is yours."

He therewith handed the kingdom over to him.

Devadatta went to Prince Ajātasattu and said to him: "Great king, send some men to take the monk Gotama's life."

So Prince Ajātasattu gave orders to some men: "Do as the Lord Devadatta says." And Devadatta told one of the men: "Go, friend; the monk Gotama lives in such and such a place. Take his life and return by such and such a path." Then he posted two men on that path, telling them: "Take the life of the man who will be coming along by that path, and return by this path." Then he posted four men on that path ... eight men on that path ... sixteen men on that path ....

Then the one man took his sword and shield and fixed his bow and quiver, and he went to where the Blessed One was. But as he drew near, he grew frightened, till he stood still, his body quite rigid. The Blessed One saw him thus and said to him: "Come, friend, do not be afraid." Then the man laid aside his sword and shield and put down his bow and quiver. He went up to the Blessed One and prostrated himself at his feet, saying: "Lord, I have transgressed, I have done wrong like a fool confused and blundering, since I came here with evil intent, with intent to do murder. Lord, may the Blessed One forgive my transgression as such for restraint in the future."

"Surely, friend, you have transgressed, you have done wrong like a fool confused and blundering, since you came here with evil intent, with intent to do murder. But since you see your transgression as such and so act in accordance with the Dhamma, we forgive it; for it is growth in the Noble One's Discipline when a man sees a transgression as such and so acts in accordance with the Dhamma and enters upon restraint for the future."

Then the Blessed One gave the man progressive instruction .... Eventually the spotless, immaculate vision of the Dhamma arose in him .... He became independent of others in the Teacher's Dispensation. He said: "Magnificent, Lord! ... Let the Blessed One receive me as his follower .... "

The Blessed One told him: "Friend, do not go back by that path; go by this path." And he dismissed him by the other path.

Then the two men thought: "How is this? The one man is a long time coming." They followed up the path till they saw the Blessed One sitting at the root of a tree. They went up to him, and after paying homage to him, they sat down at one side. The Blessed One gave them progressive instruction. Eventually they said: "Magnificent, Lord! ... Let the Blessed One receive us as his followers .... "

Then the Blessed One dismissed them by another path. The same thing happened with the four, the eight and the sixteen men.

Now the one man went to Devadatta and told him: "I have not taken the Blessed One's life, Lord. The Blessed One is mighty and powerful."

"Enough, friend; do not take the monk Gotama's life. I will take the monk Gotama's life myself."

At that time the Blessed One was walking up and down in the shade of the Vulture Peak Rock. Then Devadatta climbed the Vulture Peak Rock, and he hurled down a huge stone, thinking: "I shall take the monk Gotama's life with this."

Two spurs of the rock came together and caught the stone; but a splinter from it drew blood on the Blessed One's foot. Then he looked up and said to Devadatta: "Misguided man, you have made much demerit; for with evil intent, with intent to do murder, you have drawn the blood of a Perfect One."

Then the Blessed One addressed the bhikkhus thus: "Bhikkhus, this is the first deed with immediate effect on rebirth that Devadatta has stored up, in that with evil intent, with intent to do murder, he has drawn the blood of a Perfect One."

Vin. Cv. 7:3

FIRST VOICE. Now at that time, when the Blessed One's foot had been hurt by the splinter, he suffered severe bodily feelings that were painful, sharp, racking, harsh, disagreeable and unpleasant. Mindful and fully aware, he bore them without vexation, and spreading out his cloak of patches folded in four, he lay down on his right side in the lion's sleeping pose with one foot overlapping the other, mindful and fully aware.

Then Māra the Evil One came to him and addressed him in stanzas:

"What, are you stupefied, that you lie down?
Or else entranced by some poetic flight?
Are there not many aims you still must serve?
Why do you dream away intent on sleep
Alone in your secluded dwelling place?"

"I am not stupefied that I lie down,
Nor yet entranced by some poetic flight.
My aim is reached, and sorrow left behind.
I sleep out of compassion for all beings
Alone in my secluded dwelling place."

Then Māra understood: "The Blessed One knows me, the Sublime One knows me." Sad and disappointed, he vanished at once.

S. 4:13

SECOND VOICE. The bhikkhus heard: "It seems that Devadatta has tried to murder the Blessed One." They walked up and down and round and round the Blessed One's dwelling. They made a loud noise, a great clamour, performing recitations for the guarding, safeguarding and protecting of the Blessed One. When he heard this, he asked the venerable Ānanda: "Ānanda, what is this loud noise, this great clamour, this sound of recitation?"

"Lord, the bhikkhus have heard that Devadatta has tried to murder the Blessed One," and he told what they were doing.

"Then, Ānanda, tell those bhikkhus in my name: 'The Master calls the venerable ones.' "

"Even so, Lord," the venerable Ānanda replied. And he went to the bhikkhus and told them: "The Master calls the venerable ones."

"Even so," they replied. And they went to the Blessed One. The Blessed One said to them: "It is impossible, bhikkhus, it cannot happen, that anyone can take a Perfect One's life by violence. When Perfect Ones attain final Nibbāna, it is not through violence on the part of another. Go to your dwellings, bhikkhus; Perfect Ones need no protecting."

At that time there was a savage elephant at Rājagaha called Nāḷagiri, a man-killer. Devadatta went into Rājagaha to the elephant stables. He said to the mahouts: "We are known to the king and influential. We can get those in low places promoted, and we can get food and wages increased. So when the monk Gotama comes down this road, let the elephant Nāḷagiri loose into the road." "Even so, Lord," they replied.

Then when it was morning, the Blessed One dressed, and taking his bowl and outer robe, he went into Rājagaha for alms with a number of bhikkhus. Then the Blessed One entered that road. The mahouts saw him, and they turned the elephant Nāḷagiri loose into the road. The elephant saw the Blessed One coming in the distance. When he saw him, he raised his trunk, and with his ears and tail erect, he charged towards the Blessed One.

The bhikkhus saw him coming in the distance. They said: "Lord, the savage elephant Nāḷagiri, the man-killer, is loose in the road. Lord, let the Blessed One turn back; Lord, let the Sublime One turn back."

"Come, bhikkhus, do not be afraid. It is impossible, it cannot happen, that anyone can take a Perfect One's life by violence. When Perfect Ones attain final Nibbāna, it is not through violence on the part of another."

A second and a third time the bhikkhus said the same thing and received the same answer.

Now at that time people in the palaces and houses and huts were waiting in suspense. Those of them without faith or confidence, the unwise and indiscreet, said: "The Great Monk who is so handsome will get hurt by the elephant." And the faithful and confident, the wise and discreet, said: "Soon tusker will be contending with tusker."

Then the Blessed One encompassed the elephant Nāḷagiri with thoughts of loving-kindness. The elephant lowered his trunk, and he went up to the Blessed One and stood before him. The Blessed One stroked the elephant's forehead with his right hand and addressed him with these stanzas:

> O elephant, do not attack a tusker,
> For it is hurtful to attack a tusker;
> There is no happy destiny beyond
> For one who kills a tusker.
> Have done with vanity and recklessness;
> The reckless have no happy destiny.
> So do you act in suchwise that you go
> To a happy destination.

The elephant Nāḷagiri took the dust of the Blessed One's feet with his trunk and sprinkled it on his head, after which he retreated backwards for as long as the Blessed One was in sight. Then he went to the elephant stables and stood in his own place. It was thus that he was tamed. Now at that time people sang this stanza:

> Some tame by means of sticks,
> And some with goads and whips;
> But here a Sage has tamed a tusker,
> Using neither stick nor weapon.

People were annoyed, they murmured and protested: "This wretch Devadatta is actually wicked enough to try to kill the monk Gotama who is so mighty and powerful!" And Devadatta's gain and honour shrank away while the Blessed One's gain and honour grew greater.

Vin. Cv. 7:3

Now after Devadatta's gain and honour had shrunk away, he and his adherents used to go and eat together among families, informing them beforehand of whatever they wanted. People were annoyed, and they murmured and protested: "How can the monks, sons of the Sakyans, go and eat together among families, informing them beforehand of whatever they want? Who does not enjoy nice things? Who does not like good things?" Bhikkhus who had few wants were likewise annoyed. They told the Blessed One. The Blessed One asked Devadatta: "Is it true, as it seems, that you are doing this?"

"It is true, Lord."

The Blessed One rebuked him, and after giving a talk on the Dhamma, he addressed the bhikkhus thus: "Now, bhikkhus, I shall allow bhikkhus to eat among families in groups of not more than three. This is for three reasons: for the restraint of wrong-minded persons and the comfort of reasonable persons, in order that those of evil wishes may not form a faction and cause a schism in the Sangha, and out of compassion for families. But eating in groups should be treated according to the procedure already laid down."

Vin. Cv. 7:3; Vin. Sv. Pāc. 32

Devadatta went to Kokālika, Kaṭamoraka-Tissa, Khaṇḍādeyīputta, and Samuddadatta, and he said: "Come, friends, let us create a schism and a breach of concord in the monk Gotama's Sangha." Kokālika said: "The monk Gotama is mighty and powerful, friend. How can we do that?"

"Come, friends, we can go to the monk Gotama and demand five points of him: 'Lord, the Blessed One has in many ways commended one of few wishes, who is contented, devoted to effacement, scrupulous and amiable, given to diminution (of attachment), and energetic. Now here are five points that conduce to those states. Lord, it would be good if bhikkhus were forest dwellers for life and any who went to live in a village were censured; if they were eaters of begged-for almsfood for life and any who accepted an invitation were censured; if they were refuse-rag wearers for life and any who wore a robe given by householders were censured; if they were tree-root dwellers for life and any who dwelt in buildings were censured; if they were not to eat fish or meat for life and any who did so were censured.' The monk Gotama will never grant them. So we can inform people about these five points. It will be possible with these five points to create a schism and a breach of concord in the monk Gotama's Sangha; for people admire self-denial."

Then Devadatta went with his adherents to the Blessed One, and after paying homage to him, he sat down at one side. Having done so, he said: "Lord, the Blessed One has in many ways commended one of few wishes, who is contented, devoted to effacement, scrupulous and amiable, given to diminution (of attachment) and energetic. Now here are five points that conduce to these things...." And he enumerated the five points.

"Enough, Devadatta. Let him who wishes be a forest dweller; let him who wishes dwell in a village. Let him who wishes be an eater of begged-for almsfood; let him who wishes accept invitations. Let him who wishes be a refuse-rag wearer; let him who wishes wear a robe given by householders. Living at the root of a tree is allowed by me for eight months of the year, but not during the rains. I have allowed fish and meat that is pure in the three aspects—when it is not seen or heard or suspected to have been killed for one personally."

Devadatta was happy and elated then: "The Blessed One does not grant these five points." He got up together with his adherents, and after paying homage to the Blessed One, he departed, keeping him on his right.

He went into Rājagaha and proceeded to inform people about the five points thus: "Friends, we have been to the monk Gotama and demanded these five points of him ..." and he told them the five points, concluding: "The Blessed One does not grant these five points. But we undertake to live by them."

Then unwise people lacking faith said: "These monks, sons of the Sakyans, are scrupulous in effacement; but the monk Gotama lives in luxury, thinking of luxury." But the wise and faithful were annoyed, and they murmured and protested: "How can Devadatta aim at creating a schism and a breach of concord in the Sangha?"

Bhikkhus heard them disapproving. Those bhikkhus who had few wants disapproved likewise, and they told the Blessed One. He asked Devadatta: "Devadatta, is it true, as it seems, that you are aiming at creating a schism and a breach of concord in the Sangha?"

"It is true, Lord."

"Enough, Devadatta. Do not try to create a schism and a breach of concord in the Sangha. He who breaks the Sangha's concord reaps misery lasting the rest of the age; he ripens out in hell for the rest of the age. But he who reunites the Sangha already split reaps the highest reward of merit and enjoys heaven for the rest of the age. Enough, Devadatta, do not try to create a schism in the Sangha: a schism in the Sangha is a grave thing."

Vin. Cv. 7:3: Vin. Sv. Sangh. 10

When it was morning, the venerable Ānanda dressed, and taking his bowl and outer robe, he went into Rājagaha for alms. Devadatta saw him, and he went up to him and said: "Now, friend Ānanda, beginning from today I shall keep the holy day of the Uposatha and carry out acts of the Sangha apart from the Blessed One and the Sangha of bhikkhus."

On his return the venerable Ānanda told the Blessed One. Knowing the meaning of this, the Blessed One then uttered this exclamation:

Good can be easily done by the good;
Good is not easily done by the bad.
Evil is easily done by the bad;
Noble ones cannot do evil deeds.

On the next Uposatha day Devadatta held a ballot: "Friends, we went to the Blessed One and we demanded the five points of him. He refused. Now we undertake to live by these five points. Let any venerable ones in favour of these five points take a voting ticket."

At that time there were five hundred bhikkhus from Vesālī, sons of the Vajjians. They were new bhikkhus with no discretion of their own. Thinking: "This is the Dhamma, this is the Discipline, this is the Master's teaching," they took voting tickets. Having now created a schism in the Sangha, Devadatta left for Gayāsīsa with the five hundred bhikkhus.

Vin. Cv. 7:3; Ud. 5:8

FIRST VOICE. The Blessed One was living at Rājagaha on the Vulture Peak Rock. It was soon after Devadatta's departure. Then when the night was well advanced, Brahmā Sahampati, of marvellous appearance and illuminating the whole of the Vulture Peak, went to the Blessed One, and after paying homage to him, he stood at one side. Then he addressed these stanzas to the Blessed One:

The act of giving fruit destroys
The aloe, plantain and bamboo;
And fame destroys the wastrel too,
As foaling does the she-mule.

S. 6:12; cf. A. 4:68

SECOND VOICE. Sāriputta and Moggallāna went to the Blessed One. They told him: "Lord, Devadatta has created a schism in the Sangha and has set out for Gayāsīsa with five hundred bhikkhus."

"Do you not both feel pity for those new bhikkhus, Sāriputta? Go, before they come to ruin."

"Even so, Lord," they replied. And they left for Gayāsīsa. After they had gone, a bhikkhu stood not far from the Blessed One, weeping. The Blessed One asked him: "Why are you weeping, bhikkhu?"

"Lord, when the Blessed One's chief disciples, Sāriputta and Moggallāna, have gone to Devadatta, they will go over to his teaching too."

"It is impossible, bhikkhu, it cannot happen, that Sāriputta and Moggallāna should go over to Devadatta's teaching. On the contrary, they will convert the bhikkhus who have gone over."

Devadatta was sitting teaching the Dhamma surrounded by a large assembly. He saw the venerable Sāriputta and the venerable Moggallāna coming in the distance. He told the bhikkhus: "See, bhikkhus, the Dhamma is well proclaimed by me. Even the monk Gotama's chief disciples, Sāriputta and Moggallāna, come to me and come over to my teaching."

When this was said, Kokālika warned Devadatta: "Friend Devadatta, do not trust them. They are in the grip of evil wishes."

"Enough, friend; they are welcome since they have come over to my teaching."

Devadatta then offered the venerable Sāriputta one half of his seat: "Come, friend Sāriputta, sit here."

"Enough, friend," the venerable Sāriputta replied, and taking a seat, he sat down at one side. The venerable Moggallāna did likewise. Now when Devadatta had instructed, urged, roused and encouraged the bhikkhus with talk on the Dhamma for much of the night, he said to the venerable Sāriputta: "Friend Sāriputta, the Sangha of bhikkhus is still free from fatigue and drowsiness. Perhaps a talk on the Dhamma may occur to you. My back is paining me, so I will rest it."

"Even so, friend," the venerable Sāriputta replied. Then Devadatta laid out his cloak of patches folded in four, and he lay down on his right side in the lion's sleeping pose, one foot overlapping the other. But he was tired, and he dropped off to sleep for a while, forgetful and not fully aware.

Then the venerable Sāriputta advised and admonished the bhikkhus with talk on the Dhamma using the marvel of reading minds, and the venerable Moggallāna advised and admonished them with talk on the Dhamma using the marvel of supernormal power, till the spotless, immaculate vision of the Dhamma arose in them: All that is subject to arising is subject to cessation.

Thereupon the venerable Sāriputta addressed the bhikkhus: "Bhikkhus, we are going back to the Blessed One. Whoever upholds the Blessed One's Dhamma let him come with us." And so the venerable Sāriputta and the venerable Moggallāna took the five hundred bhikkhus with them back to the Bamboo Grove.

Kokālika roused Devadatta: "Friend Devadatta, get up! The bhikkhus have been led away by Sāriputta and Moggallāna! Did I not tell you not to trust them because they have evil wishes and are in the grip of evil wishes?" And then and there hot blood gushed from Devadatta's mouth.

The venerable Sāriputta and the venerable Moggallāna went to the Blessed One. They said: "Lord, it would be well for bhikkhus who have sided with the creator of a schism in the Sangha to take the admission again."

"Enough, Sāriputta. Do not suggest that bhikkhus who have sided with the creator of a schism in the Sangha should take the admission again. Have them confess to a serious transgression. But how did Devadatta act?"

"Lord, Devadatta acted exactly as the Blessed One has done when, after instructing, urging, rousing and encouraging the bhikkhus for much of the night, he has said to me: 'Sāriputta, the Sangha of bhikkhus is still free from fatigue and drowsiness. Perhaps a talk on the Dhamma may occur to you. My back is paining me, so I will rest it.' "

Then the Blessed One addressed the bhikkhus: "Once, bhikkhus, there were some elephants living near a big pond in a forest. They would go into the pond and pull up lotus stalks with their trunks; and when they had washed them quite clean, they would chew them up and swallow them free from mud. That was good for both their looks and their health, and they incurred no death or deadly suffering because of that. But some young calves, uninstructed by those elephants, went into the pond and pulled up lotus stalks with their trunks; but instead of washing them quite clean, they chewed them up and swallowed them along with mud. That was not good for either their looks or their health, and they incurred death and deadly suffering because of that. So too, bhikkhus, Devadatta will die miserably through imitating me."

> Through aping me he will die wretchedly
> Just like the calf that eats the mud as well
> When copying the tusker eating lotus,
> Watchful in the river, shaking off soil.

Vin. Cv. 7:4

"Bhikkhus, a bhikkhu is fit to go on a mission when he has eight qualities. What are the eight? Here a bhikkhu is one who listens, who gets others to listen, who learns, who remembers, who recognizes, who gets others to recognize, who is skilled in the consistent and the inconsistent, and who does not make trouble. A bhikkhu is fit to go on a mission when he has these eight qualities. Now Sāriputta has these eight qualities; consequently he is fit to go on a mission."

> He does not falter when he comes
> Before a high assembly;
> He does not lose his thread of speech,
> Or cover up his message.
> Unhesitatingly, he speaks out;
> No questioning can ruffle him—
> A bhikkhu such as this is fit
> To go upon a mission.

Vin. Cv. 7:4; A. 8:16

"Bhikkhus, Devadatta is overcome and his mind is obsessed by eight evil things, for which he will inevitably go to the states of privation, to hell, for the duration of the age. What are the eight?

They are gain, lack of gain, fame, lack of fame, honour, lack of honour, evil wishes, and evil friends. Devadatta will go to the states of privation, to hell, for the duration of the age because he is overcome and his mind is obsessed by these eight things.

"Bhikkhus, it is good constantly to overcome each and all of these eight things as they arise. And with what benefit in view does a bhikkhu do so? While taints and fever of defilement might arise in him who did not constantly overcome each and all of these things as they arise, there are no taints and fever of defilement in him who constantly overcomes each and all of these things as they arise. Therefore, bhikkhus, train yourselves thus: 'We shall constantly overcome each and all of these things as they arise.'

"Devadatta is overcome and his mind is obsessed by three evil things, for which he will inevitably go to the states of privation, to hell, for the duration of the age. What are the three? They are evil wishes, evil friends, and stopping halfway with the attainment of the mere earthly distinction of supernormal powers."

Vin. Cv. 7:4; A. 8:7; Iti. 89

NARRATOR TWO. The Canon does not relate the actual circumstances of Devadatta's death. According to the Commentary the earth opened and he was swallowed up and engulfed in hell, to remain there till the destruction of the hells on the advent of the next cycle of world contraction. The Commentary—but not the Canon—also relates that after King Bimbisāra's abdication, his son Ajātasattu had him imprisoned and later put to death. The accession of the ambitious Ajātasattu was followed by wars between the two dominant kingdoms of Magadha and Kosala—between nephew and uncle.

FIRST VOICE. Thus I heard. The Blessed One was living at Sāvatthī. Now at that time Ajātasattu Vedehiputta, King of Magadha, mustered a four-constituent army with elephants, cavalry, charioteers and infantry, and he marched into the Kāsi country against Pasenadi, King of Kosala. King Pasenadi heard about it, and himself mustering a four-constituent army, he advanced into the Kāsi country to engage King Ajātasattu in battle. The two kings fought. In that war King Ajātasattu beat King Pasenadi, who retreated to his own royal capital, Sāvatthī. Bhikkhus gathering alms in Sāvatthī heard about this, and they went and told the Blessed One. He said:

"Bhikkhus, Ajātasattu Vedehiputta, King of Magadha, has bad friends, bad allies, bad intimates; Pasenadi, King of Kosala, has good friends, good allies, good intimates. But King Pasenadi will pass this night in suffering as one who is beaten."

Conquest begets enemies;
One vanquished has a bed of pain,
A man at peace can lie in quiet—
No conquest or defeat for him.

Later the two kings fought as before. But in that battle King Pasenadi captured King Ajātasattu alive. Then it occurred to King Pasenadi: "Though this Ajātasattu Vedehiputta, King of Magadha, has injured me who did him no injury, still he is my nephew. Why should I not confiscate all his elephants, his horses, his chariots and his infantry, and let him go alive?" Bhikkhus gathering alms in Sāvatthī heard about this, and they went and told the Blessed One. Knowing the meaning of this, the Blessed One then uttered this exclamation:

A man may plunder as he will.
When others plunder in return,
He, plundered, plunders them again.
The fool believes he is in luck
As long as evil does not ripen;
But when it does, the fool fares ill.

The slayer gets himself a slayer,
The victor finds a conqueror,
The abuser gets himself abused,
The persecutor persecuted;
The wheel of deeds turns round again
And makes the plundered plunderers.

S. 3:14-15

14
OLD AGE

First Voice. Thus I heard. Once when the Blessed One was living at Sāvatthī King Pasenadi of Kosala came to see him at midday. The Blessed One asked him: "Where are you coming from at midday, great king?"

"Lord, I am now much exercised in the administration of those things that have to be done by anointed warrior kings who are drunk with authority and obsessed with lust for sensual pleasures, who have stabilized their countries and survive the conquest of a wide stretch of the earth."

"What is your opinion, great king? If a trustworthy and reliable man came to you from the east and said: 'Please know, sire, that I come from the east. There I saw a huge mountain as high as the heavens advancing and crushing every living thing. Do what should be done by you, sire.' And then a man came from the west, and another from the north, and another from the south, and each reported the same thing. Now with such a mighty menace impending, with merciless destruction of humanity, with human existence no more possible to retain, what should you do?"

"At such a time as that, Lord, what else can I do but walk in the Dhamma, walk in righteousness, cultivate what is wholesome and make merit?"

"I tell you, great king, I declare to you: ageing and death are closing in upon you. With ageing and death closing in upon you, great king, what should you do?"

"With ageing and death closing in upon me, Lord, what else can I do but walk in the Dhamma, in righteousness, cultivate what is wholesome and make merit? As for the things that can be done by anointed warrior kings drunk with authority and obsessed with lust for sensual pleasures, who have stabilized their countries and survive the conquest of a wide stretch of the earth—I mean fighting battles with elephants, horses, chariots and infantry—there is no scope or use for those battles when ageing and death are closing in upon me. In my court there are ministers expert in spells able to confound advancing enemies; but there is no scope or use for those battles when ageing and death are closing in upon me. In my court there is ample gold and bullion stored away underground and laid up in storerooms to buy over advancing enemies with money; but there is no scope or use for those battles when ageing and death are closing in upon me. When ageing and death are closing in upon me, Lord, what else can I do but walk in the Dhamma, walk in righteousness, cultivate what is wholesome and make merit?"

"So it is, great king, so it is. When ageing and death are closing in upon you, what else can you do but walk in the Dhamma, walk in righteousness, cultivate what is wholesome and make merit?"

S. 3:25

Once when the Blessed One was living at Sāvatthī in the Eastern Monastery, the Palace of Migāra's Mother, he had arisen from retreat in the evening and was sitting warming his back in the rays of the setting sun. The venerable Ānanda went up to him and paid homage. While he was rubbing the Blessed One's limbs he said: "It is wonderful, Lord, it is marvellous! Now the colour of the Blessed One's skin is no more clear and bright; all his limbs are flaccid and wrinkled, his body is bent forward, and there seems a change in the sense faculties of his eyes, ears, nose, tongue and bodily sensation."

"So it is, Ānanda, so it is. Youth has to age, health has to sicken, life has to die. Now the colour of my skin is no more clear and bright; all my limbs are flaccid and wrinkled, my body is bent forward, and there seems a change in the sense faculties of my eyes, ears, nose, tongue and bodily sensation."

So the Blessed One said. When the Sublime One had said this, the Master said further:

Shame on you, sordid Age!
Maker of ugliness.
Age has now trampled down
The form that once had grace.
To live a hundred years
Is not to cheat Decay
That gives quarter to none
And tramples down all things.

S. 48:41

Once the Blessed One was living at Sāmagāma in the Sakyan country just after the Nigaṇṭha Nāthaputta had died at Pāvā. The Nigaṇṭhas had split after his death into two factions, and they were brawling, wrangling, squabbling and wounding each other with verbal arrows: "You do not know this Dhamma and Discipline. How will you get to know this Dhamma and Discipline? Your way is wrong. My way is right. I am consistent. You are inconsistent. What should have been said first you said last. What should have been said last you said first. What you had threshed out has been turned upside down. Your teaching has been refuted. You are worsted. Go and learn better, or disentangle yourself if you can." It seemed as if there was internecine strife among the Nigaṇṭha Nāthaputta's pupils. And his white-clothed lay disciples were as disappointed, dismayed and disgusted with his pupils as they were with his ill-declared Dhamma and Discipline that was one hard to penetrate, leading nowhere, unconducive to peace, proclaimed by one not fully enlightened, with its shrine now broken and left without a refuge.

Then the novice Cunda, who had spent the rains at Pāvā, went to the venerable Ānanda and told him what had happened. They went together to the Blessed One and the venerable Ānanda informed him of what the novice Cunda had said. He added: "Lord, I thought: 'Let there be no disputes when the Blessed One is gone. Disputes are for the misfortune and unhappiness of many, for the harm, misfortune and suffering of gods and men.' "

"Ānanda, what is your opinion? These teachings that I have directly known and taught to you—I mean the four foundations of mindfulness, the four right endeavours, the four bases for success, the five spiritual faculties, the five powers, the seven enlightenment factors and the Noble Eightfold Path—-do you see even two bhikkhus that describe them discordantly?"

"No, Lord, but there are people who live submissive to the Blessed One now who might, when he is gone, create disputes in the Sangha about livelihood and about the Code of Monastic Rules. Such disputes would be for the misfortune and unhappiness of many."

"Dispute over livelihood or over the Code of Monastic Rules is trifling, Ānanda. But should disputes arise in the Sangha about the path or the way of practice, such disputes as those would indeed be for the misfortune and unhappiness of many."

M. 104

At one time the Blessed One was living at Vesālī in the grove outside the city to the west. It was then that Sunakkhatta, a son of the Licchavis, had just left this Dhamma and Discipline, and he was making this statement at meetings in Vesālī: "The monk Gotama has no distinction higher than any human state worthy of a noble one's knowledge and vision. The monk Gotama teaches a Dhamma merely hammered out by thought, following his own line of inquiry as it occurs to him, and whoever is taught that Dhamma for his benefit, it only leads to the complete exhaustion of suffering in him when he practises it, (but not to anything else)."

The venerable Sāriputta heard this, and he told the Blessed One. "Sāriputta, the misguided man Sunakkhatta is a man of anger, and it is in anger that these words of his are spoken. Thinking to disparage the Perfect One, he actually praises him; for it is praise of the Perfect One to say: 'And whoever is taught that Dhamma for his benefit, it only leads to the complete exhaustion of suffering in him when he practises it.'

"Now as one who has lived it out I have had direct experience of the kind of holy life known as that with four factors: I have practised the extremes of asceticism, of roughness, of scrupulousness, and of seclusion.

"This was my asceticism,[1] I went naked, rejecting conventions, licking my hands, not coming when asked, not stopping when asked; I did not accept a thing brought, or a thing specially made, or an invitation; I received nothing from out of a pot, from out of a bowl, across a threshold, across a stick, across a pestle, from two eating together, from a woman with child, from a woman giving suck, from where a woman was lying with a man, from where food was being distributed, from where a dog was waiting, from where flies were buzzing; I accepted no fish or meat, I drank no spirits or wine or fermented liquors. I kept to one house, to one morsel; I kept to two houses, to two morsels .... I kept to seven houses, to seven morsels. I lived on one saucerful, on two saucerfuls ... on seven saucerfuls a day; I took food once each day, once each two days ... once each seven days; and so, up to once each fortnight, I dwelt pursuing the practice of taking food at stated intervals. I was an eater of greens, or millet, or wild rice, or hide-parings, or moss, or rice-bran, or rinsings, or sesamum flour, or grass, or cowdung; I lived on forest roots and fruits as a feeder on windfalls. I clothed myself in hemp, in hemp mixture, in shrouds, in refuse rags, in tree bark, in antelope hide, in kusa-grass fabric, in bark fabric, in wood fabric, in head-hair wool, in animal wool, in owls' wings. I was one who pulled out hair and beard, pursuing the practice of pulling out hair and beard. I was one who stood continuously, rejecting seats. I was one who squatted continuously, devoted to maintaining the squatting position. I was one who used a mattress of spikes; I made a mattress of spikes my bed. I dwelt pursuing the practice of bathing in water for the third time by nightfall. In fact, I dwelt pursuing the practice of torment and torture of the body in its many aspects. Such was my asceticism.

"This was my roughness. Just as the bole of a tinduka tree, accumulating over years, cakes and flakes off, so too the dust and dirt, accumulating over years, caked on my body and flaked off. It did not occur to me: 'Oh, let me rub this dust and dirt off with my hand, or let another rub this dust and dirt off with his hand'—it never occurred to me thus. Such was my roughness.

"This was my scrupulousness. I was always mindful in stepping to and fro, so much so that I was full of pity even for a drop of water thus: 'Let me not hurt the tiny creatures in the crevices of the ground.' Such was my scrupulousness.

"This was my seclusion. I would go away into some wood and stay there. Just as a forest-bred deer, on seeing human beings, flees from grove to grove, from thicket to thicket, from hollow to hollow, from hillock to hillock, so too, when I saw a cowherd, or a shepherd, or someone gathering grass or sticks, or a woodsman, I would flee from grove to grove, from thicket to thicket, from hollow to hollow, from hillock to hillock. Why was that? So that they should not see me or I them. Such was my seclusion.

"I would go on all fours to the byres when the cattle had gone out and the cowherds had left them, and I would feed on the young sucking-calves' dung. As long as my own excrement and urine lasted, I fed on my own urine and excrement. Such was my great distortion in feeding.

"I would go away into some awe-inspiring grove and live there—a grove so awe-inspiring that normally it would make a man's hair stand up if he were not free from lust. I would dwell by night in the open and by day in the grove when those cold wintry nights came during the 'eight days of frost.' I would dwell by day in the open and by night in the grove in the last month of the hot season. And there came to me spontaneously this stanza never heard before:

"Chilled by night and scorched by day,
Alone in awe-inspiring groves,
Naked, no fire to sit beside,
The hermit still pursues his quest.

"I would make my bed in a charnel ground with the bones of the dead for a pillow. And cowherd boys came up and spat on me, made water on me, threw dirt at me, and poked sticks into my ears. But I never thought ill of them. Such was my equanimity.

"There are some monks and brahmans who assert and believe that purification comes through food; and they say: 'Let us live on kola fruits,' And they eat kola fruits, and they eat kola-fruit powder, and they drink kola-fruit water, and they make many kinds of kola-fruit concoctions. Now I have had the experience of eating a single kola fruit a day. But, Sāriputta, it might be that you think the kola fruit was bigger at that time; yet you should not regard it so. The kola fruit was then at most the same size as now. Through feeding on a single kola fruit a day, my body reached a state of extreme emaciation.... Again, there are some monks and brahmans who assert and believe that purification comes through food, and they say: 'Let us live on beans.' ... They say: 'Let us live on sesamum.' ... They say: 'Let us live on rice.' ... Now I have had the experience of eating a single bean ... a single sesamum seed ... a single rice grain a day .... But by that rite, that observance, that practice of difficult feats, I acquired no distinction higher than the human state worthy of a noble one's knowledge and vision. Why not? Because I did not gain the noble understanding, which, on being attained, leads to the complete exhaustion of suffering in him who practises it, because it belongs to the noble state and leads forth (from the world).

"There are some monks and brahmans who assert and believe that purification comes through some particular round of rebirths. 'But it is impossible to find the round of rebirths that I have not already traversed in this long journey—-except for the Pure Abodes;[2] for had I been born in the Pure Abodes, I should never have come back to this world.

"There are some monks and brahmans who assert and believe

that purification comes through sacrifice. But it is impossible to find the kind of sacrifice that has not already been offered up by me in this long journey, as an anointed warrior-caste king or as a rich member of the brahman caste.

"There are some monks and brahmans who assert and believe that purification comes through fire-worship. But it is impossible to find the kind of fire that has not already been worshipped by me in this long journey, as an anointed warrior-caste king or as a rich member of the brahman caste.

"There are some monks and brahmans who assert and believe thus: 'As long as this good man is still young, a black-haired boy, blessed with youth, in the first phase of life, so long is he perfect in lucid understanding. But when this good man is old, aged, burdened with years, advanced in life, and come to the last stage, being eighty, ninety or a hundred years old, then the lucidity of his understanding is lost.' But it should not be regarded so. I am now old, aged, burdened with years, advanced in life, and come to the last stage: my years have turned eighty. Now suppose I had four disciples with a hundred years' life, a hundred years' span, perfect in mindfulness, attentiveness, memory and lucidity of understanding—just as a well-equipped archer, trained, practised and tested, could easily shoot a light arrow across a palm's shadow; suppose they were even to that extent perfect in mindfulness, attentiveness, memory and lucidity of understanding—and suppose they continuously asked about the four foundations of mindfulness, and I answered when asked, and they remembered each answer, and they never asked subsidiary questions, or paused except to eat, drink, chew and taste and to make water and evacuate and to rest in order to get rid of drowsiness: still the Perfect One's exposition of the Dhamma, his explanations of the factors of the Dhamma, and his replies to questions, would be unexhausted. But meanwhile those four disciples of mine with their hundred years' life, their hundred years' span, would have died at the end of those hundred years. Sāriputta, even if you have to carry me about on a bed, there will still be no change in the lucidity of the Perfect One's understanding."

M. 12

NARRATOR ONE. In the Buddha's last years a number of vexatious events occurred—events, that is, which would have been vexatious to ordinary judgement. It has just been told how a former bhikkhu, Sunakkhatta (once a personal attendant of the Buddha's), had renounced him and was speaking against him in public, belittling his worldly supernormal powers, whereupon the Buddha uttered his "lion's roar," his declaration that there was no self-mortification that he had not practised, no method of self-purification that he had not tried. Then he was soon to lose his two chief disciples. Meanwhile, King Pasenadi of Kosala, his devoted supporter for more than forty years, was now increasingly bothered by political upsets.

NARRATOR TWO. King Pasenadi was the same age as the Buddha and accordingly in his eightieth year. He had been troubled by desultory and profitless wars with his nephew, King Ajātasattu of Magadha, and by periodical unrest in his own kingdom. As the result of a palace intrigue, his army chief, General Bandhula, was accused of plotting against him and was put to death. Later, however, he learnt that the general was innocent. Remorse haunted him. In order to make some amends, perhaps, he had the general's nephew, Dīgha Kārāyana, promoted to that post.

Commentary to M. 89 and D. 16

NARRATOR ONE. King Pasenadi went to the Buddha for advice. When his devoted consort, Queen Mallikā, had died, he went in deep dejection to the Buddha, who was then at Sāvatthī, to seek consolation.

See A. 5:49

NARRATOR TWO. The king's palace and his brilliant capital now no longer gave him any pleasure. He left it for a time to wander from place to place with a large retinue, but with no special plan.

NARRATOR ONE. During these nostalgic and uneasy wanderings the old king's path sometimes crossed that of the Buddha, and then he would go to see him. His death is not recorded in the Tipiṭaka; but one discourse is placed by the Commentary among the events that immediately preceded it. Here is the account of their last meeting.

FIRST VOICE. Thus I heard. At one time the Blessed One was living in the Sakyan country at a Sakyan town called Medaḷumpa.

Now on that occasion King Pasenadi of Kosala had arrived at Nāgaraka for some business or other. Then he told Dīgha Kārāyana: "My friend, have the state coaches summoned. Let us go to the pleasure park to see a pleasant view."

"Even so, sire," Dīgha Kārāyana replied. When the coaches were ready, he informed the king: "Sire, the state coaches are ready. Now it is time for you to do as you think fit."

So King Pasenadi mounted a state coach, and he drove with the full pomp of royalty in the direction of the park. He went thus as far as the road was passable for carriages; then he dismounted and proceeded on foot. While he was walking and wandering for exercise he observed roots of trees that inspired trust and confidence in him; they were quiet and undisturbed by voices, with an atmosphere of aloofness, where one could lie hidden from people, favourable for retreat. The sight of them reminded him of the Blessed One. Then he said: "Dīgha Kārāyana, my friend, these roots of trees are like those ... where we used to do honour to the Blessed One, accomplished and fully enlightened. Where is he living now, the Blessed One, accomplished and fully enlightened?"

"There is a Sakyan town called Medaḷumpa, sire. The Blessed One, accomplished and fully enlightened, is living there now."

"How far is it from Nāgaraka to Medaḷumpa?"

"It is not far, sire; some three leagues. There is still daylight enough left to go there."

"Then have the coaches made ready, my friend. Let us go and see the Blessed One, accomplished and fully enlightened."

"Even so, sire," Dīgha Kārāyana replied. So the king drove from Nāgaraka to the Sakyan town of Medaḷumpa, arriving there while it was still day. He went towards the park, driving as far as the road was passable for carriages. Then he dismounted and proceeded on foot.

Now on that occasion several bhikkhus were walking up and down in the open. The king approached them and asked: "Venerable sirs, where is he living now, the Blessed One, accomplished and fully enlightened? We should like to see the Blessed One, accomplished and fully enlightened."

"That is his dwelling, great king, with the door shut. Go up to it quietly and on to the porch without hurry; then cough and tap on the panel. The Blessed One will open the door to you."

King Pasenadi took off his sword and royal turban then and there, and he consigned them to Dīgha Kārāyana. Dīgha Kārāyana thought: "So the king is going into secret session now: have I got to wait here alone now?"

The king went up to the door as directed. When he tapped on the panel, the Blessed One opened the door. The king went into the dwelling, and he prostrated himself at the Blessed One's feet. He covered the Blessed One's feet with kisses, and he caressed them with his hands, pronouncing his name thus: "Lord, I am King Pasenadi of Kosala; Lord, I am King Pasenadi of Kosala."

"But, great king, what benefit do you see in doing such extreme honour to this body and in showing such friendship?"

"Lord, I believe this to be true of the Blessed One: The Blessed One is fully enlightened; the Dhamma is well proclaimed by the Blessed One; the Sangha of the Blessed One's disciples has entered upon the good way. Now, Lord, I see some monks and brahmans leading the holy life within limits for ten, twenty, thirty, forty years; and then later on I see them enjoying themselves furnished with all the five kinds of sense pleasures and indulging in them. Here, however, I see bhikkhus leading the holy life in all its perfection as long as life and breath last. Indeed, Lord, I see nowhere else a holy life so perfected as here. That is why I believe this to be true of the Blessed One: The Blessed One is fully enlightened; the Dhamma is well proclaimed by the Blessed One; the Sangha of the Blessed One's disciples has entered upon the good way.

"Again, Lord, kings quarrel with kings, warrior nobles with warrior nobles, brahmans with brahmans, householders with householders, mother with child, child with mother, father with child, child with father, brother with brother, brother with sister, sister with brother, friend with friend. But here I see bhikkhus enjoying concord, living as undisputing as milk with water and regarding each other with kindly eyes. Indeed, Lord, I see nowhere else any assembly so harmonious. That is also a reason why I believe this to be true of the Blessed One.

"Again, Lord, I have walked and wandered from park to park and from garden to garden, and I have seen there some monks and brahmans who were lean, wretched, unsightly, jaundiced, with veins knotted on their limbs, hardly such, one would think, as to make people want to look at them again. I thought: 'Surely these venerable ones are leading the holy life dissatisfied, or they have committed some crime and are hiding it, that they are like that.' I went up to them and asked why they were like that, and they replied: 'We have the family sickness, great king.' But here I see bhikkhus smiling and cheerful, sincerely joyful, plainly delighting, their faculties fresh, unexcited, unruffled, living by what others give, dwelling with minds like the wild deer. I thought: 'Surely these venerable ones perceive extraordinary successive distinctions in the Blessed One's dispensation that they are like that.' That is also a reason why I believe this to be true of the Blessed One.

"Again, Lord, as an anointed warrior-noble king, I am able to have executed those who should be executed, to fine those who should be fined, and to exile those who should be exiled. Yet when I am sitting in council, they interrupt me. Though I say, 'Gentlemen, do not interrupt me when I am sitting in council, wait till the end of my speech,' still they interrupt me. But here I see an audience of several hundred bhikkhus, and while the Blessed One is expounding the Dhamma there is not even the sound of hawking or throat-clearing among his disciples. Once the Blessed One was expounding the Dhamma to an audience of several hundred, and a disciple of the Blessed One's cleared his throat. Then one of his companions in the holy life nudged him with his knee, saying: 'Quiet, venerable sir, do not make a noise. The Master is expounding the Dhamma.' I thought: 'It is wonderful, it is marvellous! An audience can be so well disciplined, it seems, without either punishment or weapon.' Indeed, Lord, I see nowhere else any audience so well disciplined. That is also a reason why I believe this to be true of the Blessed One.

"Again, Lord, I have seen here certain warrior-noble scholars, certain brahman scholars, certain wise householder scholars, certain monk scholars, that were clever and knew others' theories as a hair-splitting marksman knows archery: one would think they must surely go about demolishing false views with the understanding they possess. They hear: 'The monk Gotama will visit such and such a village or town.' They formulate a question: 'If he is asked like this, he will answer like this, and so we shall refute his theory; and if he is asked like this, he will. answer like this, and so we shall refute his theory.' They hear: 'The monk Gotama has come to visit such and such a village or town.' They go to the monk Gotama. The monk Gotama instructs, urges, rouses and encourages them with talk on the Dhamma. After that they do not even ask him the question, so how should they refute his theory? In actual fact they become his disciples. That is also a reason why I believe this to be true of the Blessed One.

"Again, Lord, there are Isidatta and Purāṇa, my two carpenters, who accept food and keep from me, and whose provider of livelihood and bringer of fame I am. In spite of that they are less respectful to me than they are to the Blessed One. Once when I had gone out with an army on manoeuvres and was testing these carpenters, I happened to put up in a very cramped dwelling. Then these two carpenters spent much of the night in talk on the Dhamma, after which they lay down with their heads towards where they had heard the Blessed One was and their feet towards me. I thought: 'It is wonderful, it is marvellous! Surely these good men perceive extraordinary successive distinctions in the Blessed One's Dispensation.' That is also a reason why I believe this to be true of the Blessed One: The Blessed One is fully enlightened; the Dhamma is well proclaimed by the Blessed One; the Sangha of the Blessed One's disciples has entered upon the good way.

"Again, Lord, the Blessed One is a warrior noble and I am a warrior noble; the Blessed One is a Kosalan and I am a Kosalan; the Blessed One is eighty and I am eighty. These are reasons why I think it proper to do such extreme honour to the Blessed One and to show such friendship. And now, Lord, we depart. We are busy and have much to do."

"It is time now, great king, to do as you think fit."

Then King Pasenadi of Kosala got up from his seat, and after paying homage to the Blessed One, he departed, keeping him on his right.

Soon after he had gone the Blessed One addressed the bhikkhus thus: "Bhikkhus, this King Pasenadi has uttered monuments to the Dhamma before rising from his seat and departing. Learn the monuments to the Dhamma. Remember them, for they are conducive to welfare, and belong to the fundamentals of the holy life."

That is what the Blessed One said. The bhikkhus were satisfied, and they delighted in his words.

M. 89

Narrator One. What happened to the king after he left the interview is told only in the Commentary.

Narrator Two. When the king went to the Buddha's dwelling leaving the royal insignia with Dīgha Kārāyana, the latter was resentful and suspicious. He began to fancy that the king had had his uncle the general executed after an earlier private interview with the Buddha, and now he wondered if his own turn was about to come. As soon as the king had gone inside the dwelling, Dīgha Kārāyana left, taking the insignia with him back to the encampment. There he told the king's son, Prince Viḍuḍabha, to occupy the throne forthwith, threatening to do so himself unless he was obeyed. The prince agreed. Then leaving behind one horse, a sword, and one lady of the zenana there, Dīgha Kārāyana and the rest of the retinue set off post haste to Sāvatthī, after telling the lady in waiting to warn the king not to follow if he valued his life. When the king came out from the Buddha's dwelling and saw no one there, he went to the camping place. There the lady in waiting told him what had happened.

He decided to turn for help to his nephew, King Ajātasattu. On the long journey to Rājagaha he ate coarse food of a kind he was not used to and drank a lot of water. It was late when he arrived at Rājagaha and the city gates were closed, so he had to pass the night hours in the common resthouse. During the night he was attacked by a violent illness; towards dawn he expired. The lady in waiting in whose arms he died set up a loud lamentation: "My lord the king of Kosala who ruled two countries has died a pauper's death and is now lying in a common pauper's resthouse outside a foreign city!" The news was carried to King Ajātasattu, who at once ordered a royal funeral. Afterwards he made a becoming show of indignation by ordering a punitive attack against his cousin, now King Viḍuḍabha, but he soon allowed his ministers to persuade him that, with the old king dead, such an attempt might be inexpedient as well as vain, and he duly recognized his cousin's succession.

15
THE LAST YEAR

Narrator One. The events that follow happened within a year ending with the Buddha's attainment of final Nibbāna. All these events, except for the mention of the final passing of the two chief disciples, are contained in one record or sutta. It is only now in fact that a chronological relation of events is resumed in the Canon.

First Voice. Thus I heard. At one time the Blessed One was living on the Vulture Peak Rock at Rājagaha. King Ajātasattu was then anxious to attack the Vajjians. He was saying: "I will exterminate these Vajjians who are so mighty and powerful, I will destroy them, I will bring them to rack and ruin."

King Ajātasattu then told the brahman Vassakāra, a Magadhan minister: "Come, brahman, go to the Blessed One and say: 'Lord, Ajātasattu Vedehiputta, King of Magadha, pays homage with his head at the Blessed One's feet, and asks if he is free from affliction and sickness and enjoying health, strength and happiness.' And say: 'Lord, Ajātasattu Vedehiputta, King of Magadha, is anxious to attack the Vajjians. He says: "I will exterminate these Vajjians who are so mighty and powerful, I will destroy them, I will bring them to rack and ruin." ' Note well what his answer is and report it to me; for Perfect Ones never lie."

"Even so, sire," Vassakāra replied. Then he had a number of state coaches summoned. Mounting one of them, he drove out of Rājagaha towards the Vulture Peak Rock as far as the way was passable for carriages. Then he alighted and went on foot to where the Blessed One was. He greeted him and sat down at one side. When he had done so, he delivered his message.

The Blessed One addressed himself to the venerable Ānanda, who was standing behind him, fanning him: "Ānanda, have you heard whether the Vajjians hold frequent and well-attended meetings?"

"They do, Lord."

"As long as they do so, Ānanda, they can be expected to prosper and not decline. Have you heard whether they assemble in concord, rise in concord, and do their duty as Vajjians in concord—whether they avoid enacting the unenacted or abolishing existing enactments and proceed in accordance with the ancient Vajjian laws as enacted—whether they honour, respect, revere and venerate the Vajjian elders and think they should be heeded whether they live without raping and abducting the women and girls of their clans—whether they honour, respect, revere and venerate the Vajjian shrines both in town and country without allowing the lawful oblations, hitherto given and made, to lapse—whether lawful protection, defence and guarding is provided among the Vajjians for Arahants so that Arahants who have not come to the realm may come and Arahants who have come may live happily?"

"They do, Lord."

"As long as they do so, Ānanda, they may be expected to prosper and not decline."

Then the Blessed One spoke to Vassakāra: "Once, brahman, when I was living at Vesālī in the Sārandada Shrine, I taught the Vajjians these seven things that prevent decline. As long as they persist and are taught among them, the Vajjians may be expected to prosper and not decline."

When this was said, Vassakāra remarked: "If the Vajjians possess a single one of them, Master Gotama, they may be expected to prosper and not decline, so what can be said if they possess all seven? Indeed, Master Gotama, King Ajātasattu will never get the better of the Vajjians by fighting, unless he buys them over and sows dissension among them. But now we must go, Master Gotama. We are busy and have much to do."

"It is time now, brahman, to do as you think fit."

Vassakāra was satisfied. Delighting in the Blessed One's words, he got up, and after expressing his appreciation, went away. As soon as he had gone the Blessed One told the venerable Ānanda: "Ānanda, go and summon all the bhikkhus who are living in the neighbourhood of Rājagaha to meet in the service hall."

"Even so, Lord," he replied. When he had done this, he informed the Blessed One. Then the Blessed One got up from his seat and went to the service hall, where he sat down on a seat made ready. Then he addressed the bhikkhus: "Bhikkhus, I shall teach you seven things that prevent decline. Listen and attend carefully to what I shall say."

"Even so, Lord," they replied.

The Blessed One said: "As long as bhikkhus hold frequent and well-attended meetings—as long as they assemble in concord, rise in concord and do their duty as members of the Sangha in concord—as long as they avoid enacting the unenacted or abolishing the existing enactments and proceed in accordance with the training precepts as enacted—as long as they honour, respect, revere and venerate the senior bhikkhus who are experienced, long gone forth and fathers and guides of the Sangha, and think they should be heeded—as long as when craving that leads to renewal of being arises they do not fall into its power—as long as they esteem forest abodes—as long as they maintain mindfulness in themselves so that decent companions in the holy life who have not come to them may come and decent companions in the holy life who have come may live happily—so long may they be expected to prosper and not decline.

"Another seven things that prevent decline: as long as bhikkhus avoid delighting, rejoicing and taking pleasure in being busy, in gossiping, in sleeping, and in society; as long as they have no evil wishes and avoid falling under their spell; as long as they have no evil friends and avoid falling under their spell; as long as they do not stop half-way with the attainment of only the lower, worldly distinctions—so long may they be expected to prosper and not decline.

"Another seven things that prevent decline: as long as bhikkhus have faith, conscience, and a sense of shame, are learned, energetic, and mindful, and possess understanding, so long may they be expected to prosper and not decline.

"Another seven things that prevent decline: as long as bhikkhus maintain in being the enlightenment factors of mindfulness, investigation-of-states, energy, happiness, tranquillity, concentration, and equanimity, so long may they be expected to prosper and not decline.

"Another seven things that prevent decline: as long as bhikkhus develop the perceptions of impermanence, of not-self, of loathsomeness in the body, of danger, of abandoning of lust, of fading away of lust, and of cessation of lust, so long may they be expected to prosper and not decline."

D. 16; A. 7:20

"Six things that prevent decline: as long as bhikkhus maintain both publicly and privately towards their companions in the holy life, bodily, verbal and mental acts of loving-kindness; as long as they are impartial and indiscriminate sharers with virtuous companions in the holy life of lawful gain lawfully acquired, even of what is contained in the bowl; as long as bhikkhus among their companions in the holy life live both publicly and privately possessed of virtues that are unbroken, untorn, unblotched, unmottled, emancipating, commended by the wise, not misinterpreted, and conducive to concentration; as long as bhikkhus live possessed of the noble ones' view that leads out (from the round of rebirths), that leads to the complete exhaustion of suffering for him who gives effect to it—so long may they be expected to prosper and not decline.

"As long as these things that prevent decline persist and are taught among the bhikkhus, they may be expected to prosper and not decline."

And while the Blessed One was living there at Rājagaha on the Vulture Peak Rock, he often gave this talk on the Dhamma to the bhikkhus: "Such is virtue, such is concentration, such is understanding; concentration fortified with virtue brings great benefits and great fruits; understanding fortified with concentration brings great benefits and great fruits; the heart fortified with understanding becomes completely liberated from taints: from the taint of sensual desire, the taint of being, the taint of views, and the taint of ignorance."

When the Blessed One had lived at Rājagaha as long as he chose, he said to the venerable Ānanda: ,Come, Ānanda, let us go to Ambalaṭṭhikā."

"Even so, Lord," the venerable Ānanda replied. Then the Blessed One journeyed to Ambalaṭṭhikā with a large community of bhikkhus. While there he lived in the King's House in Ambalaṭṭhikā.

And while the Blessed One was living there too he often gave this talk on the Dhamma to the bhikkhus: "Such is virtue, such is concentration, such is understanding; concentration fortified with virtue brings great benefits and great fruits; understanding fortified with concentration brings great benefits and great fruits; the heart fortified with understanding becomes completely liberated from taints: from the taint of sensual desire, the taint of being, the taint of views, and the taint of ignorance."

When the Blessed One had stayed at Ambalaṭṭhikā as long as he chose, he said to the venerable Ānanda: "Come, Ānanda, let us go to Nālandā."

"Even so, Lord," the venerable Ānanda replied. Then the Blessed One journeyed to Nālandā with a large community of bhikkhus. While there he lived in the Pāvārika Mango Grove in Nālandā.

D. 16

Then the venerable Sāriputta went to the Blessed One and said: "Lord, I am convinced of this: that there never has been, never will be, and is not, any other monk or brahman more distinguished in enlightenment than the Blessed One."

"That is a grand and bold statement to make, Sāriputta, an uncompromising lion's roar to utter. Are all past Blessed Ones, accomplished and fully enlightened, then, known to you by reading their minds with your mind thus: 'Such was their virtue, such their concentration, such their understanding, such the attainment they abode in, such the manner of their deliverance'?"

"No, Lord."

"Are all future Blessed Ones, accomplished and fully enlightened, then known to you by reading their minds in that way?"

"No, Lord."

"Am I, now, accomplished and fully enlightened, then known to you by reading my mind in that way?"

"No, Lord".

"Then how can you make this grand and bold statement and utter this uncompromising lion's roar?"

"Lord, I have no knowledge of reading with my mind the minds of past, future and present accomplished and fully enlightened ones. Nevertheless, a certainty about the Dhamma is known to me. Suppose a king had a frontier city with strong ditches, ramparts and bastions and a single gate, and he had a wise, clever, sagacious gatekeeper there who stopped those whom he did not know and admitted only those whom he knew; and since he had himself gone round the path encircling the city and had seen no gaps in the ramparts or any hole even big enough for a cat to pass through, he might conclude that living beings above a certain size must go in and out through the gate—so too, Lord, a certainty about the Dhamma is known to me. All the past Blessed Ones, accomplished and fully enlightened, had their minds well established upon the four foundations of mindfulness; after abandoning the five hindrances, the defilements of the heart that weaken understanding, they have discovered the supreme full enlightenment by maintaining in being the seven enlightenment factors. All the future Blessed Ones, accomplished and fully enlightened, will do likewise. The Blessed One now, accomplished and fully enlightened, has done likewise."

D. 16; S. 47:12

And while the Blessed One was living there at Nālandā in the Pāvārika Mango Grove, he often gave this talk on the Dhamma to the bhikkhus: "Such is virtue, such is concentration, such is understanding; concentration fortified with virtue brings great benefits and great fruits; understanding fortified with concentration brings great benefits and great fruits; the heart fortified with understanding becomes completely liberated from taints: from the taint of sensual desire, the taint of being, the taint of views, and the taint of ignorance."

When the Blessed One had lived at Nālandā as long as he chose, he said to the venerable Ānanda: "Come, Ānanda, let us go to Pāṭaligāma."

"Even so, Lord," the venerable Ānanda replied. Then the Blessed One journeyed to Pāṭaligāma with a large community of bhikkhus.

The followers at Pāṭaligāma heard: "It seems the Blessed One has arrived at Pāṭaligāma." Then they went to the Blessed One, and after paying homage to him, they sat down at one side. When they had done so, they said: "Let the Blessed One accept a resthouse." The Blessed One consented in silence. Seeing that he consented, they rose from their seats, and after paying homage to him, keeping him on their right, they went to the resthouse. They completely spread it with coverings, and they prepared seats and put out a big water trough and hung up an oil lamp. Then they told the Blessed One what they had done, adding, "Now it is time, Lord, for the Blessed One to do as he thinks fit."

Then the Blessed One dressed, and taking his bowl and outer robe, he went to the resthouse. After washing his feet, he entered it and sat down by the central pillar facing the east. And the bhikkhus of the Sangha, after washing their feet, entered the resthouse and sat down by the western wall facing the east with the Blessed One before them. And the followers from Pāṭaligāma, after washing their feet, entered the resthouse and sat down by the eastern wall facing the west with the Blessed One before them. Then the Blessed One addressed the followers from Pāṭaligāma thus:

"Householders, the unvirtuous man incurs these five dangers through failing in virtue. What five? Here the unvirtuous man who fails in virtue suffers a great loss of wealth through negligence. Secondly, he acquires a bad name. Thirdly, whatever assembly he goes into, whether of warrior-nobles or brahmans or householders or monks, he lacks assurance and wants confidence. Fourthly, he dies confused. Fifthly, on the dissolution of the body, after death, he reappears in a state of privation, in an unhappy destination, in perdition, even in hell.

"But the virtuous man acquires these five benefits through perfection of virtue. What five? Here the virtuous man who has perfected virtue attains great wealth through diligence. Secondly, he acquires a good name. Thirdly, whatever assembly he goes into, whether of warrior-nobles or brahmans or householders or monks, he has assurance and does not want confidence. Fourthly, he dies unconfused. Fifthly, on the dissolution of the body, after death, he reappears in a happy destination, even in a heavenly world."

Then when the Blessed One had instructed, urged, roused and encouraged the followers from Pāṭaligāma for much of the night, he dismissed them, saying: "Householders, the night is far spent; now it is time for you to do as you think fit."

"Even so, Lord," they replied, and getting up from their seats, they paid homage to the Blessed One and departed, keeping him on their right. Soon after they had gone the Blessed One went to an empty room.

At that time Sunidha and Vassakāra, Magadhan ministers, were having a city built at Pāṭaligāma in order to keep the Vajjians at bay. Hosts of deities were then haunting the fields there by the thousands. Now mighty deities sway the minds of mighty kings and ministers to build cities in places haunted by them. Mediocre deities sway the minds of mediocre kings and ministers to build cities in places haunted by them. Minor deities sway the minds of minor kings and ministers to build cities in places haunted by them. With the divine eye, which is purified and surpasses the human, the Blessed One saw those deities. Then when the night was near dawn the Blessed One rose, and he asked the venerable Ānanda: "Ānanda, who is having a city built at Pāṭaligāma?" "Sunidha and Vassakāra are having it done, Lord."

"They are doing it as though they had been counselled by the gods in the Heaven of the Thirty-three," the Blessed One said, and he told what he had seen. He added: "Of all the resorts of noble ones and of all trading centres, Pāṭaliputta[1] will be the greatest of such cities as the place where the treasure-bags are unsealed. It risks three dangers: from fire, water, and dissension."

Then Sunidha and Vassakāra went to the Blessed One and invited him for the following day's meal. After the meal was over, when the Blessed One had eaten and no longer had the bowl in his hand, they took lower seats and sat down at one side. Then the Blessed One gave the blessing with these stanzas:

Where a wise man makes his abode,
There let him feed the virtuous
Who live the good life self-controlled,
And offer to the local gods—
This honour and respect for them
They will return to him in kind
Because their love for him is like
A mother's love for her own child;
And when a man is loved by gods,
He always sees auspicious things.

Then the Blessed One rose from his seat and went away. But on that occasion Sunidha and Vassakāra followed behind the Blessed. One, thinking: "The gate by which the Blessed One leaves shall be called the Gotama Gate; the ford by which he crosses the Ganges shall be called the Gotama Ford." And the gate by which the Blessed One left was called the Gotama Gate. But when the Blessed One came to the River Ganges, it was full and so brimming that crows could drink from it. Some people wanting to go to the further bank were looking for boats, others were looking for floats, and others were lashing rafts together. Then, as quickly as a strong man might extend his flexed arm or flex his extended arm, the Blessed One vanished with the Sangha of bhikkhus on the near bank of the Ganges and stood on the further bank. He saw the people who wanted to get across looking for boats, looking for floats, and lashing rafts together. Knowing the meaning of this, he then uttered this exclamation:

> While those who would cross the flooded stream
> Are bridge-building, avoiding deeps,
> While people lash their rafts together,
> The wise already are across.

D. 16; Ud. 8:6; Vin. Mv. 6:28

Then the Blessed One said to the venerable Ānanda: "Come, Ānanda, let us go to Koṭigāma."

"Even so, Lord," the venerable Ānanda replied. Then the Blessed One journeyed to Koṭigāma with a large community of bhikkhus. There the Blessed One stayed in Koṭigāma. And there he addressed the bhikkhus thus: "Bhikkhus, it is through not discovering, not penetrating, four truths that both you and I have had to travel and trudge through this long round. What four? They are the noble truth of suffering, the noble truth of the origin of suffering, the noble truth of the cessation of suffering, and the noble truth of the way leading to the cessation of suffering. But when these Four Noble Truths are discovered and penetrated, craving for being is cut off, craving that leads to being is abolished, and there is no renewal of being."

And while the Blessed One was living there at Koṭigāma, he often gave this talk on the Dhamma to the bhikkhus: "Such is virtue, such is concentration, such is understanding; concentration fortified with virtue brings great benefits and great fruits; understanding fortified with concentration brings great benefits and great fruits; the heart fortified with understanding becomes completely liberated from taints: from the taint of sensual desire, the taint of being, the taint of views, and the taint of ignorance."

D. 16; Vin. Mv. 6:29

When the Blessed One had stayed at Koṭigāma as long as he chose, he said to the venerable Ānanda: "Come, Ānanda, let us go to Nādikā."

"Even so, Lord," the venerable Ānanda replied. Then the Blessed One journeyed to Nādikā with a large community of bhikkhus. While there he lived in the Brick Hall in Nādikā.

Then the venerable Ānanda went to the Blessed One. He said: "Lord, the bhikkhu named Sāḷha died at Nādikā: what was his destination? What was his rebirth? The bhikkhunī named Nandā, the lay follower named Sudatta, the woman lay follower named Sujātā, the lay followers named Kakudha and Kālinga and Nikaṭa and Kaṭissabha and Tuṭṭha and Santuṭṭha and Bhadda and Subhadda—these died at Nādikā: what was their destination? What was their rebirth?"[2]

"The bhikkhu Sāḷha, Ānanda, by realization himself here and now, entered upon and dwelt in the deliverance of mind and the deliverance by understanding that are taintless through exhaustion of taints. The bhikkhunī Nandā, with the destruction of the five more immediate fetters, reappeared spontaneously elsewhere, there to attain Nibbāna without ever returning from that world. The lay follower Sudatta, with the destruction of three fetters and with the attenuation of lust, hate and delusion, became a once-returner, who will return once to this world to make an end of suffering. The woman lay follower Sujātā, with the destruction of three fetters, became a stream-enterer, no more subject to perdition, certain of rightness, and destined to enlightenment. The lay followers Kakudha, Kālinga, Nikaṭa, Kaṭissabha, Tuṭṭha, Santuṭṭha, Bhadda and Subhadda and also fifty lay followers all became non-returners. Ninety lay followers became once-returners. Over five hundred lay followers became stream-enterers.

"Now it is natural for human beings to die; but if you come and ask this question each time one dies, it wearies the Perfect One. So I shall give you an exposition of the Dhamma called 'the Mirror of the Dhamma,' possessed of which a noble disciple can predict for himself: 'There is no more hell for me, no more animal birth, no more ghost world, no more states of privation, unhappy destinations or perdition; I am a stream-enterer, no more subject to perdition, I am certain of rightness and destined to enlightenment.'

"And what is the exposition of the Dhamma called 'the Mirror of the Dhamma'? Here a noble disciple has absolute confidence in the Buddha: 'That Blessed One is such since he is accomplished, fully enlightened, perfect in knowledge and conduct, sublime, the knower of worlds, the incomparable leader of men to be tamed, the teacher of gods and men, enlightened, blessed.' He has absolute confidence in the Dhamma: 'The Dhamma is well proclaimed by the Blessed One, its effect is visible here and now, it is timeless (not delayed), it invites inspection, it is onward-leading, and it can be directly experienced by the wise.' He has absolute confidence in the Sangha: 'The Sangha of the Blessed One's disciples has entered on the good way, has entered on the straight way, has entered on the true way, has entered on the proper way, that is to say, the four pairs of men, the eight types of persons[3]—this Sangha of the Blessed One's disciples is fit for gifts, hospitality, offerings and reverential salutation, as an incomparable field of merit for the world.' He is perfect in the virtues beloved of noble ones, unbroken, untorn, unblotched, unmottled, emancipating, commended by the wise, not misapprehended, and conducive to concentration. This is the exposition of the Dhamma called 'the Mirror of the Dhamma,' possessing which a noble disciple can predict for himself: 'There is no more hell for me, ... I am a stream-enterer, no more subject to perdition, I am certain of rightness and destined to enlightenment.' "

And while the Blessed One was living there at Nādikā in the Brick Hall, he often gave this talk on the Dhamma to the bhikkhus: "Such is virtue, such is concentration, such is understanding; concentration fortified with virtue brings great benefits and great fruits; understanding fortified with concentration brings great benefits and great fruits; the heart fortified with understanding becomes completely liberated from taints: from the taint of sensual desire, the taint of being, the taint of views, and the taint of ignorance."

D. 16

When the Blessed One had stayed at Nādikā as long as he chose, he said to the venerable Ānanda: "Come, Ānanda, let us go to Vesālī."

"Even so, Lord," the venerable Ānanda replied. Then the Blessed One journeyed to Vesālī with a large number of bhikkhus. While there he lived in Ambapālī's Grove in Vesālī. There he addressed the bhikkhus thus: "Bhikkhus, a bhikkhu should live mindful and fully aware; this is our instruction to you. And how should a bhikkhu live mindful? Here a bhikkhu abides contemplating the body as a body, ardent, fully aware, mindful, having put away covetousness and grief for the world. He abides contemplating feelings as feelings, ardent, fully aware, mindful, having put away covetousness and grief for the world. He abides contemplating consciousness as consciousness, ardent, fully aware, mindful, having put away covetousness and grief for the world. He abides contemplating mental objects as mental objects, ardent, fully aware, mindful, having put away covetousness and grief for the world. And how is a bhikkhu fully aware? Here a bhikkhu is fully aware in moving to and fro, in looking ahead and away, in flexing and extending the limbs, in wearing the outer patched cloak, the bowl and other robes, in eating, drinking, chewing and tasting, in evacuating the bowels and making water, in walking, standing, sitting, going to sleep, waking, talking and keeping silent. A bhikkhu should live mindful and fully aware: this is our instruction to you."

D. 16; cf. D. 22

Now Ambapālī the courtesan heard that the Blessed One had come to Vesālī and was living in her mango (*amba*) grove. She had a number of state coaches made ready. She mounted one of them and drove with them out of Vesālī towards her own mango grove, going thus as far as the way was passable for carriages. Then she alighted and went on foot to where the Blessed One was. She paid homage to him and sat down at one side. When she had done so, the Blessed One instructed, urged, roused and encouraged her with talk on the Dhamma. Then she said to him: "Lord, let the Blessed One together with the Sangha of bhikkhus accept tomorrow's meal from me." The Blessed One consented in silence. When she saw that he had consented, she rose from her seat, and after paying homage to him, departed, keeping him on her right.

But the Licchavis of Vesālī also heard that the Blessed One was living in Ambapālī's mango grove. They too had a number of state coaches made ready, and mounting them, they drove out of Vesālī. Some were in blue, painted blue, clothed in blue with blue ornaments. Some were in yellow, painted yellow, clothed in yellow with yellow ornaments. Some were in red, painted red, clothed in red with red ornaments. Some were in white, painted white, clothed in white with white ornaments.

Ambapālī the courtesan met the young Licchavis head on, axle to axle, wheel to wheel, yoke to yoke. Then they said to her: "Hey, Ambapālī, why are you meeting the young Licchavis head on, axle to axle, wheel to wheel, yoke to yoke?"

"Sirs, I have just invited the Sangha of bhikkhus headed by the Blessed One for tomorrow's meal."

"Hey, Ambapālī, hand over that meal to us for a hundred thousand."

"Sirs, I would not hand over tomorrow's meal even if you gave me Vesālī with all its lands."

Then the Licchavis snapped their fingers: "Oh, the mango girl has beaten us, the mango girl has outwitted us!"

They drove on towards Ambapālī's grove. The Blessed One saw them coming in the distance. He told the bhikkhus: "Let the bhikkhus who have never seen the deities in the Heaven of the Thirty-three look at the band of Licchavis, let them observe the band of Licchavis, let them imagine the deities of the Heaven of the Thirty-three to be like this band of Licchavis."

The Licchavis drove as far as the way was passable for carriages. Then they alighted and went on foot to where the Blessed One was. They paid homage to him and sat down at one side. Then the Blessed One instructed, urged, roused and encouraged them with talk on the Dhamma. Afterwards they said to him: "Lord, let the Blessed One together with the Sangha of bhikkhus accept tomorrow's meal from us."

"I have already accepted tomorrow's meal, Licchavis, from Ambapālī the courtesan."

Then the Licchavis snapped their fingers: "Oh, the mango girl has beaten us, the mango girl has outwitted us!"

However, they were happy and satisfied with the Blessed One's words, and they got up from their seats and departed, keeping him on their right.

So when the night was over, the courtesan Ambapālī had various kinds of good food prepared in her own park, and she had the time announced: "It is time, Lord, the meal is ready."

When the Blessed One had eaten and no longer had the bowl in his hand, Ambapālī took a low seat and sat down at one side. She said: "Lord, I present this mango grove to the Sangha of bhikkhus headed by the Blessed One." The Blessed One accepted the park, and after he had instructed her with talk on the Dhamma, he rose from his seat and went away.

And while the Blessed One was living there at Vesālī in Ambapālī's grove, he often gave this talk on the Dhamma to the bhikkhus: "Such is virtue, such is concentration, such is understanding; concentration fortified with virtue brings great benefits and great fruits;

understanding fortified with concentration brings great benefits and great fruits; the heart fortified with understanding becomes completely liberated from taints: from the taint of sensual desire, the taint of being, the taint of views, and the taint of ignorance."

D. 16; Vin. Mv. 6:30

When the Blessed One had lived in Ambapālī's grove as long as he chose, he said to the venerable Ānanda: "Come, Ānanda, let us go to Beluvagāmaka."

"Even so, Lord," the venerable Ānanda replied. Then the Blessed One journeyed to Beluvagāmaka with a large community of bhikkhus. While there he lived in Beluvagāmaka. There he addressed the bhikkhus thus: "Come, bhikkhus, take up residence for the rains in the neighbourhood of Vesālī wherever you have friends or companions or acquaintances. I shall take up residence for the rains here at Beluvagāmaka.'

"Even so, Lord," they replied. And they did so.

After the Blessed One had taken up residence for the rains, a severe sickness attacked him with violent and deadly pains. He bore them without complaint, mindful and fully aware. Then he thought: "It is not right for me to attain final Nibbāna without having addressed my attendants and taken leave of the Sangha of bhikkhus. Suppose I forcibly suppressed this sickness by prolonging the will to live?" He did so. And then the sickness abated.

The Blessed One recovered from that sickness. Soon afterwards he came out from the sick-room and sat on a seat made ready at the back of the dwelling. The venerable Ānanda went to him and said: "I have been used to seeing the Blessed One in comfort and in health, Lord. Indeed, with the Blessed One's sickness I felt as if my body were quite rigid, I could not see straight, my ideas were all unclear. However, Lord, I comforted myself knowing that the Blessed One would not attain final Nibbāna without a pronouncement about the Sangha of bhikkhus."

"But, Ānanda, what does the Sangha expect of me? The Dhamma I have taught has no secret and public versions: there is no 'teacher's closed fist' about good things here. Surely it would be someone who thought thus: 'I shall govern the Sangha' or 'The Sangha depends on me' who might make a pronouncement about the Sangha? A Perfect One does not think like that. How then can he make a pronouncement about the Sangha? Now I am old, Ānanda, my years have turned eighty: just as an old cart is made to carry on with the help of makeshifts, so too, it seems to me, the Perfect One's body is made to carry on with the help of makeshifts. For the Perfect One's body is only at ease when with non-attention to all signs and with cessation of certain kinds of feeling, he enters upon and dwells in the signless heart-deliverance. So, Ānanda, each of you should make himself his island,[4] himself and no other his refuge; each of you should make the Dhamma his island, the Dhamma and no other his refuge. How does a bhikkhu do that? Here a bhikkhu abides contemplating the body as a body, ardent, fully aware and mindful, having put away covetousness and grief for the world. He abides contemplating feelings as feelings ... contemplating consciousness as consciousness ... contemplating mental objects as mental objects, ardent, fully aware, mindful, having put away covetousness and grief for the world. Either now or when I am gone, it is those, whoever they may be, who make themselves their island, themselves and no other their refuge, who make the Dhamma their island, the Dhamma and no other their refuge, who will be the foremost among my bhikkhus—of those, that is, who want to train."

D. 16; S. 47:9

NARRATOR TWO. Although it is not explicitly so stated in the Piṭakas, the Buddha appears to have visited Sāvatthī at this point, and it was while he was staying there that the news of the death of the two chief disciples reached him.

FIRST VOICE. The Blessed One was living at one time at Sāvatthī in Jeta's Grove, Anāthapiṇḍika's Park. But at that time the venerable Sāriputta was living at Nālagāmaka in the Magadhan country: he was afflicted, suffering and gravely ill. The novice Cunda was his attendant. With that sickness the venerable Sāriputta attained final Nibbāna. Then the novice Cunda took the venerable Sāriputta's bowl and robes; and he went to the venerable Ānanda in Jeta's Grove at Sāvatthī. He paid homage to him and said: "Lord, the venerable Sāriputta has attained final Nibbāna. These are his bowl and robes."

"Friend Cunda, this should be told to the Blessed One for his information; we should see the Blessed One and tell him this. Let us go and tell him."

"Even so, Lord," the novice Cunda replied. They went together to the Blessed One and paid homage to him. Then they sat down at one side, and the venerable Ānanda said: "Lord, this novice Cunda has told me that the venerable Sāriputta has attained final Nibbāna, and that these are his bowl and robes. Indeed, Lord, when I heard this, I felt as though my body were quite rigid; I could not see straight, and all my ideas were unclear."

"Why, Ānanda, do you think that by attaining final Nibbāna he has taken away the code of virtue or the code of concentration or the code of understanding or the code of deliverance or the code of knowledge and vision of deliverance?"

"Not that, Lord. But I think how helpful he was to his fellows in the holy life, advising, informing, instructing, urging, rousing and encouraging them; how tireless he was in teaching them the Dhamma. We remember how the venerable Sāriputta fed us and enriched us and helped us with the Dhamma."

"Ānanda, have I not already told you that there is separation and parting and division from all that is dear and beloved? How could it be that what is born, come to being, formed, and subject to fall, should not fail? That is not possible. It is as if a main branch of a great tree standing firm and solid had fallen; so too, Sāriputta has attained final Nibbāna in a great community that stands firm and solid. How could it be that what is born, come to being, formed, and bound to fall, should not fall? That is not possible. Therefore, Ānanda, each of you should make himself his island, himself and no other his refuge; each of you should make the Dhamma his island, the Dhamma and no other his refuge."

S. 47:13

At one time the Blessed One was living with a large community of bhikkhus in the Vajjian country at Ukkācelā on the banks of the Ganges. It was soon after Sāriputta and Moggallāna had attained final Nibbāna. On that occasion the Blessed One was sitting in the open surrounded by the Sangha of bhikkhus. Then, after surveying the silent Sangha of bhikkhus, he addressed them thus: "Now the assembly seems to me as though it were empty. The assembly is empty for me now that Sāriputta and Moggallāna have attained final Nibbāna. There is nowhere that one can look to and say, 'Sāriputta and Moggallāna are living there.' The Blessed Ones in the past, accomplished and fully enlightened, each had a pair of disciples the equal of Sāriputta and Moggallāna, and so will those in the future. It is wonderful, it is marvellous in the disciples how they give effect to the Master's teaching and carry out his advice, and how they are dear to the Sangha and loved and respected and revered by the Sangha! It is wonderful, it is marvellous in the Perfect One that when such a pair of disciples has attained final Nibbāna, he neither sorrows nor laments! How could it be that what is born, come to being, formed, and bound to fall, should not fall? That is not possible."

S. 47:14

One morning the Blessed One dressed, and taking his bowl and robe, he went into Vesālī for alms. When he had wandered for alms in Vesālī and had returned from his alms round after his meal, he spoke to the venerable Ānanda: "Take a mat, Ānanda, let us go to the Cāpāla Shrine to pass the day."

"Even so, Lord," the venerable Ānanda replied, and he took a mat and followed after the Blessed One to the Cāpāla Shrine. There the Blessed One sat down on a seat made ready, and the venerable Ānanda paid homage to him and sat down at one side. When he had done so, the Blessed One said: "Vesālī is agreeable, Ānanda, and so are the Udena Shrine, the Gotamaka Shrine, the Sattambaka Shrine, the Bahuputta Shrine, the Sārandada Shrine and the Cāpāla Shrine. When anyone has maintained in being and developed the four bases for success, made them the vehicle, made them the foundation, established, consolidated and properly undertaken them, he could if he wished live out the age or what remains of the age. Ānanda, the Perfect One has done all that; he could if he wished live out the age or what remains of the age."

Even when such a broad hint, such a plain sign, was given by the Blessed One, still the venerable Ānanda could not understand it. He did not beg the Blessed One: "Lord, let the Blessed One live out the age, let the Sublime One live out the age, for the welfare and happiness of many, out of compassion for the world, for the good and welfare and happiness of gods and men," so much was his mind under Māra's influence. A second and a third time the Blessed One said the same thing, and the venerable Ānanda's mind remained under Māra's influence.[5] Then the Blessed One told the venerable Ānanda: "You may go, Ānanda, now it is time to do as you like."

"Even so, Lord," he replied, and rising from his seat he paid homage to the Blessed One. Then, keeping him on his right, he went away to sit down at the root of a nearby tree.

Soon after he had gone, Māra the Evil One came to the Blessed One and stood at one side. He said: "Let the Blessed One attain final Nibbāna now, let the Sublime One attain final Nibbāna now. Now is the time for the Blessed One to attain final Nibbāna. These words were once spoken by the Blessed One: 'I will not attain final Nibbāna, Evil One, until the bhikkhus, bhikkhunīs, laymen followers and laywomen followers, my disciples, are wise, disciplined, perfectly confident, and learned, until they remember the Dhamma properly, practise the way of the Dhamma, practise the true way, and walk in the Dhamma, until after learning from their own teachers they announce and teach and declare and establish and reveal and expound and explain, until they can reasonably confute the theories of others that arise and can teach the Dhamma with its marvels.' But now all that has been accomplished. Let the Blessed One attain final Nibbāna now. These words were spoken by the Blessed One: 'I will not attain final Nibbāna, Evil One, until this holy life has become successful, prosperous, widespread, and disseminated among many, until it is well exemplified by men.' But now all that has been accomplished. Let the Blessed One attain final Nibbāna now."

When this was said, the Blessed One replied: "You may rest, Evil One. Soon the Perfect One's attainment of final Nibbāna will take place. Three months from now the Perfect One will attain final Nibbāna."

It was then, at the Cāpāla Shrine, that the Blessed One, mindful and fully aware, relinquished the will to live. When he did so, there was a great earthquake, fearful and hair-raising, and the drums of heaven resounded. Knowing the meaning of this, the Blessed One then uttered this exclamation:

> The sage renounced the life-affirming will
> Both measurable and immeasurable,
> And concentrated inwardly and happy too
> He shed his self-becoming like a coat of mail.

The venerable Ānanda thought: "It is wonderful, it is marvellous! That was a great earthquake, a very great earthquake; it was fearful and hair-raising, and the drums of heaven resounded. What was the cause, what was the reason for the manifestation of that great earthquake?"

He went to the Blessed One, and after paying homage to him, he sat down at one side. When he had done so, he asked the Blessed One about the earthquake.

"There are eight causes, Ānanda, eight reasons for the manifestation of great earthquakes. What are the eight? This great earth stands in water, the water stands in air, and the air in space. There are occasions when great winds blow (great forces move); the great winds blowing (great forces moving) make the water quake; the water quaking makes the earth quake. This is the first reason. Again, a monk or brahman may possess supernormal power and have reached mind-mastery, or deities may be mighty and powerful. One who has maintained in being the perception of earth limitedly and the perception of water measurelessly can rock this earth and make it quake and shake and tremble. This is the second reason. Again, when a Bodhisatta, mindful and fully aware, passes away from the Heaven of the Contented and descends into his mother's womb, then the earth rocks and quakes and shakes and trembles. This is the third reason. Again, when a Bodhisatta, mindful and fully aware, comes forth from his mother's womb, then the earth rocks .... This is the fourth reason. Again, when a Perfect One discovers the supreme full enlightenment, then the earth rocks .... This is the fifth reason. Again, when a Perfect One sets the matchless Wheel of the Dhamma rolling, then the earth rocks .... This is the sixth reason. Again, when a Perfect One, mindful and fully aware, relinquishes the will to live, then the earth rocks .... This is the seventh reason. Again, when a Perfect One attains final Nibbāna with the Nibbāna element without result of past clinging left, then the earth rocks ....This is the eighth reason."[6]

D. 16; A. 8:70; Ud. 6:1

"Once, Ānanda, when I was newly enlightened, while I was living at Uruvelā on the banks of the Nerañjarā River at the root of the Goatherd's Banyan Tree, Māra the Evil One came to me and said: 'Let the Blessed One attain final Nibbāna now.' Then the Blessed One went on to tell all that had passed between him and Māra. Then he said: "And now, Ānanda, this very day at the Cāpāla Shrine the Blessed One, mindful and fully aware, has relinquished his will to live."

When he heard this, the venerable Ānanda said: "Lord, let the Blessed One live out the age, let the Sublime One live out the age, for the welfare and happiness of many, out of compassion for the world, for the good, the welfare and the happiness of gods and men."

"Enough, Ānanda, do not ask that of the Perfect One now; the time to ask that of the Perfect One has now gone by."

A second time the venerable Ānanda made the same request and received the same answer. The third time the Blessed One said:

"Have you faith in the Perfect One's enlightenment, Ānanda?"

"Yes, Lord."

"Then why do you press the Perfect One up to the third time?"

"Lord, I heard and learned this from the Blessed One's lips: 'When anyone has maintained in being and developed the four bases for success, made them the vehicle, made them the foundation, established, consolidated and properly undertaken them, he could if he wished live out the age, or what remains of the age.' "

"Have you faith, Ānanda?"

"Yes, Lord."

"Then, Ānanda, the wrongdoing is yours, the fault is yours; for even when such a broad hint, such a plain sign, was given by the Perfect One, you could not understand it, and you did not beg the Perfect One to live out the age for the good, the welfare and happiness of gods and men. If you had done so, the Perfect One would have refused you twice, and then, at the third time, he would have consented. So, Ānanda, the wrongdoing is yours, the fault is yours. Once when I was living at Rājagaha on the Vulture Peak Rock, there too I told you: 'Rājagaha is delightful, Ānanda, and so is Vulture Peak Rock. When anyone has maintained in being and developed the four bases for success ... he could if he wished live out the age, or what remains of the age. Ānanda, the Perfect One has done this. He could if he wished live out the age or what remains of the age.' But even when such a broad hint, such a plain sign, was given by the Perfect One, you could not understand it, and you did not beg the Perfect One: 'Lord, let the Blessed One live out the age, let the Sublime One live out the age, for the welfare and happiness of many, out of compassion for the world, for the good and welfare and happiness of gods and men.' If you had done so, the Perfect One would have refused you twice, and then, at the third time, he would have consented. So, Ānanda, the wrongdoing is yours, the fault is yours. Once too when I was living at Rājagaha in the Nigrodha Park ... on the Robbers' Cliff ... on the slopes of the Vebhāra ... in the Sattapaṇṇi Cave ... on the Black Rock on the slopes of Isigili ... under the Overhanging Rock of the Serpents' Pool in the Cool Grove ... in the Park of the Hot Spring ... in the Bamboo Grove, the Squirrels' Sanctuary ... in Jīvaka's Mango Grove ... in the Deer Park at Maddakucchi ... Once too when I was living here at Vesālī in the Udena Shrine ... in the Gotamaka Shrine ... in the Sattamba Shrine ... in the Bahuputta Shrine ... in the Sārandada Shrine ... and now too, here in the Cāpāla Shrine today .... Have I not already told you, Ānanda, that there is separation and parting and division from all that is dear and beloved? How could it be that what is born, come to being, formed, and bound to fall, should not fall? That is not possible. Something has been given up by the Perfect One, dropped, let go, abandoned, relinquished by him; his will to live has been renounced. The unequivocal words have been uttered by the Perfect One: 'Soon the Perfect One's attainment of final Nibbāna will take place; three months from now the Perfect One will attain final Nibbāna.' It is impossible for the Perfect One to go back on those words. Let us go to the Hall with the Pointed Roof in the Great Wood, Ānanda."

"Even so, Lord," the venerable Ānanda replied, and when they went there the Blessed One addressed the venerable Ānanda: "Ānanda, go and summon all the bhikkhus in the neighbourhood of Vesālī to meet in the service hall."

"Even so, Lord," the venerable Ānanda replied. When he had done that, he informed the Blessed One. Then the Blessed One went to the service hall and sat down on the seat made ready, and he addressed the bhikkhus thus:

"Bhikkhus, I have now taught you things that I have directly known; these you should thoroughly learn and maintain in being, develop and constantly put into effect so that this holy life may endure long; you should do so for the welfare and happiness of many, out of compassion for the world, for the good and welfare and happiness of gods and men. And what are these things? They are the four foundations of mindfulness, the four right endeavours, the four bases for success, the five spiritual faculties, the five spiritual powers, the seven enlightenment factors, and the Noble Eightfold Path. I have taught you these things, having directly known them.

These you should thoroughly learn ... for the good and welfare and happiness of gods and men."

Then the Blessed One addressed the bhikkhus thus: "Indeed, bhikkhus, I declare this to you: It is in the nature of all formations to dissolve. Attain perfection through diligence. Soon the Perfect One will attain final Nibbāna." So the Blessed One said. The Sublime One having said this, the Master said further:

> Ripe is my age and little life remains to me:
> I leave you and depart; my own refuge is made.
> Be diligent and mindful, be virtuous, O bhikkhus,
> With thoughts well concentrated keep watch over
>   your hearts.
> Who lives out diligently this Dhamma and Discipline
> Will leave the round of rebirths and make an end of pain.

When it was morning, the Blessed One dressed, and taking his bowl and outer robe, he went into Vesālī for alms. When he had wandered for alms in Vesālī and was returning from his alms round after his meal, he turned to gaze at Vesālī with an elephant's gaze. Then he said to the venerable Ānanda: "Ānanda, this will be the Perfect One's last sight of Vesālī. Come, Ānanda, let us go to Bhaṇḍagāma."

"Even so, Lord," the venerable Ānanda replied. Then the Blessed One journeyed to Bhaṇḍagāma with a large community of bhikkhus. While there he lived in Bhaṇḍagāma. And there he addressed the bhikkhus thus: "Bhikkhus, it is through not discovering, not penetrating four things that both I and you have had to travel and trudge thus through this long round. What are the four? They are the noble one's virtue, the noble one's concentration, the noble one's understanding, and the noble one's deliverance. But when these four things have been discovered and penetrated, then craving about being is cut off, craving that leads to being is abolished, and there is no renewal of being."

D. 16; cf. A. 4:1

And while the Blessed One was living there at Bhaṇḍagāma, he often gave this talk on the Dhamma to the bhikkhus: "Such is virtue, such is concentration, such is understanding; concentration fortified with virtue brings great benefits and fruits; understanding fortified with concentration brings great benefits and great fruits;

the heart fortified with understanding becomes completely liberated from taints: from the taint of sensual desire, the taint of being, the taint of views, and the taint of ignorance."

When the Blessed One had lived at Bhaṇḍagāma as long as he chose, he said to the venerable Ānanda: "Come, Ānanda, let us go to Hatthigāma."

"Even so, Lord," the venerable Ānanda replied. Then the Blessed One journeyed to Hatthigāma with a large community of bhikkhus.

And similarly he visited Ambagāma and Jambugāma. When he had lived at Jambugāma as long as he chose, he said to the venerable Ānanda: "Come, Ānanda, let us go to Bhoganagara."

"Even so, Lord," the venerable Ānanda replied. Then the Blessed One journeyed to Bhoganagara with a large community of bhikkhus. While there he lived in the Ānanda Shrine in Bhoganagara. And there he addressed the bhikkhus thus: "Bhikkhus, I shall teach you the four principal authorities. Listen and attend carefully to what I shall say."

"Even so, Lord," they replied. The Blessed One said this:

"Here, bhikkhus, a bhikkhu may say: 'I heard and learned it from the Blessed One's own lips; this is the Dhamma, this is the Discipline, this is the Master's teaching.' Or a bhikkhu may say: 'In a certain dwelling place there is a community with elders and leaders; I heard and learned it from the lips of that community; this is the Dhamma, this is the Discipline, this is the Master's teaching.' Or a bhikkhu may say: 'In a certain dwelling place many elder bhikkhus live who are learned, expert in the traditions, memorizers of the Discipline, memorizers of the Codes; I heard it from those elders' own lips; this is the Dhamma, this is the Discipline, this is the Master's teaching.' Or a bhikkhu may say: 'In a certain dwelling place an elder bhikkhu lives who is learned, expert in the traditions, a memorizer of the Discipline, a memorizer of the Codes; I heard and learned it from that elder's own lips; this is the Dhamma, this is the Discipline, this is the Master's teaching.'

"Now such a bhikkhu's statement should be neither approved nor disapproved. Without either approving or disapproving, those words and syllables of his should be well learned and then verified in the Vinaya (Discipline) or confirmed in the Suttas (Discourses). If they are found to be not verified in the Vinaya or confirmed in the Suttas, the conclusion to be drawn is this: 'Certainly this is not the Blessed

One's word, it has been wrongly learned by that bhikkhu or by that community or by those elders or by that elder,' and you should accordingly reject it. If, however, they are found to be verified in the Vinaya and confirmed in the Suttas, the conclusion to be drawn is this: 'Certainly this is the Blessed One's word. It has been rightly learned by that bhikkhu or by that community or by those elders or by that elder.' You should remember these four principal authorities."

D. 16; A. 4:180

And while the Blessed One was living there in Bhoganagara in the Ānanda Shrine, he often gave this talk on the Dhamma to the bhikkhus: "Such is virtue, such is concentration, such is understanding; concentration fortified with virtue brings great benefits and great fruits; understanding fortified with concentration brings great benefits and great fruits; the heart fortified with understanding becomes completely liberated from taints: from the taint of sensual desire, the taint of being, the taint of views, and the taint of ignorance."

D. 16

Then, when the Blessed One had lived at Bhoganagara as long as he chose, he said to the venerable Ānanda: "Come, Ānanda, let us go to Pāvā."

"Even so, Lord, the venerable Ānanda replied. Then the Blessed One journeyed to Pāvā with a large community of bhikkhus. While there he lived in the mango grove in Pāvā belonging to Cunda the goldsmith's son.

Cunda the goldsmith's son heard that the Blessed One was living in his grove. He then went to the Blessed One, and after paying homage to him, he sat down at one side. Then the Blessed One instructed, urged, roused and encouraged him with talk on the Dhamma. Afterwards Cunda said to the Blessed One: "Lord, let the Blessed One with the Sangha of bhikkhus accept tomorrow's meal from me."

The Blessed One consented in silence. When Cunda saw that he had accepted, he rose from his seat, and after paying homage to the Blessed One, he departed, keeping him on his right.

When the night was over, he had good food of various kinds

prepared at his house and plenty of hog's mincemeat,[7] after which he had the time announced: "It is time, Lord, the meal is ready." Then, it being morning, the Blessed One dressed, and taking his bowl and outer robe, he went with the Sangha of bhikkhus to Cunda the goldsmith's son's house. He sat down on the prepared seat. Then he told Cunda: "Serve the hog's mincemeat you have had prepared to me, Cunda; but serve any other food you have had prepared to the Sangha of bhikkhus."

"Even so, Lord," Cunda replied, and so he did. Then the Blessed One told him: "Cunda, if any hog's mincemeat is left over, bury it in a hole. I do not see anyone other than the Perfect One in this world with its deities, its Māras and its Brahmās, in this generation with its monks and brahmans, with its princes and men, who could digest it if he ate it."

"Even so, Lord," Cunda replied, and he buried the left-over hog's mincemeat in a hole. Then he went to the Blessed One, and after paying homage to him, he sat down at one side. Then the Blessed One instructed him with a talk on the Dhamma after which he got up from his seat and departed.

It was after the Blessed One had eaten the food provided by Cunda the goldsmith's son that a severe sickness attacked him with a flux of blood accompanied by violent deadly pains. He bore it without complaint, mindful and fully aware. Then he said to the venerable Ānanda: "Come, Ānanda, let us go to Kusinārā."

"Even so, Lord," the venerable Ānanda replied.

On the way the Blessed One left the road and went to the root of a tree. He said to the venerable Ānanda: "Ānanda, please fold my outer robe in four and lay it out; I am tired and I will sit down."

"Even so, Lord," the venerable Ānanda replied. The Blessed One sat down on the seat made ready. When he had done so, he said: "Ānanda, please fetch me some water. I am thirsty and I will drink."

The venerable Ānanda said: "Lord, some five hundred carts have just gone by; the water has been churned up by the wheels; it is flowing poorly and is thick and cloudy. The River Kakutthā is not far off with clear, pleasant, cool water and smooth banks, and is delightful. The Blessed One can drink there and cool his limbs."

A second time the Blessed One asked and received the same reply. A third time the Blessed One said: "Ānanda, please fetch me some water. I am thirsty and I will drink."

"Even so, Lord," the venerable Ānanda replied. He took a bowl and went to the stream. Then the stream, which had been churned up by the wheels and was flowing poorly, thick and cloudy, flowed clear and limpid and clean as soon as the venerable Ānanda came to it. He was astonished. Then he took water for drinking in the bowl, and he returned to the Blessed One and told what had happened, adding: "Lord, let the Blessed One drink the water, let the Sublime One drink the water." And the Blessed One drank the water.

D. 16; Ud. 8:5

Now at that time a Mallian named Pukkusa, a disciple of Āḷāra Kālāma's, came by on the road from Kusinārā to Pāvā. He saw the Blessed One sitting at the root of a tree, and he went up to him. After paying homage to him he sat down at one side and said: "It is wonderful, Lord, it is marvellous what a peaceful abiding those achieve who have gone forth into homelessness. Once when Āḷāra Kālāma was on a journey, he left the road and sat down at the root of a nearby tree for his daytime abiding. Then as many as five hundred carts went by quite close to him. Afterwards a man came following behind that caravan of carts, and he approached Āḷāra Kālāma and asked: 'Lord, did you see five hundred carts go by?' —'I did not, friend.'—'But, Lord, did you hear the noise?'—'I did not, friend.'—'But how then, Lord, were you asleep?'—'I was not, friend.'—'But how then, Lord, were you conscious?'—'I was, friend.'- 'So then, Lord, you were conscious and awake, yet you neither saw the five hundred carts go by quite close nor heard the sound, although your outer robe is spattered with mud?'—'Just so, friend.' Then, Lord, that man thought: 'It is wonderful, it is marvellous what a peaceful abiding those achieve who have gone forth into homelessness; for while they are conscious and awake, they neither see five hundred carts go by nor hear the sound!' And after he had expressed his great confidence in Āḷāra Kālāma he went on his way."

"What do you think, Pukkusa? Which is harder and more difficult to do—that a man who is conscious and awake should neither see five hundred carts go by quite close nor hear the sound of them, or that a man who is conscious and awake while it is raining torrents with lightning flashing and thunder pealing should neither see them nor hear the sound?"

"Lord, what do five hundred, or six or seven or eight or nine hundred or even a thousand carts count? It is far harder and more difficult for a man who is conscious and awake when it is raining torrents with lightning flashing and thunder pealing neither to see them nor to hear the sound."

"Once, Pukkusa, I was living near Ātumā in a threshing barn. It was raining torrents then with lightning flashing and thunder pealing, and two ploughmen who were brothers were killed and four oxen as well. Then a crowd of people came out from Ātumā, and they went to the two brothers and the oxen that had been killed. But by that time I had come out from the threshing barn and was walking up and down outside in the open in the doorway. Then a man came up to me from out of the crowd, and after paying homage to me, he stood at one side. I asked him: 'Why has this crowd of people gathered, friend?'—'Lord, it has been raining torrents with lightning flashing and thunder pealing, and two ploughmen who were brothers have been killed and four oxen as well; that is why there is this crowd of people gathered here. But you, Lord, where were you?'—'I was here, friend.'—'But did you see it, Lord?'—'I did not, friend.'—'But did you hear the sound, Lord?'—'I did not, friend.'—'But were you asleep, Lord?'—'I was not, friend.'—'But were you conscious, Lord?'—'I was, friend.'—'So then, Lord, you were conscious and awake while it was raining torrents with lightning flashing and thunder pealing yet you neither saw it nor heard the sound?'—'Just so, friend.' Then that man thought: 'It is wonderful, it is marvellous what a peaceful abiding those achieve who have gone forth into homelessness; for though they are conscious and awake while it rains torrents with lightning flashing and thunder pealing, yet they neither see it nor hear the sound!' And after he had expressed his complete confidence in me, he paid homage and departed, keeping me on his right."

"Lord, I let the faith I had in Āḷāra Kālāma be, as it were, blown away by a high wind or carried off by a swift-flowing river. Magnificent, Lord, magnificent, Lord! ... I go to the Blessed One and to the Dhamma and to the Sangha for refuge. Beginning from today, Lord, let the Blessed One receive me as his follower who has gone to him for refuge for as long as breath lasts."

Then Pukkusa the Mallian told a man: "Please fetch me a pair of cloth-of-gold robes pressed and ready to wear."

"Yes, Lord," the man answered, and he brought them. Then Pukkusa took them to the Blessed One: "Lord, let the Blessed One out of compassion accept from me this pair of cloth-of-gold robes pressed and ready to wear."

"Then, Pukkusa, you may clothe me in one and Ānanda in the other."

"Yes, Lord," he replied, and he did so. Then the Blessed One instructed, urged, roused and encouraged Pukkusa the Mallian with a talk on the Dhamma, after which Pukkusa got up from his seat, paid homage to the Blessed One and departed, keeping him on his right.

Soon after he had gone, the venerable Ānanda placed the pair of cloth-of-gold robes pressed and ready to wear on the Blessed One's body. But then it seemed as if their brilliance died out. The venerable Ānanda said: "It is wonderful, Lord, it is marvellous how pure and bright the colour of the Blessed One's skin is! When I placed this pair of cloth-of-gold robes pressed and ready to wear on the Blessed One's body, it seemed as if their brilliance died out."

"So it is, Ānanda, so it is. There are two occasions when the colour of the Perfect One's skin becomes exceptionally clear and bright. What are the two? They are the eve of his discovery of the supreme full enlightenment and the eve of his attainment of final Nibbāna with the Nibbāna element without result of past clinging left. In fact, Ānanda, it is in the last watch of this coming night, between the twin sāla trees in the Mallians' sāla-tree grove at the turn into Kusinārā, that the Perfect One will attain final Nibbāna."

"Even so, Lord," the venerable Ānanda replied.

Then the Blessed One approached the River Kakutthā with a large community of bhikkhus, and he went down into the water and bathed and drank, after which he came out again and went to a mango grove. There he said to the venerable Cundaka: "Cundaka, please fold my outer robe in four and lay it out. I am tired and I will lie down."

"Even so, Lord," the venerable Cundaka replied, and he did so. Then the Blessed One lay down on his right side in the lion's sleeping pose with one foot overlapping the other, mindful and fully aware, having decided the time he would wake. And the venerable Cundaka sat down there in front of the Blessed One.

D. 16

The Blessed One said to the venerable Ānanda: "Ānanda, it is possible that someone might provoke remorse in the goldsmith's son Cunda thus: 'It is no gain, it is a loss for you, Cunda, that the Perfect One attained final Nibbāna after getting his last almsfood from you.' Now any such remorse of his must be countered thus: 'It is a gain, it is a great gain for you, Cunda, that the Perfect One attained final Nibbāna after getting his last almsfood from you. I heard and learned this from the Blessed One's own lips, friend Cunda: "These two kinds of almsfood have equal fruit and equal ripening, and their fruit and ripening is far greater than any other's. What are the two? They are the almsfood after eating which a Perfect One discovers the supreme full enlightenment and the almsfood after eating which a Perfect One attains final Nibbāna with the Nibbāna element without result of past clinging left. Cunda the goldsmith's son has stored up a deed that will lead to longevity, to good position, to happiness, to fame and to heaven." ' Any remorse of his must be countered thus."

Knowing the meaning of this, the Blessed One then uttered this exclamation:

> When a man gives, his merit will increase;
> No enmity can grow in the restrained.
> The skilled shun evil; they attain Nibbāna
> By ending greed and hatred and delusion.

D. 16: Ud. 8:5

Then the Blessed One said to the venerable Ānanda: "Come, Ānanda, let us go to the further bank of the River Hiraññavatī to the Mallians' sāla-tree grove at the turn into Kusinārā."

"Even so, Lord," the venerable Ānanda replied. Then the Blessed One went with a large community of bhikkhus to the further bank of the Hiraññavatī and on to the Mallians' sāla-tree grove at the turn into Kusinārā. Then he said to the venerable Ānanda: "Ānanda, please make a couch ready for me with its head to the north between the twin sāla trees. I am tired and I will lie down."

"Even so, Lord," the venerable Ānanda replied, and he did so. Then the Blessed One placed himself in the lion's sleeping pose on his right side with one foot overlapping the other, mindful and fully aware.

Now on that occasion the twin sāla trees were quite covered with blossoms though it was not the season. They scattered and sprinkled and strewed them on the Blessed One's body out of veneration for him. And heavenly mandārava flowers and heavenly sandalwood powder fell from the sky and were scattered and sprinkled and strewn over the Blessed One's body out of veneration for him. And heavenly music was played and heavenly songs were sung in the sky out of veneration for him.

Then the Blessed One said to the venerable Ānanda: "Ānanda, the twin sāla trees are quite covered with blossoms though it is not the season. They scatter and sprinkle and strew them on the Perfect One's body out of veneration for him. And heavenly mandārava flowers and heavenly sandalwood powder fall from the sky and are scattered and sprinkled and strewn over the Perfect One's body out of veneration for him. And heavenly music is played and heavenly songs are sung in the sky out of veneration for him. But this is not how a Perfect One is honoured, respected, revered, venerated or reverenced: rather it is the bhikkhu or bhikkhunī, or the man or woman lay follower, who lives according to the Dhamma, who enters upon the proper way, who walks in the Dhamma, that honours, respects, reveres and venerates a Perfect One with the highest veneration of all. Therefore, Ānanda, train thus: 'We will live in the way of the Dhamma, entering upon the proper way and walking in the Dhamma.' "

Just then, however, the venerable Upavāna was standing in front of the Blessed One, fanning him. Then the Blessed One dismissed him, saying: "Go away, bhikkhu; do not stand in front of me."

The venerable Ānanda thought: "The venerable Upavāna has long been an attendant on the Blessed One, near to him and closely associated with him. Yet at the last moment the Blessed One dismisses him, saying: 'Go away, bhikkhu; do not stand in front of me.' What is the reason for this?" He asked this question of the Blessed One who replied: "Ānanda, most of the deities from ten world systems have come to see the Perfect One. For twelve leagues all round the sāla-tree grove there is not a place the size of the pricking of a horse-hair's tip not occupied by deities. They are protesting: 'We have come from far to see the Perfect One. Every now and then Perfect Ones arise in the world, accomplished and fully enlightened. Tonight in the last watch the Perfect One's attainment of final Nibbāna will take place. And this eminent bhikkhu is standing in front of the Blessed One obstructing us so that at the last moment we shall not be able to see the Perfect One.' Deities are protesting, Ānanda."

"But, Lord, what deities has the Blessed One in mind?"

"There are deities who are percipient of earth in space; they are tearing their hair and weeping, stretching out their arms and weeping, falling down and rolling back and forth, crying out: 'So soon the Blessed One will attain final Nibbāna! So soon the Sublime One will attain final Nibbāna! So soon the Eye will vanish from the world!' And there are deities who are percipient of earth in earth who are doing likewise. But those deities who are free from lust resign themselves, mindful and fully aware: 'Formations are impermanent. How could it be that what is born, come to being, formed and bound to fall should not fall? That is not possible.' "

"Lord, formerly bhikkhus who had spent the rains in different parts used to come to see the Perfect One. So we were able to see and to show respect to admirable bhikkhus. But, Lord, when the Blessed One is gone we shall not be able to do so any more."

"Ānanda, there are four places for a faithful clansman to see which may be his inspiration. What are the four? Here the Perfect One was born: that is a place for a faithful clansman to see which may be his inspiration. Here the Perfect One discovered the supreme full enlightenment: that is a place for a faithful clansman to see which may be his inspiration. Here the Perfect One set rolling the matchless Wheel of the Dhamma: that is a place for a faithful clansman to see which may be his inspiration. Here the Perfect One attained final Nibbāna with the Nibbāna element without result of past clinging left: that is a place for a faithful clansman to see which may be his inspiration. Faithful bhikkhus and bhikkhunīs, and men and women lay followers, will come, saying: 'Here the Perfect One was born' and 'Here the Perfect One discovered the supreme full enlightenment' and 'Here the Perfect One set rolling the matchless Wheel of the Dhamma' and 'Here the Perfect One attained final Nibbāna with the Nibbāna element without result of past clinging left.' And all those who travel to visit shrines with confident hearts reappear on the dissolution of the body, after death, in a happy destination, even in a heavenly world."

"Lord, how are we to treat women?"

"Do not see them, Ānanda."

"Lord, if they are seen, how should we treat them?"

"Do not address them, Ānanda."

"Lord, if we do address them, how should we treat them?"

"Mindfulness should be maintained, Ānanda."

"Lord, how should we treat the Perfect One's remains?"

"Ānanda, do not preoccupy yourselves about venerating the Perfect One's remains. Please strive for your own goal, devote yourselves to your own goal, dwell diligent, ardent and self-controlled for your own good. There are wise warriors and brahmans and householders who believe in the Perfect One; they will see to venerating the Perfect One's remains."

"But, Lord, how should one treat the Perfect One's remains?"

"Treat the Perfect One's remains in the same way that the remains of a Universal Monarch[8] who turns the Wheel of Righteousness are treated."

"But, Lord, how should one treat the remains of a Universal Monarch who turns the Wheel of Righteousness?"

"They wrap his remains in new cloth; then they wrap them in well-beaten cotton; then they wrap them in new cloth. And proceeding in that way, they wrap them in five hundred twin layers. Then they place them in an iron oil vessel which they close with another vessel. Then they make a pyre with all kinds of scents and burn the remains. Then they build a monument to him at the four crossroads. That is how they treat the remains of a Universal Monarch who turns the Wheel of Righteousness; and the Perfect One's remains should be treated in the same way. The Perfect One's monument should be built at the four crossroads; and whoever shall put flowers or scents on it, or whitewash it, or shall worship it, or feel confidence in his heart there, that will be long for his welfare and happiness. There are these four who are worthy of a monument. What four? A Perfect One, accomplished and fully enlightened; a Paccekabuddha; a Perfect One's disciple who is an Arahant; and a Universal Monarch who turns the Wheel of Righteousness. And what is the aim in view of which any one of these four is worthy of a monument? There are many who feel confidence in their hearts, thinking: 'This is the monument of that Blessed One, accomplished and fully enlightened' or 'This is the monument of that Blessed One, a Paccekabuddha' or 'This is the monument of a disciple of that Blessed One' or 'This is the monument of that righteous and lawful king.' When they feel confidence in their hearts there, then on the dissolution of the body, after death, they reappear in a happy destination, even in a heavenly world."

Then the venerable Ānanda went inside a dwelling, and he stood leaning against the door bar and wept: "I am still only a learner whose task has yet to be completed. My teacher is about to attain final Nibbāna—my teacher who has compassion on me!"

Then the Blessed One asked the bhikkhus: "Bhikkhus, where is Ānanda?"

"Lord, he has just gone inside a dwelling, and he is standing leaning against the door bar weeping: 'I am still only a learner whose task has yet to be completed. My teacher is about to attain final Nibbāna—my teacher who has compassion on me!' "

The Blessed One told a bhikkhu: "Come, bhikkhu, go to Ānanda and say to him in my name: 'The Teacher calls you, friend Ānanda.' "

"Even so, Lord," the bhikkhu replied, and he went to the venerable Ānanda and told him: "The Teacher calls you, friend Ānanda."

"Even so, friend," the venerable Ānanda replied, and he went to the Blessed One, and after paying homage to him, he stood at one side. The Blessed One said to him: "Enough, Ānanda, do not sorrow, do not lament. Have I not already repeatedly told you that there is separation and parting and division from all that is dear and beloved? How could it be that what is born, come to being, formed, and bound to fall should not fall? That is not possible. Ānanda, you have long and constantly attended on the Perfect One with bodily acts of loving-kindness, helpfully, gladly, sincerely and without reserve; and so too with verbal acts and mental acts. You have made merit, Ānanda. Keep on endeavouring and you will soon be free from taints."

Then the Blessed One addressed the bhikkhus thus: "Bhikkhus, the accomplished fully enlightened ones in the past also had attendants who were to them what Ānanda is to me. And the accomplished fully enlightened ones in the future will also have attendants who will be to them what Ānanda is to me. Ānanda is wise, bhikkhus. He knows: 'This is the time for bhikkhus to come and see the Perfect One; this is the time for bhikkhunīs to come and see the Perfect One; this is the time for men lay followers ... for women lay followers to come and see the Perfect One; this is the time for kings, kings' ministers, sectarians and sectarians' disciples to come and see the Perfect One.' "

D. 16

"There are four wonderful and marvellous things in a Universal Monarch who turns the Wheel of Righteousness. What four? If an assembly of warrior-nobles or brahmans or householders or monks should come to see him, the assembly is glad to see him. If he speaks there, the assembly is glad at his speech. But when he is silent again, the assembly is still unsated. So too there are four wonderful and marvellous things in Ānanda. What four? If an assembly of bhikkhus or bhikkhunīs or men lay followers or women lay followers should come to see Ānanda, the assembly is glad to see him. If he speaks there, the assembly is glad at his speech. But when he is silent again, the assembly is still unsated."

D. 16; A. 4:129-30

When he had spoken thus, the venerable Ānanda said: "Lord, let the Blessed One not attain final Nibbāna in this little mud-walled town, this backwoods town, this branch township. There are other great cities like Campā, Rājagaha, Sāvatthī, Sāketa, Kosambī and Benares. Let the Blessed One attain final Nibbāna there where there are many prominent warrior-nobles and brahmans and householders who believe in the Perfect One. They will venerate the Perfect One's remains."[9]

"Do not say so, Ānanda, do not say 'A little mud-walled town, a backwoods town, a branch township.' There was once a king called Sudassana the Great. He was a righteous lawful Universal Monarch who turned the Wheel of Righteousness, a conqueror of the four quarters, who had stabilized his country, and who possessed the seven treasures. His capital city was Kusinārā, then called Kusavatī, and it was twelve leagues wide from east to west and seven leagues broad from north to south. The royal capital, Kusavatī, was as mighty and prosperous with as many inhabitants and as crowded with people and full of plenty as the royal capital city of the gods called Ālakamandā. The royal city of Kusavatī never lacked the ten kinds of sounds, that is to say, the sounds of elephants, horses, chariots, drums, tabors, lutes, songs, cymbals, gongs, and the cries of 'Eat! Drink! Taste!' as the tenth sound."

D. 16, 17

"Now, Ānanda, go into Kusinārā and announce to the Mallians of Kusinārā: 'Tonight, Vāseṭṭhas, in the last watch, the Perfect One's attainment of final Nibbāna will take place. Come forth, Vāseṭṭhas, come forth, lest you regret it later and think: "The Perfect One's attainment of final Nibbāna took place in our own town precincts and we did not get to see the Perfect One in the last hour." ' "

"Even so, Lord," the venerable Ānanda replied. He dressed, and taking his bowl and outer robe, he went into Kusinārā with another bhikkhu. Now at that time the Mallians of Kusinārā had met together in their assembly hall for some business or other. The venerable Ānanda went to the assembly hall and announced to them: "Tonight, Vāseṭṭhas, in the last watch, the Perfect One's attainment of final Nibbāna will take place. Come forth, Vāseṭṭhas, lest you regret it later and think: 'The Perfect One's attainment of final Nibbāna took place in our own town precincts and we did not get to see the Perfect One in the last hour.' "

When they heard this from the venerable Ānanda, the Mallians with their young men and maidens and matrons were dismayed and aghast. Overcome by grief, some tore their hair and wept, some stretched out their arms and wept, some fell down and rolled back and forth, crying out: "So soon the Blessed One will attain final Nibbāna! So soon the Sublime One will attain final Nibbāna! So soon the Eye will vanish from the world!"

Dismayed and aghast, overcome by grief as they were, the Mallians with their young men and maidens and matrons went to the venerable Ānanda in the Mallians' sāla-tree grove at the turn into Kusinārā. Then he thought: "If I let the Mallians of Kusinārā salute the Blessed One singly, the night will be over before they can finish. Suppose I get them to salute the Blessed One with a single representative for each clan thus: 'Lord, the Mallian named so-and-so, with his children, his wife and his retinue and friends, salutes the Blessed One with his head at the Blessed One's feet'?" And he did so. And in that way he got them to salute the Blessed One within the first watch.

However, a wanderer called Subhadda was staying in Kusinārā at that time. He heard: "Tonight, in the last watch, the monk Gotama's attainment of final Nibbāna will take place." Then he thought: "I have heard from senior eiders, teachers among the wanderers, that Perfect Ones appear in the world from time to time, accomplished and fully enlightened. And tonight, in the last watch, the monk Gotama's attainment of final Nibbāna will take place. While there is this doubt in me, yet I have confidence in the monk Gotama that he can teach me the Dhamma in such a way that I can rid myself of this doubt."

He went to the Mallians' sāla-tree grove at the turn into Kusinārā, and he approached the venerable Ānanda and told him all that had occurred to him, adding, "If only I might see the monk Gotama, Master Ānanda."

The venerable Ānanda said: "Enough, friend Subhadda, do not trouble the Perfect One. The Blessed One is tired."

The wanderer Subhadda made the same request a second and a third time and received the same reply. The Blessed One heard their conversation. Then he told the venerable Ānanda: "Enough, Ānanda, do not keep Subhadda out; let him see the Perfect One. Whatever he may ask of me, he will ask it only for the sake of knowledge, not to cause trouble, and what I can tell him he will quickly understand."

Then the venerable Ānanda told the wanderer Subhadda: "Go, friend Subhadda, the Blessed One gives you permission."

He went to the Blessed One and exchanged greetings with him, and when this courteous formal talk was finished, he sat down at one side. Then he said to the Blessed One: "Master Gotama, there are these monks and brahmans, each with his community, with his group, leading a group, each a renowned and famous philosopher reckoned by many as a saint—I mean Pūraṇa Kassapa, Makkhali Gosāla, Ajita Kesakambalin, Pakudha Kaccāyana, Sañjaya Belaṭṭhiputta, and the Nigaṇṭha Nāthaputta. Have they all had direct knowledge as they claim, or have none of them had direct knowledge, or have some of them had direct knowledge and some not?"

"Enough, Subhadda. Whether they have all had direct knowledge as they claim, or none of them have had direct knowledge, or some of them have had direct knowledge and some not, let that be. I shall teach you the Dhamma, Subhadda. Listen and attend carefully to what I shall say."

"Even so, Lord," he replied.

"Subhadda, in whatever Dhamma and Discipline the Noble Eightfold Path is not found, there the (first) monk is not found, the second monk is not found, the third monk is not found, the fourth monk is not found.[10] In whatever Dhamma and Discipline the Noble Eightfold Path is found, there the (first) monk is found, the second monk is found, the third monk is found, the fourth monk is found. The Noble Eightfold Path is found in this Dhamma and Discipline, Subhadda, and it is only here that the (first) monk is found, the second monk is found, the third monk is found, the fourth monk is found. Others' doctrines are devoid of monks. And if these bhikkhus live rightly, the world will not be devoid of Arahants, of Accomplished Ones.

> Aged twenty-nine, Subhadda, I went forth
> Seeking after what is wholesome;
> And more than fifty years have now gone by
> Since then, Subhadda, the time when I went forth.
> Outside this dispensation never a monk is there
> Who treads the way of Dhamma even in part.

"Nor is there the second monk, nor the third monk, nor the fourth monk. Others' doctrines are devoid of monks. But if these bhikkhus live rightly, the world will not be devoid of Arahants."

Then the wanderer Subhadda said: "Magnificent, Lord, magnificent Lord! The Dhamma has been made clear in many ways by the Blessed One, as though he were righting the overthrown, revealing the hidden, showing the way to one who is lost, holding up a lamp in the darkness for those with eyes to see visible forms. I go to the Blessed One for refuge and to the Dhamma and to the Sangha of bhikkhus. I should like to receive the going forth and the admission from the Blessed One."

"One who has already been a sectarian, Subhadda, and wants the going forth and the admission in this Dhamma and Discipline is usually put on probation for four months. At the end of the four months, if the bhikkhus are satisfied, they give him the going forth and admit him to the state of a bhikkhu. But I know that there are personal exceptions here."

"Lord, if that is so, then let me be put on probation for four years; and at the end of the four years, if the bhikkhus are satisfied, they will give me the going forth and admit me to the state of a bhikkhu."

But the Blessed One told the venerable Ānanda: "Now, Ānanda, give Subhadda the going forth."

"Even so, Lord," the venerable Ānanda replied.

Then the wanderer Subhadda said to the venerable Ānanda:[11] "It is a gain for you, friend Ānanda, it is a great gain that you have been anointed here in the Master's presence with the pupil's anointing."

And the wanderer Subhadda received the going forth under the Blessed One and he received the admission. Then not long after his admission, dwelling alone, withdrawn, diligent, ardent and self-controlled, the venerable Subhadda, by realization himself with direct knowledge, here and now entered upon and dwelt in that supreme goal of the holy life for the sake of which clansmen rightly go forth from the house life into homelessness. He knew directly: "Birth is exhausted, the holy life has been lived out, what was to be done is done, there is no more of this to come." And the venerable Subhadda became one of the Arahants. He was the last of the Blessed One's disciples to testify.

Then the Blessed One addressed the venerable Ānanda: "Ānanda, you may think: 'The word of the Teacher is a thing of the past; now we have no more Teacher.' But you should not regard it so. The Dhamma and Discipline taught by me and laid down for you are your Teacher after I am gone. Up till now bhikkhus have addressed each other with the word 'friend'; but it should not be done after I am gone. A senior bhikkhu should address a junior bhikkhu by his name or his family name, or as 'friend.' A junior bhikkhu should address a senior bhikkhu as 'lord' or as 'venerable one.' The Sangha can, if it wishes, abolish the lesser and minor rules when I am gone. The higher penalty should be imposed on the bhikkhu Channa when I am gone."[12]

"But, Lord, what is the higher penalty?"

"Whatever the bhikkhu Channa wants, whatever he says, he should not be spoken to or advised or instructed by the bhikkhus.'

D. 16

Then the Blessed One addressed the bhikkhus thus: "Bhikkhus, it may be that some bhikkhu has a doubt or a problem concerning the Buddha or the Dhamma or the Sangha or the path or the way of progress. Ask, bhikkhus, so that you may not regret it afterwards thus: 'The Teacher was face to face with us, and we could not bring ourselves to ask in the Blessed One's presence.' "

When this was said, the bhikkhus were silent. A second and a third time the Blessed One spoke the same words, and each time they were silent. Then he addressed them thus: "Bhikkhus, perhaps you do not ask because you are in awe of the Teacher. Let a friend tell it to a friend."

When this was said, they were silent. Then the venerable Ānanda said to the Blessed One: "It is wonderful, Lord, it is marvellous! I have such confidence in the Sangha of bhikkhus that I believe there is not one bhikkhu with a doubt or a problem concerning the Buddha or the Dhamma or the Sangha or the path or the way of progress."

"You, Ānanda, speak out of confidence. But the Perfect One has knowledge that here in this Sangha of bhikkhus there is not one bhikkhu who has any doubt concerning the Buddha or the Dhamma or the Sangha or the path or the way of progress. The most backward of these five hundred bhikkhus is a stream-enterer, no more subject to perdition, certain of rightness, and destined to enlightenment."

Then the Blessed One addressed the bhikkhus thus: "Indeed, bhikkhus, I declare this to you: It is in the nature of all formations to dissolve. Attain perfection through diligence."[13]

D. 16; A. 4:76

This was the Perfect One's last utterance.

Then the Blessed One entered upon the first meditation. Emerging from that, he entered upon the second meditation. Emerging from that, he entered upon the third meditation. Emerging from that, he entered upon the fourth meditation. Emerging from that, he entered upon the base consisting of the infinity of space. Emerging from that, he entered upon the base consisting of the infinity of consciousness. Emerging from that, he entered upon the base consisting of nothingness. Emerging from that, he entered upon the base consisting of neither-perception-nor-non-perception. Emerging from that, he entered upon the cessation of perception and feeling.

Then the venerable Ānanda said to the venerable Anuruddha: "Lord, the Blessed One has attained final Nibbāna."

"No, friend. The Blessed One has not attained final Nibbāna; he has attained the cessation of perception and feeling."

Then the Blessed One, emerging from the cessation of perception and feeling, entered upon the base consisting of neither-perception-nor-non-perception. Emerging from that, he entered upon the base consisting of nothingness. Emerging from that, he entered upon the base consisting of the infinity of consciousness. Emerging from that, he entered upon the base consisting of the infinity of space. Emerging from that, he entered upon the fourth meditation. Emerging from that, he entered upon the third meditation. Emerging from that, he entered upon the second meditation. Emerging from that, he entered upon the first meditation. Emerging from that, he entered upon the second meditation. Emerging from that, he entered upon the third meditation. Emerging from that, he entered upon the fourth meditation. And on emerging from the fourth meditation, the Blessed One attained final Nibbāna.

With the Blessed One's attainment of final Nibbāna there was a great earthquake, fearful and hair-raising, and the drums of heaven resounded.

With the Blessed One's attainment of final Nibbāna Brahmā Sahampati uttered this stanza:

> No being in the world but shall lay down
> The temporary compound of its person,
> And even such a teacher without peer
> In all the world, perfected, with the powers,
> Enlightened, has attained complete extinction.

D. 16; S. 6:15

With the Blessed One's attainment of final Nibbāna, Sakka, Ruler of Gods, uttered this stanza:

> Formations are impermanent,
> Their very nature is to rise and fall,
> And there is none arises but must cease:
> True bliss lies in their stilling.

D. 16; S. 6:15

With the Blessed One's attainment of final Nibbāna, the venerable Anuruddha uttered this stanza:

> One even such as he, his mind at rest,
> Remained bereft of breathing; having no wants,

> The Seer completes his time, intent on peace.
> He bore his feelings with untrammelled heart:
> His heart's release was like a flame's extinction.

With the Blessed One's attainment of final Nibbāna, the venerable Ānanda uttered this stanza:

> Oh, then was paralyzing fear;
> Oh, then the hair stood up with horror—
> The Enlightened One supremely graced
> Attained the ultimate extinction.

D. 16; S. 6:15

And with the Blessed One's attainment of final Nibbāna, some bhikkhus who were not without lust stretched out their arms and wept, and they fell down and rolled back and forth: "So soon the Blessed One has attained final Nibbāna! So soon the Sublime One has attained final Nibbāna! So soon the Eye has vanished from the world!" But those who were free from lust, mindful and fully aware, said: "Formations are impermanent. How could it be that what is born, come to being, formed, and bound to fall should not fall? That is not possible."

Then the venerable Anuruddha addressed the bhikkhus: "Enough, friends, do not sorrow, do not lament. Has it not already been declared by the Blessed One that there is separation and parting and division from all that is dear and beloved? How could it be that what is born, come to being, formed, and bound to fall should not fall? That is not possible. Deities are protesting, friends."

"But, Lord, what sort of deities has the venerable Anuruddha in mind?"

"Friends, there are deities percipient of earth in space; they are tearing their hair and weeping, stretching out their arms and weeping, failing down and rolling back and forth, crying out: 'So soon the Blessed One has attained final Nibbāna! So soon the Sublime One has attained final Nibbāna! So soon the Eye has vanished from the world!' And there are deities percipient of earth in earth who are doing likewise. But deities who are free from lust, mindful and fully aware, say: 'Formations are impermanent. How could it be that what is born, come to being, formed, and bound to fall should not fall? That is not possible.' "

The venerable Anuruddha and the venerable Ānanda spent the rest of the night in talk on the Dhamma. Then the venerable Anuruddha said to the venerable Ānanda: "Go, friend, go into Kusinārā and announce to the Mallians of Kusinārā: 'Vāseṭṭhas, the Blessed One has attained final Nibbāna. Now it is time for you to do as you think fit.' "

"Even so, Lord," the venerable Ānanda replied. And it being morning, he dressed, and taking his bowl and outer robe, he went to Kusinārā with another bhikkhu. Now at that time the Mallians of Kusinārā had met together in their assembly hall for some business or other. The venerable Ānanda went to the assembly hall and announced to them: "Vāseṭṭhas, the Blessed One has attained final Nibbāna."

When they heard this from the venerable Ānanda, the Mallians of Kusinārā with their young men and maidens and matrons were dismayed and aghast. Overcome by grief, some tore their hair and wept, some stretched out their arms and wept, some fell down and rolled back and forth, crying out: "So soon the Blessed One has attained final Nibbāna! So soon the Sublime One has attained final Nibbāna So soon the Eye has vanished from the world!"

Then the Mallians of Kusinārā gave men orders: "Collect scents and flowers and all the instruments of music in Kusinārā." And they took the scents and flowers and musical instruments and also five hundred lengths of cloth to where the Blessed One's body lay in the Mallians' sāla-tree grove at the turn into Kusinārā. And they spent that day in paying honour, respect, reverence and veneration to the Blessed One's body with dances, songs, music, garlands and scents, and in making cloth canopies and pavilions. Then they thought: "It is too late now to burn the Blessed One's body today; we shall do it tomorrow." And so they passed the second day, and the third and fourth and fifth and sixth days.

On the seventh day they thought: "Let us bear the Blessed One's body southwards outside the town to a place south of the town, paying honour, respect, reverence and veneration to the Blessed One's body with dances, songs, music, garlands and scents, and there to the south of the town let us burn the Blessed One's body."

Then eight leading Mallians bathed their heads and put on new garments. Thinking to lift up the Blessed One's body, they could not do so. They asked the venerable Anuruddha the reason.

"You, Vāseṭṭhas, have one intention, while the deities have another."

"Then, Lord, what is the deities' intention?"

"Your intention, Vāseṭṭhas, is this: 'Let us bear the Blessed One's body southwards outside the town to a place south of the town, paying honour, respect, reverence and veneration to the Blessed One's body with dances, songs, music, garlands and scents, and there to the south of the town let us burn the Blessed One's body.' The deities' intention is this: 'Let us bear the Blessed One's body northwards to the north of the town, paying honour, respect, reverence and veneration to the Blessed One's body with dances, songs, music, garlands and scents, and then entering by the north gate, let us bear it through the middle to the middle of the town, after which let us go out by the east gate, and there where the Mallians have a shrine called Makuṭabandhana to the east of the town, there let us have the Blessed One's body burnt."

"Lord, let it be as the deities intend."

Now at that time Kusinārā was all strewn knee deep with mandārava flowers, even to the middens and rubbish heaps.

So, paying honour, respect, reverence, and veneration to the Blessed One's body with both divine and human dances, songs, music, garlands and scents, the deities with the Mallians of Kusinārā bore the Blessed One's body northwards to the north of the town, and entering by the north gate, they bore it through the middle to the middle of the town, and going out by the east gate to where the Mallians have a shrine called Makuṭabandhana to the east of the town, there they set it down.

Then the Mallians of Kusinārā said to the venerable Ānanda: "Lord Ānanda, how are we to treat the Perfect One's remains?"

"Treat the Perfect One's remains, Vāseṭṭhas, as the remains of a Universal Monarch who turns the Wheel of Righteousness are treated."

"But, Lord Ānanda, how is that done?"

"They wrap the remains of a Universal Monarch who turns the Wheel of Righteousness in new cloth, Vāseṭṭhas; then they wrap them in well-beaten cotton; then they wrap them in new cloth. And proceeding in that way they wrap them in five hundred twin layers. Then they place them in an iron oil vessel, which they close with another iron vessel. Then they make a pyre with all kinds of scents and burn the remains. Afterwards they build a monument to him at the four crossroads. That is how they treat the remains of a Universal Monarch who turns the Wheel of Righteousness. And as his remains are treated so should the Perfect One's remains be treated. The Perfect One's monument should be built at the four crossroads; and whoever shall put flowers or scents on it, or whitewash it, or shall worship it or feel confidence in his heart there, that will be long for his welfare and happiness."

Thereupon, the Mallians of Kusinārā gave men orders to collect all the Mallians' beaten cotton. And then they wrapped the Blessed One's body in new cloth; and after that they wrapped it in beaten cotton; and after that they wrapped it in new cloth; and having wrapped the Blessed One's body in that way in five hundred twin layers, they put it into an iron oil vessel which they closed with another oil vessel. Then they built a pyre with all kinds of scents and they mounted the Blessed One's remains on the pyre.

D. 16

Now at that time the venerable Mahā-Kassapa was travelling on the high road from Pāvā to Kusinārā with a large number of bhikkhus, with five hundred bhikkhus. Then he left the road and sat down at the root of a tree. Meanwhile a mendicant ascetic who had picked up a mandārava flower in Kusinārā was travelling by that road. The venerable Mahā-Kassapa saw him coming. He asked him: "Do you know our Teacher, friend?"

"Yes, friend, I know him. The monk Gotama attained final Nibbāna seven days ago today. That is how I got this mandārava flower."

Some of the bhikkhus who were not free from lust stretched out their arms and wept, and they fell down and rolled back and forth: "So soon the Blessed One has attained final Nibbāna! So soon the Sublime One has attained final Nibbāna! So soon the Eye has vanished from the world!" But those bhikkhus who were free from lust, mindful and fully aware, said: "Formations are impermanent. How could it be that what is born, come to being, formed, and bound to fall should not fall? That is not possible."

But there was one sitting in the assembly called Subhadda who had gone forth in old age. He said to those bhikkhus: "Enough, friends, do not sorrow, do not lament. We are well rid of the Great Monk. We have been frustrated by his saying 'This is allowed to you; this is not allowed to you.' But now we shall do as we like and we shall not do as we do not like."

Then the venerable Mahā-Kassapa addressed the bhikkhus thus: "Enough, friends, do not sorrow, do not lament. Has it not already been declared by the Blessed One that there is separation and parting and division from all that is dear and beloved? How could it be that what is born, come to being, formed, and bound to fall should not fall? That is not possible."

D. 16; Vin. Cv. 11:1

Four leading Mallians who had bathed their heads and put on new garments thought: "Let us light the Blessed One's pyre." But they were unable to do so. Then they asked the venerable Anuruddha for the reason.

"The deities have a different intention, Vāseṭṭhas."

"But, Lord, what is the deities' intention?"

"The deities' intention is this, Vāseṭṭhas: 'There is the venerable Mahā-Kassapa travelling on the high road from Pāvā to Kusinārā with a large community of bhikkhus, with five hundred bhikkhus. The Blessed One's pyre shall not be lit until the venerable Mahā-Kassapa has saluted the Blessed One with his head.' "

"Then, Lord, let it be as the deities intend."

The venerable Mahā-Kassapa came to the Blessed One's pyre at the Mallians' Makuṭabandhana Shrine at Kusinārā. When he had done so, he arranged his robe on one shoulder, and raising his hands palms together, he circumambulated the pyre three times to the right. Then the Blessed One's feet were revealed, and he saluted the Blessed One's feet with his head. And the five hundred bhikkhus arranged their robes on one shoulder, and they did as the venerable Mahā-Kassapa had done. But as soon as they had finished, the pyre caught alight of itself. And just as when butter or oil burns it produces neither cinder nor ash, so too, in the burning of the Blessed One's body, neither the outer skin nor the inner skin nor the flesh nor the sinews nor the oil of the joints produced any cinder or ash; only the bones remained. And of the five hundred twin wrappings only two were burnt: the innermost and the outermost.

When the Blessed One's body was consumed, a cascade of water poured down from the sky and extinguished the pyre, and water welled up from underground and extinguished the pyre, and the

Mallians of Kusinārā extinguished the pyre with all kinds of scented waters.

Then the Mallians kept the Blessed One's bones in the assembly hall for seven days, and they made a lattice frame of spears set round with a rampart of bows; and they honoured, respected, revered and venerated them with dances, songs, music, garlands and scents.

King Ajātasattu of Magadha heard: "The Blessed One, it seems, has attained final Nibbāna at Kusinārā." Then he sent an envoy to the Mallians of Kusinārā with the demand: "The Blessed One was a warrior; I too am a warrior. I am worthy of a share of the Blessed One's bones. I too will build a monument and hold a ceremony."

And the Licchavis of Vesālī heard likewise, and they too sent an envoy with the demand: "The Blessed One was a warrior; we too are warriors. We too are worthy of a share of the Blessed One's bones. We too will build a monument and hold a ceremony."

And the Sakyans of Kapilavatthu heard likewise, and they too sent an envoy with the demand: "The Blessed One was the greatest of our blood; we too are worthy of a share of the Blessed One's bones. We too will build a monument and hold a ceremony."

And the Bulians of Allakappaka heard likewise, and they too sent an envoy with the demand: "The Blessed One was a warrior; we too are warriors. We too are worthy of a share of the Blessed One's bones. We too will build a monument and hold a ceremony."

And the Koliyans of Rāmagāma heard likewise, and they too sent an envoy with the demand: "The Blessed One was a warrior; we too are warriors. We too are worthy of a share of the Blessed One's bones. We too will build a monument and hold a ceremony."

And the brahman of Veṭha Island heard likewise, and he too sent an envoy with the demand: "The Blessed One was a warrior; I am a brahman. I too am worthy of a share of the Blessed One's bones. I too will build a monument and hold a ceremony."

And the Mallians of Pāvā heard likewise, and they too sent an envoy with the demand: "The Blessed One was a warrior; we too are warriors. We too are worthy of a share of the Blessed One's bones. We too will build a monument and hold a ceremony."

When this had been said, the Mallians assembled the envoys and answered them thus: "The Blessed One attained final Nibbāna in the precincts of our town. We will not give up the bones of the Blessed One."

Then the brahman Doṇa addressed the assembled group with these stanzas:

Sirs, hear a word from me: our Wakened One
Preached patience. So it ill becomes us now
That we should come to clash over a share
In that exalted personage's bones.
Sirs, let us all unite in harmony
And in agreement to make up eight parts.
Let monuments be set up far and wide,
That many may gain trust in the Seer.

"Then, brahman, you yourself should divide up and distribute the Blessed One's bones fairly into eight equal parts."

"Even so, sirs," he replied, and he divided up and distributed the Blessed One's bones fairly into eight equal parts. Then he asked the assembled group: "Give me this vessel, sirs; I too will build a monument and hold a ceremony." And they gave him the vessel.

The Moriyans of Pipphalivana heard: "The Blessed One, it seems, has attained final Nibbāna at Kusinārā." Then they sent an envoy with the demand: "The Blessed One was a warrior; we too are warriors. We too are worthy of a share of the Blessed One's bones. We too will build a monument and hold a ceremony."

"There is no share of the Blessed One's bones left. They have all been distributed. You may take the ashes from here." So they took the ashes.

Then Ajātasattu Vedehiputta, King of Magadha, had a monument built to the Blessed One's bones, and he held a ceremony. And all the others did likewise. So there were eight monuments to the Blessed One's bones, and one to the vessel, and one to the ashes. That is how it happened.

D. 16

16
THE FIRST COUNCIL

NARRATOR ONE. After the Buddha's attainment of final Nibbāna, the bhikkhus dispersed from Kusinārā. The Elder Mahā-Kassapa now emerges as the most prominent figure in the Sangha of bhikkhus.

NARRATOR TWO. He had earlier been mentioned by the Buddha as fourth in the long list of specially distinguished disciples. The first was the Elder Kondañña, the first convert; the second and third were the Elders Sāriputta and Moggallāna, the two chief disciples, now attained to final Nibbāna. There are many stories of the Elder Mahā-Kassapa in the Canon, where he appears as a stern, rugged figure, uncompromising in his devotion to asceticism, and more than once administering a blunt rebuke to the Elder Ānanda for indulging in gentle acts of altruism when he might have been doing more lasting good in that way by completing his own perfection—the perfection already reached by the Elder Mahā-Kassapa himself.

NARRATOR ONE. Here is an incident belonging to this interim period which well illustrates his character.

FIRST VOICE. Thus I heard. At one time the venerable Mahā-Kassapa was living at Rājagaha in the Bamboo Grove, the Squirrels' Sanctuary. Now at that time the venerable Ānanda was wandering in the Southern Hills with a large community of bhikkhus. It was then that thirty of his co-residents gave up the bhikkhus' training and reverted to what they had abandoned, most of them being youths.

When the venerable Ānanda had wandered in the Southern Hills as long as he chose, he went to the venerable Mahā-Kassapa in the Bamboo Grove at Rājagaha. After paying homage to him he sat down at one side. The venerable Mahā-Kassapa said: "Friend Ānanda, for the sake of what benefit did the Blessed One make known the rule that not more than three bhikkhus together should eat among families?"

"He did so, Lord Kassapa, for the sake of three benefits: for the restraint of wrong-minded persons and the comfort of reasonable persons, in order that those of evil wishes may not form a faction in the Sangha, and out of compassion for families."

"Then, friend Ānanda, why do you go wandering with these new bhikkhus who are unguarded in the doors of their sense faculties, who do not know the right measure in eating, who are not devoted to wakefulness? One would think you were wandering about destroying crops. One would think you were wandering about destroying families. Your following is breaking up. Your new converts are falling away. And still this boy does not know his own measure!"

"Lord Kassapa, there are actually white hairs growing on my head; so let us have done with the venerable Kassapa's calling me a boy."

"But that is what you are, friend Ānanda. You go wandering with these new bhikkhus who are unguarded in the doors of their sense faculties, who do not know the right measure in eating, who are not devoted to wakefulness. One would think you were wandering about destroying crops. One would think you were wandering about destroying families. Your following is breaking up. Your new converts are falling away. And still this boy does not know his own measure!"

The bhikkhunī Thullānandā[1] heard this. She thought: "It seems that the Lord Ānanda, the Videhan Seer, is displeased with the Lord Kassapa for calling him a boy," and she was offended and uttered words of displeasure: "How can the Lord Mahā-Kassapa, who used to be a sectarian, dream of displeasing the Lord Ānanda, the Videhan Seer, by calling him a boy?"

The venerable Mahā-Kassapa heard her saying this. Then he said to the venerable Ānanda: "Indeed, friend Ānanda, the bhikkhunī Thullānandā has spoken hastily without reflecting. Since I shaved off my hair and beard and put on the yellow robe to go forth from the house life into homelessness, I have never looked to any teacher other than the Blessed One, accomplished and fully enlightened. Formerly when I was a layman I thought: 'House life is crowded and dusty; life gone forth is wide open. It is not easy, living in a household, to lead a holy life as utterly perfect and pure as a polished shell. Suppose I shaved off my hair and beard, put on the yellow robe, and went forth from the house life into homelessness?' Later I made a patched cloak out of rags. Then I shaved off my hair and beard and put on the yellow robe for the sake of those in the world who are Arahants, and I went forth from the house life into homelessness.

"When I had gone forth, while I was journeying by road, I saw the Blessed One between Rājagaha and Nālandā sitting in the Bahuputta Shrine. When I saw him I thought: 'If ever I acknowledge a Master, let me acknowledge only the Blessed One. If ever I acknowledge a Sublime One, let me acknowledge only the Blessed One. If ever I acknowledge a Fully Enlightened One, let me acknowledge only the Blessed One.' Then, prostrating myself there at his feet, I said: 'Lord, the Blessed One is my teacher; I am his disciple. The Blessed One is my teacher; I am his disciple.' Then the Blessed One said: 'Kassapa, if anyone were to say without knowing "I know" or without seeing "I see" to so single-hearted a disciple as you, his head would burst. But knowing I say "I know," seeing I say "I see." Therefore, Kassapa, you should train thus: "A keen conscience and sense of shame shall be established in me in relation to the elder bhikkhus, new bhikkhus and those of middle seniority." And you should train thus: "I shall hear the Dhamma with a ready ear, listening and attending and giving my whole mind to anything conducive to the wholesome." And you should train thus: "I shall never fail to practise gladly mindfulness occupied with the body." You should train thus.' Then after the Blessed One had given me this advice, he rose from his seat and departed.

"I ate the country's almsfood as a debtor for only seven days. On the eighth day final knowledge arose. Then the Blessed One left the road and went to the root of a tree. I folded my patched cloak of rags in four, and I said to him: 'Lord, let the Blessed One sit here, so that it may be long for my welfare and happiness.' The Blessed One sat down on the seat made ready. Then he said: 'Your patched cloak of rags is soft, Kassapa.'—'Let the Blessed One accept the patched cloak of rags from me, Lord, out of compassion.'—'But will you wear my hemp-cloth refuse-rag robe that I cast off, Kassapa?'

'Lord, I shall wear the Blessed One's hemp-cloth refuse-rag robe that he casts off.' I gave the Blessed One my patched cloak of rags, and I took in exchange the Blessed One's hemp-cloth refuse-rag robe that he cast off. If it can be said of anyone: 'He is the Blessed

One's own son, born of his mouth, born of the Dhamma, created by the Dhamma, an heir of the Dhamma, a receiver of hemp-cloth refuse-rag robes cast off,' it is of me indeed that that should be said."

NARRATOR ONE. He went on to tell how he was able, whenever he wished, to enter upon and abide in the four meditations and also the four formless states and the cessation of perception and feeling too, besides having acquired the five kinds of worldly direct knowledge, that is to say, supernormal powers, the divine ear element, penetration of minds, recollection of past life, and the divine eye by which to see beings' passing away and reappearing according to their deeds. He concluded:

FIRST VOICE. "Whenever I wish, then by realization myself with direct knowledge here and now, I enter upon and dwell in the deliverance of mind and deliverance by understanding that are taintless with the exhaustion of taints. He would imagine that a tusker elephant fourteen feet high or more could be eclipsed by a palm leaf who would fancy that he himself could eclipse me in the matter of these six kinds of direct knowledge."

The bhikkhunī Thullānandā later fell from the holy life.

S. 16:11

NARRATOR TWO. It is still only a few weeks after the Parinibbāna.

THIRD VOICE. The venerable Mahā-Kassapa said: "Now, friends, let us rehearse the Teaching and the Discipline, the Dhamma and the Vinaya. Already wrong teachings and wrong discipline have been courted, and right teachings and right discipline have been flouted. And already upholders of wrong teachings and wrong discipline have been strong, and upholders of right teachings and right discipline have been weak."

"Then, Lord, let the Elder convoke an assembly of bhikkhus."

So the venerable Mahā-Kassapa convoked an assembly of one less than five hundred Arahants; for the bhikkhus had said: "There is the venerable Ānanda. Though he is still only a learner—a stream-enterer—still he is incapable of going to an unhappy destination through desire, anger, delusion or fear. He has mastered much of the Dhamma and Discipline of wide variety in the Blessed One's presence. Let the Elder summon the venerable Ānanda too."

So he summoned the venerable Ānanda too. Then he asked the bhikkhus: "Where shall we do the rehearsing?"

The elder bhikkhus thought: "Rājagaha is a big resort with plenty of accommodation. Why not go to Rājagaha and stay there for the rains?" So the venerable Mahā-Kassapa placed a resolution before the Sangha to that effect:

"Let the Sangha hear me, friends. If it seems proper to the Sangha, let the Sangha authorize as follows: that these five hundred bhikkhus stay at Rājagaha for this rains for the purpose of rehearsing the Dhamma and the Discipline, and that no other bhikkhus stay at Rājagaha for this rains. This is the resolution. Let the Sangha hear me, friends; the Sangha authorizes as follows: that these five hundred bhikkhus stay at Rājagaha for this rains for the purpose of rehearsing the Dhamma and the Discipline, and that no other bhikkhus stay at Rājagaha for this rains. Let him who agrees to this keep silent; let him who does not agree speak out. The Sangha agrees that this resolution is authorized by the Sangha, therefore the Sangha keeps silent. So I record it."

Then the elder bhikkhus met in Rājagaha to rehearse the Dhamma and the Discipline. However, they considered: "The repair of what is broken and dilapidated was recommended by the Blessed One. So, friends, let us see to this during the first month. In the second month we shall meet together for the rehearsal."

Meanwhile the time came when the venerable Ānanda thought: "The meeting is tomorrow. It is not seemly for me to go to the meeting place as a mere learner." He spent much of the night in contemplation of the body. When the night was near dawn, he thought "I shall lie down"; but he kept mindful of the body. Before his head touched the pillow and after his feet left the ground, his heart was in this interval liberated from taints through not clinging. So the venerable Ānanda went to the assembly as an Arahant.

Then the venerable Mahā-Kassapa placed a resolution before the Sangha: "Let the Sangha hear me, friends; if it seems proper to the Sangha, I shall interrogate the venerable Upāli on the Discipline."

Then the venerable Upāli placed a resolution before the Sangha: "Let the Sangha hear me, Lords; if it seems proper to the Sangha, I, being interrogated on the Discipline by the venerable Mahā-Kassapa, shall answer."

Then the venerable Mahā-Kassapa said to the venerable Upāli:

"Friend Upāli, where was the First Defeat declared?"
"At Vesālī, Lord."
"On whose account?"
"On account of Sudinna Kalandaputta."
"Dealing with what subject?"
"Dealing with sexual intercourse."

NARRATOR TWO. The Elder Mahā-Kassapa then interrogated the Elder Upāli about the subject matter of the First Defeat, its source, the person, the declaration, the modifications, the offence, and what was no offence. Then he interrogated him likewise about the other three Defeats—those of stealing, killing human beings, and knowingly making a false claim to spiritual attainments. In this manner he interrogated him on the two Codes, namely, the bhikkhus' Pātimokkha or Code of Monastic Rules and that of the bhikkhunīs, and also on all the other rules laid down. The Elder Upāli answered each question.

THIRD VOICE. Then the venerable Mahā-Kassapa placed a resolution before the Sangha: "Let the Sangha hear me, friends; if it seems proper to the Sangha, I shall interrogate the venerable Ānanda on the Dhamma."

Then the venerable Ānanda placed a resolution before the Sangha: "Let the Sangha hear me, Lords; if it seems proper to the Sangha, I, being interrogated on the Sangha by the venerable Mahā-Kassapa, shall answer."

Then the venerable Mahā-Kassapa said to the venerable Ānanda: "Friend Ānanda, where was the Brahmajāla Sutta spoken?"

"Between Rājagaha and Nālandā, Lord, in the king's resthouse at Ambalaṭṭhikā"

"On whose account?"

"On account of the wanderer Suppiya and the brahman student Brahmadatta."

NARRATOR TWO. The Elder then interrogated him about the source of the Brahmajāla Sutta, the first in the Collection of Long Discourses, and about the person. After that, he interrogated him about the Sāmaññaphala Sutta in the same way. In this manner he interrogated him on all the appropriate discourses in all the four Main Collections of the Sutta Piṭaka.

THIRD VOICE. Then the venerable Ānanda told the elder bhikkhus: "Lords, at the time of the Blessed One's attainment of final Nibbāna he told me: 'If it wishes, the Sangha can abolish the minor and lesser rules when I am gone.' "

"But, friend Ānanda, did you ask the Blessed One what these minor and lesser rules were?"

"I did not, Lords."

NARRATOR TWO. The elders expressed different opinions about which rules, apart from the four Defeats, ought to be taken as the minor and lesser rules. Then the venerable Mahā-Kassapa placed a resolution before the Sangha.

THIRD VOICE. "Let the Sangha hear me, friends; there are certain of our training rules that involve laymen, by which laymen know what is allowed to monks who are sons of the Sakyans and what is not. If we abolish these minor and lesser rules, there will be those who say: 'The training rules proclaimed by the monk Gotama to his disciples existed only for the period ending with his cremation; they kept his training rules as long as he was present, but now that he has attained final Nibbāna they have given up keeping his training rules.' If it seems proper to the Sangha, let not what is undeclared be declared, and let not what is declared be abolished; let the Sangha proceed according to the training rules as they have been declared." The resolution was placed before the Sangha and passed.

Then the elder bhikkhus said to the venerable Ānanda: "Friend Ānanda, this was a wrongdoing on your part: that you did not ask the Blessed One which were the minor and lesser rules. Acknowledge that wrongdoing."

"It was through want of mindfulness, Lords, that I did not ask the Blessed One that. I do not see it as a wrongdoing. Nevertheless, out of faith in the venerable ones, I acknowledge it as a wrongdoing."

"This, too, was a wrongdoing on your part: that you trod on the Blessed One's rains-cloth when you were sewing it. Acknowledge that wrongdoing."

"It was not out of disrespect for the Blessed One, Lords, that I did so. I do not see it as a wrongdoing. Nevertheless, out of faith in the venerable ones, I acknowledge it as a wrongdoing."

"This, too, was a wrongdoing on your part: that you had the Blessed One's remains saluted first by women. They were weeping, and the Blessed One's remains were smeared with their tears. Acknowledge that wrongdoing."

"I had them do so, Lords, in order that the time should not be unsuitable for them. I do not see it as a wrongdoing. Nevertheless, out of faith in the venerable ones, I acknowledge it as a wrongdoing."

"This, too, was a wrongdoing on your part: that even when such a broad hint, such a plain sign, was given you by the Blessed One, you did not beg the Blessed One: 'Lord, let the Blessed One live out the age, let the Sublime One live out the age, for the welfare and happiness of many, out of compassion for the world, for the good and welfare and happiness of gods and men.' Acknowledge that wrongdoing."

"It was because my mind was under the influence of Māra that I did not ask the Blessed One that. I do not see it as a wrongdoing. Nevertheless, out of faith in the venerable ones, I acknowledge it as a wrongdoing."

"This, too, was a wrongdoing on your part: that you interested yourself in the going forth of women in the Dhamma and Discipline proclaimed by the Perfect One. Acknowledge that wrongdoing."

"I did so, Lords, thinking that this Mahāpajāpatī Gotamī was the sister of the Blessed One's mother, was his nurse, his foster mother, his giver of milk she suckled the Blessed One when his own mother died. I do not see it as a wrongdoing. Nevertheless, out of faith in the venerable ones, I acknowledge it as a wrongdoing."

Vin. Cv. 11:1-10

Now at that time the venerable Purāṇa was wandering in the Southern Hills with a large community of bhikkhus, with five hundred bhikkhus. Then after the Dhamma and Discipline had been rehearsed by the elders, when the Elder Purāṇa had stayed in the Southern Hills as long as he chose, he went to the elders in the Bamboo Grove at Rājagaha. They said to him: "Friend Purāṇa, the Dhamma and Discipline have been rehearsed by the elders. Do you support that rehearsal?"

"Friends, the Dhamma and Discipline have been well rehearsed by the elders. I, however, shall remember them as I heard them from the Blessed One's own lips."

Vin. Cv. 11:11

NARRATOR ONE. Now here is one last incident, which shows the young Sangha living on after its founder's passing and established as a viable body—a body which has survived uninterruptedly and flourished for two and a half millennia until the present day.

THIRD VOICE. Thus I heard. At one time the venerable Ānanda was living at Rājagaha in the Bamboo Grove, the Squirrels' Sanctuary, not long after the Blessed One had attained final Nibbāna.

At that time, however, King Ajātasattu Vedehiputta of Magadha was having Rājagaha fortified, since he was mistrustful of King Pajjota of Avanti.

In the morning the venerable Ānanda dressed, and taking his bowl and outer robe, he went into Rājagaha for alms. Then it occurred to him: "It is still too early to wander for alms in Rājagaha. Suppose I went to where the defence minister Moggallāna the brahman's works are in progress?"

He did so. The brahman saw him coming. Then he said: "Let Master Ānanda come. Welcome to Master Ānanda. It is long since Master Ānanda came this way. Let Master Ānanda be seated. There is this seat made ready."

The venerable Ānanda sat down on the seat made ready, while the brahman took another lower seat and sat down at one side. He said: "Master Ānanda, is there any single bhikkhu who possesses in all ways and every way those qualities that Master Gotama possessed?"

"There is not, brahman. For the Blessed One was the arouser of the unarisen path, the producer of the unproduced path, the declarer of the undeclared path, the path knower, path seer, skilled in the path. But now when the disciples dwelling in conformity with that path become possessed of it, they do so after him."

Their talk meanwhile was left unfinished here, however, for the brahman Vassakāra the Magadhan minister, who was inspecting the works at Rājagaha, came to where the venerable Ānanda was, where the defence minister Moggallāna's works were in progress. He exchanged greetings, and when this courteous formal talk was finished, he sat down at one side. He said: "For what talk are you gathered here now? And what was your talk meanwhile that was left unfinished?"

The venerable Ānanda told him the conversation that had just taken place. He added: "This was our talk meanwhile that was left unfinished, for then you arrived."

"Master Ānanda, is there any single bhikkhu nominated by Master Gotama thus: 'This one will be your refuge when I am gone,' whom you can have recourse to now?"

"No such bhikkhu was nominated by the Blessed One who knows and sees, accomplished and fully enlightened."

"Then, Master Ānanda, has any single bhikkhu been chosen by the Sangha, elected by a majority of elder bhikkhus thus: 'This one will be our refuge when the Blessed One is gone,' whom you can have recourse to now?"

"There is no such bhikkhu, brahman."

"But if there is no refuge, Master Ānanda, what reason for concord is there?"

"We are not without refuge, brahman. We have a refuge. The Dhamma is our refuge."

"But, Master Ānanda, how should the meaning of these statements be regarded?"

"The Blessed One who knows and sees, accomplished and fully enlightened, has made known the training rules for bhikkhus, and he has set forth the Pātimokkha Code of Monastic Rules. As many of us as live within one village district meet together on the day of the Uposatha each half moon, and when we do so we appoint him who is familiar with the Pātimokkha. If a bhikkhu has committed an offence, a transgression, since this Code of Monastic Rules is recited, it is according to the Dhamma, according to the precept, that we have him act: it is not persons, surely, that have us act, but rather it is the Dhamma that has us act."

"Is there any single bhikkhu, Master Ānanda, whom you now honour, respect, revere and venerate, and on whom you live in dependence, honouring and respecting him?"

"There is such a bhikkhu, brahman."

"But, Master Ānanda, when you were asked: 'Is there any single bhikkhu nominated by Master Gotama thus: "This one will be your refuge when I am gone"?' you replied that there was no such bhikkhu. And when you were asked: 'Then has any single bhikkhu been chosen by the Sangha, elected by a majority of Elder bhikkhus, thus: "This one will be our refuge when the Blessed One is gone," whom you can have recourse to now?' you replied that there was no such bhikkhu. And when you were asked: 'Is there any single bhikkhu whom you now honour, respect, revere and venerate, and on whom you live in dependence, honouring and respecting him?' you replied that there is such a bhikkhu. How then should the meaning of these statements be regarded?"

"Brahman, ten things that inspire faith and confidence have been described by the Blessed One who knows and sees, accomplished and fully enlightened. We honour, respect, revere and venerate him among us in whom these things are evidenced, and we live in dependence on him, honouring and respecting him. What are the ten?

"Here a bhikkhu is virtuous, restrained with the Pātimokkha restraint, perfect in conduct and resort; seeing fear in the slightest fault, he trains by giving effect to the precepts of training. He is well taught, and he remembers and records what he has heard; the teachings that are good in the beginning, good in the middle and good in the end with the meaning and the letter, which explain a holy life that is utterly perfect and pure, those teachings he learns well, remembers, consolidates by word of mouth, looks over in his mind, and thoroughly penetrates with right view. He is contented with his robes, almsfood, lodging, and medicine. He obtains at will, with no trouble or reserve, all the four meditations which belong to the higher mentality and provide a pleasant abiding here and now. He wields the various kinds of supernormal powers: having been one, he becomes many; having been many, he becomes one; he appears and vanishes; he goes unhindered through walls, through enclosures, through mountains, as though in space; he dives in and out of the earth as though it were water; seated crosslegged he travels in space like a winged bird; with his hand he touches and strokes the moon and sun so powerful and mighty; he wields bodily mastery even as far as the Brahma-world. With the divine ear element, which is purified and surpasses the human, he hears both kinds of sounds, the divine and the human, those that are far as well as near. He penetrates with his mind the mind of other beings, of other persons; he understands mind affected by lust as affected by lust ... (see Ch. 12, p. 243) ... and unliberated mind as unliberated. He recollects his manifold past life ... (see Ch. 2, p. 23). With the divine eye, which is purified and surpasses the human, he sees beings passing away and reappearing ... (see Ch. 2, p. 24) ... He understands how beings pass on according to their deeds. By realization himself with direct knowledge he here and now enters upon and abides in the deliverance of mind and the deliverance by understanding that are taintless with the destruction of taints. These are the ten things."

When this was said, the brahman Vassakāra turned to General Upananda and asked: "What is your opinion, general? If it is in this way that these worthy people honour him who should be honoured, then do they not do rightly? For if they did not do so, whom indeed should they honour, respect, revere and venerate, and whom should they live in dependence on, honouring and respecting him?"

The brahman Vassakāra then asked the venerable Ānanda: "Where is Master Ānanda living now?"

"I am living in the Bamboo Grove now, brahman."

"I hope, Master Ānanda, that the Bamboo Grove is agreeable and quiet, undisturbed by voices, a place with an atmosphere of aloofness, where one can lie hidden from people, and favourable for retreat?"

"Indeed, brahman, that the Bamboo Grove has all those qualities is owing to guardian protectors like yourself."

"Indeed, Master Ānanda, that the Bamboo Grove has those qualities is owing to the good people who acquire meditation and practise it; for these good people do acquire meditation and practise it. Once Master Gotama was living at Vesālī in the Hall with the Pointed Roof in the Great Wood. Then I went there and approached him. And there Master Gotama talked about meditation in many ways. Master Gotama was one who practised meditation and he was accustomed to meditation. In fact, Master Gotama commended all kinds of meditation."

"The Blessed One did not commend all kinds of meditation, brahman; nor did he condemn all kinds of meditation. What kinds did the Blessed One not commend? Here someone abides with his heart possessed by lust, a prey to lust, and he does not rightly understand the escape from lust. He still puts lust first for all he meditates and over-meditates and unmeditates and remeditates again. And likewise he is possessed by ill will, by lethargy and drowsiness, by agitation and worry, or by uncertainty. The Blessed One did not commend such meditation.

"And what kind of meditation did the Blessed One commend? Here someone, quite secluded from sensual desires, secluded from unwholesome states, enters upon and abides in the first meditation, which is accompanied by thinking and exploring, with happiness and pleasure born of seclusion. And he enters upon and abides in the second, the third, and the fourth meditations. The Blessed One commended such meditation."

"Then, Master Ānanda, it seems that Master Gotama condemned the kind of meditation that deserves condemnation and commended the kind that deserves commendation. And now, Master Ānanda, we depart; we are busy and have much to do."

"It is time now, brahman, to do as you think fit."

Then the brahman Vassakāra, the Magadhan minister, got up from his seat, and after he had approved and agreed with the venerable Ānanda's words, he went on his way. Soon after he had gone the defence minister, the brahman Moggallāna, said: "Master Ānanda has not answered our question."

"Did we not tell you, brahman, 'There is no single bhikkhu who possesses in all ways and every way those qualities that the Blessed One, accomplished and fully enlightened, possessed; for the Blessed One was the arouser of the unarisen path, the producer of the unproduced path, the declarer of the undeclared path, the path knower, the path seer, skilled in the path; but now, when the disciples dwelling in conformity with that path become possessed of it, they do so after him'?"

M. 108

NARRATOR TWO. Meanwhile King Ajātasattu was bent on the destruction of his too powerful neighbour, the Vajjian Confederacy with its capital at Vesālī northeast across the Ganges. In order to help him achieve this end, Vassakāra posed as a conspirator against him; he had himself denounced as a traitor and fled to Vesālī for asylum. The next three years were spent by him in artful dissemination of mistrust and mutual suspicion among the members of the confederacy. When he judged the moment ripe, he secretly informed King Ajātasattu. The rulers of Vesālī were now too disunited to defend their country, and Ajātasattu was soon able to round off a successful invasion with an extensive massacre of the population. This was the end of Vajjian independence. King Viḍūḍabha of Kosala quickly followed his cousin's example by overrunning the Sakyan and Koliyan territory on his northeastern border, treating the people there in the same way.

NARRATOR ONE. That closes the first scene of Indian history. For the next century and a half, till the rise of the Maurian Empire with its new dynasty, nothing is recorded but the names of kings of Magadha and the account of the Second Council of Arahants one hundred years after the Parinibbāna. By that time, though, the great northern kingdom of Kosala had vanished (how we do not know), and Chandragupta (the "Sandrocottos' of the Greek traveller Megasthenes), as heir of the old Magadha, had command of all the Ganges valley with his capital now at Patna (Pāṭaliputta).

An account of the Second Council was added to the Vinaya Piṭaka no doubt at the time of that council. The Canon was recited again, and it was then, it may be assumed, that the few suttas dealing with the period after the First Council were incorporated in the Sutta Piṭaka. At a third council held during the reign of the Emperor Asoka (Chandragupta's grandson), the Abhidhamma Piṭaka was completed by adding a book on heresies, and the Tipiṭaka virtually closed.

Eighteen differing "schools" had sprung up by this time. The Theravāda (Doctrine of the Elders) became dominant under Asoka, who himself embraced Buddhism. His son (or by some traditions, his nephew), the Arahant Mahinda, brought the Pali Tipiṭaka with its Commentary to Ceylon,[2] while other elders went to other countries. It is this Pali Tipiṭaka which has been preserved till today in Ceylon, and in Burma, Thailand and Cambodia, where the Theravāda still flourishes.

If we accept the observations of the Chinese traveller I-tsing, who came to India (but not to Ceylon) at the end of the seventh century, the Theravāda was dominant in all the southern half of India, while the Sarvāstivāda (whose Canon, in Sanskrit, is held to be less old than the Pali) dominated the northern half, though other schools were widely disseminated in many parts. The Sarvāstivāda Canon spread northward and eastward, and the Pali Canon southward and eastward. The Mahāyāna, which I-tsing (himself a Sarvāstivādin) seems to suggest had roots in his time in all or most of the schools, is usually claimed to have sprung from one of them, namely the Mahāsanghika. Though flourishing from time to time in Ceylon and Burma, it was never able to suppress its older rival in those countries. But in India, Buddhism in all its forms seems to have entirely disappeared by the fifteenth century.

NOTES

CHAPTER 1

1. The word *bhagavant* is here rendered unliterally by "Blessed One." A literal rendering is impossible. Ācariya Buddhaghosa, in his *Visuddhimagga* (VII, 53ff.), gives a variety of explanations.

2. The word *bhikkhu* (Sanskrit: *bhikshu*) has been left in the original. Etymology now derives the word from *bhikkhā* (alms). But there is also an older "semantic" derivation: *saṃsāre bhayaṃ ikkhatī ti bhikkhu* ("he sees fear in the round of rebirths, thus he is a 'fear-seer' "). A bhikkhu is a fully admitted member of the monastic order (Sangha); but his admission involves no irrevocable vows.

3. *The Heaven of the Contented (tusita).* The cosmology of the time describes many heavens: notably six paradises in which the pleasures of all the senses are enjoyed; above those, twelve Brahmā heavens (the "World of High Divinity"), where consciousness is quite purified of present lust, though not of the future potentiality for it, and where (according to the Commentary) material form is rarefied by absence of the three senses of smell, taste and bodily touch and of sex; they correspond to the states attainable by human beings in the four meditations. Extra to these (as it were, refinements of the fourth) are the four "formless" states of infinity where all perceptions of material form and of difference are transcended: the infinity of space and of consciousness, and nothingness, and reduced perception of nothingness. Rebirth in all is impermanent and followed by renewed rebirth unless Nibbāna, the Unformed, is attained.

4. In this set phrase the Commentary has been followed in the rendering of *sadevamanussānaṃ* by "with its princes and men." The whole sense requires it, and deva is the normal form of address to a king.

5. *Kaṇhasiri* would mean "Dark Splendour" (the Sanskrit equivalent of *kaṇha* is *krishna*).

6. These circumstances are elsewhere stated to be constant for all Bodhisattas in their last existence (D. 14). But it is only of the former Buddha Vipassī (D. 14), not of the Buddha Gotama, that the story of the "four messengers"—the old man, the sick man, the corpse, and the monk—

is told in the Tipiṭaka itself. Later accounts ascribe this to the Buddha Gotama too.

CHAPTER 2

1. *Kusala*: wholesome, profitable. (Nyp.)

2. *Akusala*: originally translated here by "unprofitable." (Nyp.)

3. What the last lines (omitted here but included in Ch. 4, p. 61) of this song refer to is placed by the Commentary one year later than the rest.

4. The Dictionary of the Pali Text Society gives "junket" for *kummāsa*, which the Commentaries, however, explain as made of wheat (*yava*).

5. Discourses describing the Enlightenment in different terms are: in terms of dependent arising (S. 12:10, 65; cf. D. 14); of the three true knowledges or sciences (M. 4, 100); gratification, inadequacy (danger), and escape in the case of the five aggregates (S. 22:26), the elements (S. 14:31), sensual desires (S. 35:117; M. 14), feeling (S. 36:24), the world (A. 3:101); in terms of the four right endeavours (A. 5:68), of the four foundations of mindfulness (S. 47:31), of the four bases for success (S. 51:9), of abandonment of evil thoughts (M. 19), etc.

6. For dependent arising see Ch. 12.

7. Or: thorough consideration, wise reflection (*yoniso manasikāra*). (Nyp.)

CHAPTER 3

1. There is a constant punning, if that is the word for it, between the words *brāhmaṇa* (divine-caste, a recluse, a priestly divine), *brahma* (divine, heavenly, perfect), and *Brahmā* (divinity, the High Divinity, or divinities beyond the gods of the six sensual paradises). The brahmanical priesthood is drawn from this caste, for which a special connection with Brahmā is claimed, and it is that fact which can justify the rendering "divine." Normally the word is left untranslated. Other echoes are: the "divine abidings" (*brahmāvihara*: Ch. 10, p. 177) of loving-kindness, etc., the holy or "divine life" (*brahmacariya*) or "pure conduct," which is so by virtue of the "divine" characteristic of chastity, the "divine vehicle" (*brahmayāna*: Ch. 12, p. 251), and so on.

2. The placing of this and the following incidents here is indicated by the texts themselves. The *Mālālankāravatthu* puts the Temptation by Māra's daughters here too; but Ācariya Buddhaghosa ascribes that to the first year after the Enlightenment (see Ch. 4, p. 62). One other incident, not included here, of some brahmans who reproached the Buddha for not showing respect to them (cf. Ch. 9, p. 124), is related at A. 4:22.

3. These are two difficult verses. It is really necessary to translate the word *bhava* more or less consistently by "being" rather than by "becoming." The "essentials of existence" are elsewhere explained as referring to all components of existence ranging from objective chattels to subjective craving and attitudes.

4. "Extinction" and "Nibbāna" have been used interchangeably throughout. "Extinction" is to be taken as extinguishment of the fires (S. 35:28, quoted at Ch. 4, p. 64) of lust, hate and delusion, and the consequences thereof. It should not be taken to mean "extinguishment of a living person" (see Ch. 11, p. 203). Modern etymology derives the word *nibbāna* (Skr: *nirvāṇa*) from the negative prefix *ni(r)* plus the root *vā* (to blow). The original meaning was probably extinction of a fire by ceasing to blow on it with bellows (e.g. a smith's fire). It seems to have been extended to the extinction of fire by any means, e.g. the going out of a lamp's flame (*nibbāyati*: M. 140; *nibbanti*: Sn. 2:1, v. 14). By analogy it was extended to the extinction of lust and the rest, completely achieved by the Arahant during his life. On his physical death the five-aggregate process will dissolve without renewal. Nibbāna is wrongly identified as "extinction of an existing self" and likewise as the perpetuation of self (see Ch. 12, pp. 228-235).

5. The Pali for "one of the haughty, haw-haw-ing kind" is *huhunka-jātika*, which the Commentary says means "one who says 'hum, hum' out of pride."

6. Instead of "that goes in one way only" the compound *ekāyana* is usually translated by "the only way"; but see the use of the compound in M. 12.

7. "Let those who hear show faith" (*ye sotavanto pamuñcantu saddhaṃ*) is a passage much controverted by scholars. The rendering usually adopted is "Let them who hear renounce their faith"; but this meaning jars with the spirit of the teaching. Also it depends on interpreting the word vissajjentu (with which the Commentary glosses *pamuñcantu*) as "let them give up"; but that word can also mean "let them give out" or "let them put forth." Thus *pamuñcantu*—"let them show, bring out." That this is how the Commentary takes it is confirmed by the end of the commentarial paragraph: *sabbo jano saddhā-bhājanaṃ upanetu* ("Let everyone bring forward his vessel of faith": Comy. to M. 26), in which the *upanetu* paraphrases *pamuñcantu.* The idiom also occurs at Sn. 1146 (where, unfortunately, it has sometimes been confounded with another idiom *saddhā-vimutto*—"one liberated by faith").

8. "All-transcender" (*sabbābhibhū*): a derivative of the root *bhū* (to be), in the sense of "beyond being" or "who has overcome all being." *Abhibhū* (which will be encountered again later) is paraphrased by some translators with "mastery" (as in *abhibhāyatana*) or "Overcomer" as an epithet of *Mahā-brahmā.* It

can be taken as one of the instances of the use of a current word by the Buddha in a transforming context.

9. The "aggregates affected by clinging" (*upādānakkhandha*) are discussed in Ch. 12.

10. *Bhāvetabbaṃ*: "must be cultivated, developed." (Nyp.)

CHAPTER 4

1. The story of the sleeping minstrels is told only of the venerable Yasa in the Tipiṭaka itself, though later versions ascribe it also to the Bodhisatta as the immediate motive for his renunciation.

2. This rendering of *sāmukkaṃsika* is based on the commentary to A.7:12. There is no doubt that the P.T.S. Dictionary is wrong here.

3. This refers to a stream-enterer (sotāpanna). (Nyp.)

4. There seems no reason to read into the words *attānaṃ gaveseyyātha* ("you should seek yourselves") more than that contained in the Delphic "know thyself." In Pali the word *attā* (self) is not used in the plural form, and there is nothing abnormal in the singular form applied to a group (also Indian alphabets have no capitals).

5. The Commentary says the "five floods" are "those of lust, etc., connected with the five sense-doors," the "sixth" being "the flood of defilement connected with the mind-door."

6. The "ten ways of life" are the noble ones' ten ways of life (D. 33); for the ten powers, see Ch. 11, p. 185; the "ten things" are the ten kinds of action, wholesome and unwholesome (see e.g. M. 9); the "ten factors" are the ten states of the adept (D. 33): so the Comy.

CHAPTER 5

1. "Habit of treating it (the physical body) as the basis for all his inferences" (*kāyanvayatā*) refers to the way of thinking which assumes the physical body as the basic reality, the empirical truth, and builds its system upon that (materialism, in fact, the physiological view of mind, or the view of consciousness as an "epiphenomenon" upon matter). Both this standpoint and the opposite, which treats matter as subordinate to mind, are discussed at the beginning of M. 36.

2. According to the Theragāthā Commentary, the River Rohiṇī runs southwards and separates the Sakyan country on the west from the Koliyan on the east. Rājagaha lay far to the south across the Ganges, so one travelling from there via the Vajjian and then the Koliyan country would cross the river facing west.

3. *Pabbajjā*: the novice ordination. (Nyp.)

4. The "four bases for success" (or roads to power) are described as "the basis for success that has concentration due to desire-to-act and has for its determination the endeavour-to-control" (M. 16). That is the first. The other three substitute respectively "energy," "(natural purity of) mind," and "inquiry" for "desire-to-act." They represent four types of approach to development, according to idiosyncrasy.

5. The date of the Elder Ānanda's going forth seems not quite certain. His verses spoken by him in the Theragāthā point to a much later date. It is not clear too whether the word rājā (here rendered by "who is governing") applied to Bhaddiya the Sakyan means "king" (in which case King Suddhodana's death is implied) or simply "regent." The commentarial placing has been followed here.

CHAPTER 6

1. A figurative expression for an Arahant. (BB.)

2. There is actually no evidence to show when this Māra incident occurred.

3. "Whom the virtuous bhikkhu's fire shall burn": here is Ācariya Buddhaghosa's comment: "A bhikkhu who abuses in return an abuser ... is incapable of burning with the bhikkhu fire. But when he (the bhikkhu) does not abuse an abuser in return, he (the abuser) fails with respect to him and is burned by the fire of his (the bhikkhu's) virtue, that is, he gets no sons or daughters, and no cattle, etc.; the meaning is that they are brought to naught, 'like palm stumps'; being burned by the bhikkhu fire, they become like a palm with its crown cut off and only the trunk remaining; the meaning is that they have no more increase by sons, daughters, and so on."

CHAPTER 7

1. The *Mālālankāravatthu* says that this rains was spent at Rājagaha in the Bamboo Grove, which must be wrong.

2. At least two of the more abstruse discourses in the Sutta Piṭaka (M. 44 and S. 44:1) were delivered by bhikkhunīs. A number of women were singled out for special virtues (A. 1:14), and there is a collection of verses uttered by them on reaching Arahantship (Therīgāthā, Eng. trans. *Psalms of the Sisters* by Mrs. C. A. F. Rhys Davids).

3. "Roses" is not literal for *atimuttaka*, but simply seemed preferable to the rather grim "gaertnera racemosa" offered by the Dictionary.

CHAPTER 8

1. There is a difference of opinion on the meaning of the word *yamāmase*: whether it should be rendered "we should restrain ourselves" or "we may be destroyed."

CHAPTER 9

1. The word *kevalī* ("has reached the Absolute") seems only to be used by the Buddha when speaking to brahmans.

2. Some of the puns in this passage strain the resources of the translator badly. "Teaches that there is no ought-to-do" (*akiriyavādī*) means one who says that acts are amoral and have no ripening, good or bad. "Teaches nihilism" (*ucchedavādī*) means one who believes that some sort of a soul or self has temporary permanence but is cut off at some point. It contains an assumption about a soul temporarily existing. "One to lead away" (*venayika*) is the most difficult. The word *vineti* (lit. "to lead away") means both to lead away and, metaphorically, to discipline. To "lead away" is also used by the Buddha in the sense of leading disciples away from suffering, and by his opponents to abuse him as one who leads people away to the destruction, furnished by nihilism, the "abyss of nothingness," and as a consequence he is for them one "to be led away," i.e to be got rid of.

3. There is a word-play on the word *sutta*, literally "thread" and metaphorically "thread of argument" or stringing together of connected ideas; it is in this latter sense that the Buddha's discourses are called "suttas," because the teaching is put together in them in the form of a connected thread of argument.

4. "Loathsomeness" is a term for the object of contemplation consisting in either the "thirty-one parts of the body" (thirty-two in the Commentaries) or the decay of corpses (Ch. 12, pp. 241 and 242). Its purpose is to reduce attachment to the physical body by demonstrating its unattractiveness and transitoriness.

5. The word *padhāvino* (travellers) appears in the same phrase in M. 50 but spelled there *pathāvino* (P.T.S. ed.). The Comy. to M. 50 has been followed. The P.T.S. Dict. gives both words but with different meanings though the separate inclusion of *padhāvin* there is an error.

6. "If you will believe in": literally, *sace... ajjhosissasi* means "if you will accept," or as the Comy. says: "If, through believing (i.e. accepting), swallowing, assimilating, you will assume with craving, conceit and views."

7. The emphasis is all on the notion of being ("to be or not to be"). The allotment of utterances and the readings are taken from the Burmese ed., which

is more reliable here than any other and has *nāpahosiṃ* instead of *nāhosi.* All the clauses from that with "earth" down to "all" should be read (e.g.) thus: *sabbaṃ kho ahaṃ brahme sabbato abhiññāya yāvatā sabbassa sabbattena ananubhūtaṃ, tad abhiññāya sabbaṃ nāpahosiṃ, sabbasmiṃ nāpahosiṃ, sabbato nāpahosiṃ, sabbam me ti nāpahosiṃ, sabbaṃ nābhivadiṃ* ("Having had direct knowledge of all as all ...."). In both this sutta and D. 11 the line, *Viññāṇam anidassanam anantaṃ sabbatopabhaṃ* ("The consciousness that makes no showing ...") is spoken by the Buddha (this page and also p. 150). The line has puzzled many. The Majjhima Commentary allows much greater latitude than the Dīgha Commentary and puts forward a derivation from the root *bhū* (to be) for *pabhaṃ* (or *pahaṃ*). Following this hint, though not quite on the lines suggested by the Comy., we could take *sabbatopabhaṃ* to be made up of *sabbato* and a contracted form of the present participle of *pahoti* (= *pabhavati*), i.e. pahaṃ (= pabhaṃ). This ties up with the preceding *sabbato abhiññāya ... sabbaṃ nāpahosiṃ;* however, the sense then requires a suppressed negative, i.e *sabbatopahaṃ* = *sabbato apahaṃ* ("claiming no being apart from all"). The letters h and bh are easily mistaken for each other in Sinhalese. In D. 11, in which the same line occurs, the Buddha is probably quoting from this discourse. We have here material for the nucleus of an interesting ontological study.

CHAPTER 10

1. The "Octets" are the Aṭṭhaka-vagga of the Sutta-nipāta.

2. A Paccekabuddha is one who becomes enlightened without the guidance of a Buddha. He does not attempt to enlighten others. (BB)

3. If this passage is read as a general injunction to disregard all instruction, then it would be impossible to carry out; for one could only carry it out by not carrying it out (a well-known logical dilemma). But the rest of the discourse should make clear the sense intended. For faith (saddhā) see Ch. 11, p. 200.

4. The caring for the sick enjoined here applies to bhikkhus caring for sick bhikkhus. The general practice of medicine by bhikkhus upon the laity is considered as one of the wrong means of livelihood for a bhikkhu and is not allowed.

5. This song, known as the "Song of Loving-kindness" (Mettā Sutta), is the most popular of all for recitation today. If the concealed direct-speech passage (in " ... " in the rendering) is overlooked, the architecture of the sutta is lost; it is not an injunction to an audience, but a description of the thoughts of one practising the divine abiding of loving-kindness. (The *iti* which normally terminates direct-speech passages in Pali is often left out in verse.) "This is divine

abiding here, they say" means that they (i.e noble ones, those who have realized extinction of lust, hate and delusion) say that this abiding equals in this very life the pure consciousness enjoyed in the higher heavens. The last four lines point out that while the four divine abidings lead to heaven, they do not ensure attainment of the unformed (unconditioned) Nibbāna (the cessation of birth, ageing and death) unless coupled with insight into the impermanent nature of all that is arisen and conditioned, whether formed or formless, and including all modes of heavenly existence (cf. e.g. A. 4:125-26).

CHAPTER 11

1. The first line of this riddle refers to defilements of lust, hate and delusion, the second to virtue, the third and fourth to the moment of enlightenment. So Comy.

2. *Papañca.* For a different interpretation of this difficult term, see *Concept and Reality in Early Buddhist Thought* by Bhikkhu Ñāṇananda (Kandy: BPS, 1971), where, on p. 21, an alternative rendering of the following verse and its commentarial explanation are given. (Nyp.)

3. The verb *maññati* ("to conceive conceits") has for its corresponding nouns in the Suttas both *maññanā* (conceiving) and *māna* (conceit). Used in the sense of conceiving that "this is that" or simply that "it is," it has a fundamental ontological significance (cf. M. 1 and M. 49) in the ascription of "being" (*bhava*) to what is perceived. For its sense of the "conceit I am" (*asmi-māna*) see Ch. 12, pp. 232-34. When conceiving that "I am better than another," etc., it is conceit as pride (*atimāna*). It is important to preserve this thread of meaning in the Suttas.

4. Or perfect confidence (*vesārajja*). (Nyp.)

5. Or wisdom-deliverance (*paññā-vimutti*). (Nyp.)

6. The "ten undeclared matters" (*avyākata*) (see Ch. 12, p. 208) of which these are four, all assume something which is affirmed whether the answer given is yes or no. The Greeks used to ask "Do you use a thick stick when you beat your wife?" and whether the answer was "yes" or "no" the conclusion was "Well, you do beat your wife, then." For reasons why the Buddha refuses to answer, see the end of this chapter.

7. The word *tathāgata* (here rendered unliterally by "Perfect One") was first used by the Buddha of himself soon after the Enlightenment (Ch. 3, p. 34.) Later it is also used by him of Arahants. The Commentary derives it variously (taking seven pages over it): "because he is *tathā āgato*, thus-come, by the aspiration to enlightenment, as did the former Buddhas; because he is *tathā*

gato, thus-gone, by practice and realization, by the way of the former Buddhas; because he is *tatha-lakkhaṇaṃ āgato*, come upon the characteristic of reality," etc.

CHAPTER 12

1. The "five aggregates affected by clinging" (*upādāna-kkhandha*) are best regarded as five convenient "classes" or categories under which any arisen component of experience (in its widest sense) can be grouped for analysis and discussion; they have no existence of their own separate from the components that represent them. Their representatives do not occur separately. Also they are structurally interdependent, rather as a glass tumbler implies at once the feature of *material* (glass), *affective* (attractiveness, or the reverse or indifference), *individual characteristics* (shape, colour, etc.), *determined* (formed) *utility* (all these constituting the "name-and-form"), and *consciousness of all this*, which it is not.

2. "Earth" represents solidity, "water" cohesion, "fire" both temperature and ripening, "air" both extension (distension) and motion.

3. "Whatever has the characteristic of forming should be understood, all taken together, as the formations aggregate .... (It) has the characteristic of agglomerating ... (and) its function is to accumulate." *The Path of Purification (Visuddhimagga)*, tr. by Ñāṇamoli, XIV, 131. (Nyp.)

4. *Cetanā*; usually translated by "volition," "will." (Nyp.)

5. This is in the sense of necessary condition.

6. On dependent arising see *The Path of Purification*, Ch. XVII.

7. *Sīlabbat'upādāna*—clinging to rites and rituals. (Nyp.)

8. "Contact" is the contact between the "in-oneself" and the "external" (e.g. eyesight-cum-seen), which is only made possible by the presence of consciousness (e.g. eye-consciousness). It is thus a basic factor in the essential complexity of anything arisen, perceived and formed, whether five-sensory or idea or both.

9. "Name-and-form" is the perceiving and the percept together, experienced and recognized ("named"). It is the "imagery-cum-matter,' which together make the individualized and determined subjective perception of an object; but it does not, in the Suttas, include the consciousness in virtue of which that is possible. Later literature includes consciousness within "name," thus favouring an underivable "mind-matter" opposition.

10. Other renderings of *cetanā* (here "choice") are "volition" and "intention."

11. It is necessary to avoid confusing the "formless" (*arūpa*), which is a variety of being (*bhava*), with the "unformed" (or "unconditioned," *asankhata*), which is what has no formation (or condition, *sankhāra*). The latter is a term for Nibbāna. The "formless" is always conditioned.

12. The details of the first three truths have so far given only analytical details. Here we also have descriptions of how they should be viewed.

13. That means that there is no moral significance in these acts. (Nyp.)

14. A plantain or banana trunk consists of nothing but sheaths with no core.

15. "Formed" is *sankhata*, also rendered "compounded" or "conditioned"; "unformed" is *asankhata*, also rendered "uncompounded" or "unconditioned." The latter is identified as Nibbāna. (Nyp.)

16. *Citta*: mind, mentality, cognizance. (Nyp.)

17. "Embodiment": *sakkāya* = *sa* (either "existing" or "own") plus *kāya* (body). The identification of self (*attā*) with one or more of the five aggregates thus constitutes an "embodiment" of that self, and that establishes a wrong view. (Note: *Sakkaāyadiṭṭhi* is more usually rendered "personality view"—Nyp.)

18. Or "attachment to rites and rituals" (*sīlabbata-parāmāsa*). (Nyp.)

19. The exercise described is one in mental observation, not in bodily development or breath-control as in hathayoga. This sutta, the Satipaṭṭhāna Sutta, is much recited today as a basis for meditating. Its subject, the establishment of mindfulness, forms the cornerstone of the Buddha's instruction.

20. According to the Commentary, "externally" means someone else's body, etc. (but it could also refer to pure objectivity seen in one's own body too); this first paragraph of the refrain emphasizes concentration. The second paragraph, on origination and fall (decay), refers to insight (right view). The third paragraph describes the full awareness in one who has attained final realization.

21. According to the Commentary, "experiencing the whole body (of breaths)" means being fully aware of the entire in-breath and out-breath. "Tranquillizing the bodily formation" means making the breath become increasingly subtler and calmer. (BB)

22. "Materialistic" (*āmisa*) refers to such physical things as food, clothing, etc.; here the feeling connected with them.

23. "Contracted" by lethargy; "exalted" from the sensual state to a state of meditation; "surpassed" in meditation or in realization.

24. "Hindrance" should be taken rather in the sense of, as it were, a hedge

that keeps one in the traffic-stream of lust, hate and delusion, rather than an obstacle that blocks the way.

25. See "right speech" (p. 238) for full text.

26. See "right mindfulness" (p. 240) for full text.

CHAPTER 14

1. The austerities described here are in the main those recommended in the Jain religion.

2. The "Pure Abodes" are a part of the higher Brahma-world (*brahmaloka*) inhabited only by non-returners (see Ch. 12, p. 236), who are reborn there on their death, and live there without returning to any other world till they attain final Nibbāna.

CHAPTER 15

1. The village of Pāṭaligāma here changes its name to Pāṭaliputta with the building of the new town (today called Patna). Later it became famous as the capital of Asoka's empire, which had grown out of the kingdom of Magadha.

2. The Commentary says that the Janavasabha Sutta (D. 18) was delivered at this point.

3. The "four pairs of men, the eight types of person" are explained as the attainer of the path and the attainer of its fruition in the case of each of the four stages (paths) of realization. "Fruition" is stated to follow immediately upon the attainment of any one of these stages (see Sn. 2:1, vv. 5 and 6). This is one of the meanings of the word "timeless" (or "not delayed") applied to the Dhamma a few lines above, in the sense that the successful attainment of the path does not require waiting for a time, say till after death, for its fruition.

4. The word *dīpa* can mean either "island" or "lamp." The Commentary explains by "island."

5. It is worth noting that the Buddha decided to teach his doctrine on the invitation of a Divinity (Ch. 3, p. 38), and that he relinquished his vital determination in the absence of an invitation to prolong it, owing to the intervention of Māra ("Death").

6. In the text an account follows here of the eight kinds of assembly, the eight bases for transcendence, and the eight liberations, omitted here for lack of space.

7. "Hog's mincemeat" (*sūkara-maddava*): the expression has been a subject of discussion from very early times. The Commentary to this sutta says: "It is meat already on sale in a market (see Vin. Mv. 6:31), of an *ekajeṭṭhaka* pig that

is neither too young nor too old. That, it seems, is both soft and succulent. The meaning is that it was prepared and carefully cooked. (But some say that *sūkara-maddava* is the name of a recipe for cooking soft boiled rice with the five products of the cow, just as 'cow-drink' is the name of a beverage. Others say that it is a kind of elixir that comes within the science of elixirs, and that Cunda prepared that elixir thinking 'Let the Blessed One not attain final Nibbāna.' But the deities of the four continents and their two thousand islands infused nutritive essence into it.)" (Note: the bracketed passage is not in all editions.)

Besides this, the Udāna Commentary says: "*Sūkara-maddava*, according to the Great Sinhalese Commentary (Note: no longer extant) is tender succulent pork meat already on sale in the market. Some, however, say that it is not pig's meat but the shoots of bamboo trampled by pigs. Others say that it is a kind of mushroom that grows in places trampled by pigs. But yet others say that it is an elixir, and that the goldsmith, having heard that the Blessed One was to attain final Nibbāna that day, thought 'Perhaps after using it he will remain longer,' and so gave it to the Master out of desire to lengthen his life span" (Comy. to Ud. 8:5). Meat eating was allowed by the Buddha subject to three conditions: that it was not seen or heard or suspected that the animal had been killed for the benefit of the eater of the meat (M. 55, Vin. Mv. 6:31, cf. A. 4:44; also Vin. Cv. 7:4 quoted at Ch. 13, p. 266). We shall probably never know what was intended. "Hog's mincemeat" has been chosen because it is non-committal and near the original: *sūkara* = pig, *maddava* = sweet; cf. "bulls' eyes," "angel on horseback," etc.

8. The Indian myth of the Universal Monarch who turns the Wheel of Righteousness (Pali: *cakkavatti*; Skr.: *cakravartin*) is given in D. 26 and M. 129.

9. According to the Commentary the Mahā Sudassana Sutta (D. 17) was delivered at this point.

10. The four "monks" are explained as the stream-enterer, once-returner, non-returner and Arahant.

11. The Commentary says that Subhadda made this remark under the erroneous impression that, like certain teachers of other sects, the Buddha in his last moments was conferring on his pupil the right to give the admission and to succeed him as head of the Sangha. He is not the same person as the Subhadda mentioned a few pages later.

12. The story of how Prince Siddhattha Gotama, the Bodhisatta, left his home in the night with his groom, Channa, and his horse, Kanthaka, is

not in the Canon, though there is a reference to Kanthaka in the canonical Vimānavatthu (vv. 7:7). That story is given in full in Ācariya Buddhaghosa's Introduction to the Jātaka Commentary. This bhikkhu Channa (identified with the groom) appears in the Vinaya (Pār. 4; Sangh. 12, etc.) as proud, obstinate and intolerant of correction. In the Suttas it is told how he repented after the Parinibbāna and asked for help from the Elder Ānanda. As the result of that Elder's talk, he became an Arahant (S. 22:90).

13. Perhaps Prof. T. W. Rhys Davids' "Work out your salvation with diligence," which T. S. Eliot has made classic literature by quoting it in his *Waste Land*, ought to have been retained; but it seems rather too free. The last words in Pali are: *Handa 'dāni bhikkhave āmantayāmi vo: Vaya-dhammā sankhārā; appamādena sampādetha.*

CHAPTER 16

1. The bhikkhunī Thullānandā appears often in the Vinaya as a proud, clever and factious woman, and the cause of a number of rules being laid down.

2. Ceylon: present-day Sri Lanka. (BB)

LIST OF SOURCES

Text	PTS Vol. & Page		Subject	Page
VINAYA: MAHĀVAGGA				
1:1-4	i,	1-4	after the enlightenment	30-34
1:5		4-7	the decision to teach	37-39
1:6		7-14	the first five disciples	39-47
1:7-20		15-34	the teaching spreads	48-60
1:21-22		34-39	the Fire Sermon, etc.	64-69
1:23-24		39-44	the two chief disciples	70-73
1:54		82-83	return to Kapilavatthu	77-79
2:1-2		101-2	the observance days	156-57
2:3		102	reciting the Pātimokkha	160
3:1		137	the rains residence	99-100
5:1		179-83	the simile of the lute	170-71
5:13		194-97	Soṇa Kuṭikaṇṇa	165-67
6:28		226-31	the last journey	291-94
6:30		231-33	the courtesan Ambapālī	297-99
8:12,13		287-89	rules on robes	164-65
8:15		290-94	Visākhā	151-56
8:26		301-3	attending on the sick	177-79
10:1-5		337-57	the quarrel at Kosambī	109-19
VINAYA: CULLAVAGGA				
5:33	ii,	139-40	"Learn in one's own language"	173
5:33		140	"Long life to you, Lord!"	173
6:4		154-59	Anāthapiṇḍika	87-91
6:5-9		159-65	the partridge's holy life	92-95
7:1		180-84	the Sakyans go forth	80-84
7:2-4		184-203	Devadatta	257-71
9:1		236-40	eight qualities of the ocean	160-63
10:1		253-56	the going forth of women	104-7
10:5		258-59	the Dhamma in brief	336-40
11:1.1		284-85	the Master is gone	329-30

11:1.1-11		285-90	the First Council	336-40

VINAYA: SUTTA-VIBHANGA

Pārā. 1	iii,	1-4	the foremost in the world	123-25
Pārā. 1		6-11	the rains at Verañjā	126-29
Sangh. 10		171-72	schism in the Sangha	265-67
Pāc. 32	iv,	71-72	eating among families	264-65
Pāc. 92		173	the size of robes	196

DIGHA NIKĀYA

2	i,	73-76	the four jhānas	246-48
9		195-202	three theories of self	203-4
11		221-23	Kevaḍḍha Sutta	147-50
14	ii,	7	six former Buddhas	183
14		7	facts about Gotama	183
15		57	birth, ageing and death	226
16		72-166	Mahāparinibbāna Sutta	286-332
22		291-304	right mindfulness	240-46
22		307-11	on Four Noble Truths	212-13
22		311	right view	228
22		311-13	path factors 2-7	237-40
22		313	right concentration	246-48
26	iii,	75-76	the Buddha Metteyya	199-200
33		211	beings maintained by nutriment	227
33		217	three formations	217
33		234	five higher fetters	236

MAJJHIMA NIKĀYA

2	i,	7-8	the thicket of views	232-33
4		17-18	living in the jungle	15-16
8		41-42	four formless states	249
8		46	"Meditate, bhikkhus!'	250-51
10		56-63	right mindfulness	240-46
12		69-72	Buddha's powers and confidences	185-86
12		77-83	Buddha's austere practices	276-79
13		90	right intention	237
14		91	overcoming sensual desires	237
21		129	simile of the saw	237
22		133-35	similes of snake and raft	255-56

22	137-38	self and self's property	233-34
22	140	Buddha misrepresented	203
22	142	those who have faith	250
25	160	attainment of cessation	249-50
26	163	the going forth	10
26	163-66	Bodhisatta's quest	13-14
26	167	attainment of enlightenment	28
26	167-73	the decision to teach	37-39
28	190-91	"Who sees dependent arising"	226
36	240	the going forth	10
36	240-46	struggle for enlightenment	16-19
36	246-47	finding the path	21
36	247-49	attainment of enlightenment	23-25
36	249-51	a deluded man's abiding	194-95
38	259	consciousness is conditioned	218
38	261	four nutriments	227
38	262-64	conditionality	226
38	266-69	the gradual training	251-54
38	270	cessation of suffering	255
39	275-76	the five hindrances	254
39	276-78	the four jhānas	246-48
41	288	right speech	238
43	292, 293	functions of consciousness	218
44	300	views of self	232
44	301	three formations	217
44	302-3	three types of feeling	216
47	320	faith backed by evidence	200
49	326-31	Brahmā's belief in eternity	143-47
61	414-15	to Rāhula: on lying	84-86
62	420-21	to Rāhula: on meditation	122-23
62	423-25	four elements and space	214-15
64	433	five lower fetters	235-36
67	456-59	Buddha dismisses the Sangha	141-43
72	485-86	the thicket of views	203
74	497-501	discourse with Dīghanakha	73-75
75	508	Nibbāna the greatest bliss	229
86	ii, 97-105	conversion of Angulimāla	134-39
87	108-12	sorrow from dear ones	96-98
89	118-25	Pasenadi's homage to Buddha	280-84
90	126-27	question of omniscience	185
91	133-40	Buddha's marks and conduct	186-93

104		243-45	disputes in the Sangha	275
107	iii,	4-6	Buddha shows the way	200-201
108		7-15	with the Master gone	341-45
109		16	causes of the aggregates	219
109		16	clinging and aggregates	219
117		71	noble right concentration	248
117		71-72	right view	225
117		75	wrong livelihood	239
118		80-81	four types of noble ones	236
123		118-24	Buddha's wonderful qualities	2-5
128		152-54	the quarrel at Kosambī	111-13
128		154-57	living in concord	113-15
129		169	the blind turtle	250
135		203	beings own their actions	220-21
143		261	Anāthapiṇḍika's death	100-101
147		277-80	Rāhula attains Arahantship	132-33
148		285	underlying tendencies	222
152		302	"Meditate, bhikkhus!"	250-51

SAMYUTTA NIKĀYA

1:23	i,	13	disentangling the tangle	250
1:72		39	world led by mind	221
2:26		61-62	the world's end	206
3:1		68-70	Pasenadi meets Buddha	98-99
3:11		77-79	Arahants hard to know	174-75
3:14-15		82-85	victory and defeat	271-72
3:25		100-102	ageing and death approach	273-74
4:1		103	useless penance	36
4:6		106-7	a sage feels no fear	91-92
4:13		110-11	"I sleep out of compassion"	262
4:20		116-17	can one rule without force?	79-80
4:24		122-24	dialogue with Māra	60-61
4:25		124-27	Māra's daughters	61-64
6:1		136-38	"Should I teach Dhamma?"	37-39
6:2		139-40	respect for Dhamma	36-37
6:12		153-54	fame destroys the wastrel	267-68
7:11		172-73	Kasi Bhāradvāja	120-22
10:8		210-12	purchase of Jetavana	87-91
12:2	ii,	2-4	dependent arising: factors	219-20
12:15		17	to Kaccāyana on right view	226-27
12:17		18-20	who makes suffering?	207-8

12:20		25-26	specific conditionality	226
12:37		64-65	this body is not yours	221
12:43		72	origin of suffering	220
12:61		94-95	mind like a monkey	230
12:63		98	four kinds of nutriment	227
12:65		104-6	the ancient path	25-27
15:1		178	beginningless the round	212
16:11		217-22	Mahā-Kassapa's greatness	333-36
16:13		223-25	how Dhamma disappears	163-64
17:35-36		258-59	Devadatta gains renown	257-58
21:8		281	advice to Nanda	84
21:10		282-84	living alone	169
22:2	iii,	4	what does Buddha preach?	236-37
22:26		27-28	gratification, danger, escape	28
22:46		45	the three characteristics	229
22:47		46-47	self-theories and "I am"	234
22:48		47, 48	five aggregates of clinging	215-18
22:49		48	conceit is blindness	235
22:51		51	right view	229
22:56		59-61	the aggregates analyzed	214-18
22:59		66-68	Discourse on Non-self	46-47
22:79		86, 87	the aggregates explained	214-18
22:81		94-95	at Pārileyyaka	116
22:83		105	"I am" is derivative	235
22:87		119-24	advice to Vakkali; suicide	196-99
22:89		130-31	Khemaka on "I am"	235
22:94		138-39	"no dispute with the world"	230
22:95		142	the lump of foam, etc.	228
35:1	iv,	1	the three characteristics	229
35:19		13	the eye, etc.	230
35:28		19-20	Fire Sermon	64-65
35:43		28	all is impermanent	229
35:82		52	why is it called "world"?	231
35:85		54	void is the world	231
35:93		67	consciousness and duality	218
35:116		95	"world" in noble discipline	231
35:145		132	old kamma and new kamma	221
35:155		142	right view	229
35:197		174	venomous snakes	228
35:197		174	the empty village	228
38:1		251	what is Nibbāna?	228

38:2		252	what is Arahantship?	236
43:1-44		359-73	epithets of Nibbāna	256
44:2		380-84	the Perfect One after death	201-3
44:10		400-401	is there a self?.	209-10
45:4	v,	4-5	the divine vehicle	251
45:8		9-10	path factors defined	228-48
47:9		152-54	"Be your own refuge"	299-300
47:12		159-61	Sāriputra's lion's roar	290-91
47:13		161-63	death of Sāriputta	300-301
47:14		163-64	"The assembly seems empty"	301-2
47:18		167	four foundations of mindfulness	35-36
47:19		169	guard oneself, guard others	246
47:42		184	origin and disappearance	246
47:43		185	four foundations of mindfulness	35-36
48:41		216-17	"How the Buddha has aged!"	274
48:57		232-33	the five faculties	35
54:9		320-22	suicides in the Sangha	168-69
56:11		421-24	the First Sermon	42-44
56:11		421	truth of suffering	212
56:23		433	Buddha discovers the truths	182-83
56:27		435	the four truths are real	214
56:29		436	penetration of the truths	213-14
56:31		437-38	simile of siṃsapa leaves	206-7
56:37		442	right view like dawn	224

ANGUTTARA NIKĀYA

3:33	i,	134	how kamma ripens	221
3:33		135	extinction of kamma	222
3:38		145-46	Bodhisatta's youth	8-9
3:47		152	the formed and unformed	229
3:55		159	choosing wrongly	220
3:55		159	Nibbāna here and now	222
3:61		177	origin and cessation of suffering	212-13
3:65		188-93	Kālāma Sutta	175-77
3:73		219-20	knowledge and concentration	195-96
3:83		230	"Too many rules!"	164
3:134		286	the three characteristics	229
4:21	ii,	20-21	respect for Dhamma	36-37
4:23		23-24	why called a Perfect One	183-84
4:24		25	he conceives no conceits	184
4:36		37-39	"What will you be?"	187-88

4:46		49-50	the world's end	206
4:68		73	fame destroys the wastrel	267-68
4:76		79-80	the last utterance	323-24
4:77		80	four incalculables	221
4:129-30		132-33	Ānanda's qualities	319
4:180		168	four principal authorities	308-9
5:123-24	iii,	143-44	qualities of a nurse	178-79
5:172-73		203-4	the five precepts	238-39
5:177		208	five prohibited trades	239
5:196		240-41	Bodhisatta's dreams	22
6:55		374-75	simile of the lute	170-71
6:63		415	choice is action	217
6:63.		415	ripening of action	221
6:63		416	ripening of suffering	231
7:20	iv,	17-18	things that prevent decline	286-88
7:46		51	fortifying the mind	232
8:7		160	Devadatta's obsession	270-71
8:11		172-76	the foremost in the world	123-25
8:16		196	fit for a mission	270
8:20		204-8	eight qualities of the ocean	160-63
8:51		274-77	the going forth of women	104-7
8:53		280-81	the Dhamma in brief	107-8
8:70		308-13	relinquishing the will to live	302-4
8:83		338-39	the root of all things	246
9:3		354-58	advice to Meghiya	129-32
9:20		394-95	what is most fruitful?	230
10:21	v,	33-36	Buddha's ten powers	185-86
10:27,28		50, 55	beings maintained by nutriment	227
10:60		110-11	Nibbāna is peaceful	228
10:72		135-36	ten thorns	167-68
10:94		189-90	he speaks with discrimination	193-94
10:95		193-95	unprofitable questions	208-9

KHUDDAKA-PĀṬHA

2	2	beings maintained by nutriment	227

DHAMMAPADA

3-6	how enmity ceases	112-13
153-54	the house builder is seen	29
328-30	walk alone	113

UDĀNA

1:1-3	1-3	at the root of the Bodhi Tree	30-31
1:4	3	what is a brahman?	33
2:1	10	Mucalinda	33-34
3:2	21-24	Nanda and the nymphs	102-4
3:10	32-33	contemplating the world	32
4:1	34-37	advice to Meghiya	129-32
4:5	41-42	the Pārileyyaka elephant	115-16
4:8	43-45	the murder of Sundarī	139-41
5:3	48-50	Suppabuddha the leper	171-72
5:4	51	"Do you dislike pain?"	179
5:5	51-56	eight qualities of the ocean	160-63
5:6	57-59	Soṇa Kuṭikaṇṇa	165-67
5:8	60-61	Devadatta splits the Sangha	267
5:9	61	dispute in the Order	112
6:1	62-64	relinquishing the will to live	302-4
6:2	64-66	Arahants hard to know	174-75
6:3	66	"What earlier was," etc.	182
6:4	66-68	blind men and elephant	210-11
6:9	72	like moths drawn to flame	179
7:7	77	diversification abandoned	182
8:1-3	80-81	utterances on Nibbāna	223
8:7	90-91	the forked road	79
8:5	81-84	the last meal	309-11
8:5	84-85	Cunda's merit	314
8:6	85-90	at Pāṭaligāma	291-94
8:8	91-92	dear ones bring sorrow	155-56

ITIVUTTAKA

22	14-15	do not fear merit	186-87
24	17	the heap of bones	250
38	31-32	Buddha's two thoughts	186
44	38	two elements of Nibbāna	223-24
49	43-44	extremist views	233
73	62	cessation most peaceful	223
89	85	Devadatta's obsession	270-71
100	101-2	two kinds of gifts	200
112	121-22	why called a Perfect One	183-84

SUTTA-NIPĀTA

1:4	12-14	to Bhāradvāja	120-22
1:8	25-26	Mettā Sutta	180-81
3:1	72-74	the going forth	11-13
3:2	74-77	Māra's squadrons	19-21
3:2	77-78	Māra's disappointment	61
3:11	131-36	the visit of Asita	6-8
4:2	152	in the face of Death	228
5:7	206-7	no measuring a sage	224

THERAGĀTHĀ

527-33	"Let the Sakyans see you"	76-77

INDEX

Abhidhamma 109, 346
abstaining 238
action (*kamma*) 24, 187, 217, 220f., 225,238
adept (*sekha*) 195-96
admission (*upasampadā*) 45, 50, 51, 52, 53, 106f., 269
affliction (*vyābādha*) 177,220, 237
ageing 9, 10, 25, 212, 219, 273f.
aggregate (*khandha*) 28, 43, 214ff., 219, 234, 235, 244
air (*vāyo*) 123, 215
Ajātasattu 257f., 271, 285, 286f., 331, 332, 341, 345
Ajita Kesakambali 98, 321
Āḷāra Kālāma 13f., 39, 311
all 64; 145f., 227
Ambalaṭṭhikā 84, 289f.
Ambapālī 296ff.
Ānanda 1, 2, 79, 82, 105, 133, 183, 289 passim, 333f., 336f., 338, 341ff.
Anāthapiṇḍika 87ff., 118
Angulimāla 134ff.
annihilation 124, 203, 233
Aññāta Kondañña 44f.
Anotatta, Lake 56
Anupiyā 80
Anurādha 201ff.
Anuruddha 80ff., l14f., 324, 325f., 326ff., 330
Arahant 47, 52, 58f., 70, 105, 162, 174, 223, 235, 236, 322
asceticism 276
Asita 6ff.
Asoka 346
Assaji 70f.
attention (*manasikāra*) 25, 53, 220, 232f., 246
austerity 193
authorities, the four principal 308f.

Baka Brahmā 143ff.
base (*āyatana*) 26, 27, 244f.
beauty (*subha*) 168
beginning (*ādi*) 212
being (*bhava*) 25, 32, 146, 219, 233, 294
Benares (*Bārānasi*) 41,44
Bhaddiya (1) 45
Bhaddiya (2) 81ff.
Bhagu 82, 113f.
Bhalluka 34
Bhāradvāja 120ff.
bhikkhu 99
bhikkhunī 106, 154
Bījaka 158
Bimbisāra 11, 65ff., 96, 157, 170, 260, 271
birth 10, 219
blind men 210f.
Bodhisatta 3ff., 10, 15, 22, 304
Bodhi Tree 30
body (*kāya*) 75, 197, 206, 221, 230, 240ff.
Brahmā (*Mahā-Brahmā*) 148f., 187. See also *Baka; Sahampati*
Brahman 33, 124
Brahmāyu 188, 192
breath, breathing 122, 131,169, 240
Buddha—see *Enlightened One*
burning 64

caste 162
cessation 26f., 43, 213, 222ff., 228, 249f.
Chandragupta 346

Channa 323
characteristic 229
chief disciple 72, 183
choice (*cetanā*) 217, 220, 221, 237
clinging (*upādāna*) 25, 32, 214, 215, 219, 220
compassion (*karuṇā*) 177, 250
conceit (*maññanā, māna*) 32
concentration (*samādhi*) 164, 195f., 246ff., 309
concord l14f., 286f., 288
conditionality 25ff., 37, 226
confidence (*pasāda*) 200, 295f., 343
consciousness
citta: 217, 230, 243,246
viññāṇa: 26, 46, 64, 133, 217f., 219, 220, 227,229
contact (*phassa*) 25, 64, 133, 220, 227, 246
contemplation (*anupassanā*) 35f., 240
corpse 242
Council 337ff.
craving (*taṇhā*) 25, 43, 212, 220
Cunda the goldsmith's son 309f., 314
Cunda the novice 275
Cundaka 313

death 9, 10, 25, 96f., 156, 219, 273f.
Deathless, the 10, 28, 35, 39, 41f., 70, 71, 121, 229, 256
decline, prevention of 286ff.
defeat 159
deliverance 28, 30, 53, 186, 196, 255, 307
delusion (*moha*) 32, 64, 176, 194, 220, 221, 222
dependent arising (*paṭicca-samuppāda*) 25, 30f., 212f., 219f., 225, 226, 227
desire (*chanda*) 218, 236f., 243f.
Devadatta 82,257 passim
Dhamma 37, 38ff., 41f., 44f., 49, 52, 65, 71, 107f., 117, 127f., 157, 162, 172, 194, 197, 200, 203, 206, 208, 226, 255f., 290, 295, 299, 300, 315, 336f., 338, 342
Dīgha Kārāyana 280, 281, 285
Dīghanakha 73ff.
diligence 324
dispute 275
divine ear element 343
divine eye 24, 186, 343
Divine Kings, the four (*Catummahārājā*) 34, 45, 55f., 148
divine vehicle (brahma-yāna) 251
doctrine 206 passim
Doṇa 187, 332
doubt 175
dream 21f.

earth (*paṭhavī*) 123, 127, 144, 145, 214
earthquake 303f.
effort 53, 239
element (*dhātu*) 100, 123, 145, 148f.
elephant l15f., 210f., 263f.
embodiment (*sakkāya*) 232
endeavour (*padhāna*) 239, 306
energy (*viriya*) 131,239
enlightenment (*bodhi*) 22ff., 98, 183, 290
enlightenment factor (*bojjhanga*) 245, 288, 290
entity, great (*mahā-bhūta*) 75, 148f., 214
equanimity (*upekkhā*) 177, 245
escape (*nissaraṇa*) 28, 32, 223
essentials of existence (*upadhi*) 32, 37, 225, 228
eternal, eternity 143ff., 230, 233f.
evil 177, 271
extinction—see *Nibbāna*
eye 64, 100, 132, 220, 221, 244, 253

faculty (*indriya*)
(a)of sense: 223, 234, 251f.
(b) spiritual: 35, 306
faith (*saddhā*) 39, 120, 159, 200
fear 15, 32
feeling (*vedanā*) 5, 25, 36, 46, 64, 75, 215f., 220, 222, 227, 242, 244, 246
fetter (*saṃyojana*) 235f.
fire (*tejo, aggi*) 16f., 55, 99, 123, 144, 215

Fire Sermon 64f.
fire worship 55f., 66, 279
form (*rūpa*) 46, 122, 214f., 220, 223, 228, 230, 244
formations (*sankhārā*) 37, 46, 216f., 220, 231, 244, 324, 326
formed (*sankhata*) 216f., 229, 301
formless (*arūpa*) 223, 249

Ganges 162, 293
Gayā 40, 54, 64, 267f.
giving, gift (*dāna*) 155, 187, 200, 230, 314
gladness (*muditā*) 177
Goatherds' Banyan 33, 60, 304
god (*deva, devatā*) 6, 187, 293. See also *deity; divinity*
going forth (*pabbajjā*) 10, 11, 45, 50, 78, 80f., 104f.
Gotama 183
gratification (*assāda*) 28
Great Man 188ff.

harmlessness 186
hate (*dosa*) 64, 175, 220, 221, 237
heaven 3, 24, 45, 109, 172, 221, 292
hell 24, 159, 172, 221, 292
hindrance (*nīvaraṇa*) 243f., 254, 255, 291
holy life (*brahmacariya*) 10, 51, 127f., 207, 276

ignorance (*avijjā*) 24, 30, 212, 213, 220, 222
ill will (*vyāpāda*) 131, 177, 244, 254
impermanent (*anicca*) 28, 32, 46, 75, 131,132f., 229f., 288, 325
imperturbability (*āneñja*) 23, 217
incalculables, the four 221
India (*Jambudipa*) 57
infinity 208, 223, 249, 324
insight (*vipassanā*) 43
intention (*sankappa*) 42, 237
intrepidity (*vesārajja*) 186
Isidatta 284
Isipatana 40, 48

Jain—see *Nigaṇṭha*
Janapadakalyāṇi 102
Jeta's Grove 90f.
joy (*somanassa*) 28, 248

Kaccāna, Mahā 165f.
Kaccāyana 226f.
Kakusandha Buddha 127f., 183
Kālāmans 175f.
Kāḷudāyi 75
Kamma—see *action*
Kapilavatthu 76, 104, 183, 331
Kāsi (= Benares) 40, 271
Kasi Bhāradvāja 120
Kassapa Buddha 35, 127f., 183
Kassapa of Gayā 54f., 59
Kassapa, Mahā 163, 329ff., 333ff.
Kassapa, Pūraṇa 98, 195, 321
Kassapa of the River 54f., 60
Kassapa of Uruvelā 54ff.
Kassapa the naked ascetic 207
Kevaḍḍha 147
Khattiya—see *warrior-noble*
killing 79, 176, 238f., 252
Kimbila 82, 114
knowledge (*ñāṇa, vijjā*) 23ff., 42ff., 195f.
Kokāḷika 265, 269
Kolita 72
Koliyans 76, 331, 345
Koṇāgamana Buddha 127, 183
Kondañña—see *Aññāta Kondañña*
Kosala 12, 79f., 95f., 104, 345
Kosambī 109ff.
Kusinārā 314, 319ff.

learner (*sekha*) 50, 195, 318
liberation 32, 162, 199
Licchavi 167, 297ff., 331
lies 85, 238
livelihood 11, 42, 239
loathsomeness (*asubha*) 131, 288
love (*pema*) 250
loving-kindness (*mettā*) 131, 177, 180, 186f., 264, 289, 318

Lumbinī 6
lust (*lobha, rāga*) 32, 37, 64, 74, 131, 236, 288, 316

Magadha 38, 56, 95, 345
Mahā-Kaccāna—see *Kaccāna*
Mahā-Kassapa—see *Kassapa*
Mahānāma 45
Mahānāma the Sakyan 80f., 195f.
Mahāpajāpatī Gotamī 77, 104ff., 118, 340
Makkhali Gosāla 98, 195, 321
Mallians 80, 311, 320, 327ff., 330ff.
Mallikā 96ff., 280
Māra 19ff., 31, 36, 52ff., 60ff., 79f., 91f, 143f., 146f, 199, 249, 250, 262, 304
Māra's Daughters 61ff.
marvel 77, 147f., 269
matted-hair ascetic 54, 55, 174
Maurian empire 346
Māyā, Queen 183
meat-eating 266
meditation (*jhāna*) 21, 23, 167f., 195, 246ff., 324f., 344f.
Meghiya 129ff.
merit (*puñña*) 19, 186f., 217, 274
Metteyya Buddha 199f.
mind, mental (*mano*) 64f., 133, 217, 230, 244f.
mindfulness (*sati*) 20, 23, 35, 61, 132, 240ff., 277, 288, 317
miracle—see *marvel*
misapprehension (*parāmāsa*) 236
mission 270
Moggallāna the brahman 341
Moggallāna, Mahā 70ff., 118, 126ff., 141ff., 160ff., 183, 258, 268ff., 301f.
monk (samaṇa) 304, 321f. See also *bhikkhu*
monument 317f., 331f.
moon 15, 223, 343
mortification 42, 125
Mucalinda 33

Nāgasamāla 79
Nāga serpent 33, 55, 91
naked ascetic 152, 174
Nāḷagiri 263f.
Nālaka 8
name-and-form (nāma-rūpa) 26f, 150, 213, 220, 246
Nanda 77, 102ff., 196
Nandiya 114
neither-painful-nor-pleasant (*adukkham-asukha*) 215, 216, 222, 248
neither-perception-nor-non-perception (*nevasaññānāsaññā*) 14, 249, 324f.
Nerañjarā 19, 60
Nibbāna (extinction) 29, 32, 35ff., 131f., 199, 222ff, 228, 236, 256, 324ff.
Nigaṇṭha (Jain) 98, 174, 194, 275
Noble Eightfold Path—see *path*
Noble Truth (*ariya-sacca*)—see *truth*
non-being (*vibhava*) 32, 146, 233
non-cruelty (*avihiṃsā*) 237
non-delusion (*amoha*) 176
non-hate (*adosa*) 176
non-ill will (*avyāpāda*) 237
non-lust (*alobha*) 176
non-returner (*anāgāmī*) 162, 236
nothingness (*ākiñcañña*) 13, 249, 324f.
not-self (*anattā*) 46ff., 75, 131, 229, 231, 232ff.
nun—see *bhikkhunī*
nutriment (*āhāra*) 227, 246

objects, mental (*dhammā*) 64, 133, 240, 243ff., 300
ocean 161ff.
omniscient 183ff.
once-returner (*sakadāgāmī*) 162, 236
ordinary man (*puthujjana*) 232f., 234f.
origin (*samudaya*) 26, 43, 212, 219ff.

pain, painful (*dukkha*) 32, 35, 45, 179, 212ff., 219ff. See also *suffering; unpleasant*
Pakudha Kaccāyana 98, 321
Pārileyyaka 115, 120
partridge, story 93f.,
Pasenadi, King 96ff., 135ff., 174f., 185,

273f., 280, 282ff.
Pāṭaligāma 291ff.
Pāṭaliputta (Patna) 293, 346
Path, Noble Eightfold 22, 27, 43, 224ff., 251ff., 321f., 341
Pāṭimokkha (Monastic Rules) 127, 131, 160ff., 342, 343
perception (*saññā*) 5, 46, 133, 216f., 220, 288
Perfect One (*tathāgata*) 34, 41, 183ff., 203, 302ff., 315f., 320f.
Piṭaka 346
pleasure, pleasant (*sukha*) 21, 23, 46, 75, 132, 215ff., 242, 247, 248
power (*bala*) 185, 310
power, supernormal (*iddhi*)—see *supernormal power*
proud 33
Pukkusa 311ff.
Purāṇa (a carpenter) 284
Purāṇa (a monk) 340
Pūraṇa Kassapa—see *Kassapa*
purity, purification 7, 35, 36

raft, simile of 256
Rāhula 77ff., 84f., 118, 122ff., 132f.
rains 99f., 111, 299
Rājagaha 65, 68, 70, 259, 286ff., 337
Rājāyatana Tree 34
rebirth 278
refuge (*saraṇa*) 34, 49, 51, 53, 256, 301
relishing (*nandī, abhinandanā*) 32, 212, 222, 252, 255
renunciation (*nekkhamma*) 237
resistance (*paṭigha*) 222
restraint (saṃvara) 131, 187, 312f.
robe 164f., 196, 334
Rohitassa 206
round of births (saṃsāra) 212, 278
rule (*sikkhāpada*) 163, 164, 275

Saccaka Nigaṇṭhaputta 194
sacrifice 279
Sahampati, Brahmā 35f., 38f., 142, 267f., 325
Sakka, Ruler of Gods 6, 57, 68, 102f., 187, 325
Sakyan (*Sakka*) 6, 7, 21, 76, 77, 80ff.
Sangha 53, 95, ll0ff., 128f., 159, 160ff. 258f., 265ff., 267, 296, 299f., 323, 324, 339, 341ff.
Sañjaya 70ff.
Sañjaya-Belaṭṭhiputta 98, 321
Sāriputta 70ff., 78, 84, 93, 117, 122, 127ff., 143, 183, 259ff., 268ff., 290f., 300f.
Sāvatthī 90, 96, 102, 134, 135ff., 139
schism 109ff., 257ff., 269
seclusion, secluded 21, 34, 131, 186, 246
self (*attā*) 46ff., 209f., 227, 229, 230, 232ff.
Senānigāma 14, 52
Seniya Bimbisāra—see *Bimbisāra*
sensual desire, sensuality (*kāma*) 15, 20, 23, 25, 35, 42, 130, 159, 212, 236, 237, 246
sexual intercourse 158, 158f. 199, 338
sick 153, 178, 178f.
sickness 9, 195, 299, 310
Sikhī Buddha 127, 183
siṃsapa trees 206
Sīvaka 88
skeleton 242
sleep 194
snake simile 255f.
sneeze 173
Soṇa Kolivisa 170f.
Soṇa Kuṭikaṇṇa 165ff.
soul (*jīva*) 208
space (*ākāsa*) 123, 215, 249
speech 11, 43, 238
stealing 238
stream-enterer (-entry) (*sotāpanna*) 83, 105, 162, 232, 236, 295
Subhadda (1) 320ff.
Subhadda (2) 329f.
success, basis for (*iddhipāda*) 80, 305, 306
Suddhodana, King 6, 75, 77, 104, 183
Sudinna 157ff., 338
suffering (*dukkha*) 24ff., 30ff., 43ff.,

131, 203, 206ff., 211, 212ff., 227, 228ff., 252, 255. See also *pain* and *unpleasant*
Sundarī 140
supernormal power (*iddhi*) 49, 147, 343
Suppabuddha 171f.

Tagarasikhī 172
taint (*āsava*) 24f., 47, 50, 75, 121, 186, 188, 194, 236, 249f.
talk 131, 193
Tapussa 34
Tathāgata—see *Perfect One*
Tekula 173
Thera 169
thinking, thought (*vitakka*) 5, 21, 23, 130ff., 186, 247
thorns 168
tradition 175
training rule 158f., 163f.
treasures, the seven 188
truth (*sacca*) 43, 182f., 212ff., 227, 294

Uddaka Rāmaputta 14, 39f.
Udena, King 109
unborn (*ajāta*) 223
uncertainty (*vicikicchā*) 14, 49, 244, 254
undeclared, unanswered (*avyākata*) 203, 208
underlying tendency (*anusaya*) 222, 234f.
understanding (*paññā*) 13, 35, 131, 174, 186, 196, 225
unformed (*asankhata*) 223, 229, 256
unwholesome (*akusala*) 21, 23, 86, 131, 164, 175ff., 182, 186, 252, 255
Upaka 40
Upāli 1f., 82ff., 337f.
Upatissa 72
Upavāna 315
Uposatha (observance day) 111, 160, 161
Uruvelā 14, 30, 40, 52, 54, 304
Uttara 188f.
Uttarakuru 56, 127
Uttiya 208f.

Vacchagotta 209
Vajirī, Princess 97
Vajjians 287, 345
Vajjiyamāhita 193
Vakkali 196f.
vanity (*mada*) 9
Vassakāra 286f., 292ff., 341f. 344f.
Verañjā 123, 126ff.
Vesālī 104, 105, 296ff., 345
Vessabhū Buddha 127, 183
Viḍūḍabha 97, 285, 345
view (*diṭṭhi*) 24, 42, 74, 224, 225, 232ff., 291, 296
Vipassī Buddha 127, 183
virtue (*sīla*) 130, 195, 239, 292, 296, 307,309
Visākhā 118, 151ff.
volition—see *choice*
Vulture Peak Rock 261f., 305

wanderer (*paribbājaka*) 70, 140f., 156f., 193
warrior-noble (*khattiya*) 12, 98, 162, 183, 283
water (*āpo*) 123, 215, 228, 241
way (*paṭipadā*) 25, 42ff., 213, 224ff., 251ff., 275
wheel (*cakka*) 6, 7, 40, 44f., 185, 187, 317, 319
wholesome (*kusala*) 86, 131, 176f., 182, 275
will—see *choice*
wine 239
women 104ff., 159, 316f.
world (*loka*) 3, 24, 32, 144, 180, 183, 206, 208, 226f., 228, 229, 231, 234, 236, 240

Yamelu 173
Yasa 48ff.

PRINCIPAL DATES

See E. J. Thomas, *The Life of the Buddha*, Routledge & Kegan Paul; also *Cambridge History of India*, Vol. I.

Event	Date (approximately)
Birth of the Buddha	563 B.C.
The Renunciation of the House Life	534*
The Enlightenment	528*
The Parinibbāna	483*
The First Council	483*
The Second Council	383*
Chandragupta (Sandrocottos)	313
Asoka (begins reign)	274
The Third Council (at Patna)	253
Arrival in Ceylon of the Arahant Mahinda	243
Death of Asoka	237
Committal to writing of Tipiṭaka in Ceylon	80
End of the Ceylon Chronicle (Dīpavaṃsa)	330 A.C.
End of the Ceylon Chronicle (Mahāvaṃsa)	330
Ācariya Buddhaghosa	430

*Dates marked by asterisks are according to the reckoning of European scholars; the Sinhalese reckoning places them about sixty-one years later.

ABOUT THE AUTHOR

Osbert Moore (as the author was known in lay life) was born on the 25th June, 1905, in England. He graduated at Exeter College, Oxford, and during the Second World War he served as an army staff-officer in Italy. It was at that time, by reading an Italian book on Buddhism, that his interest in that teaching was aroused. This book—*The Doctrine of Awakening* by J. Evola—was later translated by a friend and fellow-officer, Harold Musson, who, in 1948, accompanied Osbert Moore to Ceylon. In 1949, both received novice ordination as Buddhist monks, at the Island Hermitage, Dodanduwa; and in 1950, the higher ordination as bhikkhus, at the Vajirarama Monastery, Colombo. Osbert Moore, our author, received the monastic name of Ñāṇamoli, and his friend that of Ñāṇavīra. Both returned soon to the Island Hermitage (an island monastery situated in a lagoon) where the Venerable Ñāṇamoli spent almost his entire monk life of eleven years. Only very rarely did he leave the quietude of the island, and it was on one of these rare occasions, on a walking tour undertaken with the senior monk of the Hermitage, that he suddenly passed away on 8th March 1960, through heart failure. He had not yet completed his 55th year. His death took place at a lonely little village, Veheragama near Maho.

In addition to the present volume, he translated, from the original Pali into lucid English, some of the most difficult texts of Theravāda Buddhism. These translations, listed below, were remarkable achievements in quantity as well as in quality. His translations show the highest standard of careful and critical scholarship and a keen and subtle mind philosophically trained. His work in this field is a lasting contribution to Buddhist studies.

BHIKKHU ÑĀṆAMOLI: A BIBLIOGRAPHY

Published by the Buddhist Publication Society

The Path of Purification (*Visuddhimagga*) by Bhadantācariya Buddhaghosa. Trans. 1956. 5th ed. 1991.

The Practice of Loving-kindness. Texts compiled and translated from the Pali. (Wheel No. 7) 1958.

Three Cardinal Discourses of the Buddha. Trans. with introduction and notes. (Wheel No. 17) 1960.

Pathways of Buddhist Thought. Essays. (Wheel No. 52/53) 1963.

Mindfulness of Breathing (*ānāpānasati*). Texts compiled and translated from the Pali. 1964.

A Thinker's Notebook. Posthumous papers. 1972.

Published by the Pali Text Society

Minor Readings and The Illustrator. Trans. of Khuddakapāṭha and Commentary. 1960.

The Guide. Trans. of Nettippakaraṇa. 1962.

The Piṭaka Disclosure. Trans. of Peṭakopadesa. 1964.

The Path of Discrimination. Trans. of Paṭisambhidāmagga. 1982.

The Dispeller of Delusion. Trans. of Sammohavinodanī. 2 vols. 1987, 1991.

Published by Wisdom Publications

The Middle Length Discourses of the Buddha. Trans. of Majjhima Nikāya.

Published by BPS Pariyatti Editions

The Path of Purification (*Visuddhimagga*) by Bhadantācariya Buddhaghosa. Trans. 1956. First BPE edition 1999.

Of related interest from BPE Pariyatti Editions
Available at bookstores and from Pariyatti Book Service,
800-829-2748
or www.pariyatti.com.

THE PATH OF PURIFICATION
VISUDDHIMAGGA

The classic manual of Buddhist doctrine and meditation by Bhadantācariya Buddhaghosa

TRANSLATED FROM THE PALI BY BHIKKHU ÑĀṆAMOLI

"Bhadantācariya Buddhaghosa's Visuddhimagga ... represents the epitome of Pāli Buddhist literature, weaving together its many strands to create this wonderful meditation manual, which even today retains the clarity it revealed when it was written ... I welcome this new edition of Bhikkhu Ñāṇmoli's celebrated English translation of the Path of Purification. I offer my prayers that readers, wherever they are, may find in it advice and inspiration to develop that inner peace that will contribute to creating a happier and more peaceful world."

—*from the Appreciation by H.H. the Dalai Lama*

960 PAGES
ISBN 1-928706-01-0 (pbk) $38.00
1-928706-00-2 (cloth) $50.00

THE VISION OF DHAMMA

BUDDHIST WRITINGS OF NYANAPONIKA THERA

Core issues in the teachings of the Buddha are explained in lucid and accessible language in this esteemed work by Nyanaponika Thera, the German monk-scholar who helped establish the Buddhist Publication Society. The Vision of Dhamma explores topics such as *Kamma (Karma), Nibbāna (Nirvana), Devotion and Buddhism*, and *The Way to Freedom from Suffering*. First published in 1971, this U. S. edition provides renewed access to the scholar's deep understanding of traditional Buddhist literature and Western culture and philosophy.

"This book has been an essential training manual for me, along with many other teachers of Buddha-Dhamma in the West….."

—Sharon Salzberg, author, *Loving-Kindness: The Revolutionary Art of Happiness*; cofounder, Insight Meditation Society

ISBN 1-928706-03-7,
368 PAGES, $19.00

THE NOBLE EIGHTFOLD PATH:

WAY TO THE END OF SUFFERING

Bhikkhu Bodhi

The Noble Eightfold Path clearly outlines a practical method of gaining understanding and freedom from suffering in life. Bhikkhu Bodhi's training in Western philosophy and decades of study of the Buddha's teachings help him explain in crisp and lucid language how to apply these steps in daily life and practice. The American-born monk is currently president and editor of the Buddhist Publication Society in Sri Lanka.

"Bhikkhu Bodhi's great gift to us all is his clear and authentic transmission of the Buddha's teaching. *The Noble Eightfold Path* expresses the essence of the spiritual path and lives up to the author's wonderfully high standards. This book is a wonderful contribution to the Dhamma in the West."

—Joseph Goldstein, author, *Insight Meditation: The Practice of Freedom*

ISBN 1-928706-07-X
128 PAGES $10.95

A COMPREHENSIVE MANUAL OF ABHIDHAMMA

THE PHILOSOPHICAL PSYCHOLOGY OF BUDDHISM

General Editor: Bhikkhu Bodhi

Bhikkhu Bodhi presents concise surveys of the central topics of Abhidhamma, the Buddhist analysis of mind and mental processes. Covered are: states of conciousness and mental factors, the functions and processes of the mind, the material world, dependent arising, and the methods and stages of meditaion.

"Bhikkhu Bodhi gives his explanation of the four-fold ultimate realities in a very clear, calm, exact and expressive way. He brings to the subject a distinctively passionate voice and profound care and respect for the unfathomable wisdom of the Buddha. This is a brilliant gem of a guidebook and will lead the reader to new dimensions of the wisdom of the Buddha."

—Rina Sircar, PhD.
World Peace Buddhist Chair
California Institute of Integral Studies
Author, *The Psycho-Ethical Aspects of Abhidhamma*

ISBN 1-928706-02-9
432 PAGES $24.00